TRANS/ACTING CULTURE, WRITING, AND MEMORY

TransCanada Series

The study of Canadian literature can no longer take place in isolation from larger external forces. Pressures of multiculturalism put emphasis upon discourses of citizenship and security, while market-driven factors increasingly shape the publication, dissemination, and reception of Canadian writing. The persistent questioning of the Humanities has invited a rethinking of the disciplinary and curricular structures within which the literature is taught, while the development of area and diaspora studies has raised important questions about the tradition. The goal of the TransCanada series is to publish forward-thinking critical interventions that investigate these paradigm shifts in interdisciplinary ways.

Series editor:
Smaro Kamboureli, Canada Research Chair in Critical Studies in Canadian Literature, School of English and Theatre Studies and Director, TransCanada Institute, University of Guelph

For more information, please contact:

Smaro Kamboureli
Professor, Canada Research Chair in Critical Studies in Canadian Literature
School of English and Theatre Studies
Director, TransCanada Institute
University of Guelph
50 Stone Road East
Guelph, ON N1G 2W1
Canada
Phone: 519-824-4120 ext. 53251
Email: smaro@uoguelph.ca

Lisa Quinn
Acquisitions Editor
Wilfrid Laurier University Press
75 University Avenue West
Waterloo, ON N2L 3C5
Canada
Phone: 519-884-0710 ext. 2843
Fax: 519-725-1399
Email: quinn@press.wlu.ca

TRANS/ACTING CULTURE, WRITING, AND MEMORY

ESSAYS IN HONOUR OF BARBARA GODARD

EDITORS
Eva C. Karpinski
Jennifer Henderson
Ian Sowton
Ray Ellenwood

WILFRID LAURIER UNIVERSITY PRESS

This book has been published with the help of a grant from the Canadian Federation for the Humanities and Social Sciences, through the Awards to Scholarly Publications Program, using funds provided by the Social Sciences and Humanities Research Council of Canada. Wilfrid Laurier University Press acknowledges the support of the Canada Council for the Arts for our publishing program. We acknowledge the financial support of the Government of Canada through the Canada Book Fund for our publishing activities.

Library and Archives Canada Cataloguing in Publication

    Trans/acting culture, writing, and memory : essays in honour of Barbara Godard / Eva C. Karpinski ... [et al.], editors.

(TransCanada Series)
Includes bibliographical references.
Issued also in electronic formats.
ISBN 978-1-55458-839-8

    1. Canadian literature—History and criticism—Theory, etc. 2. Canada—Civilization. 3. Canada—Intellectual life. 4. Feminism and literature—Canada. 5. Collective memory and literature—Canada. 6. Translating and interpreting—Canada. I. Godard, Barbara II. Karpinski, Eva C. III. Title: Transacting culture, writing, and memory. IV. Series: TransCanada series

PS8061.T72 2013   C810.9   C2012-907190-0

Electronic monograph in multiple formats.
Issued also in print format.
ISBN 978-1-55458-862-6 (PDF).—ISBN 978-1-55458-863-3 (EPUB)

    1. Canadian literature—History and criticism—Theory, etc. 2. Canada—Civilization. 3. Canada—Intellectual life. 4. Feminism and literature—Canada. 5. Collective memory and literature—Canada. 6. Translating and interpreting—Canada. I. Godard, Barbara II. Karpinski, Eva C III. Title: Transacting culture, writing, and memory. IV. Series: TransCanada series (Online)

PS8061.T72 2013   C810.9   C2012-907191-9

Cover design by Daiva Villa, Chris Rowat Design. Front-cover photograph by Kate Eichhorn. Text design by James Leahy.

© 2013 Wilfrid Laurier University Press
Waterloo, Ontario, Canada
www.wlupress.wlu.ca

Every reasonable effort has been made to acquire permission for copyright material used in this text, and to acknowledge all such indebtedness accurately. Any errors and omissions called to the publisher's attention will be corrected in future printings.

No part of this publication may be reproduced, stored in a retrieval system, or transmitted, in any form or by any means, without the prior written consent of the publisher or a licence from the Canadian Copyright Licensing Agency (Access Copyright). For an Access Copyright licence, visit http://www.accesscopyright.ca or call toll free to 1-800-893-5777.

Contents

Editors' Introduction vii
  EVA C. KARPINSKI AND JENNIFER HENDERSON

Prolegomenon: Reader at Work: An Appreciation of Barbara Godard 1
  DANIELLE FULLER

Part One: Textual/Visual Production: Critical Interventions

1 Incisive Literary Critic, Brilliant Theorist, Engaged Teacher, Inspired Translator, Public Intellectual, and Committed Activist—All in the Feminine: The Early Barbara Godard 23
  LOUISE H. FORSYTH

2 Cultural Memory and Tragic Affect in Nancy Huston's *The Mark of the Angel* 41
  PAMELA MCCALLUM

3 Language and Interdisciplinarity: (Re-)contextualizing Nicole Brossard's *Picture Theory* 59
  KARL E. JIRGENS

4 Writing the Museum: Visual Art and Literature: Denise Desautels and Louise Warren 77
  CLAUDINE POTVIN

Part Two: Culture/Policy/Institutions

5 Negotiating Literatures in Contiguity: France Daigle in/and Québec 95
  LIANNE MOYES AND CATHERINE LECLERC

6 A Lack of Public Memory, a Public Memory of Lack 119
  PHANUEL ANTWI

7 "The Toil and Spoil of Translation": A Godardian Reading of the *Study-Guide: Discover Canada/Guide d'étude: Découvrir le Canada* (2010)   149
LEN M. FINDLAY

8 Notes toward Thinking Transsexual Institutional Poetics   167
TRISH SALAH

Part Three: Translation/Transculturation

9 *Voyage autour de la traduction*: The Translator as Writer and Theorist   193
ALESSANDRA CAPPERDONI

10 Taking Deleuze in the Middle, or Doing Intellectual History by the Letter   211
JASON DEMERS

11 Gail Scott and Barbara Godard on "The Main": Borders, Sutures, Micro-cosmopolitan Interconnectivity, and Translation Studies   225
GILLIAN LANE-MERCIER

Part Four: Public Memory and the Archive

12 Linked Histories and Radio-Activity in Marie Clements's *Burning Vision*   245
SOPHIE MCCALL

13 Memory as Fracture: French Mnemotechniques in the Erasure of the Holocaust   267
MICHAEL DORLAND

14 Gender in the Shaping of Public Memory: *Arms (Monumental) for Montreal*   287
SUE LLOYD

15 Contested Memories: Canadian Women Writers in and out of the Archive   297
BARBARA GODARD

Coda: In the Stacks of Barbara Godard, or Do Not Confuse the Complexity of This Moment with Chaos   325
LISA SLONIOWSKI

Contributors   339
Index   347

Editors' Introduction

EVA C. KARPINSKI AND JENNIFER HENDERSON

This book was conceived as a collection of essays written in honour of Barbara Godard, one of the most original and wide-ranging literary critics, theorists, teachers, translators, and public intellectuals Canada has ever produced. The idea of preparing this publication was first mentioned at an event held in Toronto in December 2008, which celebrated Godard's contribution to Canadian scholarship and academic culture and also launched a major collection of her own essays titled *Canadian Literature at the Crossroads of Language and Culture*, edited by Smaro Kamboureli.[1] Our vision was of a book that would extend her work in a number of fields through engagements with her published texts, a book that would continue conversations with this inspiring thinker. The present collection brings together seventeen essays by well-established and emerging Canadian scholars, several former colleagues and students of Barbara Godard, but all readers of her work, connected through their own studies to the vast and profound influence of Godard's writing on the study of Canadian literature, culture, and theory.

The authors explore and extend this body of work in the spirit of creative interchange and intergenerational relay of ideas, as their essays resonate with Godard's innovative scholarship situated at the intersection of such fields as literary, cultural, and arts criticism; feminist semiotics; translation studies; and social and institutional analysis. In pursuit of unexpected linkages and connections, the essays venture beyond generic and disciplinary borders, paying homage to a particular transdisciplinary practice, developed in the course of one career, but extremely influential in the way that it framed questions and modelled interventions for the study of Canadian and Québécois literatures and cultures.

The reference to "trans/acting" in the title of this volume draws attention to the importance of both performance and the *trans-* that in Barbara Godard's work mobilized a semiotic proliferation through such constructs as transformance, translation, transculturation, transversality, transcreation, and transcoding. In fact, one might say that "trans/position" is what would best describe where Godard situates herself, working from a "within/without" epistemic location (Godard, "Deterritorializing Strategies" 169). *Trans-* also implies multidirectional mappings as opposed to linear, narrative approaches that she avoided in her practice (Godard, "Critical Discourse" 88). Indeed, this multidirectionality is what the essays gathered here have tried to capture. They engage with different archives ranging from Canadian government policies and documents, to publications concerning white supremacist organizations in southern Ontario, online materials from a Toronto-based transsexual/transgender arts festival, a photographic mural installation commemorating the Montreal Massacre, and the works of such writers and artists as Marie Clements, Nicole Brossard, France Daigle, Nancy Huston, Yvette Nolan, Gail Scott, Denise Desautels, Louise Warren, Rebecca Belmore, Vera Frenkel, Robert Lepage, and Janet Cardiff. Through their critical performances, the authors find new and surprising ways of explicating hegemonies and tensions between and within French- and English-speaking Canada, Aboriginal and non-Aboriginal populations, racialized groups, and those subjects who challenge and resist the normativities of Canadian culture. Taken together, the selections demonstrate that Canadian cultural studies, although conceived from a national standpoint, is in fact open to transnational flows of concepts and theories, and is itself one of the forces shaping contemporary global understandings of feminism, translation, the politics of literary and cultural institutions; the memorializing of gendered, racial, and colonial trauma; and the limits of narrative.

The volume opens with a Prolegomenon that reviews Barbara Godard's multi-faceted work. Danielle Fuller's "Reader at Work: An Appreciation of Barbara Godard," traces the contours of Godard's scholarly oeuvre with a particular focus on what might be broadly termed her feminist materialist contributions to cultural theory and criticism. The essay marks the intellectual influences, institutional locations, and political currents that informed and inspired Godard's scholarly and creative life. Detailing elements of

Godard's life history, Fuller provides a vivid rendering of Godard, the "reader at work," as a polymath who made significant contributions to Canadian studies, feminist translation theory, and Canadian literary criticism, but also as a worker who insisted on reading past the social and cultural conditions that might have held her in place. As Fuller remarks, Godard's primary genre was the essay.[2] She defied the academic market, which produces the "author" and the "book" and celebrates individual success, coherence, and unity. In her 1999 essay "A Literature in the Making," Godard reflects on "the author-function" as a guarantee of cohesion and exceptionality, linked to an "expectation of unity in the receiving-cultural field" (293). She resisted the draw and the consolidating effect of the "author-function" through her facility to cover an exceptional range of ideas, her penchant for collaboration, and her polyglossia and heteroglossia, that is, her receptiveness to many languages and critical idioms allowing them to co-exist in proximity to each other. As a result, a lot of her work exists in dispersion, in scattered sites of discourse, and we have only one volume of her collected essays in *Canadian Literature at the Crossroads of Language and Culture*, which Fuller reviews in more detail. Although this anthology consolidates the scholarly portrait of Godard the Canadianist, focusing primarily on her interventions into Canadian studies, Canadian critical theory, and the cultural traffic between anglophone Canada and Québec, there are multiple openings in these essays toward an "elsewhere," especially in her enactment of "relational logic" between here and there, which, according to Fuller, propelled Godard "across the political border-lines of nation-states." Taking her cue from Godard's own self-reflexive practice, and signalling her own formation as a reader of Godard's work, Fuller constructs her essay in such a way that it shifts between formal, scholarly and intimate registers.

Fuller's presentation provokes several questions about Barbara Godard as a reader. What kinds of reading strategies did she develop? How did she transform our relationship to knowledge? How did she help to reorient a set of existing relations within the many fields of her study? Through her pursuit of emergent discourses and literatures, Godard not only played a role in opening up the academic field for the institutionalization of Canadian literature and the introduction of women's writing into the curricula in the 1970s, but she added complexity and nuance to the profession, already in her early essays on Sheila Watson, Audrey Thomas, Isabella Valancy Crawford, Anne Hébert, and Margaret Atwood. She brought up the question of "a female aesthetics" in her 1984 essay on Alice Munro, around the same time as she pioneered literary theory courses for undergraduate

English departments across Canada ("The Critic" 28). In the groundbreaking essay "The Canadian Discourse as the Discourse of the Other," Godard used Deleuze and Guattari's concept of minor literature to argue that Canadian literature is a deterritorialized literature. But most significant, in the 1980s and beyond, was her part in provoking/occasioning, synthesizing, collecting feminist literary and cultural criticism in Canada and Québec, and in providing key meta-statements on it. In "Critical Discourse in/on Quebec" she gives an account of the emergence of feminist criticism in Québec in the mid-1970s in the writing of Suzanne Lamy and the poets Nicole Brossard, France Théoret, and others. Beginning with her early 1980s articles on Brossard, she continued to produce paradigm-setting feminist literary criticism in such edited collections as *Gynocritics/La gynocritique* (which mapped out the scene of Canadian feminist theory and writing),[3] *Collaboration in the Feminine* (which gathered writings on women and culture from the feminist journal *Tessera* that she co-founded), and more recently *Wider Boundaries of Daring* (which broadened the scope of the new modernist studies in Canada by restoring women's visibility in the canon).

However, Godard departs from a liberal paradigm of feminism toward a more radical perspective, insisting that "women should ally themselves with other oppressed elements in society to engage in a critique of institutions and the way they reproduce the relationships of domination" ("Critical Discourse" 101–2). Her criticism and theory share precisely this kind of alignment with the marginalized and the supplemental as she consistently engages with such terrain as Québec and Acadian literature and culture, lesbian poetics, indigenous literatures, translation, or African Canadian writing. She was one of the first non-indigenous critics writing about Aboriginal women's literature in her 1985 CRIAW pamphlet "Talking About Ourselves: The Literary Productions of Native Women," her study of orality in "Voicing Difference: The Literary Production of Native Women" (1986), and "The Politics of Representation: Some Native Canadian Women Writers" (1990). Although produced from a site of relative academic privilege, Godard's critical writing positions itself as emergent, minority discourse vis-à-vis currently dominant and historically residual discourses ("Critical Discourse" 89). Her stance of becoming "minor" is a strategic move that enables her to capture the fault lines of institutional practices of theory, criticism, art, literature and activism, produced in a given historical moment in a specific social context. This is where we can locate the strengths of her methodology of reading and critical practices. Influenced by Mikhail Bakhtin and Gilles Deleuze, she privileges dialogism, heterogeneity, and unexpected linkages, while attending both to signification and communication as social processes. She carefully contextualizes, historicizes, and approaches literature/texts through a politicized lens, viewing form and genre as ideological constructions. Paying attention to which lines of force operate in the utterance, she always asks: "who is speaking, to whom, under what conditions" ("The Politics of Representation" 132). Her critical enunciations are epistemic performances, an invitation to thinking along in recording the process of meaning-making rather than revealed knowledge. Significantly, she ends one of her essays, "Structuralism/Post-structuralism," a meta-synthesis of various textual strategies used by Canadian critics, with an open invitation to others to unravel the thread and bring in new theories and new readings to the fray. In what follows, we hope to show how the contributors to this volume heed Godard's call.

Part One: Textual/Visual Production: Critical Interventions, contains a sampling of essays focused on interpretive strategies, and coheres around the thematic threads of this collection as a whole. The section begins with Louise Forsyth's contribution, "Incisive Literary Critic, Brilliant Theorist, Engaged Teacher, Inspired Translator, Public Intellectual, and Committed Activist—All in the Feminine: The Early Barbara Godard." Combining biography, literary history, and criticism, Forsyth's essay pays tribute to Godard as a prolific producer and broker of feminist culture and women's writing in Canada. She identifies several areas where Godard has left her mark, including her role in developing feminist theory through analysis of "the discursive, ontological, and epistemological sources" of women's marginalization; her rewriting of a Canadian literary canon to make it more inclusive of heterogeneity and difference; her contributions to literary criticism and methodology, underpinned by her fluency in multiple idioms of theory and her ability to systematize different approaches and trends; and her efforts to foster translation and translation studies from a gendered, politicized angle. Forsyth highlights the first three decades of Godard's career, begun in the 1960s, contextualizing her formative years through the political, social, and intellectual radicalism of the time. In collaboration with Frank Davey, Godard first brought experimental writing from Québec to English Canada through the Coach House Québec Translation series. Forsyth pays special attention to Godard's sustained encounters with Nicole Brossard, discussing the importance for Godard of Brossard's first three novels published in the series, *A Book, Turn of a Pang*, and *French Kiss*, along with Godard's own translation of *L'Amèr: These Our Mothers* (1983). Their long friendship and collaboration resulted in Godard's further translations of *Amantes:*

Lovhers (1986), *Picture Theory* (1991; rpt. rev. 2006), and *Intimate Journal* (2004) and her critical essays on Brossard and several entries in British and American encyclopedias and literary dictionaries.[4] Most notable among these essays are the early piece "*L'Amèr* or Exploding Chapter: Nicole Brossard at the Site of Feminist Deconstruction" (1984), the influential "'Producing Visibility for Lesbians': Nicole Brossard's Quantum Poetics" (1995), and "Life (in) Writing: Or a Writing-Machine for Producing the Subject" (2005).

The next essay, "Cultural Memory and Tragic Affect in Nancy Huston's *The Mark of the Angel*," Pamela McCallum offers a reading of an author whose work is seldom discussed in Canadian literary criticism, but who is linked to Godard's interests in cultural memory and history and her work on French language and translation. In her 1999 novel set in Paris during the years of the Algerian war, Nancy Huston, who publishes in both French and English and translates her own work, explores the complexities of historical memories, the possibilities of redemption and change, and the tragedies of repetition and reversal. McCallum's essay has been written in sync with Godard's fascination with culture as "contact, flow, intersection" ("Culture at the Crossroads" 11) and her interest in capturing those moments in cultural memory when one narrative gives way to another. Drawing on the British Marxist critic Raymond Williams's writing on modern tragedy and revolution, McCallum traces a theory of affect that is important in understanding social and political change. With the help of trauma theory, she reads Huston's novel in terms of its inscription of affective relationships with such tragic and emancipatory events in modern history as Europe's liberation from Nazism, the Algerian war, and the Hungarian revolution, and their effects on the protagonists. McCallum argues that Huston's novel represents "modern tragedy" in the sense outlined by Williams: the blockage of human longings and aspirations toward transformation, both social and individual, in historical impasses that resist change. In Huston's classical love triangle—involving Raphael, a talented Parisian musician, Saffie, his young German wife, and her lover, Andràs, a Hungarian refugee—the violence of war, resistance, and defeat are allegorically condensed. The interrelationships among these three survivors of the brutalities of the mid-twentieth century form a condensed structure through which yearning and frustration are played out with tragic consequences.

The following essay, Karl Jirgens's "Language and Interdisciplinarity: (Re-)contextualizing Nicole Brossard's *Picture Theory*," extends current debate on contemporary neo-baroque literary expression by applying a critical method that develops the views of Ludwig Wittgenstein, Gilles Deleuze, Julia Kristeva, and Espen Aarseth, so as to illuminate important achievements of contemporary inter-media, language-based artists and authors such as Vera Frenkel, Janet Cardiff, and Nicole Brossard. Moving through commentaries on these inter-media artists and contemporary artist/writers, the essay comes to centre on Godard's interpretation of Nicole Brossard's innovative novel, *Picture Theory*. Jirgens provides a post-Einsteinian perspective on Brossard's feminist and self-reflexive portrayal of "double-time" in reference to the diegetic flux evident in shifting narrative patterns. Her text relies on holographic techniques in order to explore a porous border between the virtual and the actual. The essay cross-references Pablo Picasso's and Gertrude Stein's Cubism, with Wittgenstein's notion of "picture theory," Blanchot's sense of silence, and Kristeva's paragrammatics, to illuminate Godard's reception of Brossard's novel. Jirgens recognizes Godard's translation of Nicole Brossard's *Picture Theory* as a diegetic performance, affirming a feminism that defines itself in its own terms. His essay relates to Godard in many other ways, resonating with her theoretical interest in performance[5] and the impact of new media on language and print culture, evidenced in her participation in the panel "Five New Manifestoes on the Book" during the Toronto Scream Festival in July 2009. She also examined multimedia forms in her review of collaborative installations of the moving image combining film, video, photography, and paper media in "Theatres of Perception: The Filmworks of Barbara Sternberg and the Paperworks of Rae Davis" (1999). Moreover, Godard's interest in contemporary developments associated with the neo-baroque—the aesthetics of the fold that involves a play with perspectives, media, and frames of vision—is evident in her "Relational Logics," where she discusses Brazilian discourses of cultural "cannibalism."

    This section concludes with Claudine Potvin's "Writing the Museum: Visual Art and Literature: Denise Desautels and Louise Warren." Writing *à côté* Godard's work on Québec women writers, begun in the early 1980s and continued in bilingual *Gynocritics/La Gynocritique* and *Tessera* as well as in such essays as "Critical Discourse in/on Quebec" (1990) and "A Literature in the Making" (1999), Potvin examines the interface between the literary and the visual arts in two works: a poetic collection by Denise Desautels (*Leçons de Venise*) and a novel by Louise Warren (*Tableaux d'Aurélie*). These texts incorporate works of art as their structural components either through the inclusion of visual representations of art works within the book and a dialogue between words and images, or through the insertion of the visual dimension within the narrative. Potvin develops the notion of "text-museum" so as to explore the overlapping frames of postmodern visual aesthetics, women's literary practice, and feminist epistemology. The "text-museum" creates a pictorial effect, a visual trace, as the image challenges the author and the reader when art finds itself inscribed/described within the text. In the case of a written representation of the image, the transparency of the visual model is recuperated by the complexity of language. In the first part, Potvin takes us for a museum walk with Desautels, who mediates the sculptures of Michel Goulet in a series of fragments refracting images and objects caught in the gaze, fracturing gender and memory. In the second part she analyzes Warren's novel as a kind of *Künstlerroman* with the narrator-painter who confounds visuality and textuality while painting and writing her story. Potvin prudently proposes to look at the transactions between the visual and the textual as translation from the image to the narrative that produces a *tableau* effect. She argues that Desautels and Warren's references to visual arts question the politics, semantics, and aesthetics of the "official" gaze, which has viewed and evaluated women and art throughout history.

The essays in Part Two acknowledge their indebtedness to a branch of Godardian scholarship on the relations between cultural production, state policy, and the institutions of culture, a scholarly interest rooted in her early exposure to the sociology of literature and the literary institution in her studies in Montreal and Bordeaux. From her days as a graduate student at the Université de Montréal in the early 1960s, working across departments in order to pursue a comparative Canadian literature program that did not yet exist in this country, to later writing in which she reflected on the ways in which discourses supporting public funding for the arts in Canada had opened possibilities for "training and practice which have constituted the habitus making materially possible who I am," Godard never ceased to address the power/knowledge nexus that produced her worlds ("Feminist Speculations" 49). Beginning in the mid-1990s, however, she pursued institutional critique and analysis of policy discourse with a sense of the urgency of naming the rapid and sweeping shifts in public policies and institutions brought about by neo-liberal restructuring of the state. She published a genealogy of the discourses and models of value in Canada Council and Ontario Arts Council reports over thirty years, tracking the "perennial" nature of crises but also key resignifications of terms such as "culture," "the artist," "unity," and "interest" ("Feminist Speculations"). For an essay collection on the past and future of Canadian universities, she contributed reflections on the corporatized post-secondary institution as (not mincing words) a "mass-marketer for the high-tech industries," "interact[ing] with students in their play" ("The Risk" 28). Not unrelatedly, she began a research project on the history of 1960s student activism in English Canada that would look back to the importance for her generation of anti-colonial struggles, via their particular resonance in Québec, as well as the international antinuclear movement.[6] Although she was self-reflexive regarding the melancholy edge of her witnessing of historical shifts—asking "what is this thing I don't know how to lose, or for whose loss I have found no valid compensation[?]"—Godard was also intervening in public discourses to call for more historical consciousness, for recognition of contingency in the case of the "single framing of the social: the bottom line," and for knowledge of the history of local forms of global consciousness ("Feminist Speculations" 53, 63).

Insofar as the project on the sources and locations of early 1960s student activism seemed to be spurred by her "discovery" in the University of Toronto archives of "a history of action on the Quebec question," it was a project through which she was returning, albeit in a more historiographic vein, to earlier work on English Canadian readings of Québec ("The Critic" 18). "A Literature in the Making" provides an account of English translation as a "second literary system," alongside criticism, producing a Québec corpus for English Canada that is embedded in a "system of differential positions" ("A Literature" 273, 275). Lianne Moyes and Catherine Leclerc use Godard's 1999 essay as their point of departure in their opening contribution to Part Two: Culture/Policy/Institutions, "Negotiating Literatures in Contiguity: France Daigle in/and Québec." Drawing in particular upon Godard's analysis of interactions between cultural fields, Moyes and Leclerc consider the (dis)connections between Québec and Acadian literatures. Their essay asks what is at stake for an Acadian writer in being integrated into Québec letters when the reception and consecration of a writer's work comes at the risk of appropriation and decontextualization. Whereas Godard turned her critical ear toward English-speaking Canada and its relationship to French-speaking Québec, Moyes and Leclerc attend to the multiple, contending, and contradictory relations between French Canada, Québec, and English Canada. Such a mapping allows for analysis of positions—Acadian and Québécois—that are minoritized by and with regard to Canada, as well as for analysis of the crucial role played by Québec literature as a sphere of influence and support for French-language literatures outside its borders. Following Godard, they also show that "issues of gender are operative" (Godard, "A Literature in the Making" 280) in institutional mediations of cultural production. Daigle's novels, Moyes and Leclerc argue, speak eloquently to the conflictual relationship of Acadian writers to the pressures of "passing by way of Québec" in order to be published and received.

Also building on Godard's model of reading for the fields within which differential values and distinctions are produced—and shifted, when the boundaries are reconceived—is Phanuel Antwi, in an essay that extends Godard's assertion that the North–South axis and transversal lines of an American "hemispheric imaginary" can be traced, even in the absence of direct contact between writers ("Relational Logics" 318). Like Godard, Antwi is interested in the encounters and relationalities that come into view when received practices of comparison, often serving to shore up national cultures, are bypassed. Antwi departs from Godard's model of reading for representations of contact and exchange in the minor literatures of the Americas, however, by using traces of "racial feeling" as a thread to connect North American practices of ritualized racial claim-staking. Rather than minor literatures, it is the theatrical displays of the Orange Order, the KKK, and the "old boys" at Upper Canada College (in blackface minstrelsy) that Antwi compares. Thus, "A Lack of Public Memory, a Public Memory of Lack" proposes a continental racial imaginary that would cut across the interprovincial and East–West habits of comparison of cultural historians, habits that, according to Antwi, have entrenched a myth of Ontarian restraint.

At another level, Antwi's essay gestures at some of the ways in which insisting on the existence of an archive of feeling, here an archive of hateful affect, might provide a means of moving black history in Ontario beyond the two poles of structured absence and a provincial "heritage" industry. Like Antwi's essay, Trish Salah's relates to the two branches of Godard's scholarship centred on institutional critique and archive theory. Salah's "Notes Toward Thinking Transsexual Institutional Poetics" extends Godard's particular interest in gendered practices of inscription into the cultural economy in the direction of questions of transgender cultural production. In order to theorize the ways in which subjects crossing sex and/or gender enter into and disappear from gendered economies of cultural value, Salah deploys Godard's revision of Pierre Bourdieu's concept of distinction in her 2002 article, "Feminist Periodicals and the Production of Cultural Value." Examining the archive of the Toronto-based Transsexual/Transgender arts festival, Counting Past 2: Film, Video, Performance, Spoken Word with Transsexual Nerve, Salah mobilizes Godard's insistence on the differential valuation of gendered cultural labour to trace the devaluation of trans sex worker labour, even within trans discourses. At the same time, Salah's essay asks what difference transsexuality makes to feminist theorizing and oppositional practices of sexual difference, suggesting that transgender cultural work both reiterates and displaces feminist analysis of sexual difference. Institutional feminisms have sometimes operated as regulatory discourses on gender, performing authorizing, contouring, and censuring functions, and Salah's essay demonstrates some of the ways they have been contested by transgender discourses. In this way, Salah renews a question Godard asked herself as she wondered what it meant for her to provide her "feminist speculations on value" in the era of a shrinking public sphere: "Am I carrying the heavy burden Virginia Woolf laid on the 'daughters of educated men' to protect 'culture and intellectual liberty'? [Is it] easier for them to question established values than for their brothers?" ("Feminist Speculations" 53). Salah renews that question by posing it in relation to feminism itself as an arbiter of certain institutionalized values.

Part Two concludes with an essay that takes its cues from Godard's practice of bringing an arsenal of socio-semiotics and fine-grained textual analysis situated within vectors of power to bear in the reading of recent state policy, a type of cultural criticism that she also practised in "Notes from the Cultural Field" and on the pages of *Fuse* and *Border/lines* magazines. Len Findlay's essay, "'The Toil and Spoil of Translation': A Godardian Reading of the *Study-Guide: Discover Canada/Guide d'étude: Découvrir le Canada* (2010)" focuses on the revised citizenship test study guide produced by the Conservative government of Stephen Harper. Godard was sharply attuned to the changing means by which the Canadian state has managed linguistic and cultural heterogeneity alongside the reproduction of inequality and the suppression of indigenous sovereignties. Some of her late observations concerned the rhetoric of technological innovation and the promise of the "equalizing effects" of "continuous change" as the register in which the value of ethnocultural "diversity" spun as "social morphing" is now produced and circulated ("Feminist Speculations" 62). Findlay locates an approach to reading the pedagogy of the revised study guide in a less obvious place: in what he sees as Godard's elaboration of a theory of translation as the performance of power relations between dominant and subordinate languages. In "Writing Between Cultures" (1997), Godard moves through the cultural turn in translation studies to frame an account of translation in Canada as a passage between languages that is always shaped by historical moment and by specific understandings of "the modalities of linguistic and cultural interference," modalities that do not always correspond to the normative English sense of translation as textual equivalence ("Writing" 204). In her detailed comparison of works in seventeenth-century French and modern English that are energized by different understandings of translation, Godard shows how the "toils and spoils of translation" are already documented in certain texts. Findlay tests this approach in his reading of *Discover Canada/Découvrir le Canada*, a bilingual text designed to represent Canada to citizens and potential citizens as an inclusive and prosperous democracy committed to equal justice for all. His Godardian reading reveals the play of state desire and state anxiety throughout the document, both in what is claimed and in how claims are translated from one official language into the other. The treatment of Aboriginal languages is especially revealing, consigned as they are to a non-place between official and immigrant cultures and within neo-colonial relations of ruling.

Findlay's exercise in mediating the semiotics of translation in a bilingual document constructing citizenship for the Eurocentric settler colonial state reminds us of the crucial aspect of translation for Godard, namely its political implications. In her comments on neo-liberal cultural policies, she perceives cutting funds to arts organizations and privileging support for the individual artist precisely as the state's attempt to contain the political potential of art, to stifle those institutional forms of arts production that can *translate* "artists' discourse from the symbolic to the political with the power to affect the world around it" ("Feminist Speculations" 70). The politicizing of translation is a distinct feature of Godard's approach to the concept and pragmatics of translation in its triple modality as theory, institution, and craft as the essays in Part Three: Translation/Transculturation further demonstrate. For Godard, translation functions as theory and method of contact, movement, transformation at the border of different semiotic systems, "a dynamic mechanism through which cultural fields develop relations with each other" ("A Literature in the Making" 278). Her fascination with the vitality of translation as a machine for interdiscursive production of meaning is voiced in her definitions of translation as "creative transposition" ("The Translator as She" 196) and a clinamen or "creative swerve" ("Deleuze and Translation" 56). Whether she talks about translation's role as implicated in colonial instrumentality and in policy-making within the multilingual Canadian state, or as part of the system of publication and dissemination, a space of dialogue between anglophone and francophone women writers in feminist journals, Godard insists on asking who and what gets translated and how it structures the field of cultural production.[7] Similarly, she views the craft of translation through a political lens, claiming the role of feminist translator as an active co-producer rewriting the dominant codes of language and representation.⁸ We can distinguish three overlapping areas of Godard's theoretical innovation in translation studies related to feminist theories, Deleuzian philosophy, and post-colonial and indigenous thought, each of which has been addressed by our contributors.

Part Three opens with Alessandra Capperdoni's "'Voyage autour de la traduction': The Translator as Writer and Theorist," dedicated to Barbara Godard's feminist theorizing of translation. In "A Literature in the Making" Godard pinpoints the exact historical moment in the early 1980s, when the question of sexual difference emerged as a new problematic in translation studies in her own essay "Translating and Sexual Difference" (1984) and in Kathy Mezei's analysis of male translators' treatment of texts by women writers (310). Godard subsequently elaborated a feminist theory of translation in such essays as "The Translator as She" (1985), "Theorizing Feminist Discourse/Translation" (which appeared in the 1989 issue of *Tessera*, "*La Traduction au féminin*/Translating Women"), and "Translating (with) the Speculum" (1991). Her performative model of translation as rewriting with a difference emerges from her theorizing of feminist discourse and her study of transformation of gender and genre in adaptations of novels for the stage in "(Re)Appropriation as Translation" (1990). Feminist translation rejects the notion of "fidelity" to the original and thus moves away from mimetic theories of transparency in foregrounding a visible effect of translation. The dualism of source-target gives way to productive, intersubjective border encounters. Consequently, a traditional gendered view of translation as passive imitation is replaced by a new authority of the translator as co-creator who "flaunts the signs of her manipulation of the text" ("Theorizing" 94) in the process of dialogical rewriting and transcoding. At the same time, neutrality of translation gives way to political and ethical considerations that "highlight all the socio-cultural mediations affected by translation, especially the ideological, cognitive, and affective aspects" ("A Literature in the Making" 311).

Drawn to this interweaving of praxis and thought in Godard's conceptualizations of translation, Capperdoni discusses Godard's central role in the shaping of a Canadian feminist theory of writing and translation through a methodology that brought together translation practice, feminist thought, and feminist theories of writing. She registers key moments in Godard's interventions into feminist translation theory, from her early essays, to women's conferences, the founding of the journal *Tessera*, and her translations of Nicole Brossard, France Théoret, and Antonine Maillet. The essay reads these translations in the context of Godard's contribution to Canadian and Québécois feminist theories of writing since the 1970s and her facilitation of the dialogue between such francophone feminist writers and theorists as Brossard, Susanne Lamy, Madeleine Gagnon, Lousie Dupré, and Louise Cotnoir and anglophone feminists Kathy Mezei, Daphne Marlatt, Betsy Warland, and Gail Scott. Godard recognizes the translational aspect of feminist discourse, specifically in its practice of fiction-theory, "a dual activity of reading and (re)writing" ("Theorizing" 47) that blurs the boundaries between critical and creative writing as it becomes a dynamic site of feminist *poiesis* transforming dominant systems of representation through inscriptions of gender. Godard's central role in articulating feminist translation as feminist poetics, as Capperdoni shows, begins with the important prefaces to her translations of Brossard's *Lovhers* (1986), *Picture Theory* (1991), and *Intimate Journal* (2004), and Théoret's *The Tangible Word* (1991).

The second essay in this section, Jason Demers's "Taking Deleuze in the Middle, or Doing Intellectual History by the Letter," bounces off Godard's preoccupation with feminist discourse by returning to her essay "Translating (with) the Speculum" (1991) and her account of translating Brossard's *L'Amèr*, which allows him to unfold Godard's "associative theory of translation" articulated in her two essays "Deleuze and Translation" (2000) and "Signs and Events: Deleuze in Translation" (2005). In her analysis of the translations of Luce Irigaray's *Speculum de l'autre femme* and Hélène Cixous's *Vivre l'orange* in the Speculum essay, Demers locates a shift from metaphor to metonymy, or from representational to combinatory economies of translation. On the other hand, Godard-translating-Brossard-discovering-Deleuze "in the middle" reveals intersubjective foldings constituted through the process of translation. Exploring how Godard teased out and theorized the somewhat obscured preoccupation with translation in the work of Gilles Deleuze, Demers focuses on her expansion of the Deleuzian concepts of the fold, the event, and transcreation that contain "an implicit theory of translation" (Godard, "Deleuze" 56). Godard recognizes in Deleuze's pragmatic thought about language and his attentiveness to "the heterogeneity of 'assemblages'" the possibility of deriving "a micro-politics of 'translation'" or "an analytic framework for the transformative work of translation" ("Signs" 4). Events such as texts or translations can be viewed as assemblages of complex foldings and unfoldings of intersubjective relations. To choose transcreative becoming or translation that privileges the letter (the signifier) over the one that privileges meaning (the signified) signals the choice of abundance, proliferation, and polysemy. As Demers explains, an associative or combinatory theory of translation not only operates by, but actively encourages movement and ramification rather than simple substitution. Taking this theory of translation as a cue, the essay goes on to look at what it would mean to do intellectual history associatively. It reads Deleuze and Félix Guattari's capitalism and schizophrenia books in association with the international social movements that were in the midst of unfolding at the turn of the 1970s, when the books were being written.

This section concludes with Gillian Lane-Mercier's essay, "Gail Scott and Barbara Godard on 'The Main': Borders, Sutures, Micro-cosmopolitan Interconnectivity, and Translation Studies." Lane-Mercier's essay examines the productive resonances between Gail Scott's novel, *The Obituary* (2010), Barbara Godard's 1996 article entitled "Writing from the Border: Gail Scott on 'The Main,'" and the concept of micro-cosmopolitanism recently defined in the area of translation studies by Michael Cronin. Scott's writing and Godard's analysis point to ways of going beyond the translational paradigms inspired by Antoine Berman and Lawrence Venuti, thereby anticipating new routes of reflection on the theory and practice of translation in the age of globalization that converge with Cronin's concept. Indeed, if, as Cronin states, "translation incarnates the fundamental characteristics of a micro-cosmopolitan vision of […] inward/outward interconnectedness" predicated on non-linearity, mobility, random bifurcation, non-equilibrium, and conflicting loyalties, then it is possible to see in the notions of "suture" (Scott) and "metonymic accretion" (Godard) the conceptual and material contours of a new paradigm for translation studies. This new paradigm enables the foregrounding of alternative forms of connectivity that entail an "open-ended interdependency" (Cronin) in which a question such as "Who am ... WE?" (Scott) can be rethought. Combining local differentiation and global connection, micro-cosmopolitan translation includes the possibility of multiple affiliations and solidarities from below, from marginalized social spaces, languages, and identities that are revealed to be layered, palimpsestic, and culturally diverse. Lane-Mercier argues that any account of metonymic accretion must factor in an analysis of power so as to address such negative forms of interconnectivity as economic oppression, violence, war, and genocide of indigenous peoples. Following Godard, she also echoes Demers's argument, thus bringing Deleuze into the fold in her view of translation as "strained encounters" at the borders. Lane-Mercier's vision of translation "increasingly becoming an intrinsic, inward-bound phenomenon called upon to mediate language or community rights, ethnic solidarities, cultural difference, cultural memory and loss within a given local setting" recalls Godard's discussion in "Writing Between Cultures" (1997) of two different imperial moments that produce two models of translation: a vertical, colonial "con/version" (in the writing of Marie de l'Incarnation) and a transversal, indigenous "re/version" as resistance writing (in Daniel David Moses's play *Almighty Voice and His Wife*).

The essays in Part Four coalesce around Public Memory and the Archive, themes that preoccupied Godard in the last two decades of her life. Her work in a field that was, at the time, in the process of being consolidated into "memory studies" was, like many other contributions, mobilized by a specific event and the questions of adequate memorialization that it raised: in Godard's case, this was the December 6, 1989, Montreal Massacre. In 2000 and 2001, she presented a number of papers on feminist monuments produced in response to the 1989 murder of female engineering students at the École Polytechnique; however, a decade earlier, she had framed a less direct response to this event as co-editor of companion issues of the journal, *Tessera*, devoted to "Memory Work/des mémoires des femmes" and "Feminist(s) Project(s)/Projet (des) féministes," respectively.[9] These issues bear the mark of Godard's feminist and transdisciplinary engagement with questions of memory as her introductory comments move between psychoanalytic ground—where she counters an image of female subjectivity as melancholic, declaring that nostalgic "return to the maternal is not always possible, nor indeed desirable, especially where change is at stake"—and institutional critique that warns about the dangers of losing the records of women's "attempt to make their mark on a temporality of a collective subject" (Binhammer et al. 8, 10). Indeed, the context for Godard's turn to the themes of public memory and the archive also involved major changes in government policy in the 1990s that seemed to bring an end to an era of state-funded feminist work on behalf of women's autonomy in Canada. For Godard, this process of state restructuring called for the marking of profound losses but also for guarding against forgetting. These concerns took her in the direction of the theory and politics of the archive. The archive as "a subject as well as a process of cultural production" was the topic of a graduate seminar she taught at York University, beginning in 2007 (Godard, "Theorizing the Archive").

Part Four of this book contains essays that reflect the scope of Godard's interest in memory work as a field of humanities research grounded in the burdens of specific historical experiences, but also a vein of artistic practice capable of staging complex textualities and reading positions. Together, these essays also fracture and multiply the publics of public memory through their considerations of different national, minoritized, and transnational spaces of collective remembrance. The section opens with Sophie McCall's reading of Marie Clements's *Burning Vision*, a play about the "selective memory" that holds apart the interpenetrating histories of dispossession and displacement of indigenous and migrant groups in Canada. Reading the play in terms of its ethical and sensory implication of the audience in the question of what "reconciliation" might mean if it were detached from settler-nationalist imperatives, McCall demonstrates the ways the play displaces a master trope of state-directed memory work. Her essay extends Godard's theorization of resistance literature as a "re-accentuation" of discourse producing epistemic breaks with respect to a given semiotic field in her 1990 essay, "The Politics of Representation: Some Native Canadian Women Writers." Godard's essay was written in response to the "appropriation of voice" debates within the Canadian literary institution in the late 1980s, and thus oriented around what McCall refers to as a "Native–white axis" insofar as it attempted to counter the subtle rhetorical violence of liberal defences of the freedom of the imagination by identifying the "semiotic field of the Native" in Canadian literature that is organized around the production of settler indigenization as value (Godard 117). In McCall's extension and updating of Godard's insights, it is a concept of national reconciliation associated with clarity and closure, isolated historical wrongs, and compartmentalized communities that shapes the semiotic field with which Clements's play contends. *Burning Vision* insists on interconnectivity and implication through chance historical convergences that link disparate communities, notably the diasporic and indigenous ones held apart by the "Native–white axis." The play traces the journey of uranium from its origins underground in Sahtu Dene territory into the bomb that was dropped on Hiroshima. In McCall's reading, the play proposes an alternative to the state-driven model of reconciliation by dramatizing a process of sharing testimony across the boundaries of language, history, and geography, flowing from a Dene-centred understanding of historical accountability. Clements's use of code-switching between English, Japanese, and Slavey foregrounds the "disequilibrious range of differences" through which this sharing must occur as translation. The interpenetrating worlds of the play are not equivalent, never completely commensurable, as the non-verbal soundscape of clicks, ticks, heartbeats, feedback, and static also suggests, but this insistent soundscape also makes the play itself "radioactive, ... an agent of contamination that implicates the audience in linked histories."

Michael Dorland's essay, "Memory as Fracture: French Mnemotechniques in the Erasure of the Holocaust," draws the connection between

Godard's late work on struggles over memory in the Canadian context and earlier French scholarship on collective memory, its topographies, and its transmission through social institutions. Godard knew the postwar French intellectual context well as a student at L'École des études pratiques and as a teacher at the Université de Paris VIII in the 1960s, but the intellectual moment of the turn from structuralism to post-structuralism in which she was immersed predated by several decades France's public reckoning with what Dorland calls the "French Judeocide," and the widening of the discussion of French Holocaust memory, which had been restricted to a small group of scholars. For Dorland, the French struggles and debates over Holocaust memory may be seen as constituting a template for other memory struggles insofar as they lay out the contradictions between lived memory, historiography, and commemoration; they involve—through the contributions of early postwar studies by French Jewish historians—a historical sense informed by an accumulation of catastrophic antecedents, "calling for a form of reflexivity regarding Western culture as a whole"; and finally, insofar as the French debates regarding representation produced new figures of testimony and witness.

Dorland's concluding review of the French debates about the politics and aesthetics of memorializing traumatic experience provides a bridge to Sue Lloyd's "Gender in the Shaping of Public Memory: Arms (Monumental) for Montreal," an essay about her creation of a site-specific photographic mural commemorating the fourteen women killed at L'École Polytechnique. Lloyd was commissioned to create this mural by York University in 1998 for installation on the wall of a student centre lounge. In 2003, Godard invited the artist to address a seminar she had organized, "Gender in the Shaping of Public Memory: Issues in the Canadian Context." Like so many of Godard's characteristic gestures of prompting and convening, the invitation occasioned these reflections by Lloyd on her approach to creating a monument to murdered women. As Lloyd recounts, Godard's question, "How does gender figure in memorializing practices?" led her to further questions of her own: When memorializing practices involve visual representations, what are the possibilities for representing the female body, for providing a sense of gendered embodiment that maintains critical distance from received motifs of mourning? Her essay provides an account of how she developed a conceptual strategy for her photographic mural by working with an idea of the "impossible" figure, one who exceeds recognition and flouts dualistic logic. In *Arms for Montreal*, she wanted to provide an embodied representation of the women, but at the same time to maintain a tension around that embodiment; similarly, she wanted to invoke the women's association with engineering, but without affirming symbols of the profession in a public memorialization of female lives lost in its pursuit.

Part Four concludes with an essay by Barbara Godard herself, which represents her only published work in the fields of memory and archive studies, "Contested Memory: Canadian Women Writers in and out of the Archive" (first published in 2007 in the Tokyo-based *Annual Review of Canadian Studies*). The essay examines the representational practices of the archive, the monument, and performance involved in Canadian contests over memory, contests that Godard saw as being related to the condition of a culturally divided settler/invader society additionally riven by conflicts of gender. In this essay Godard moves across these three representational practices by analyzing, first, the coincidence of the project of creating a women's movement archive with the archival turn in narrative fiction by Canadian women writers in the 1970s and 1980s. She then turns to some of the many counter-monuments of December 6, 1989, that "make visible women's troubling position in the symbolic economy," reflecting on the place of the mutilated female body in public art. As Godard observes, the murder of the fourteen women students was a pivotal event in the history of women in Canada that made questions of memory a focus for many feminists in this country from the 1990s on. Violence against Aboriginal women, specifically, has a longer history entwined with the policies of the settler state and the social relations and practices that the state normalized. In the final section of her essay, then, Godard turns to the use of performance and ritual in the work of Rebecca Belmore, Marie Clements, and the theatre collective, the Turtle Gals, who have worked to insert the history of this systemic violence in public space as a defamiliarizing spectacle.

Finally, bookended by the images of Godard's library taken by her former student and collaborator Kate Eichhorn, Lisa Sloniowski's essay "In the Stacks of Barbara Godard, or Do Not Confuse the Complexity of This Moment with Chaos" functions as a coda to this volume. Sloniowski recounts her several encounters with Godard shortly before her passing, which led to the project of archiving her "personal and idiosyncratic" collection of books and papers for York's libraries. Memories and descriptions of Godard's archive are interspersed with the librarian's theoretical reflection and feminist questioning of hegemonic technologies of archivization that rationalize exclusion of certain forms of lived experience and privilege linear, individualized, provenance-based approaches over rhizomatic, intertextual networks and connections preserved by the collector. Godard constructed her own system, consistent with her philosophy of relational and dialogic thinking, which also preserved "the historical palimpsest" of her development as an intellectual, critic, and activist. Exposure to this collection inspires Sloniowski to challenge dominant institutional practices and to rethink the subject in a feminist archival theory. Her engaging ethnography not only conveys a vivid sense of the physicality and materiality of Godard's archive but also stages a theoretically productive, albeit posthumous, exchange between the archivist and the collector whose absorption into a public institution constitutes a double moment of feminist resistance and triumph. What Sloniowski's experience clearly demonstrates is that Godard's work of spurring new knowledge in unexpected ways never ends. And with this reassurance that Godard's becoming-archive exceeds any attempts to contain her, here is where we leave her, in the library.

Notes

1. The symposium, called "Inspiring Collaborations," was organized by Godard's graduate students and colleagues. Most of the materials from the symposium are available in the Barbara Godard Collection at YorkSpace, York University's online archive.
2. According to Godard's academic CV, over the course of her forty-year-long career, she authored two books, edited six books and five special issues while she had over eighty essays published as book chapters and close to 120 articles in journals.
3. It appeared after a five-year delay in 1987. It included the "Bibliography of Feminist Criticism in Canada and Quebec" and the program of the 1981 Dialogue Conference, which brought together francophone and anglophone critics and writers.
4. For example, *Encyclopedia of World Literature in the 20th Century* (1999), *Contemporary World Writers* (1993), *Oxford Companion to Canadian Literature* (1997), *Feminist Writers* (1996), and *Lesbian Histories and Cultures* (2000).
5. See Godard's article "Between Performance and Performativity: Translation and Theatre in the Canadian/Quebec Context."
6. Godard elaborates on this project on the 1960s in her interview with Smaro Kamboureli. See "The Critic, Institutional Culture, and Canadian Literature," 18–19. She presented her paper, "Quebec, the National Question and Student Activism in the 1960s," at the conference New World Coming: The Sixties and the Shaping of Global Consciousness, at Queen's University in 2007.
7. See her analysis of the reception of Québec women's writing in English Canada in "A Literature in the Making" (1999), or of the belatedness of translations of Deleuze into English ("Signs").

8   For examples of her analysis of translation as a craft, see her discussion of translations of Gabrielle Roy, Marie-Claire Blais, and Anne Hébert in "A Literature in the Making," as well as her discussion of the translation and reception of Luce Irigaray and Hélène Cixous in "Translating (with) the Speculum."
9   Godard's presentations on the feminist monuments were "Sacrificial Logics: The Politics of Feminist Memorializing," Canadian Women's Studies Association, Congress of the Social Sciences and Humanities, Edmonton, May 27, 2000; "The Politics of Feminist Memorializing after December 6, 1989," University Art Association of Canada, University of Manitoba, Winnipeg, November 3, 2000; and "Symbolic Economies and Making Space for Women: The Politics of Feminist Memorializing after December 6, 1989." Espacios de Género/Gendered Spaces Interdisciplinary Conference, Universidad Huelva, Spain, May 10, 2001.

Works Cited

Binhammer, Katherine, Louise Cotnoir, Barbara Godard, Jennifer Henderson, and Lianne Moyes. "For the Record." Introduction to "Memory Work/des mémoires des femmes." *Tessera* 14 (Summer 1993): 7–23. Print.

Godard, Barbara. "Between One Cliché and Another: Language in *The Double Hook*." *Studies in Canadian Literature* 4.1 (Summer 1978): 114–65. Print.

———. "Between Performance and Performativity: Translation and Theatre in the Canadian/Quebec Context." *Modern Drama* 43.3 (Fall 2000): 327–58. Print.

———. "The Canadian Discourse as the Discourse of the Other." *A/part: Papers from the 1984 Ottawa Conference on Language, Culture, and Identity in Canada*. Ed. G.M. Bumstead. *Canadian Literature* supp. no. 1 (May 1, 1987): 130–7. Print.

———, ed. *Collaboration in the Feminine: Writings on Women and Culture from Tessera*. Toronto: Second Story, 1994. Print.

———. "Crawford's Fairy Tales." *Studies in Canadian Literature* 4.2 (Winter 1979): 109–38. Rpt. in *Nineteenth Century Literary Criticism*. Vol. 127. Detroit: Gale, 2003. Print.

———. "Critical Discourse in/on Quebec." *Studies on Canadian Literature: Essays Introductory and Critical*. Ed. Arnold E. Davidson. New York: MLA, 1990. 271–95. Rpt. in *Canadian Literature at the Crossroads of Language and Culture*. Ed. Smaro Kamboureli. Edmonton: NeWest, 2008. 83–107. Print.

———. "The Critic, Institutional Culture, and Canadian Literature." Interview with Smaro Kamboureli. *Canadian Literature at the Crossroads of Language and Culture*. Ed. Smaro Kamboureli. Edmonton: NeWest, 2008. 17–52. Print.

———. "Culture at the Crossroads." "The Big Divide." *Resources for Feminist Research* 32.3–4 (2007): 13–28. Print.

———. "Deleuze and Translation." *Parallax* 14 (January 2000): 56–81. Print.

---. "Deterritorializing Strategies: M. Nourbese Philip as Caucasianist Ethnographer." *Ebony, Ivory, and Tea*. Ed. Zbigniew Bialis and Krzysztof Kowalczyk-Twarowski. Katowice, Poland: Wydawnictwo Uniwersytetu Slaskiego, 2004. 228–42. Rpt. in *Canadian Literature at the Crossroads of Language and Culture*. Ed. Smaro Kamboureli. Edmonton: NeWest, 2008. 161–73. Print.

---. "Feminist Periodicals and the Production of Cultural Value." *Women's Studies International Forum* 25.2 (March 2002): 209–23. Print.

---. "Feminist Speculations on Value: Culture in an Age of Downsizing." *Ghosts in the Machine: Women and Cultural Policy in Canada and Australia*. Ed. Annette Van Den Bosch and Alison Beale. Toronto: Garamond, 1998. 43–76. Print.

---, ed. *Gynocritics/La Gynocritique: Feminist Approaches to Writing by Canadian and Québécoise Women*. Toronto: ECW, 1987. Print.

---. "Heirs of the Living Body: Alice Munro and the Question of a Female Aesthetic." *The Art of Alice Munro: Saying the Unsayable*. Ed. Judith Miller. Waterloo: U of Waterloo P, 1984. 43–71. Print.

---. "*L'Amèr* or Exploding Chapter: Nicole Brossard at the Site of Feminist Deconstruction." *Atlantis* 9.2 (Spring 1984): 23–34. Print.

---. "Life (in) Writing: Or a Writing-Machine for Producing the Subject." *Nicole Brossard: Essays on Her Works*. Ed. Louise Forsyth. Toronto: Guernica, 2005. 193–210. Print.

---. "A Literature in the Making: Rewriting and the Dynamism of the Cultural Field." 1999. *Canadian Literature at the Crossroads of Language and Culture*. Ed. Smaro Kamboureli. Edmonton: NeWest, 2008. 273–313. Print.

---. "My (M)Other, My Self: Strategies for Subversion in Atwood and Hébert." *Essays on Canadian Writing* 26 (1983): 13–44. Rpt. in *The Art and Genius of Anne Hébert: Essays on Her Work*. Ed. Janis Pallister. Cranbury, NJ: Fairleigh Dickinson UP, 2001. 316–34 Print.

---. "Notes from the Cultural Field: Canadian Literature from Identity to Commodity." *Essays on Canadian Writing* 72 (2000): 209–47. Rpt. in *Canadian Literature at the Crossroads of Language and Culture*. Ed. Smaro Kamboureli. Edmonton: NeWest, 2008. 235–71. Print.

---. "The Politics of Representation: Some Native Canadian Women Writers." *Canadian Literature* 124–25 (April 1992): 5–27. 1990. Rpt. in *Canadian Literature at the Crossroads of Language and Culture*. Ed. Smaro Kamboureli. Edmonton: NeWest, 2008. 109–59. Print.

---. "'Producing Visibility for Lesbians': Nicole Brossard's Quantum Poetics." *English Studies in Canada* 21.2 (1995): 125–37. Print.

---. "(Re)Appropriation as Translation. *Canadian Theatre Review* 64 (Fall 1990): 22–31. Print.

---. "Relational Logics: Of Linguistic and Other Transactions in the Americas." 2005. Rpt. in *Canadian Literature at the Crossroads of Language and Culture*. Ed. Smaro Kamboureli. Edmonton: NeWest, 2008. 315–57. Print.

―――. "The Risk of Critique: Voices Across the Generations." *Academic Callings: The University We Have Had, Now Have, and Could Have*. Ed. Janice Newson and Claire Polster. Toronto: Canadian Scholars Press, 2010. 26–34. Print.

―――. "Signs and Events: Deleuze in Translation." *Semiotic Review of Books* 15.3 (2005): 3–10. Print.

―――. "Structuralism/Post-Structuralism: Language, Reality, and Canadian Literature." *Future Indicative: Literary Theory and Canadian Literature*. Ed. John Moss. Ottawa: U of Ottawa P, 1987. 25–51. Rpt. in *Canadian Literature at the Crossroads of Language and Culture*. Ed. Smaro Kamboureli. Edmonton: NeWest Press, 2008. 53–82. Print.

―――. *Talking About Ourselves: The Literary Productions of Native Women*. CRIAW Publication no. 11. Ottawa: CRIAW, 1985. Print.

―――. "Theatres of Perception: The Filmworks of Barbara Sternberg and the Paperworks of Rae Davis." *Image/duration: Installations of the moving image*. Ed. Tim Dallett. Ottawa: Gallery 101, 1999. 48–73. Print.

―――. "Theorizing Feminist Discourse/Translation." *Tessera* 6 (Spring 1989): 42–53. Print.

―――. "Theorizing the Archive in the Canadian Context." York University course outline for English 6997 and Social and Political Thought 6672. Fall 2007.

―――. "Translating and Sexual Difference." *Resources for Feminist Research* 13.3 (November 1984): 13–14. Print.

―――. "Translating (with) the Speculum." *TTR* 4.2 (Winter 1991): 85–121. Print.

―――. "The Translator as She." *In the Feminine: Women and Words/Les femmes et les mots*. Ed. Ann Dybikowksi et al. Edmonton: Longspoon, 1985. 193–98. Print.

―――. "Voicing Difference: The Literary Production of Native Women." *A-Mazing Space: Writing Canadian Women Writing*. Ed. Shirley Newman and Smaro Kamboureli. Edmonton: Longspoon, 1986. 87–107. Print.

―――. "Writing Between Cultures." *TTR* 10.1 (1997): 53–97. Print.

―――. "Writing from the Border: Gail Scott on 'The Main.'" *Gail Scott: Essays on Her Work*. Ed. Lianne Moyes. Toronto: Guernica, 2002. 117–41. Print.

Godard, Barbara, with Katherine Binhammer, Louise Cotnoir, Jennifer Henderson, and Lianne Moyes. "Feminist(s) Project(s)/Projets (des) féministes." *Tessera* 15 (Winter 1993): 6–13. Print.

Godard, Barbara, with Di Brandt, eds. *Wider Boundaries of Daring: The Modernist Impulse in Canadian Women's Poetry*. Waterloo: Wilfrid Laurier UP, 2009. Print.

Godard, Barbara, with Susan Knutson, Daphne Marlatt, Kathy Mezei, and Gail Scott, eds. "La Traduction au feminine/Translating Women." *Tessera* 6 (1989). Print.

Prolegomenon
Reader at Work: An Appreciation of Barbara Godard

DANIELLE FULLER

> What narrative to relate? This is the fundamental question to be addressed by the literary critic faced with a vast body of material, a pluralistic critical scene, a border/line position both inside and outside the critical institution in question, and the limitations of form imposed by the present venue.
>
> (Godard, *Canadian Literature* 83)

In their original context these words stage the problematic of composing a critique that at once introduces, surveys, and interrogates the discourse about Québec literature. They also seem appropriate to the job before me here. Which narrative of Barbara Godard should I write, given the range and quantity of her scholarly work and achievements? How should I tell a story that celebrates a career? What narrative mode should I adopt for this tale of an intellectual whom I think of as a teacher, although I have never formally been her student? To borrow from Godard again, think of what follows as a reader at work, reading again, and reading *with* the critic who is also "reading reading" (*Canadian Literature* 200). Consider this as an invitation to read on and beyond the narratives that I have selected here.

"Such Is the Evolving Nature of My Subject That, Even as I Speak, [She] Slips Away from Me" (Godard, *Canadian Literature* 53)

Barbara Godard's contribution to Canadian literature and culture was extensive and multi-faceted. As a prize-winning translator, theorist, editor, collaborator, award-winning teacher (at York University), researcher, and recipient of the Award of Merit from the Association for Canadian Studies, Godard took up multiple positions within the field of scholarship that we have come to delimit as CanLit. She was a significant intellectual figure whose feminist politics informed her professional advocacy work, social activism, teaching, and scholarship. Creating the tools—bibliographical and theoretical—as well as many primary and secondary texts that have helped to shape the paradigms of feminist Canadian criticism was a key achievement of Godard's long and distinguished scholarly career. Her accomplishments range from dazzling contributions to feminist translation theory, to her practice of "writing with the text," a style of criticism elaborated among the *Tessera* collective as "fiction-theory" (Godard, *Collaboration*). She was one of a small handful of scholars responsible for the introduction of several substantial bodies of theory and knowledge to Canadian academic criticism, from semiotics to approaches derived from comparative literature. As well as publishing prolifically across her wide range of interests, Godard was involved in the production of several innovative Canadian periodicals, labour that, when it is well done, of course, is often almost invisible to its readers. Without such labour, however, it is very difficult to sustain intellectual conversations across time and space, and Godard's substantial volume of work on periodicals was characterized by a strong commitment to introducing to the pages of Canadian journals not only new ideas and experimental writing, but also work by new generations of academic and creative writers. A founding member of *Tessera*, the feminist journal that brought together work by feminist writers and thinkers from across Canada and in both official languages, Godard also worked for many years as a contributing editor to *Open Letter* and, from 1998, as the book reviews editor for *Topia*, the journal of Canadian cultural studies. Additionally, she was the French editor of *Fireweed* (1978–80) and served on the editorial boards of a range of other periodicals.

Barbara Godard is a name known to many feminist scholars around the world, especially perhaps to students of translation and followers of Canadian and Québec women's writing. Her creatively engaged work as a translator of Nicole Brossard and Antonine Maillet, among others, represents just a fraction of her efforts as a practitioner in that field, a practice that profoundly affected her relationship with language and her analysis of its operation in various cultural, temporal, and linguistic contexts. For someone so attentive to the power of words and to the situation of those empowered and disempowered by words, it is not surprising that editing also represents a significant aspect of Godard's oeuvre. She was responsible for producing a dozen important collections published in the form of special journal issues as well as books. Among the latter is the path-breaking *Gynocritics/Gynocritiques: Feminist Approaches to Canadian and Quebec Women's Writing* (1987), winner of the Gabrielle Roy Prize. This collection included two contributions authored by Godard, one of which was a valuable bibliographical resource for feminist criticism in Canada and Québec. Like so many other projects she initiated over the last (nearly) forty years, at the time of its publication, the bibliography represented a much-needed resource for an emerging area of study that still lacked many of the basic scholarly materials required for sustained—and historically sustainable— research. The bibliography thus stands today as an essential historical record of feminist critical writing in Canada to the mid-1980s, and an important document of a period that few scholars outside Canada study. For these reasons, Godard's introduction to *Gynocritics/Gynocritiques*, "Mapmaking: A Survey of Feminist Literary Criticism in Canada/Quebec," is an essay that I continue to recommend to undergraduates in my own Canadian women's writing courses because of the intelligent critical history and theoretical orientation that it offers.

Always mindful of the "relentless presentness of the field" (*Canadian Literature* 34), a focus that is partly due to the fact that primary Canadian texts rapidly go out of print, Godard continued to produce resources to help students of Canadian literature better understand poetics and translation in theory and as a set of historical (as well as contemporary) practices. She worked with Di Brandt on *Re:Generations: Canadian Women Poets in Conversation* (2005) and on a complementary collection of critical essays *"Wider Boundaries of Daring": The Modernist Impulse in Canadian Women's Poetry* (2008). Additionally, she edited with Kate Eichhorn "Feminist Poetics Today," a special issue of *Open Letter* (2009) that revisits and extends a dialogue begun in another special issue of that journal edited by Lola Lemire Tostevin (1992), which focused on the "next generation" of feminist writers. A book of essays, *Translation Studies in Canada: Institutions, Discourses, Practices, Texts* (forthcoming), is another collection gathered by Godard that usefully signals in its title a series of concerns and sites that variously occupied her throughout her career. The selection of Godard's essays, published as *Canadian Literature at the Crossroads of Language and Culture* (2008), demonstrates similar preoccupations.

Perhaps because her written work has always moved self-reflexively between her roles as a creator and a cartographer of the CanLit field, remarking in a timely fashion upon its institutional and infrastructural struggles, intervening in and advancing its theoretical debates and parsing its discursive formations, Godard's impressive publication output was dominated by the genre of the essay. She was, in fact, the author of over two hundred essays written in French or English. These contributions appeared in a wide range of periodicals and book collections variously focused on semiotics, post-structuralism, translation and translation theory, poetics, comparative literature, feminist theory, Canadian and Québec literature, and cultural theory. Many essays have been translated into other languages, most frequently into Italian and Spanish, while several have been republished in various languages within collections produced outside Canada in Europe, the Americas, and Asia. Comparative literature scholars in Brazil and feminist scholars in India have proven to be especially receptive audiences for Godard's work, with several graduate students from both countries travelling to work with her in Canada. These young scholars number among the nearly forty doctoral students supervised by Godard and the further seventy-eight graduate students whose committees she belonged to during her long career at York University, where she taught in the Department of English, as well as for the graduate programs in social and political thought, women's studies, and French. As a teacher and visiting professor, then, Barbara Godard directly influenced generations of students around the world, as well as generating great influence across her fields of study.

Reading across the Generations

Godard's feminist theorizing of women's writing, combined with her attention to the politics of cultural production, profoundly influenced my own understanding of textual practices and critical methods. Her complex engagement with the philosophical arguments of French theorists and their followers was nearly always accompanied in her essays by careful commentary on the material conditions within which cultural texts are produced, disseminated, and interpreted. Close attention to the operation—linguistic, economic, discursive—of vectors of power results in a methodology that has often appeared to me to be layered in its process and cumulative in its effect. For a reader this can be a dizzying experience, since there are always multiple threads to follow and, certainly in my own case, to become entangled within. (The "web" is a favoured feminist metaphor of Godard's and an especially apt one). Nevertheless, I remember how important it was to me as a graduate student to learn that critical writing could be seriously playful and creative with form as well as with language and concepts, yet retain a concern with material and embodied experience. Lynette Hunter's M.A. course on Canadian writing at the University of Leeds positioned Godard's critical texts alongside those of Daphne Marlatt (*Ana Historic*, 1988) and Nicole Brossard (*These Our Mothers* in Godard's translation, 1983) to create a type of textual reproduction of the conversations about language, gender, and power in which these feminist writers were still actively engaged at that time (1990–91). Although our classroom was far away from the actual sites of those discussions, their collective intellectual energy was communicated to us and intensified by this textual juxtaposition. Prompting us to read Godard, Marlatt, and Brossard intertextually was, of course, entirely appropriate to their creative-critical project as feminist collaborators, and it is a testimony to the brilliance of Hunter's intellectual pedagogy that I still possess an almost visceral memory of those seminars. I also remember giving away my copy of *These Our Mothers* to a professional dancer who led a workshop on "feminist" erotic performance that I took around this time (too young for the second wave, some aspirant feminists of my generation who sought to be "creative" spent a fair amount of their energy on that kind of thing). I have often wondered whether, in that dancer's hands, Brossard's work underwent a further translation and what such a remediation would have looked like. Given Godard's love of music and dancing, it would certainly have been a fitting continuation of her translation practice as a form of creative rereading.

By the time I encountered Godard's work, she had already been involved in the formation of several professional associations that helped to establish Canadian literary studies as a recognizable academic "field" (including the Association for Canadian and Québécois Literatures in 1974). By the time I understood that "Canadian literature" referred to criticism as well as a set of primary texts, Godard had taught a number of well-attended courses in Canadian and Québec writing, and in literary theory at York University, always lobbying for their importance within the "English" curriculum, and actively resisting institutional moves to marginalize and/or remove them. By the time I was beginning to understand what an academic feminist discourse was and what "writing in the feminine" meant, Barbara Godard had taken part in a number of landmark Canadian feminist conferences such as Women and Words (Vancouver, 1983) which, among other things, catalyzed the group that went on to produce the first issues of *Tessera*.

Additionally, and throughout the late 1970s and the 1980s, Godard was associated with various feminist networks, reading and seminar groups (for example, the *Fireweed* collective) for whom she frequently became a "connector" figure. Such a role makes particular sense, it seems to me, for someone trained in comparative literature, bilingual in Canada's official languages, and active as a translator who came to political consciousness during the 1960s. Although it contains no explicitly autobiographical material, one of Godard's last published essays, "Quebec, the National Question and English-Canadian Student Activism in the 1960s: The Rise of Student Syndicalism" (2009), presents a compelling analysis of the student activist movement in the early years of that decade, the period during which Godard was an undergraduate student in Toronto. As her title suggests, Godard's study offers more than a carefully researched history of political exchange and communication between anglophone students based at the University of Toronto and francophone students attending universities in Québec. The essay traces a genealogy of "syndicalisme," a conceptualization of the student as a citizen as well as a member of the academy and an idea adopted by students in Québec. As Godard represents it, the notion of citizenship pertaining at the time was not always limited by the political constructions or imaginings of nation-states, whether Canada or Quebéc. Students did, of course, discuss the issues of a sovereign Québec, language rights, and social equality, as her evidence from student newspapers and the records of national and provincial student associations vividly demonstrates. But "the National Question" was not only framed by the Canadian situation. In Godard's lucid analytical narrative, we see how students from Québec and Ontario were also influenced by social movements and economic transformations occurring around the globe. She represents this period without recourse to nostalgia and in order to underline the dialectics in which activists of various ideological persuasions were inevitably caught as they learned about the "dynamics of international power" both in terms of the decolonization processes occurring in other regions of the world, and in terms of the expansion of late capitalism (289). The essay is a *tour de force* in terms of its attention to empirical detail, its nuanced readings of political position-taking and its back-and-forth movement between local circumstance and transnational contexts. Here, then, is a complex representation of one crucible within which a young Godard's politics were formed, but you need to read between the lines to find her as she plays the part of the self-effacing historian so well.

Another of Godard's genealogical critiques—this time about the state of women's studies in the mid-2000s—is more revealing of her self-formation, both in terms of her respectful but critical treatment of the life-transforming events experienced by second wave feminists, and in terms of the eloquent case she advances for feminist work on language and poetics. In "Culture at the Crossroads" (2007), Godard asks, "What counts as culture?" within the institutional constructions of women's studies, within contemporary feminism, and for members of different generations (21). If Godard's history of the Canadian student movement in the 1960s is a story of the fusion of ideas and of organizations, then her intellectual history of women's studies is a narrative about fissure: between the movement and the academy, between the humanities and the social sciences, and even between generations of feminist theorists. Godard's analysis charts "the uneasy relations of the Humanities and the Social Sciences within Women's Studies" across three decades (14), probing competing discourses of knowledge production. Taking a cue from Woolf, Godard "think[s] back through" the philosophy and experiences of the women who pioneered the teaching of women's studies in the United States and Canada by examining a series of memoirs and anthologies (16). These, she avers, "converge around an emplotment of loss" that records not only the failure of a political project that aimed to "end inequality," but also "around Women's Studies' as yet incomplete promise of interdisciplinarity in its institutionalization" (16). As Godard's examination continues, the losses mount up, persuasively, if rather depressingly, for those of us trained in the humanities. Feminist theories of gender as symbolically inscribed, which enable the analysis of language, discourse, and representation, get shunted aside in favour of those conceptualizing gender as socially organized. Sites of textual production and exchange, such as women's writing, and the work of feminist editorial collectives become devalued and overlooked as possible objects for study and research. Utility prevails under a banner promising social change. The inspirational role played by feminist visual artists, poets, writers, and theatre groups whose work informed, provoked, and motivated many women of the so-called "second wave" is forgotten or marginalized.

Godard's analysis in "Culture at the Crossroads" demonstrates the way that cultural practices fade from view when "culture" is understood as "a distinctive way of life, linked to the collective identity of a community or nation" but disaggregated from notions of "civility" and humanity expressed in "well made artefacts" (25). The "crossroads" of her title refers to this "Culture/culture" division, a division that Godard torques at the essay's end into a potentially productive dialectic. She envisions "a carrefour" or an intersection where scholarship that engages with the aesthetic, the economic, and the ethnographic can coincide and conversations across disciplines can occur (25). Her closing image of pathways converging and opening out again is an apt metaphor for her own intellectual and activist work. At many points in her long career, Godard chose the crossroads as her philosophical location and material situation, a position from which she created new collaborations, ideas, and texts. She frequently employed her ability to identify points of connection among different groups and individuals, bringing people together to work on a common issue, event, or problem, usually as a means to challenge the power relations within and beyond her own social reality. "Relationality within vectors of power" is a key concept within Godard's writing and teaching (*Canadian Literature* 27). Following Gramsci, Godard always thought about "one literature or text in relation to another, thinking dialectically or intertextually," understanding language and culture as "always positioned in relation to another temporal moment or geopolitical space" rather than considering them "in terms of identity" (*Canadian Literature* 26–27). Godard's varied activities are lent a thoughtful and fascinating framework in "The Critic, Institutional Culture, and Canadian Literature: Barbara Godard in Conversation with Smaro Kamboureli," the interview that forms a lively and detailed introduction to Godard's essays collected in *Canadian Literature at the Crossroads of Language and Culture*. The "Conversation," as Kamboureli points out, forms an important "cultural memory document" in which Godard explains her academic training, career trajectory, institutional battles, intellectual influences, and feminist practice within a narrative that is at once a personal and a public intellectual history.

Godard's account of her university education, especially her search for a suitable location for her doctoral work, is a trenchant reminder of the "youth" of Canadian literary criticism and its institutional formations. It is also a story that suggests her unending intellectual curiosity, her dogged determination, and a very pragmatic approach to institutional obstacles: she repeatedly sought out people who could offer her advice and whose knowledge opened up new opportunities and new ways of thinking to her. The dearth of established programs in Canadian literature during the late 1960s was the main reason that Malcolm Ross (the founder-editor of the New Canadian Library Series) advised her to "get out of here," "here" being the University of Toronto, which Ross himself was about to leave behind for Dalhousie University (*Canadian Literature* 21). Not only was Godard, the graduate student, relatively unusual at the time of Ross's injunction in terms of her enthusiasm for the literatures of the country she had grown up in, but her M.A. training at the Université de Montréal, where she was able to take classes in both French and English departments, had inspired a conviction that she should also work comparatively. Thus, as with so many of her subsequent intellectual endeavours, Godard was simultaneously a "path-breaker" and an "early adopter." In her doctoral work on English and French Montreal urban imaginaries she sought to "analyze literary form through a political lens" (*Canadian Literature* 21). However, not content to engage only with sociological approaches to literature, she also drew upon the work of other theoretical traditions such as phenomenology. Godard's determination to undertake comparative work in Canadian and Québec literatures eventually led her to Robert Escarpit, one of the founders of the International Association of Comparative Literature, who was working at the University of Bordeaux. She set out for France, hoping that she would be able to return to Canada to complete her studies at the Université de Montréal once their comparative literature program had been approved, but this was not to be. Instead, Godard's unintentionally extended study time in France exposed her to theories and paradigms, such as structuralism, semiotics, feminism, and institutional analysis that resonate across her oeuvre.

The reader of "Structuralism/Post-structuralism: Language, Reality, and Canadian Literature" (1987), another essay in the *Canadian Literature at the Crossroads of Language and Culture* collection, might find it helpful to imagine Godard sitting in Roland Barthes's seminars in Paris, teaching in the same department as Hélène Cixous, witnessing the post-structuralist "turn" as it was mediated (in person) through such figures as Michel Foucault and Gilles Deleuze. My point is that Barbara Godard did not only study this key period in the history of Western philosophical thought, she actually lived through and participated in it: these theorists created the swirling currents in which the young scholar swam. Reading the essay now is like stepping aboard a high-speed time-travelling ghost train that blasts through over a decade of what we used to call "high theory." Like all good ghost trains, there are some genuinely scary sights (Frye! Leavis! American New Criticism!), as well as a few ghostly apparitions to be exorcised: "nowhere in these studies are Tzvetan Todorov and Gerard Genette, whose spirit is nonetheless everywhere present" (*Canadian Literature* 66). And, just as you think you have arrived safely at the end of the ride—"The name of Derrida at last, you sigh" (*Canadian Literature* 74)—the train lurches into a new section of the labyrinthine tunnel system, where we encounter several (Canadian and French) interpretations of deconstruction and feminism before taking a final rapid swerve through Foucault and Bakhtin.

My ghost-ride metaphor is intentionally humorous and more a reflection of the ways that my own knowledge gaps make reading this essay a particularly heady experience for me. Nevertheless, the image has some critical purchase since there is a calling-out and a confrontation of spectral (theoretical) figures taking place here. Godard's critique traces "the presuppositions and ... the logic and ideology" of various "textual strategies" adopted by an array of Canadian literary critics writing in the first half of the 1980s (*Canadian Literature* 82)—what she refers to at the beginning of the essay as "the 'new criticism' of Canadian literature" (*Canadian Literature* 53). The reader may arrive at the end of her high-speed, time-defeating journey feeling a little shaken up, but she has a better sense of intellectual history and, in particular, of the critical efforts of Canadian scholars to find a language and a set of conceptual frameworks that would both explain and validate Canadian writing, while banishing forever the haunt of thematic criticism.

"Work[ing] (the) in-Between" (*Canadian Literature* 175)

Working collaboratively, collectively, and across languages, Godard maintained a deep involvement with feminist cultural production in Canada for several decades as a practitioner, and frequently initiated conversations that bridged the two so-called "literary solitudes." Sometimes this involved creating literal spaces for discussion among francophone and anglophone Canadian writers and critics by organizing conferences, workshops, or symposia. At others, she acted as a translator and selector of Québec essays, as she did early on as a contributing editor to *Open Letter*, a role she took up when the journal was restarted by Frank Davey in 1972 (*Canadian Literature* 42). While Godard's translation activities during the 1970s were at least partially prompted by the necessity of earning a living, thanks to the precariousness of her initially untenured position at York University (at one point she nearly took up the post of translation officer for the Canada Council), her translation activities in the 1980s were partly inspired by an eagerness to teach more writing from Québec to her predominantly anglophone students. For Coach House Press, which produced so many beautiful books designed with great care and printed on lavishly high-grade paper in the 1980s, Godard translated Brossard's *L'Amèr*, a book that appeared in a series of small, slim, blue, and, as I recall, somewhat less lavishly manufactured books (the series ceased publishing in 1985). It was in this format, and in Godard's "Englishing" of *These Our Mothers* that not only Godard's undergraduate students, but also many anglophone feminists outside Canada first read Brossard's work (*Canadian Literature* 42). As an intellectually creative translator of experimental Québécoise writers, Godard brought attention to work that challenged the then-dominant paradigm of English-Canadian realism. She also produced what might be more accurately described as additional interpretations of (as opposed to essays about) these works, texts that, in their turn, also rewrote and reread the originals. Frustrated by the failure of some French feminist theory to deal with "issues of gender" and to "rise to the challenges of the linguistic play in the texts" that were becoming familiar to her as a reader, critic, teacher, and translator, Godard became a theorist of feminist translation strategies (*Canadian Literature* 43). Her experiences of working with Brossard's texts were particularly inspirational in this regard and she made a series of critical interventions within the field of translation studies that have helped form a "distinctive" "Canadian school of translation theory" (*Canadian Literature* 43). Members of the audience at the panel on Brossard's work organized by Susan Rudy for the British Association for Canadian Studies conference held at Oxford in March 2009 will recall Ann-Marie Wheeler's and Louise Forsyth's engaging explications of this "school" and their expert demonstrations of feminist translation praxis via their "live" collaborative readings with Brossard.

Godard was equally adept at "translating" and interrogating critical discourses about Québec writing for an anglophone readership. "Critical Discourse in/on Quebec" (first published in 1990) and "A Literature in the Making: Rewriting and the Dynamism of the Cultural Field" (1999, translated for the 2008 essay collection from the original French by Godard) offer acute analyses of the literary-critical field (in the Bourdieusian sense) within which both fiction from and academic writing about Québec are produced, published, and received by professional readers. As such, they historicize and conceptualize a series of approaches developed within Québec but adapted from the francophone "sociology of literature" tradition, including an important Québec-Belgian dialogue that refocused critical attention on institutional analysis during the 1980s (*Canadian Literature* 96). "Critical Discourse," in particular, examines the various institutional and theoretical influences that produced critical writing about Québécois literature up to the late 1980s, not the least of which was the important emergence of feminist theory and creative-critical writing. "A Literature in the Making" extends the critique offered in "Critical Discourse" in time, but here, Godard also expands upon it to offer a theoretically accomplished and materially situated articulation of the complex intersections of English-Canadian and French-Canadian literary fields. This essay considers not only the translation of works by Marie-Claire Blais, Gabrielle Roy, and Anne Hébert into English (the "big three" from the anglophone reader's point of view) but also the ways that their popular and academic reception has been framed by other forms of translation via, for example, adaptation for television drama. Godard argues that "TV dramatization linked Roy's work to the pastoral myth and Blais's fiction to the pain of urban living," thereby elaborating upon "the dominant representation of Quebec literature in its attention to the symbolic and affective aspects of the work—restrained despair contrasted with sympathy for the characters, the poetry of their dreams, and the passion or lyricism of the novelist" (*Canadian Literature* 287). She further demonstrates how the celebration of "the work of Quebec women writers for its pathos" is a discourse employed by journalists, feminist academic critics, and translators alike (286). Interpreting Québec women's writing in terms of folklore and realism rather than paying attention to its technical skill and subtle political commentary, she contends, suits "the large-scale field of production, that of popular literature" (287). However, this practice is not simply the inevitable outcome of commodification, but rather it serves an important symbolic and ideological function that is particularly identifiable within the writing of several English-Canadian critics who conflate "the nationalist demands of Quebec with those of Canada" so that "Quebec constitutes a sort of libidinal excess for Anglophone culture" (289). Godard's treatment of various (mis)translations of Blais's writing is a particularly fascinating and compelling aspect of her argument. She shows through a detailed series of examples how translators working for mainstream English-Canadian publishers like McClelland & Stewart have followed a translation practice that promotes an "ideology of naturalization" (302) at the expense of rendering neutral the linguistic openness of the Québécois idiom and the "language politics" that it signals (301).

These two essays can be set alongside a third, "Notes from the Cultural Field: Canadian Literature from Identity to Commodity" (2000, included in the 2008 collection), which focuses primarily on the English-Canadian literary field. Here, Godard analyzes the changing symbolic role of Canadian literature within a discourse of Canadian identity as that field was altered by the internationalization of the discipline, the globalizing structures of English-language publishing, and the reorientation of Canadian cultural policy and state funding in the mid-1990s toward a notion of culture for profit rather than for community. In addition to examining the history of the Canada Council, and that of the Ontario Arts Council, Godard considers how international agencies such as the World Trade Organization have made decisions that impacted directly on the production and dissemination of Canadian writing. Godard analyzes the federal government's role in "selling Canadian knowledge industries abroad" and assigning a "cultural" role to Canadian studies associations outside Canada financed through the Department of Foreign Affairs and International Trade (DFAIT) (256). Reading policy documents produced by Chrétien's government in 1995, Godard notes the linking of the marketing of cultural goods to the promotion of Canadian trade opportunities. However, if culture was positioned by DFAIT fifteen years ago as a "secret agent in global economic struggles" (256), we have since witnessed its total elimination from foreign policy priorities. Rereading "Notes from the Cultural Field" in 2010, I am prompted to reflect upon this development as the inevitable outcome of the naturalization of capitalism within Canadian foreign policy and its concomitant curtailment of anything that explores or challenges "the concept of exchange-value as absolute" (257), or, for that matter, of creative work that might unsettle the notion that inter/national "security" is dependent on the exchange of "intelligence." As my reflection suggests, one of the valuable aspects of Godard's work for me is her consistent attention to the rhetoric, structures, and practices of governments, and educational and legal institutions. Her critiques repeatedly expose the operations of economic capital and interrogate power relations that are exercised through discourse and strategies of representation. She reminds us that the role of an intellectual is to question the society in which she lives and works, to make theory in order to unravel what appears to be "normal," and to politicize what appears to be "neutral."

"A 'Lament for a Nation'? Or Scratching Graffiti in a Prophecy of Doom?" ("Feminist Speculations" 43)

Godard's series of essays about the downsizing of federal and provincial funding for culture and the arts skewers the neo-conservative ideology of the mid-1990s with irony and humour. These pieces, published in both academic and popular periodicals, also articulate Godard's cultural nationalism and her pride in being a Torontonian—not, perhaps, identities that her feminist followers would immediately associate with the woman or her work, but certainly, for Godard, identifications that inspired a passion for the performing and textual arts and a deeply held belief in the capacity of cultural practices to trouble normative relations and to celebrate differently imagined communities. In "Feminist Speculations on Value: Culture in the

Age of Downsizing" (1998), she scrutinizes the activities and rhetoric of the Canada Council to reveal how it played a part in the "vanishing" of public culture and the "resignification" of "public interest" as economic profit (45). But Godard also pauses, in a characteristic moment of critical self-reflection, to recall the material and symbolic transformations that the Canada Council and cultural policy have wrought within the arts in Canada since the late 1950s. Remembering the changes brings recognition of "how [her] own intellectual formation has been shaped by cultural policy" (49). Movingly, she writes about the advantages denied to her mother's generation but available to hers: "I have long taken for granted the possibilities these policies opened for intellectual and artistic training and practice which have constituted the habitus making materially possible who I am. Without these policies, there would be little Canadian literature, film, painting, theatre for me to teach and translate" (49). Godard goes on to paint a vivid scene of a 1950s Toronto in which her younger self endured "one long dull wait for something, anything, to happen." Cataloguing what was available, and contrasting it with the Toronto of the 1990s, she asserts that her "pleasure in the rich diversity" of the arts is "limited only by the difficulty of making a choice among them" (50).

Godard's pleasure in live performance, which she so often shared with friends, students, and colleagues passing through her hometown, is, however, tempered by melancholia in these essays on the changing state of the arts in her local and national culture. The tactic Godard adopts in "Feminist Speculations," one of oscillation between what she terms the "genres" of "'lament for a nation'" and "scratching graffiti in a prophecy of doom" (43), continues through her essays for *Fuse* magazine. There, she reiterates her analyses of cultural funding, offering compelling and detailed case studies of the restructuring of the Ontario Arts Council (in "Privatizing the Public: Notes from the Ontario Culture Wars," 1997) and the dismantling of the Nova Scotia Arts Council (in "Upping the Anti: Of Poetic Ironies, Propaganda Machines, and the Claims for Public Sponsorship of Culture," 2002). Her instinct for recording shifts in the signification of "culture" as they actually occurred is even more discernible in her magazine writing than in her academic articles. "Upping the Anti" is especially powerful for its excavation of the tensions between aesthetic and political discourses as they played out in the Nova Scotian cultural field of 2002. Godard's careful attention to both rhetoric and economics blasts a hole through the neoliberal's love of free market economy, at the same time demonstrating how both federal and provincial governments drove a wedge between political and aesthetic discourse in order to justify their "hands-off" approach to arts funding. Especially valuable for those of us who are students of cultural politics and production in Canada is her account in this essay of the collapse of General Distribution Services and the dire ripple effect this had on independent Canadian publishing companies as well as Canadian-owned bookstores. If you want to trace the effects upon Canadian culture of corporate convergence and vertical integration in the cultural industries, "Upping the Anti" is a good starting point.

Godard continually warns us throughout her life's work on cultural policy and production that scrutinizing the "interlocking interests of politics and knowledge" is essential if, as scholars and citizens, we wish to contribute to the advancement of "democratic and social values" founded on notions of equality and a belief in the human benefits of cultural expression ("Upping" 19). "Feminist Speculations" and "Feminist Periodicals and the Production of Cultural Value: The Canadian Context" (2002), as their titles suggest, present an overtly feminist take on these issues. Both critique the "triumph of exchange value" as advocated and enacted by Canadian state organizations and each essay sets out thoroughly researched examples of its consequences for feminist labour and feminist texts ("Feminist Periodicals" 209). "Feminist Periodicals" presents a lively record of the production of periodicals by and for women in Canada from "a highpoint in the recognition of feminist culture," which Godard identifies as occurring in 1985–86, to the demise of many feminist magazines a decade later (209). Impressively, Godard also addresses a significant omission in Bourdieu's materialist analysis of the relationship between cultural and economic value by introducing gender as a category that troubles his model of social stratification. Her insights into "the gendered processes of social reproduction and creation of cultural value" in this essay thus represent not only an important contribution to Canadian women's cultural history, but also a notable addition to cultural theory (211).

In common with much of Godard's scholarship from this period of her career, the analysis in "Feminist Periodicals" reveals in candid detail how "art serves ... as an alternative to participatory democracy" as the public sphere disappears in an era of neo-liberal free market capitalism (221). Godard's is a thoroughly "interested" history of feminist labour and expression in terms of her emotional and political commitment to the value of the work involved in producing and disseminating feminist periodicals. By showing why and how this particular example of cultural practice matters, she offers a counter to the "disinterestedness" of neo-liberalism: a "disinterestedness" that, in Bourdieusian terms, is integral to the economic structures of late capitalism, but also, as Godard notes, a "distinterestedness" that enacts an elision of both "culture" and "Culture" in its disavowal of the collective and its ignoring of communally produced art. In other words, much of the literary-cultural infrastructure constructed in the decades following the Massey Commission was swept away in the mid-late 1990s by a business model that was predicated on a for-profit conceptualization of Canadian arts, rather than on a notion of culture inflected by ideals of democratic access to the means of expression and production. When read alongside a series of pieces from an earlier phase of Godard's career, these essays on feminist cultural production identify all too clearly which cultural groups and communities lose out most when the market is given free rein by government agencies.

"A Country in Translation" (*Canadian Literature* 202)

During the period from the mid-1980s to the mid-1990s, small Canadian presses, supported by state funding, were responsible for producing a significant quantity of innovative and sometimes theoretically informed poetry and prose authored within various cultural communities from across Canada. Godard was an early commentator on much of this writing, especially performance and print texts produced by First Nations peoples and African Canadians. This area of her work is especially well represented by two essays first published in the 1990s that examine Aboriginal Canadian texts from the colonial and contemporary eras. Both "Writing Between Cultures" (1997) and "The Politics of Representation: Some Native Canadian Women Writers" (1990) are reprinted in *Canadian Literature at the Crossroads of Language and Culture*. Godard's critical work in this area stands out because it has always been respectful of the dynamics of specific oral and textual practices, while remaining intellectually rigorous and alert to the power politics and legacies of colonialism. While many other Euro-American critics were still unpacking racist cultural stereotypes in the late 1980s, some even falling into the trap of reproducing them, Godard tackled difficult questions about the politics and processes of cultural transfer between oral and written modes of articulation, between the stage and the page, between indigenous and non-indigenous audience-spectators. She deconstructed the roadblocks of cross-cultural interpretation without ignoring the significance of the historical conditions that produced them. Meanwhile, the elaboration of "relationality" as a theory and a method propelled Godard beyond one language or medium of representation and across the political borderlines of nation-states.

Godard's analysis in "The Politics of Representation: Some Native Canadian Women Writers," first published in the journal *Canadian Literature* (1990), remains relevant and fresh, not least because of her lively opening account of a series of theatrical productions, art exhibitions, and workshops that took place during the spring of 1989 in Toronto. The energy and excitement of the writing in the early pages of this essay emerge in part from the detail of Godard's documentation of the events: titles, artists' names, locations, and dates are all carefully recorded as a prelude to an extended analysis of the "challenge to the Canadian literary tradition" enacted by Aboriginal cultural producers (110). "Politics" is an intervention into and, thanks to Godard's painstaking habit of tracing and checking her facts, a vivid record of the infamous "appropriation of voice" debates of the late 1980s. Sparked by a series of incidents, including public protests by writers Lee Maracle and Leonore Keeshig-Tobias against the stealing of Aboriginal stories by non-Aboriginal producers, the institutionalized racism of the publishing industry, as well as the cultural specificity of constructions of literary value espoused by many of its workers, was dramatically exposed. In this essay, Godard delineates the semiotic field of "the Native" as it operated in Canada in the late 1980s and shows how the words, performances, and texts of writers destabilize dominant colonial discourses while avoiding their binary traps. She argues that while texts such as Armstrong's *Slash* (1985) and Maracle's *I Am Woman* (1988) are recognizable and powerful examples of "resistance literature" produced "within a struggle for decolonization" (*Canadian Literature* 129), their texts also exceed (dominant) categories of genre and displace "conventional representational practices" through a series of "re-visionary" textual manoeuvres (133). Two more recent pieces, also included in the 2008 essay collection, carry similar concerns into a new decade and century, namely, "Deterritorializing Strategies: M. Nourbese Philip as Caucasianist Ethnographer" (2004) and "Relational Logics: Of Linguistic and Other Transactions in the Americas" (2005). The latter essay examines the "re-invention of the Americas" and the "borderline" through a series of historical events and representations by Canadian and Brazilian writers and visual artists (*Canadian Literature* 317). Significantly, these later essays implicitly refer to Godard's understanding of her own cultural nationalism as a position within an expansive field of production that was not, in her purview, delimited only by nation-state politics or policies.

"There Is No Inside/Outside Re-reading, Re-writing" (*Canadian Literature* 200)

"Everybody loves that one!" Godard responded when I suggested "Becoming My Hero, Becoming Myself: Notes Towards a Feminist Theory of Reading" (1990) for inclusion in her essay collection. The essay did not make the final cut, but the fact that Godard canvassed so many of her correspondents, former students, and colleagues as part of the initial selection process for the book is a reminder of how important, yet at the same time how habitual, the practices of collaboration had become for her. Godard's love of conversation conducted in person, in cyberspace, and in her writing created both real and imagined communities of scholars that literally spanned time and space. Perhaps one of the reasons so many of "us" nominated "Becoming My Hero, Becoming Myself" is the intense honesty involved in Godard's representation of her "self-actualization *en process*" (112). Alerted by Godard's introduction to the work of reading (and rewriting) that awaits us, the reader is invited to move back and forth between the two columns of text: Godard's theorizing ("What Are the Readers?") and her more personal account of becoming a reader ("Who Is the Reader? A Case History"). The process of reading and rereading this essay is delightful because Godard's moments of feminist self-discovery through reading are so joyful: "1963—In the summer I read *Mémoires d'une jeune fille rangée* and *Le deuxième sexe* with excitement. I've discovered the story of my life, my conflict with bourgeois society.... Now I have a new hero and a different script for my life" (116). Self-knowledge is, however, also born of frustration, pain, and anxiety, and Godard explores these emotions through the interwoven domains of her intellectual work and everyday life. She acknowledges the psychological struggles involved in her experiences of mothering and "being mothered," as she witnesses her son becoming a teenager and her mother's aging mind and body. At this point in her life, while rapidly acquiring vocabularies, theories, and ideas as she reads, teaches, thinks, and makes sophisticated sense of her self-performance, she simultaneously leaves "great white spaces in [her] diary" despite a contradictory compulsion to "confront intense moments of shock and mourning and avoid them by not writing" (120). Meanwhile, she begins additional diaries and journals as experiments in expression, genre, language, translation, and "as self-analysis, as self-construction in/by narrative" (120).

In her editorial preface to the collection of Godard's essay published in 2008, Smaro Kamboureli describes how the project "has been shaped by

[her] desire for th[e] volume to be at once cohesive and representative of the complexity and range of [Godard's] critical and theoretical concerns" (13). As Kamboureli intimates, the quantity and scope of Godard's writings are staggering. Her life's work cannot be encompassed in a single volume or commentary, but rather requires many rewritings from diversely situated readers. Always seeking new interlocutors, Godard is frequently in dialogue in her essays with named (and unnamed) Canadian critics, as well as with a startlingly large array of structuralist and post-structuralist theorists. Understanding the locations from which these essays spring is important. Fiercely self-reflexive (but un-indulgent) about her own location, Godard's praxis continues to remind the reader that, "It does matter ... from what point one enters the [hermeneutic] circle, since meaning-effects produce truth-claims having different exclusionary practices mediating who has the right to speak, about what, whose cultural values will be considered normal, natural, properly 'Canadian'" (*Canadian Literature* 200). For Godard and for her future readers, wherever and however they are located, the plot is constantly unfolding: "the words pour forth. / To be continued ..." ("Becoming" 122).

Works Cited

Armstrong, Jeannette. *Slash*. Penticton: Theytus, 1985. Print.

Brossard, Nicole. *L'Amèr: These Our Mothers*. Trans. Barbara Godard. Toronto: Coach House, 1983. Print.

Godard, Barbara. "Becoming My Hero, Becoming Myself." *Language in Her Eye*. Ed. Libby Scheier, Eleanor Wachtel, and Sarah Sheard. Toronto: Coach House, 1990. 112–22. Print.

———. *Canadian Literature at the Crossroads of Language and Culture*. Ed. Smaro Kamboureli. Edmonton: NeWest, 2008. Print.

———, ed. *Collaboration in the Feminine: Writing on Women and Culture from Tessera*. Toronto: Second Story, 1994. Print.

———. "Culture at the Crossroads." *Resources for Feminist Research* 32.3-4 (2007): 13–28. Print.

———. "Feminist Periodicals and the Production of Cultural Value: The Canadian Context." *Women's Studies International Forum* 25.2 (2002): 209–23. Print.

——— "Feminist Speculations on Value: Culture in an Age of Downsizing." *Ghosts in the Machine: Women and Cultural Policy in Canada and Australia*. Ed. Alison Beale and Annette Van den Bosch. Toronto: Garamond/Melbourne: U of Melbourne P, 1998. 43–76. Print.

———, ed. *Gynocritics/Gynocritiques: Feminist Approaches to Canadian and Quebec Women's Writing*. Toronto: ECW, 1987. Print.

———. "Privatizing the Public: Notes from the Ontario Culture Wars." *Fuse* 22.3 (1999): 27–33. Print.

———. "Quebec, the National Question, and English-Canadian Student Activism in the 1960s: The Rise of Student Syndicalism." *The Sixties in Canada: A Turbulent and Creative Decade*. Ed. M.A. Palaeologu. Montreal: Black Rose, 2009. 286–309. Print.

———, ed. *Translation Studies in Canada: Institutions, Discourses, Practices, Texts*. Toronto: Editions du GREF, forthcoming.

———. "Upping the Anti: Of Poetic Ironies, Propaganda Machines, and the Claims for Public Sponsorship of Culture." *Fuse* 25.3 (2002): 12–19. Print.

Godard, Barbara, and Di Brandt, eds. *Re:Generations: Canadian Women Poets in Conversation*. Windsor: Black Moss, 2005. Print.

———, eds. *"Wider Boundaries of Daring": The Modernist Impulse in Canadian Women's Poetry*. Waterloo: Wilfrid Laurier UP, 2008. Print.

Godard, Barbara, and Kate Eichhorn, eds. "Feminist Poetics Today." Spec. issue of *Open Letter: A Canadian Journal of Writing and Theory* 13th series, no. 9 (2009). Print.

Maracle, Lee. *I Am Woman*. Vancouver: Write-on, 1988. Print.

Marlatt, Daphne. *Ana Historic*. Toronto: Anansi, 1988. Print.

Tostevin, Lola Lemire, ed. *Redrawing the Lines: The Next Generation*. Spec. issue of *Open Letter: A Canadian Journal of Writing and Theory* 8.4 (Summer 1992). Print.

PART ONE
Textual/Visual Production: Critical Interventions

Chapter 1

Incisive Literary Critic, Brilliant Theorist, Engaged Teacher, Inspired Translator, Public Intellectual, and Committed Activist—All in the Feminine: The Early Barbara Godard

LOUISE H. FORSYTH

> To touch once again the energy which, from 1965 to 1975, coursed through the bodies and ways of thinking of a generation.
> (Brossard, "An Introduction" 9)

> Around 1985 was a high-point in the recognition of feminist culture.
> (Godard, "Making a Difference" 1)

A Restless Mind

This essay has been written in recognition of the outstanding accomplishments of Barbara Godard as a literary scholar for whom Canadian and Québec literature and women's place in society and culture—their voices and words, ideas, artistic production, desires, and collective activities— never ceased to matter. Many others have worked, as Godard did, to recognize the significant contributions made by women in a vast range of ways in the past and the present. And, like her, many have been motivated in their activities by a compelling awareness of the social and political injustices from which women have suffered and that too often still remain to be addressed. However, no one has gone as fully as she did to the discursive, ontological, and epistemological sources of women's ongoing marginalization and alienation, revealing the underlying fallacies at their roots as she went. Her detailed yet panoramic vision of a Canadian literary canon— broadly inclusive of works in many languages, giving appropriate weight to pieces relegated to the margins by virtue of the language, ethnicity, sex, sexual orientation, or geographical location of their authors, and going far beyond the narrow confines of traditional divisions of literary genres—has never been equalled. Her ability to draw on and implement a rich cocktail of theoretical perspectives—language-centred writing, formalism, structuralism, post-structuralist linguistics, socio-semiotics, feminist theories, deconstruction, theories of reception and translation, psychoanalysis—was amazing. Her production as a literary translator, translation theorist, and editor is unique in the country and the world.[1] As Kathy Mezei has said, the fields opened and occupied by Godard's scholarly and activist work show her to be one of this country's, and indeed one of the world's, most important and original thinkers: "she has contributed to forging a distinct Canadian feminist translation practice and theory" (204). Students, colleagues, and friends who spent time with Godard were invariably struck by the compelling dynamism of her mind and spirit. She was one of those responsible for making Canadian literature a recognized reality, not on the basis of tired nationalist or pastoral clichés, but on the basis of its rich artistic qualities and fascinating ideas that resonate with individuals' and communities' sense of self.

I shall recall in this chapter some of the moments along the engaged scholarly path of Barbara Godard's career in the 1960s, 1970s, and early 1980s, during which she advanced onto the conceptual, semiotic, ludic, oniric, mythic, and imaginative terrains she found most congenial. I hope that this look at the early part of her career will help us understand the ways in which some of the facets of her unique world view came together. Crucial in the course of these inspiring decades were her encounters with the texts of Québec writer Nicole Brossard—her feminism, formalism, play with words in poetry, novels, and theory, and commitment to social justice. The sparks resonating between their two brilliant minds illuminated ways of seeing, enunciating, and being, particularly in women's experiences, which had previously been unrecognized, unacknowledged, and unexpressed as legitimate points of view in human affairs.

The 1960s: A Revolutionary Decade

Cultural activists in francophone and anglophone Canada in the early years of the 1960s were preoccupied with the question of whether there were sufficiently rich bodies of literary texts that could together be called Canadian literature or *littérature québécoise*. Curricula in schools and universities provided little evidence of their existence. In all literary and artistic genres, the preference and even the knowledge almost always went in the direction of the United States, England, and France. The spirit of colonization, intimately woven into the collective psyche, still continued to oppress and repress creative energy in Québec and Canada. Literary criticism cognizant of writers of earlier periods, which might have forged criteria appropriate for the appreciation of the burgeoning Canadian literary scene, was little more than nascent. In terms of social and cultural identity, it was as though neither francophone nor anglophone Canada existed as unique and interesting in the eyes of the world or even in its own.

There were, though, some boldly experimental writers beginning to raise their pens and voices at this time of growing social unrest. They usually lived in Montreal, Toronto, or Vancouver. Knowing themselves to be marginalized, ignored, or ridiculed on society's main stages, they listened to and encouraged each other, publishing their texts in poorly funded little magazines or small publishing houses. These writers experimented with words and flaunted their creative challenges before ossified institutional structures As is evident in Godard's essay, "The Avant-garde in Canada: *Open Letter* and *La Barre du jour*," she was one of the first to recognize that the new writing published in these little magazines was the literary and cultural wave of the future. It proclaimed the possibility of actually constructing a unique Canadian identity nurtured by vibrant artistic expression. It was probably not a coincidence that *Open Letter*, *La Barre du jour*, and Coach House Press were founded the same year, 1965, despite the distance between Vancouver, Toronto, and Montreal and the lack of contact in the beginning among those who were involved, and despite, as well, the profound cultural differences between the anglophone and francophone contexts in which they were seeking to bring about literary and cultural rebirth. There was suddenly in the 1960s in both of the country's linguistic contexts an exciting proliferation of writers, musicians, artists, and activists. Godard, who had picked up the inaugural issue of *La Barre du jour*, was the first, in collaboration with Frank Davey, to take the initiative to inform anglophone writers and readers of the exciting experimental, anti-establishment writing being produced in Québec. In the special issue of *Ellipse*, she captured the essence of the two upstart magazines, while showing her passionate interest in the kind of new writing that shakes people out of their comfortable routine of complacency and conformity: "All [these lively little magazines] are united in their aim to dislodge objectified modern man, to drive him out of his fictitious well-made world, by celebrating the 'messiness' of existence, by showing that there are no plots with their beginning, middle, and end" ("The Avant-garde in Canada" 98).

This same decade of the 1960s—which was disturbing in the questions of individual and national identity it raised and the activist ramifications that followed from them—was also the time when the sexual revolution came to this country and when feminist analysis began its radical interrogation of the place and image of women in social practices and traditions, interpersonal relations, discursive and socio-cultural systems structures. The high level of anti-establishment creative energy that characterized the 1960s had a major impact on Godard's educational and professional career directions.[2]

She was a student in the 1960s at the University of Toronto, l'Université de Montréal, l'Université de Paris, and l'Université de Bordeaux. In those heady days of revolt in Canada, France, and the United States, she chose comparative studies of Canadian literature in English and French. Her courses and research also led her into close contact with many of the French theorists who were then setting on fire the world of semiotics, literary criticism, psychoanalysis, deconstruction, and post-structuralism. The intellectual path she chose shows she was eager to build on these new ways of knowing and so to appreciate, study, and write about Canadian literature differently than through established modes of scholarly and pedagogical discourse. The attention she gave to the exciting field of semiotic theory that was exploding at the time proved to be the starting point for the primary focus she maintained throughout her career on the functioning of language and other sign systems in the production of meaning and construction of socio-cultural systems.[3]

Like Godard, Nicole Brossard attended l'Université de Montréal during the exciting times of *La Révolution tranquille*. She published her first collections of poetry and co-founded *La Barre du jour* then. Although there is no indication that the two young women met during those years, it is clear that words, literature, social change, and the search for underlying causes of alienation and injustice were the primary preoccupations of both from the beginning of their careers. Brossard has stated on several occasions that this was the case for her:

> Underlying the idea of literature as an ethics, the certainty that, although it was a space conducive to the wildest imaginings, literature provided lucidity, made humans even more human—that is, compelled them to dream of a life and of passion that could set them free and lead them away from stupidity and violence. ("An Introduction" 10)

Godard and Brossard were both swept up in the swirl of intellectual, creative, and political energy that characterized much of the university and the city at a time when they were setting the course of their bold and exciting careers. When they did meet in the 1970s, there was already much fertile ground in their personal universes to produce, almost immediately, bonds of complicity between them. Much more than collaboration, they have been two brilliant women, each pursuing her course, finding bases for complicity, and resonating in spontaneous understanding with one another.

Translation and Other Radical Turns in the Early 1970s

Radical changes occurred in Québec during the first half of the 1970s. Politically, this period culminated in 1976, when the sovereignist Parti Québécois came to power for the first time. The adoption of Bill 101 was a clear indication of the top priority given to the French language by the members of the PQ. Driven by the intense political fervour of the independence movement and the priority given to language as the more or less sole shared identifying trait for the Québécois and Québécoises and the basis for cultural, social, and political unity, the arts and popular culture flourished.

Godard was always attracted by the attention paid to language issues in Québec and how this differed from anglophone Canada, where language usage is seldom problematized and the underlying role of language in the construction of ideologically determined institutions and systems has received little theoretical analysis: "feminists in France and Quebec directed their intervention in the social structures at a different level [than their English counterparts], aiming directly at the production of ideology and its conveyance and assertion through language and literature" ("Mapmaking" 14). This preoccupation with words and their structures, seen as constituting an inexhaustible, multi-layered system of symbols without which the meaning of experience and reality remains inaccessible to individuals and collectivities, remained fundamental for Godard throughout her career as literary critic, theorist, translator, and teacher.

The same decade of the 1970s that saw a definitive shift on the Québec political scene away from ossified traditions and institutions also marked a radical change in the status of women. A large percentage of Québécoises announced defiantly that they refused to play any longer the ideologically determined maternal role into which their mothers had been coerced. The transformation occurred with amazing rapidity and was marked by the creation of feminist organizations, publications of works in every literary and non-literary genre, women's bookstores, legislative and judicial initiatives, cultural, theatrical, and other performance events, social agencies and government offices responsible for the status of women, transformation of educational opportunities for girls and women, and a remarkable decline in the birth rate.

When Godard returned to Toronto from France in 1971 and took a teaching position as literary comparatist at York University, she promptly became involved with *Open Letter*, the little magazine that colleague Frank Davey first founded in Vancouver and then refounded in Toronto. The editorial responsibilities she undertook for *Open Letter* and its publishing partner, Coach House Press, particularly the co-creation in 1974 and co-management with Davey until 1986 of the Coach House Québec Translation series, represent a lasting contribution to Canadian letters. The Translation series was meant "to make francophone and anglophone writers in Canada more aware of each other's writing and writing theories" (Davey 15). Godard had taken her first steps as a translator during her student days in Montreal and Paris to pay the bills. Translation was to become intimately integrated into her overarching perspective on the literatures of Canada and her teaching and scholarly work on writers in both official languages. Her first literary translations, published in 1972 in *Open Letter*,[4] were followed until 1974 by several other "political/poetical manifestos by key Québec nationalist poets" (Mezei 206). Further to the federal government's adoption in 1969 of the Official Languages Act whereby Canada formally declared itself a bilingual country, the Canada Council created its new program in 1972 in support of literary translation. This program offered necessary financial support to professional translators and made it possible for Godard, Davey, and Coach House Press to create the Québec Translation series, which published close to twenty translations of new writing in Québec fiction, poetry, and theatre. While Victor-Lévy Beaulieu's *Jack Kerouac: essai-poulet* was the first translation in the series, experimental writing by women, particularly by Nicole Brossard, increasingly attracted the attention of Godard and Davey: "It became gradually evident to us that many of the writers that interested us were women" (Davey 7). Consequently, Brossard's first novel *Un livre* was the second translation in the series. This groundbreaking translation was followed the same year by Brossard's second novel, *Sold-out. Étreinte/illustration*. At the same time, Godard was working on her first book-length translation: Antonine Maillet's recently published *Don l'orignal*.

These encounters with the challenges of translating language-based experimental texts and Acadian dialect in a particular socio-cultural context made Godard, already fascinated by the multi-faceted elements, functions, and structures of language, aware of the creative potential of translation as an inexhaustible means of cultural renewal. Too often assumed to be a matter of relatively easy, derivative, and unproblematic passage from one language to another, translation for Godard is a conscious act of mediation that can capture the entire memory of a people. It is a complex process of interpretation, contextualization, and rewriting. It involves careful reading of the original text; awareness of the capability of words to construct meaning, value, identity, and reality; understanding the systemic differences at play between languages and their power differentials; appreciating the place and function of the source text in its socio-cultural and ideological context; paying attention to the conditions likely to determine reception in the target community; and playing imaginatively with words, expressions, structures, sounds, and rhythms in the target language: "As Bakhtin points out, language is no neutral, value-free medium, but is charged with the ideological values of a culture, saturated with the voices and points of view of everyone who has spoken it" (Godard, *Collaboration* 262). Godard was intrigued by the dialectical encounters inherent in processes of translation and their revelation of power dynamics that may normally go unrecognized. This positioning between languages and viewing them in relation to each other would typify Godard's approach not only as a translator and editor, but also as a teacher and writer of theory and literary criticism:

> Thinking one literature or text in relation to another, thinking dialectically or intertextually has been a key aspect of all my writing and teaching, informing the way I establish course syllabi as well as the topics I write on. In the literary translation I was doing at the time, and in the editing of translations for the Coach House translation series I ran with Frank Davey, such relational thinking for incommensurabilities or for convergences was at the heart of my writing practice [...] It is important to attend to the vectors of power in the relations between cultures at specific conjunctures. (*Canadian Literature* 27)

Godard and Davey originally planned to include Brossard's third novel, *French Kiss: Étreinte-exploration*, in the Coach House Translation series immediately following the first two novels. These choices for the series, along with Brossard's book of poetry also published in the early 1970s, *Mécanique jongleuse, suivi de Masculin grammaticale*, show that familiarizing herself with the enigmas of Brossard's fiction and poetic expression had a decisive impact on Godard's methodological and theoretical approach to literary criticism and translation. Recently republished by Coach House Books under the title *The Blue Books*, these translations of Brossard's first three novels form an amazingly original trilogy of the *new novel* in Québec.

Brossard's dedication of this volume to Godard highlights the importance she attached to her sensitive and astute reception of these novels: "To Barbara Godard, who first introduced my books to Coach House Press and who has been since a perspicacious reader and translator of my work" (5).

What was the importance of these novels for Godard? Why did she and Davey feel so strongly that these and subsequent texts published by Brossard should be given priority in the Coach House Québec Translation series? These three works of experimental fiction are urban novels (a break from the not-yet dormant rural and realistic novel tradition in Québec with its emphasis on theme). All play themselves out on a largely implicit but urgent contemporary socio-political background. Brossard has consistently rejected in her works of fiction creating the illusion of psychologically credible characters, constructing coherent narratives, and representing the outside world realistically because such novelistic conventions create the reassuring illusion of reality for the very deceptive appearances she seeks to debunk. While social, political, and geographical actualities are always evoked in her fiction, their status as unchanging reality is always cast in doubt. The materiality of the circumstances in which individuals have their corporeal existence, along with the materiality of words that are written and read, is complemented in these novels by flows of erotic energy that suggest to readers that all things in this world, including any sense of permanence or coherence in place or identity, are subject to change:

> I believe the same principle applies to eroticism as well as to the sexual encounters between characters, "attractive signalling figures." Living in the slipstream of words, living in the obsession of words as one lives in the obsession of sex as metaphor for an inexpressible lust for life. (Brossard, "An Introduction" 12)

Two action lines are sustained in *A Book*. One of these develops events in the lives of five young characters, three women and two men, who have few distinguishing characteristics and almost no reported dialogue. They eat, talk, sleep, put up with the heat of a Montreal summer, go to work, make love, and display an awareness of the tense yet static political situation in which they exist. Brossard captured in their relative inertia the sense of waiting that characterized the tense months before the October Crisis. The second action line, which occupies as much space of the text as the first, is the action of writing the text of *A Book*. This action involves an anonymous enunciating voice reflecting on the story's fictional events and on the act of producing them, as well as the act of reading the text, which involves the person actually holding it in her or his hands. On page 82, for example, the voice, appearing to share the moment and tension of the *someone* who is reading the book, begins with "On page eighty-two" and ends the text of that page with "At the end of page 82. Every bit as tense as the someone who is turning the page." When the book ends, the voice addresses the reader directly: "The words are yours" and then states, presuming that the reader is about to close the book, "Someone is reading. And gently closes the object" (98, 99). Almost all the verbs of *A Book* are in the present tense. Brossard's apparent intent was to make a real connection with each person who reads the book, to draw that person's attention to the act of reading at the present moment, and so to incite a lucid awareness of that person's presence in the world, the way words work on the page, and the largely unrealized potential for words to be used as fuel for meaningful action and creation in the real world. The way she puts the novel together urges readers to take their place in the world as active subjects and to get involved in public affairs as creative writers or through some other form of engaged action.

A Book shows Brossard preoccupied simultaneously with writing and reading, production and reception, creation, and recreation of meaning. It is not enough for the artist to produce a fine work. The work must be received, understood, and appreciated by another person, who may or may not give the originally intended meaning to the work, but who is active—not passive!—in constructing significance through acts of dialogue, exchange, and communication: "Reading is eye-opening: opening one's eyes onto the world, desiring it, questioning it" (Brossard, 11). Through the multiplication of such creative and communicative processes, the possibility emerges of moving beyond apathy and impotence, building a spirit of shared concerns, exploring possible courses of meaningful action, and affirming the reality of a lucid and engaged interpretive community.

The second novel of *The Blue Book* trilogy, *Turn of a Pang*, is equally playful and disrespectful of established conventions for writing novels—to the point of radical disruption of page layout, frequent typeface changes, and handwritten graffiti—but in ways that differ completely from *A Book*. *Turn of a Pang*, written after the declaration in 1970 of the War Measures Act, so widely reviled in Québec, superimposes that event on the 1942 federal plebiscite authorizing conscription, when large demonstrations in Québec against participation in World War II at the side of the British provided evidence for serious civil unrest in Québec, fuelled by a frenzy of sexual desire and norms of social activity favouring immediate gratification.

Radical Feminism, Language-Centred Writing, Women's Studies, Translation, Translation Theory

> The research I had initiated in the 1970s on questions of language, orality, folklore, and magic realism from the perspective of narratological theory was changed by my involvement in feminist dialogues. I started to think through the same issues from a feminist perspective. (Barbara Godard in conversation with Smaro Kamboureli, *Canadian Literature* 29)

Almost immediately following her return from France, Godard's activism as a Canadianist and feminist scholar and teacher began. She pushed for radically rethinking the curriculum and for setting up women's studies at York University and across Canada through her part in the Association of Canadian University Teachers of English, the Canadian Comparative Literature Association/Association canadienne de littérature comparée, and the founding of the Association of Canadian and Québec Literatures/ l'Association des littératures canadiennes et québécoises (1974). She became a member of the first *Fireweed* collective and the Toronto Area Women's Research Colloquium.

It was at this time that her highly significant work as a theorist of translation and as a theorist of translation *in the feminine* began. Her increasingly intense dialogue with Brossard and other radical Québec feminist writers saw her opening a remarkably dense and innovative path of feminist translation. Along this path she published translations of four books and many other texts by Brossard, one book by Antonine Maillet and another by France Théoret, along with numerous pieces by sixteen other Québec women writers.

Godard's enthusiastic reception of Brossard's brilliant departure into writing as a radical feminist in the early 1970s is easy to see. While never abandoning the language-centred writing that has characterized all her work, Brossard was stretching the horizons of *La Barre du jour*, where gender-based politics had not yet come into play, and positioning herself as a highly original feminist writer and thinker. The back cover of the Coach House translation of *Mécanique jongleuse, Daydream Mechanics*, describes the poems as "textual constructions of female sexuality, translations of blood-vessels into the signs of language." Similarly, the back cover of the translated *French Kiss* states that this joyously dynamic and erotic little novel "celebrates the energy of woman and language, urges its reader to 'spread' herself, 'eager' to 'ride astride grammar,' 'to ride astride the delible ink.'"

As in *A Book*, the action of *French Kiss* takes place in contemporary Montreal among five young characters, three women and two men. And like the two preceding novels, *French Kiss* experiments with and transgresses every novelistic convention, every formatting and typesetting norm. The ludic dimension of this novel is amazing. The apathy, oppression, and climate of incipient violence suggested in *A Book* have been replaced by movement, erotic energy, and indomitable presence in the streets of downtown Montreal. These francophone characters affirm orgasmically, at least for the time, their right to control their city. The primary action line of *French Kiss* is:

> Camomille [and] Marielle Desaulniers driving in real life down real Sherbrook Streets tarmac at forty miles an hour in a Plymouth, an old convertible, purple vintage 1965 [...] a cruise across the city. The whole length of Sherbrooke Street from one end to the other, east to west. West to east. A carrousel of history and geography. (*French Kiss. Or: a Pang's Progress* 12)

This textual "cruise" is a high-energy journey simultaneously along the city's principal arteries and similar "blood vessels" of "female sexuality," as in *Daydream Mechanics*. It is a triumphant assertion of repossession of a previously colonized city, of women's autonomy and freedom, and of everyone's right to sexual *jouissance*, whatever their orientation. Its verbal and imagistic frankness, combined with bold refusal to accept any conventionalized social taboos, is stunning. The novel's *French Kiss* occurs close to the centre of the book "Just Once" in a long sequence during which the two female characters stop at the heart of the city, the intersection of Sherbrooke and St. Denis streets, and engage in a long, passionate embrace: "In which the text slows down in Camomille's mouth [...] Ecstatic perfusion in Camomille's mouth [...] Prolong the desires with the telling, the narration of a long uninterrupted kiss [...] The kiss, a ball of fire." (57)

The same year that Brossard published *French Kiss* and *Mécanique jongleuse*, she was preparing the first of a series of special issues of *La Barre du jour* on feminist topics, this one on "Femme et langage." Contributors were invited to address the question: "Comment la femme qui utilise quotidiennement les mots (comédienne, journaliste, écrivain, professeur) peut-elle utiliser un langage qui, phallocratique, joue au départ contre elle?" (8–9). Brossard's text in this special issue, "*E* muet mutant," is a landmark in the development of feminist writing and theory in Québec. Godard's work at the same time shows her addressing the same thorny and complex issue of how women who are creative writers and thinkers can use language to speak their own insights without getting caught in its sexist traps. Both Godard and Brossard recognized at the time that women are necessarily bilingual. While knowing the *Master*'s language well, they can construct and share their own identities and realities only when they subvert language norms and invent words and forms of expression that explicitly work for them.

A later special issue in the feminist series of *La Barre du jour*, which she published right after her explosive novel *L'Amèr ou le chapitre effrité*, was "Le corps, les mots, l'imaginaire." In her opening text, Brossard once again stressed the priority she attached to women reading so that they would see, reflect upon, and move to take action in the lived reality of their female body, mind, and imagination:

> Donner à lire des écritures de femmes. Telles que nous sommes dans le sujet de nos textes, ce même sujet sans doute *le corps les mots l'imaginaire* qui nous regroupe dans les multiples possibles de la vie souterraine/la réalité. (10)

This particular issue seemed important to Godard, who "was feeling frustrated about the place of theory generally [among English-Canadian writers and critics]" (*Canadian Literature* 35). As a result, she played a leading role in the preparation of a special issue of *Room of One's Own*, appearing mere months later, in which many of the *Barre du jour* texts were translated, several by Godard. This issue highlighted the importance of translation for feminist writers, critics, teachers, and students.

Godard never deviated in her writing and teaching from her conviction that feminist writing in Québec was potentially of great interest in English Canada, and that the greater interest in theory among francophone writers was producing important creative texts: "I was keen to increase the writing from Quebec available in English to use in my course on English-Canadian and Quebec fiction." Godard's commitment as a public intellectual to enhancing the quality of dialogue and effectiveness of communication across language and ideologically determined barriers resulted in:

> A lot of [my] energy [going] to creating such institutional spaces for intellectual work [as Canadian literature as a field in which people could do research], Canadian literature in the 1970s, theory and especially feminism in the 1980s when it emerged as an academic field. (*Canadian Literature* 34)

Godard's achievements in expanding horizons by opening fresh linguistic and literary paths and ways of thinking have been outstanding. Her vision and work in facilitating the 1979 bilingual anthology of works by new writers of Québec, edited by Nicole Brossard, *Les Stratégies du réel. The Story so Far 6*, was remarkable. The book is a treasure full of wonderful pieces. It involved a rare collaboration between two publishing houses, one in Québec and the other in Ontario. It is the first bilingual collection to introduce to English-language readers the avant-garde writers of *La Barre du jour* and *Les Herbes rouges*. Brossard's inextinguishable exuberance as a bold, endlessly innovative, and no-holds-barred creative writer is evident in her preface to the anthology, "Les stratégies du réel," as translated by Godard:

> I conceive of this anthology as a joyous complicity with those Canadian poets who know how to take the subversive risks of rupture and emotion. Since it will always be the case in this story to write, not to stop oneself, not to refrain from. To be at the service of one's text, as of one's energy: delight of daring. (9)

Also during the later years of the 1970s, Godard was working on the daunting challenge of translating Brossard's *L'Amèr ou le chapitre effrité*, wherein the audacious extremity of play on words, ideas, and conventions covering the entire gamut of traditions and practices of patriarchal society has never been surpassed. The voice speaking in the novel proclaims her absolute rejection of the patriarchally determined maternal role and affirms the writer's complete freedom to construct her own identity and reality: "*I have murdered the womb and I am writing it*" (21). This leads her to make one of the most celebrated statements in Brossard's oeuvre: "To write: I am a woman is heavy with consequences" (45). The narrator positions herself as lesbian, caressing and dancing in turns with her baby daughter and her lover: "If it weren't lesbian, this text would make no sense at all" (16).

Kathy Mezei, placing particular emphasis on the amazing transformations produced by Godard in her translation, has called it a "*tour de force*" (211). In effect, Godard had to call upon the entire range of her experience as a literary critic, language and translation theorist, and engaged feminist in order to pull off this amazing recreation/rewriting of a revolutionary book—what she, Brossard, and others called "fiction/theory."[5] Throughout this arduous work, Godard showed, as she stated in the preface to *These Our Mothers. Or: the Disintegrating Chapter*, that she never lost her sensual delight in working with the text or in the attention she paid in all writing and teaching to the vital importance of reading where reception of the text is not an end but an infinitely spiralling beginning and an invitation to participate in an endless cycle of writing, reading, and rewriting: "May the intensity of your involvement as reader be as great as mine and you extend its creation in new directions to make this the text of bliss it works to be" (7).

Exemplary Career Making a Difference

I have tried in this piece to give some idea of the flowing together over the first years of Barbara Godard's career of many literary, intellectual, theoretical, and political currents into patterns that only she could discern and then use in widely influential ways. While I am stopping my account at this point, it does not in any way indicate that her activity diminished or even slowed down around the end of the 1970s. In 1981 she organized the Dialogue conference, one of the first conferences that brought together women writers and literary critics.[6] Shortly thereafter, she was a central presence at several groundbreaking conferences: the International Conference on Research and Teaching Related to Women, organized by Maïr Verthuy at Concordia University; l'Atelier d'études féministes, organized by Suzanne Lamy and Irène Pagès at the annual meetings of the Association des professeurs de français des universités et collèges canadiens; and the Women and Words/ Les femmes et les mots conference in Vancouver. She was subsequently the major force in the founding and managing of *Tessera*, "a bilingual, pan-Canadian periodical offering a space for women's thinking and writing" (*Collaboration in the Feminine* 9). Her wonderful translations of Brossard's *Amantes, Picture Theory,* and *Journal intime ou voilà donc un manuscrit*, of France Théoret's texts, and many other smaller translations, along with her insightful and probing theoretical works of translation theory and literary criticism, have shown the way for dialogues that nurture justice and creativity for all. Her work provides a highly original model for literary criticism and translation based on a bold synthesis of personal engagement, artistic creativity, and rigorous theoretical reflection. Her ways of seeing, thinking, writing, reading, and rewriting through translation are a sustained invitation to us to buck the norms of conformity and to see through deceptive appearances in order to discover practices embedded in systems and codes that contrive deceptive and dangerous versions of what is real through their manipulation of discursive conventions and so to rediscover the reality of the world within ourselves in acts of lucid intentionality.

Notes

1 Barbara Godard edited or co-edited several volumes, special issues of journals, and series, published translations from French to English of six books, countless translations of poems and essays, and a great number of significant

articles and chapters in books on Canadian literature in French and in English, language-centred writing, translation in Canada, translation theory, and gender and translation.
2. For details on Godard's years as a student and her reflections on several aspects of her career, see Mezei and Kamboureli.
3. The subject of Godard's M.A. thesis at the Université de Montréal was "The City of Montreal in the English and French Canadian Novel, 1945–1965" (1967) and of her doctoral thesis at the Université de Bordeaux was "God's Country: L'homme et la terre dans le roman des deux Canada" (1971).
4. These translations by Godard for *Open Letter* were by Jacques Brault, Paul Chamberland, Raoul Duguay, and Michèle Lalonde. See Mezei for bibliographical information on these translations and the many other translations made by Godard of francophone writers.
5. The expression "fiction/theory" was devised by Brossard to capture the radical significance of women writing creatively in their lucid, thinking body, motivated by their own autonomous desire and their unique perception of ethical and aesthetic dimensions. For an extensive discussion of this important concept, see *Tessera* 3 in *Canadian Fiction Magazine* 57 (1986) and *Collaboration in the Feminine: Writings on Women and Culture from* Tessera.
6. Godard's edited publication of the proceedings of the Dialogue conference appeared as *Gynocritics/La Gynocritique*, one of the first theoretical books published on feminist literary criticism.

Works Cited

Bayard, Caroline. *The New Poetics in Canada and Quebec: From Concretism to Post-modernism*. Toronto/Buffalo/London: U of Toronto P, 1989. Print.

Beaulieu, Victor-Lévy. *Jack Kerouac: A Chicken Essay*. Trans. Sheila Fischman. Toronto: Coach House, 1975. Print. Trans. of *Jack Kerouac: essai-poulet*. Montreal: Éditions du Jour, 1972.

Breen, Mary, Janice Pentland-Smith, Gayla Reid, Gail van Varsevele, Eleanor Wachtel, and Jean Wilson, eds. *Room of One's Own: A Feminist Journal of Literature and Criticism* 4.1/2 (1978). Print.

Brossard, Nicole. *Amantes*. Montreal: Éditions Quinze, 1980. *Lovhers*. Trans. Barbara Godard. Toronto: Guernica Editions, 1986. Print.

———. *French Kiss. Étreinte-exploration*. Montreal: Éditions du Jour, 1974. *French Kiss. Or: A Pang's Progress*. Trans. Patricia Claxton. Toronto: Coach House, 1986. Print.

———. "An Introduction." Trans. Susanne de Lotbinière-Harwood. *The Blue Books. A Book; Turn of a Pang; French Kiss, or, A Pang's Progress*. Trans. Larry Shouldice and Patricia Claxton. Toronto: Coach House, 2003. Print.

———. *Intimate Journal, or Here's a Manuscript*. Trans. Barbara Godard. Toronto: The Mercury, 2004. Print. Trans. of *Journal intime ou voilà donc un manuscrit*. Montreal: Les Herbes rouges, 1984.

———. *L'Amèr ou le chapitre effrité*. Montreal: Éditions Quinze, 1977. *These Our Mothers. Or: The Disintegrating Chapter*. Trans. Barbara Godard. Toronto: Coach House, 1983. Print.

———. *Le Sens apparent*. Paris: Flammarion, 1980. *Surfaces of Sense*. Trans. Fiona Strachan. Toronto: Coach House, 1989. Print.

———. Ed. *Les Stratégies du réel. The Story So Far 6*. Toronto/Montreal: Coach House/La Nouvelle Barre du Jour, 1979. Print.

———. *Mécanique jongleuse, suivi de Masculin grammaticale*. Montreal: Éditions de l'Hexagone, 1974. *Daydream Mechanics. Masculine Singular*. Trans. Larry Shouldice. Toronto: Coach House, 1980. Print.

———. *Picture Theory*. Montreal: Nouvelle Optique, 1982. *Picture Theory*. Trans. Barbara Godard. Toronto: Guernica Editions, 1991. Print.

———. "Préliminaires," "E muet mutant." *La Barre du jour* 50 (1975): 6–9, 10–27. Spec. issue on "Femme et langage." Print.

———. *Sold-out. Étreinte/illustration*. Montreal: Éditions du Jour, 1973. *Turn of a Pang*. Trans. Patricia Claxton. Toronto: Coach House, 1976. Print.

———. *Un livre*. Montreal: Éditions du Jour, 1970. *A Book*. Trans. Larry Shouldice. Toronto: Coach House, 1976. Print.

Davey, Frank. "A History of the Coach House Press Québec Translations." Paper delivered at annual meeting of ACQL/ALCQ, May 1995. Web. August 22, 2010. <http://publish.uwo.ca/~fdavey/c/chpque.htm>.

Forsyth, Louise. "Feminist Criticism as Creative Process." *In the Feminine. Women and Words. Les Femmes et les mots*. Ed. Ann Dybikowski et al. Edmonton: Longspoon, 1985. 87–94. Print.

———. "Les Numéros spéciaux de *La (Nouvelle) Barre du jour*. Lieux communs, lieux en recherche, lieu de rencontre." *Féminité, subversion, écriture*. Dirs. Suzanne Lamy et Irène Pagès. Montreal: Éditions du Remue-ménage, 1983. 175–84. Print.

Godard, Barbara. "Annotated Bibliography of the Writings of French-Canadian Women in English Translation." *Writers in Translation: An Annotated Bibliography*. Ed. Marjorie Resnick and Isabelle de Courtivron. Boston: Garland, 1984. 93–112. Print.

———. "The Avant-garde in Canada: *Open Letter* and *La Barre du jour*." *Ellipse* 23/24 (1979): 98–113. Print.

———. *Canadian Literature at the Crossroads of Language and Culture*. Ed. Smaro Kamboureli. Edmonton: NeWest, 2008. Print.

———, ed. *Collaboration in the Feminine: Writings on Women and Culture from Tessera*. Second Story, 1994. Print.

———. "Critical Discourse in/on Quebec." *Studies on Canadian Literature*. Ed. Arnold E. Davidson. New York: MLA, 1990. 271–95. Print.

———. "Fiction/Theory: Editorial"; "Becoming My Hero: Becoming Myself. Notes toward aFeminist Theory of Reading." *Canadian Fiction Magazine* 57/ *Tessera* 3 (1986): 4–6, 142–49. Print.

———. "*La Barre du jour*: vers une poétique féministe." *Féminité, subversion, écriture*. Dirs. Suzanne Lamy et Irène Pagès. Montreal: Éditions du Remue-ménage, 1983. 195–205. Print.

———. "L'Amèr or the Exploding Chapter: Nicole Brossard at the Site of Feminist Deconstruction." *Atlantis* 9.2 (1984): 23–34. Print.

———. "Language and Sexual Difference: The Case of Translation." *Atkinson Review of Canadian Studies* 2.1 (1984): 13–20. Print.

———. "Making a Difference: Feminist Challenges to Creative and Critical Practice." 2003. MS. Academic paper prepared for Workshop on Feminist Challenges to Knowledge Production IWSGS, University of Toronto.

———. "Mapmaking: A Survey of Feminist Criticism"; "Bibliography of Feminist Criticism in Canada and Quebec." *Gynocritics: Feminist Approaches to Writing by Canadian and Québécoises Women/La Gynocritique: Approches féministes à l'écriture des Canadiennes et Québécoises*. Ed. Barbara Godard. Toronto: ECW, 1987. 1–30, 231–350. Print.

———. "Nicole Brossard." *Profiles on Canadian Writing*. Ser. 6. Ed. Jeffery Heath. Toronto: Dundurn, 1985. 123–28. Print.

———. "(Re)Appropriation as Translation." *Canadian Theatre Review* 64 (1990): 22–31. Print.

———. "Redrawing the Circle." *Feminism Now*. Ed. Mary Louise Kroker. *Canadian Journal of Social and Political Theory*, 1985: 165–92. Print.

———. "Ri/post: Postmodernism and Feminism in Quebec." *Quebec Studies* 9 (1989): 131–43. Print.

———. "Structuralism/Post-Structuralism: Language, Reality, and Canadian Literature." Ed. John Moss. *Future Indicative: Literary Theory and Canadian Literature*. Ottawa: U of Ottawa P, 1987. 25–51. Print.

———. "Terroristes d'amour; terroristes du récit." *Le Discours féminin dans la littérature postmoderne au Québec*. Ed. Raija Koski, Kathy Kells, and Louise Forsyth. San Francisco: Mellen Research UP, 1993. 143–67. Print.

———. "Theorizing Feminist Discourse/Translation." *Tessera* 6 (Spring/Printemps 1989): 42–53. Print.

———. "Theorizing Feminist Discourse/Translation." *Translation, History, and Culture*. Ed. Susan Bassnett and André Lefevere. London: Frances Pinter, 1990. 87–96. Print.

———. "A Translator's Journal." *Culture in Transit: Translating the Literature of Québec*. Ed. Sherry Simon. Montreal: Véhicule, 1995. 69–82. Print.

———. "Translations"; "Letters in Canada 1986." *University of Toronto Quarterly* 57.1 (1987): 77–98. Print.

———. "Women of Letters (Reprise)." *Collaboration in the Feminine: Writings on Women and Culture from Tessera*. Ed. Barbara Godard. Toronto: Second Story, 1994. 258–306. Print.

———. "Writing and Difference: Women Writers of Québec and English-Canada"; "The Translator as She." *In the Feminine: Women and Words. Les femmes *et les mots*. Ed. Ann Dybikowski et al. Edmonton: Longspoon, 1985. 122–26; 193–98. Print.

Godard, Barbara, and Coomi S. Vevaina, eds. *Intersexions: Issues of Race and Gender in Canadian Women's Writing*. New Delhi: Creative Books, 1996. Print.

Godard, Barbara, with Kathy Mezei et al. "Translation: The Relationship between Writer and Translator." *Meta* 34.2 (1989): 209–24. Print.

Kamboureli, Smaro, ed. "The Critic, Institutional Culture, and Canadian Literature: Barbara Godard in Conversation with Smaro Kamboureli." Barbara Godard, *Canadian Literature at the Crossroads of Language and Culture*. Edmonton: NeWest, 2008. 17–52. Print.

Maillet, Antonine. *Don l'orignal*. Montreal: Leméac, 1972. *The Tale of Don l'Orignal*. Trans. Barbara Godard. Toronto: Clarke-Irwin, 1978. Print.

Mezei, Kathy. "Transformations of Barbara Godard." *Writing between the Lines: Portraits of Canadian Anglophone Translators*. Ed. Agnes Whitfield. Waterloo: Wilfrid Laurier UP, 2006. 203–24. Print.

Chapter 2

Cultural Memory and Tragic Affect in Nancy Huston's *The Mark of the Angel*

PAMELA MCCALLUM

In her memoirs of Paris in the postwar years Simone de Beauvoir writes about her experience as a participant in a large demonstration against French involvement in the escalating war in Algeria. She describes the beginning of the procession in the following words:

> And at that moment a procession appeared carrying a placard: PEACE IN ALGERIA, which soon had hundreds of people clustering behind it; others began coming from all sides.... I took hold of Sartre's arm on one side and that of someone I didn't know on the other, noticing with surprise that the boulevard suddenly stretched as far as the eye could see in front of us, quite empty.... Astonished to find itself walking along like this unmolested, the crowd became infected with tremendous gaiety. And how good I felt! Solitude is a form of death, and as I felt the warmth of human contact flow through me again, I came back to life. (619–20)

De Beauvoir's account shifts from uneasy minutes of waiting, anxious about when the procession of the secretly organized demonstration would appear, to an exhilaration born out of being part of collective action. Linking arms with her lifelong companion on one side and an unknown person with whom she shares only opposition to the war in Algeria on the other, she feels the isolation of living in a city, where Gaullist supporters of the conflict seem to be in the majority, dissolve in the collectivity of the crowd. De Beauvoir's language—"as I felt the warmth of human contact flow through me again, I came back to life"—suggests the reanimation of a spectral woman, frozen into silence by her political segregation, who is re-inspirited by the community of the demonstration. It is as if a transfusion of human contact brings her back to life. Such enlivening stimulation depicts a utopian moment, which, as might be expected, cannot be sustained. All too soon the demonstration is attacked by the police and the warmth of a revitalizing flow in de Beauvoir's figuration is replaced by more sombre images: "big splashes of blood on the street corner"; a bludgeoned man "with flesh hanging away from his face"; another unconscious with a skull fracture (620). And yet, for a time, the glimpse of the boulevard stretching before them—empty and therefore open to potential—together with the camaraderie of the crowd, seemed to represent different possibilities extending endlessly into the future.

Readers of de Beauvoir's account, however, can hardly fail to feel the tug of suppressed cultural memory for there is undoubtedly a historical amnesia at work in the crowd infected with such "tremendous gaiety." The beautiful, expansive Parisian boulevards, which appear to signify unrestricted possibilities, are already inscribed with history. Indeed, their very construction is testimony to Baron Haussman's redesign of the city streets in the nineteenth century to accommodate the control of crowds. The open spaces of Paris have often been the sites of demonstration and violent response, the shock of truncheon, sabre, and bullet against the vulnerability of human flesh. It is almost as if the crowd in its euphoric exhilaration represents a forgetting similar to what Nancy Huston calls "the mark of the angel," the gentle pressure against the lips of the not-yet-born infant who will come into the world innocent, without memory of suffering and brutalization (*Mark* 124). Just as the child must encounter the experience of the world, so the frisson of collective action will encounter the brutality of the violent conflicts that have motivated the demonstration, that have inspired the participants to come out into the streets. In her 1999 novel about Paris during the years of the Algerian war, *The Mark of the Angel*, Nancy Huston explores the complexities of historical memories, the possibilities of redemption and change, the tragedies of repetition and reversal. In what follows I will suggest that Huston's novel represents "modern tragedy" in the sense outlined by the British Marxist critic Raymond Williams: the blockage of human longings and aspirations toward transformation, both social and individual, in historical impasses that resist change. In Huston's classical love triangle—Raphael, a talented Parisian musician, Saffie, his young German wife, and her lover, András, a Hungarian refugee—the violence of war, resistance, and defeat are allegorically condensed. The interrelationships among these three survivors of the brutalities of the mid-twentieth century form a condensed structure through which yearning and frustration are played out with tragic consequences.

Raymond Williams's book *Modern Tragedy*, published in 1963, was conceived and written in the wake of the Algerian war, renewed conflict in Indochina, the Soviet invasion of Hungary, the involvement of British troops in South Arabia (now Yemen), in other words, in the same period and conflicts that are embedded in Huston's novel. Huston's narrator relentlessly challenges the reader not only to situate the interactions among the love triangle within the histories the three have survived, but also among the contemporary history of the late 1950s. If this postwar period might be seen to be a progressive moment of rebuilding Europe after six years of war and the defeat of fascism, the narrator is quick to dismiss such overly optimistic confidence. "Let's spend a while just floating on the ocean of events that are taking place on the planet Earth in the fall of 1957" (*Mark* 47), the narrator invites the reader, slyly producing an ever-intensifying list of horrors: French conscripts in Algeria learn how to torture militants; Mao Zedong "warming up for the Great Leap Forward," which will produce mass starvation (48); the Russian success with *Sputnik* intensifying the Cold War; finally, "the self-same Dwight Eisenhower whose armed forces crushed the Wehrmacht in 1945, is starting to cast sidelong glances at a little country called Vietnam" (48). It is significant that the narrator also invites readers to consider the startling, ironic reversals in history: young French soldiers learn torture techniques, reproducing Nazi interrogations of captured French resistance fighters; the Great Leap Forward in China was conceived as a strategy to increase industrial production in a war-devastated impoverished country, but created widespread famine; the "space race" of the Cold War underscored the inadvertent contribution science made to ever more deadly intercontinental weaponry; the U.S. military forces who helped to liberate Europe from Nazi occupation would soon be loosed on the population of a small Indochinese country.[1] In drawing attention to the unsettling reversals that all too often characterize history, Huston gestures toward the conception of a historically embedded modern tragedy developed by Raymond Williams.

Williams's *Modern Tragedy*, published in 1966, is in many ways a response to George Steiner's widely read book *The Death of Tragedy*.[2] Steiner had advanced the argument that Enlightenment faith in the ability of human societies to transform themselves, together with later nineteenth-century philosophy and especially Marxism, have erased the possibility for tragic thought. If the world can be remade, then older forms of thinking such as inescapable fate, so necessary to tragedy, no longer structure representation. For Williams, however, modern tragedy is located in the very tensions between the utopian visions of how societies might be transformed to incorporate values such as equality, freedom, human respect, and the disappointing trajectories of social movements that have attempted to achieve these ideals. Beginning with the turn of the French Revolution away from its Jacobin values of *liberté, égalité,* and *fraternité* into empire and restoration, through the reversals of the hopes raised by the Soviet Revolution, which sink inexorably into civil war, party purges, and Stalinist dictatorship, Williams situates modern tragedy in the contradictions between human longings for social transformation and the brutal violence that seems all too necessary for the dismantling of modes of domination in the world.

When modern aesthetics describes tragedy, the tendency is to focus on the tragic individual—the "fault in the soul" is Williams's phrase—ignoring "war, revolution, poverty, hunger; men reduced to objects and killed from lists; persecution and torture; the many kinds of contemporary martyrdom" (*Modern* 62–63). He comments, "Revolution—the long revolution against human alienation—produces, in real historical circumstances, its own new kinds of alienation, which it must struggle to understand and which it must overcome, if it is to remain revolutionary" (*Modern* 82). Thus in describing revolution as tragedy, Williams underlines processes of hatred, violence, dehumanization, and other brutalities that are put in motion in efforts to transform societies. From his perspective, the task of analysis is to restore tragic affect to the understanding of the actions of revolutionary change. As he writes, "in contemporary revolution, the detail of suffering is insistent, whether as violence or as the reshaping of lives by a new power in the state" (*Modern* 89). To attend to "the detail of suffering" is to reinstate recognition of the human emotions that are intricately entangled within movements for social change. By reconnecting the suppression of emotion in revolution to subsequent reflections on the process and its consequences, its successes and reversals, Williams restores an affective relationship with the past that has the potential to loosen blockages and release energies for future projects of social and political transformation. He quotes Brecht's poem "An Die Nachgeborenen" ("To Those Who Come After"), whose penultimate stanza notes the contradictions at the heart of revolution: Hatred, even of meanness / Contorts the features. / Anger even against injustice / Makes the voice grow harsh" (Brecht 320). To desire another way of living and to take action toward changing a society is also to commit to the possibilities of perpetuating violence in the opposition to it.

In a different but overlapping context, Deborah Gould draws on Williams's writings in *The Long Revolution* to argue that emotion can be "a key force in social change" (32). She suggests that the need for social transformation is often experienced as inarticulate feelings, as sensations, deeply felt but not consciously understood, that "something is awry, that things could be and perhaps should be different" (32). "Our affective states," Gould goes on to write, "are what temper and intensify our attentions, affiliations, investments, identifications, and attachments; they help to solidify some of our ideas and beliefs and attenuate others" (33). When Williams proposes that tragic affect is bound up with the reversals of projects for social change in the modern period, he implies that feeling the emotions aroused by and circulating within revolution, suffering, and dehumanization and their consequences—"degeneration, brutalisation, fear, hatred, envy" (*Modern* 102)—need to be experienced and understood and not deflected or dismissed. The liberation of Europe, the Hungarian revolution, the Algerian war of independence against France—these are the emancipatory moments that also mark the protagonists of Huston's novel with pain, horror, and despair. Both Saffie ("France is the country of freedom" [115]) and András ("It was my mother's dream. The City of Light in the country of Enlightenment" [115]) have come to Paris as a site of liberation; they find a city engaged in war.

The narrative of *The Mark of the Angel* centres on a love triangle: Raphael, a middle-class French classical musician, Saffie, his young wife, a recent German immigrant to France, and her lover, András, an instrument maker and a Hungarian living in Paris. Huston therefore evokes the great tradition of the nineteenth-century novel of adultery in French literature of which Stendhal's *Le Rouge et le noir* and Flaubert's *Madame Bovary* are the most well known. At the same time, Huston's characters are deeply rooted in twentieth-century history, profoundly marked with the horrifying experiences of war, occupation, and genocide. Raphael, who is perhaps least affected, suffers the loss of his father, killed in an unexplained accident in the early morning hours of occupied Paris. He witnesses the execution of young Resistance fighters in front of the family's apartment: "the messy mass of arms and legs, the bloody embrace of four comrades fallen together" (9). András has endured the destruction of the Budapest Jewish community, including the deaths of close family members, and has fled his homeland following the abortive Hungarian uprising in 1956: "weeks of fear and hunger and cold, the diarrhea, the ice-crusted fields, the waiting, the endless black nights, the inhospitable Alps, the dozens of encounters with policemen, border authorities and innkeepers, the phony papers, the phony smiles, the perpetual lack of truth and trust" (*Mark* 114). While Raphael and András have both suffered, the traumas of history are most deeply inscribed on Saffie. As a child in Germany, she had to face the death of her friend Lotte, who was crushed by debris in a bombing raid, "pinned beneath the roofbeam, her right arm and leg reduced to mush" (73); she witnessed the deaths of other children, "the little bodies are hastily carried off, their white dresses drenched in blood" (128); she encounters a dying Allied pilot, whom she sees as a black devil, "panting, bleeding, stretching his arm out toward her" (80); she watches her mother tortured and raped by Russian soldiers before she too is raped; some years later she is seduced by a French high school language teacher in a grotesque mixture of sexual touching and stories of Nazi cruelty (68–69). Over and over, a historical moment that might be read as emancipatory—the Allied attacks on Nazi Germany, the defeat of the Germans on the eastern borders by the Soviet army, the reintegration of Germany into Europe following the war—proves to be a site of pain and suffering for Saffie. These repeated brutalizations—"the unmaking of her world," to borrow a phrasing from Elaine Scarry's book *The Body in Pain*—precipitate Saffie into a dislocated state of detachment, equally indifferent to the ache of work, the caresses of lovemaking, or the touch of her infant.

In the opening pages of Huston's narrative, the reader first encounters Saffie standing indifferently outside Raphael's apartment door, waiting to apply for a job as his housekeeper. Her gestures "vague, preoccupied" (*Mark* 3) betray neither eagerness at the prospect of employment, nor anxiety about the imminent interview, but rather an unsettling blankness, a lack of reaction to the world around her. In the rigidity of her movements, in her "robot-like" stiffness, Saffie carries the markings of history in her body. Like Septimus Smith, the shell-shocked veteran of World War I in Virginia Woolf's *Mrs. Dalloway*, Huston's Saffie is an uncannily accurate literary depiction of the effects of trauma. In *Trauma and Recovery*, the psychiatrist Judith Lewis Herman describes withdrawal and indifference as classical responses of traumatized victims: psychologically damaging events, especially when repeated, dissolve the basic human assumption that the world is a secure and reasonable place in which to live. As Herman puts it, "thereafter, a sense of alienation, of disconnection, pervades every relationship, from the most intimate familial bonds to the most abstract affiliations of community and religion" (52). Saffie's failure to produce even feigned emotional contact is the cause of her dismissal from the "welcome hostess" position for which she trained in Germany; she is indifferent to Raphael's passion, lying immobile and unresponsive: "her body isn't inert; it's absent. Static, even when it moves" (*Mark* 30). Most surprising and shocking to readers is her lack of response to her own infant: she handles Emil with efficient but unloving hands, "awkward and distracted ... it's as if the child doesn't exist for her" (64).[3] Such impassive detachment is especially puzzling in the relationship between mother and child, the basic dyad that both biology and society construct as the centre of love and concern. Herman notes that traumatic experiences "call into question basic human relationships. They breach the attachments of family, friendship, love, and community. They undermine the belief systems that give meaning to human experience" (51). The lack of affect in Saffie's relationship with her small son is only the most extreme exemplification of the psychic damage she has suffered.

"Dear Lord," Raphael asks himself about Saffie's bewildering response—no resistance, no acceptance—to his sexual advances, "what can have happened to her?" (*Mark* 29). In an astonishing, ever-evolving passage of writing, Huston begins to unravel the structures of trauma that haunt Saffie's psyche. With Raphael away on a concert tour, Saffie is alone with her infant son in the Paris apartment. On a sunny spring day she has begun to hang up Emil's newly washed diapers. Huston describes Saffie's slippage into the past in this way: "As she's hanging up the white rectangles of cotton, a ray of sunlight falls on one of them and she plummets into a blur of whiteness, blinding sunlight glancing off white sheets and pillow slips ..." (66). Here the metonymic association of the shape and whiteness of the diapers with another memory of laundry, together with the glint of bright light, sets in motion an abrupt transition into a childhood experience of helping her mother hang laundered sheets in the garden of their home. Huston's narrative represents the past not so much as a memory, but rather as a spontaneous irruption, a relentless reliving of perpetual present: "She's helping her mother," Huston writes, "she can only be five or six" (66), not "she *was* helping ..." or "she *was* five or six." Mother and daughter make a playful game of the laundry, singing and laughing among the windblown sheets, so it comes as a surprise to readers that Saffie becomes aware of herself in the familiar Paris apartment with ominous feelings of fear: "panting, her heart thumping, a dreadful weight on her chest" (67). As metonymic sequences continue to unfold, readers begin to connect Saffie's experiences with the trauma of a young German girl growing up in the war and its aftermath. Her language teacher from France—a young man formally engaged in the wider project of reintegrating Adenauer's Germany into Europe—not only educated the adolescent Saffie about Nazi atrocities, but also drew her into perverse games of sexual touching, combining narratives of brutal violence with erotic caresses. Stories of how Nazi soldiers smashed the fragile skulls of "undesirable" infants, therefore, are enmeshed with Saffie's concern for the vulnerability of her own small son, whose German heritage perhaps situates him as a target for revenge.

The complex entanglements of trauma and the lived experiences of modern history in the young woman's consciousness are condensed in Huston's figure of mother and child alone in the Paris apartment. As Huston constructs the story, Saffie is cradling her baby in her arms when she experiences a flashback to what seem to be generic murders of infants, "smashing the little body against a brick wall or the side of a truck or a cement floor" (70). The multiplication of images endows the scene of horror with a surreal intensity that is both concretely specific in its reiteration of cruel deaths and vaguely abstract in its repetition of numberless ways to kill. In the account no direct source is named for the images; they might be events witnessed by Saffie, stories recounted by the French teacher, photos in a newspaper, a newsreel film, or accounts from war crimes trials or stories told by survivors. In addition, Huston's description of the mind in traumatic recollection—"stop, photo, freeze ..." (70)—underlines both the mechanical operations suggested by the allusion to photography and the agency required to commit an image to memory: "stop" and "freeze" might be actions of a witness; "photo" might be shorthand for "take a mental snapshot so as not to forget." And yet, the entanglements reach their most complex in the metonymic chains of association that connect the brutality of the soldier, sexuality, and the innocence of the child. In a grotesque and fantastic slippage through time, the narrator describes Saffie's preoccupation with an image of a Nazi soldier:

> but his body, yes, let's take his body, it's suspended outside of time and Saffie, gliding toward him with her eyes closed, gently removes his shiny black boots, then the trousers and jacket of his uniform—and gradually, as she undresses it, the Nazi's body relaxes, softens and shrinks ... turning at last into little Emil, sound asleep in his mother Saffie's arms. (70)

The abruptness of the narrator's intrusiveness—confronting the reader with Saffie's bizarre train of thought, and the vertigo of the transformation of a frightening apparition, the SS soldier, into the small sleeping child—combine to produce a powerful effect of dislocation. The twinning of sexualized gestures with the conventional figure of mother and infant work to create a profane madonna. While a psychological reading of such an image (Theweleit) would undoubtedly result in a productive interpretation, Williams's conception of modern tragedy points instead toward the social and cultural questions raised by Huston's arresting portrait. How does the child gently held in the arms of a German mother (in the war years? in the early 1920s?) grow up to be one of the black-uniformed murderers who swell the SS ranks some twenty years later? How is the potential in the new life of any human being distorted into the social violence of Nazi Germany? In dissolving the years into a regression in which the soldier becomes once again a helpless infant, Saffie's unsettling vision challenges the reader to think through the reversals of human possibility implied in the histories of the twentieth century.

But this is not all. Huston returns to mothers and children in reconstructing a crucial traumatic moment in Saffie's childhood. On the second day of Raphael's absence, Saffie's thoughts drift back to her own mother, surrounded by her five children, singing an apparently innocent nursery song, "Alle meine Entchen schwimmen auf dem See, all my little ducklings swimming in the lake" (72). The mother's voice draws the children into the metaphor of the song; they figuratively become the ducklings clustered around the female duck: "it's almost impossible to hear anything else, almost impossible, their heads in the water, their tails in the air, no, the humming vibration you feel in Mutti's flesh comes from her song, not from the bombers" (72). Once again, Huston's prose assembles metonymic chains to represent the structure of trauma: the children, having become the ducklings of their mother's song, are now transformed into another bird—the ostrich with its head in the sand, trying desperately to ignore the approach of the enemy airplanes. Similarly, the hum of vocal music—the comforting sounds of *Muttersprache*—slides into the ominous mechanical hum of engines about to release death and destruction on the people below. The madonna figure of a mother surrounded by her children, itself a conventional image of consolation and security, is defamiliarized to become a portrayal of desperation, a mother trying to protect her children with nothing but her voice to shelter them. As readers circle through these scraps of Saffie's memories, her actions in the present become less erratic and more understandable.

When the bombs fall, it is not Saffie and her family who are the victims, but rather her neighbour and childhood friend, Lotte, who lies dying under debris, "pinned beneath the roofbeam" (*Mark* 73). While the death of her friend is unquestionably traumatic, at this moment of flashback, Huston's narrative draws attention to the unmaking of the mother's world. Because Lotte was her only child, Frau Silber is transformed from "Lotte's mother" into the blankness of the bereaved woman with aching, empty arms: "Saffie's mother comes out and gently takes the arm of Lotte's—now no one's—mother, and leads her over to their house" (76). The relentless repetition of the phrasing three times within a single page ("no one's mother isn't hungry"; "no one's mother, rocking silently back and forth" 76) underlines the mother's dependence on the child for a central part of her identity. "Mother" turns out to be as helplessly fragile and as subject to arbitrary violence as the small baby in the hands of the SS soldier. After the narrator has ruthlessly led the reader through these fragments of Saffie's childhood memories, it comes as no surprise that the birth of her son fails to be a source of comfort to the young wife. To become a mother is, in Saffie's experience, to be all the more vulnerable to the brutalities of the twentieth century.

It is her affair with Andràs that initiates a process of healing for Saffie. Beginning from shared laughter and sexual desire, Saffie is drawn back into a connection with the world. In the musical instrument shop, jumbled and disordered, suggesting a disregard for hierarchy and an embrace of creativity that Raphael's bourgeois apartment can never represent, and in the Marais courtyard, crossed by the diverse ethnicities of an inner-city community, she is confronted with deeply buried anxieties: she meets black jazz musicians, shadows of the devil airman, who treat her with gentle friendliness; she takes a Jewish lover who forces her to recognize the rituals of Yom Kippur and to acknowledge the deportation of Parisian Jews during the occupation; she feels pleasure in her own body and contentment with her infant.[4] Less tender, more tenacious, but equally important is her lover's insistence that she confront her German past: little by little Saffie recounts her mother's torture and death, her experiences following the war, and finally her father's participation in Nazi medical experiments. The trauma theorist Dori Laub notes "survivors did not only need to survive so that they could tell their stories; they also needed to tell their stories in order to survive. There is, in each survivor, an imperative need to *tell* and thus to come to *know* one's story, unimpeded by ghosts from the past against which one has to protect oneself" (63; emphasis in the original). It is crucial to recognize that these accounts (119–21, 178–80) are narrated by Saffie in a spirit of communicating and acknowledging her past; the memories do not intrude unexpectedly in traumatic chains of association as her childhood experiences of the war were triggered by the white rectangles of newly washed cloths. At the same time, there is no doubt that Saffie still needs to circle toward the traumatic centre before she is able to recount her own history. When she approaches her father's complicity with Nazi medical experiments, she takes the first tentative steps by relating her veterinarian father's burial of pets, euthanized at the request of their owners, in the family's garden. Their bodies—inadequately interred—break through the surface in a way that reminds Andràs of "other hastily buried bodies—not of domestic animals, but of Jews ... corpses swelling and starting to bleed, building up pressure, finally splitting open the earth's surface" (*Mark* 137). In these sequences of shared association, readers too are drawn into the circles of reciprocal memory: when Saffie relates her mother's torture by Russian soldiers who burn the woman with a household iron, all of a sudden Saffie's obsessive cleaning and her desperate attempts to control domestic objects becomes comprehensible through the narration of the horrific events witnessed by the little girl.

Abandonment of indifference and restoration of community are focused in a remarkable *mise en scène* on the traditionally magical midsummer's eve when Saffie visits the Marais courtyard during an improvised jazz gathering. One furtive guest is the Algerian revolutionary Rachid, who has been tortured; his hands broken by the French police are described in a disturbing image of sexual impotence: "wrapped in white bandages [they] dangle uselessly between his thighs" (172). When Saffie offers him tea, he is unable to grasp the cup: "And so, crouching down in turn, the German woman holds a glass to the Algerian's lips in the courtyard of the Hungarian, amid the syncopated jazz riffs of the African-Americans" (172). At one and the same time, the act of offering tea signifies both conventions of hospitality and a poignant tenderness that does not forget the basic human need to satisfy thirst within a small community of exiles from Europe, Africa, and America.

And yet, the very condition that makes this restoration of reciprocity possible is also the dynamic of its undoing. Rachid's hands, systematically broken by a hammer, are an immobile blank whiteness, a sign of a counter-reality that will break up the utopian moment of community. Like the whiteness of the newly washed cloths that set in motion the traumatic intrusions of Saffie's childhood experiences, the pale bandages that obscure Rachid's hands—the site of the body that most concretely represents human contact—signify a dark side of French history, the counter-narratives of colonialism and oppression. Indeed, the political and ideological impetus behind the extraordinary efforts to retain Algeria as a colony of France takes shape in the humiliations of defeat, especially in Indochina. As a political radical committed to liberty for Algeria, Rachid calls attention to the contradiction within a France that claims *libérté, égalité, fraternité* in its own national self-definition, but subjects others to racism and colonization. This is the sense in which he is Saffie's rival for Andràs because he represents political involvement; he exemplifies the commitment to action that will draw Andràs away from the individualized dyad of two lovers into the contingency of history. From the perspective of Williams's tragic impasse, the love Andràs offers Saffie has its roots in a political conviction against injustice and inequality that also compels him to take up the violence of class and anti-colonial war. If Andràs, a Hungarian Jew who lost most of his family in the Nazi occupation of Budapest, is able to open himself to the possibilities of love with a young German woman, it is because of his political engagement with the utopian socialist promise of equality in the world. And yet, it is this very commitment that will inevitably conflict with personal passions of sexual attraction and love, pulling him back into political struggles, both public and covert, against the war in Algeria.

Andràs, who has shown Saffie openness to human contact with the world, who befriends American jazz musicians, the elderly Jewish widow living upstairs, and the homeless man from a nearby market, is consumed by anger that Rachid and the cause of Algerian independence mobilize: "Andràs is seething. Electrified with hatred. Longing to fight. Now. To get in there. Be Rachid's hands. Where things are happening ..." (*Mark* 187).[5] Huston's short staccato sentences evoke the rage that has pushed him out of his easygoing stance. It is the normally inarticulate Saffie who specifies the contradictions within Andràs's embrace of violence: "You mean ... you help to make war?" says Saffie, backing away from him. "You mean ... these hands, they touch clarinets ... and guns? *These hands ... are for killing people?*" (*Mark* 149; emphasis in the original). If Andràs has adopted Frantz Fanon's contemporary justification of revolutionary violence—"the colonized man finds his freedom in and through violence" (86), Fanon writes in *The Wretched of the Earth*—Saffie has experienced the brutality of armies engaged in liberating Germany from the Nazis (bombing by Americans; rape by Russians). Saffie's willingness to confront her lover and her precise description of the contradiction Andràs has embraced, focusing again on hands that are both the object of creativity (the making of instruments) and destruction (participation in acquiring armaments), adeptly demonstrates her disposition to take up an ethical position.

It is at the same time also clear that the love Andràs feels for Saffie leads him to new human responses that reverse the undoubtedly justifiable anger he feels against the Nazis and collaborators who murdered his family. To recognize the modulations in Andràs's attitudes is not to suggest he begins to forgive the brutal regime; rather it is to acknowledge the reciprocity he offers the young German woman. When Saffie hesitantly inquires about the fate of his family, Andràs reflects, "Why should I tell her? … How does this truth concern her? Must she really be forced to learn it?" (116). His choice to relate "only a part of the story" (*Mark* 116) is a self-reflective acceptance that Saffie, who was only a child during the Nazi period, cannot be made to bear responsibility for the actions of adult Nazis and Hungarian collaborators. That the historical situation in which he now finds himself—the involvement of France in a colonial war and the brutal repression of North African immigrants—blocks his utopian desire to live in a present released from history is the tragic impasse of the twentieth century, as Williams defines it. In the negotiations with the past that Andràs must work through, he is inexorably caught: he cannot offer Saffie warmth and love without his commitment to the struggle for freedom in Algeria; at the same time, his love of liberty draws him into a world of violence that destroys his friend Rachid and undermines Saffie's trust.

Raphael, who seems least marked by history and whose positioning in the narrative as the betrayed husband, and ultimately the man whose actions cause Emil's death, seems to elicit little sympathy, but alongside Saffie's slow recovery from multiple traumas and Andràs's wavering between love and hatred, Raphael articulates an aesthetics of resistance. His name, which recalls the great painter of Renaissance Rome, evokes resonances of compelling beauty and exquisite execution; his profession as a flutist in a Parisian orchestra offers the opportunity to create concerts that produce the experience of aesthetic beauty for audiences. "Music is my way of taking part in the struggle, making the world a better place to live," he explains to Saffie: "Happiness and beauty … still have to be embodied in the here and now. It's a political act to make this possible in the real world" (*Mark* 191). It is true that Raphael appears unaware of other crucial political issues—the largely middle-class audience classical music attracts, for instance. It is also true that his structural position in the novel—the betrayed husband emotionally blind to his wife's infidelities—does not invest his ideas with much weight. And yet, Raphael articulates an Enlightenment aesthetics developed from philosophers as different as Friedrich Schiller and Immanuel Kant and, on the left, advanced in Theodor Adorno's aesthetic theories.

In his well-known essay on lyric poetry, Adorno notes that aesthetic expression, "having escaped from the weight of material existence, evoke[s] the image of a life free from the coercion of reigning practices, of utility, of the relentless pressures of self-preservation" (39). Such a description might seem to take as its point of departure the autonomy of art, but Adorno points out that it implies a socially rooted and politically inflected project as a "protest against a social situation that every individual experiences as hostile, alien, cold, oppressive ... the work's distance from mere existence becomes the measure of what is false and bad in the latter" (39–40). If Raphael's music is his form of protest against what is, it comes as no surprise that he perceives the march against the Algerian war and the skirmishes between demonstrators and police as a frightening threat. He relives the panic he feels emerging from the Odéon metro into the crowd: "the emptiness in his hands, in his soul, when his Louis Lot [flute] had been knocked from his grasp and, crouching down in the fray, he'd caught sight of it in the gutter, amid gushing mud and rainwater, kicked left and right by the scuffling feet of strangers" (*Mark* 191).[6] "It was as if," he goes on, "as if I'd lost everything, the very meaning of ..." (192). Huston's style, depicting the normally lucid Raphael breaking off into incoherence, underlines the powerful affect of the experience. The language of the passage also stresses a parallel with Andràs's use of his instrument maker's skilful hands to carry a suitcase full of money to buy arms for the Algerian rebels. Raphael feels the emptiness in his hands, which move masterfully along the keys of the flute, and also in his soul, which dreads the loss of the ability to create beauty. In this case a demonstration that began peacefully—think of de Beauvoir's descriptions of the utopian moment of human community as the demonstrators move along the open boulevard—ends up in violence. It is, within the space of a few hours on one day, a condensed reminder of the reversal of utopian hopes in social transformation that Williams describes as modern tragedy.

Barbara Godard writes about how the need "to cut away from or to cut into established categories or discursive forms opens up new questionings and orderings of reality, new possibilities for creating meaning, in a gesture that problematizes the socalled [sic] naturalness or inevitability of previously available narratives" ("Culture"). *The Mark of the Angel* puts in question traditional narratives about the liberation of Europe in the 1940s and France's claim to be the continuing site of the emancipatory traditions of Enlightenment Europe. It is a world in which familiar stories are replaced with children cowering from bombing raids, the rape of women and girls, a Paris peopled with refugees and North African immigrants.[7]

Toward the end of the novel, Huston's intrusive narrator confronts the reader with a bizarre prayer, a litany asking mercy for the inability to break through cycles of suffering: "we are incapable of healing our pain" (196). "We hop," the narrator intones, "grotesquely through our time on earth, one foot in our private lives and the other in the history of our century" (196). This figure, with its powerful asymmetry and poignant distortion, conveys the difficulty of negotiating the tenderness of human love in a world given over to cruel force. Huston's novel chronicles the persistence of history's distortions: the love between Saffie and Andràs is also embedded in his support for a liberatory project that answers violence with violence, sometimes directed against civilians like the little girl Saffie of the mid-1940s. In a parallel way, Saffie is willing to implicate her small son, a child "at odds with reality" (199), in the complex web of divided allegiances and deception that eventually causes his death in his father's "enormity of despair" (217). Attempts to negotiate "private lives" and the inescapable limits of history—hopping however grotesquely—are tragic in the sense Raymond Williams described. Like the blank indeterminate whiteness of the bandages on Rachid's hands or the emptiness of the Paris apartment where "there remained not the slightest trace of Saffie's passage through Raphael's existence" (217) at the end of the novel, history distorts and even erases the yearnings and desires of the human beings that make it and inhabit it.

Notes

I am grateful to the organizers of the symposium on Nancy Huston at Mount Royal College, Calgary (now Mount Royal University), where I first presented the ideas in this article, and to the members of the post-colonial studies research group at the University of Calgary who heard a different version and offered useful feedback. Aritha van Herk, Barbara Godard, and Sandra Singer all made helpful contributions.

1. In adopting these moments of an overarching omniscient narrator—Branach-Kallas calls it a "blatant narrating voice" (190)—Huston may have been inspired by the same strategy used in Elsa Morante's novel about Roman refugees in World War II, *History: A Novel*.
2. In this paragraph and the next I am drawing on my introduction to *Modern Tragedy*. See Williams, *Modern*.
3. Saffie uses Emil, the German spelling of the name. The French spelling, Emile, situates the child, ironically, in relation to Jean-Jacques Rousseau's well-known conduct book about how to educate a son. Emil, a pawn in the deceptions of adultery, with no friends his own age, and ultimately faced with his father's rage when he discovers the unfaithfulness of the boy's mother, is an unhappy

example of how not to raise a child: "even as he learns how to talk," Huston writes, "he's being taught how to lie" (*Mark* 141).

4   Huston comments on the importance of a writer inhabiting what Proulx describes as "the convergence of different cultures and ethnicities" (85); as she writes: "Mais mon accent, au fond, j'y tiens. Il traduit la friction entre moi-même et la société qui m'entoure" (qtd. in Proulx 85). Bond describes similar tensions in Huston's writings: "Nous sommes tous doubles: individus libres et victims de toutes sortes de forces qui nous menacent, sujets parlants transformes en objects par le discours des autres" (69). Huston has also written: "Every expatriate has the conviction—deeply rooted in her subconscious and regularly rejected as preposterous by her intellect—that a part of herself, or, rather *another self*, has never stopped living *back there*" (*Losing* 91; emphasis in the original).

5   Andràs is involved in the Algerian struggle as one of the "suitcase men," the French sympathizers who helped take funds across borders for the FLN (Front de la libération nationale) in Algeria. In Schalk's words, "As late as 1961, 80 percent of the funds for the FLN cause came from Algerian workers in France, and all that money had to be conveyed secretly across the French border" (98). Huston describes the process (*Mark* 170–71). See also Harmon and Rotman, and Haroun. Young provides an overview of the influence of Fanon and this revolutionary model on subsequent African struggles.

6   De Beauvoir, safely at home, writes: "When I went down to buy something for dinner, I heard distant noises, the traffic was jammed along the Boulevard Saint-Germain; demonstrations were still going on near the Odéon, and we heard later that there had been some fighting in the Latin Quarter" (620).

7   Huston has written "A country's voluntary fictions (stories) provide better access to its reality than its involuntary fictions (History)" (*Tale-Tellers* 159).

Works Cited

Bond, David. "Nancy Huston: Identité et dédoublement dans le texte." *Studies in Canadian Literature* 26.2 (2001): 53–70. Print.

Branach-Kallas, Anna. "Lovers and/or Enemies: Love and Nationality in Nancy Huston's *The Mark of the Angel*." Steenman-Marcuse. 189–97. Print.

Brecht, Bertolt. *Poems. Part 2 1929–1938*. Ed. John Willett and Ralph Mannheim with Erich Fried. London: Eyre Methuen, 1976.

Caruth, Cathy, ed. *Trauma: Explorations in Memory*. Baltimore: Johns Hopkins UP, 1995. Print.

de Beauvoir, Simone. *Force of Circumstance*. Trans. Richard Howard. Harmondsworth: Penguin, 1968. Print.

Fanon, Frantz. *The Wretched of the Earth*. New York: Grove, 1968. Print.

Godard, Barbara. *Canadian Literature at the Crossroads of Language and Culture*. Ed. Smaro Kamboureli. Edmonton: NeWest, 2008. Print.

———. "Culture at the Crossroads." *Resources for Feminist Research* 32.3–4 (2007): 13+. *CPIQ (Canadian Periodicals)*. Web. February 2, 2011. <http://find.galegroup.com Gale document number: A184429033>.

Gould, Deborah. "On Affect and Protest." Staiger, Cvetkovich, and Reynolds. 18–44.

Harmon, Hervé, and Patrick Rotman. *Les Porteurs de valise: La résistance française à la guerre d'Algérie*. Paris: Albin Michel, 1979. Print.

Haroun, Ali. *La 7e Wilaya: La Guerre de FLN en France*. Paris: Seuil, 1986. Print.

Herman, Judith Lewis. *Trauma and Recovery: The Aftermath of Violence from Domestic Abuse to Political Terror.* New York: Basic Books, 1992. Print.

Huston, Nancy. *Longings and Belongings: Essays by Nancy Huston*. Toronto: McArthur and Co., 2005. Print.

———. *Losing North: Musings on Land, Tongue, and Self*. Toronto: McArthur and Co., 2002. Print.

———. *The Mark of the Angel*. [*L'Empreinte de l'ange*] Toronto: McArthur and Co., 1999. Print.

———. *The Tale-Tellers: A Short Study of Humankind*. Toronto: McArthur and Co., 2008. Print.

Laub, Dori. "Truth and Testimony: The Process and the Struggle." Caruth, *Trauma: Explorations in Memory*, 61–75. Print.

Morante, Elsa. *History: A Novel*. Trans. William Weaver. New York: Random House, 1984. Print.

Proulx, Patrice J. "Writing Home: Explorations of Exile and Cultural Hybridity in the Correspondence of Nancy Huston and Leila Sebbar." *L'Esprit Créateur* 40.4 (Winter 2000): 80–88. Print.

Scarry, Elaine. *The Body in Pain: The Making and Unmaking of the World*. New York: Oxford UP, 1985. Print.

Schalk, David L. *War and the Ivory Tower: Algeria and Vietnam*. New York: Oxford UP, 1991. Print.

Staiger, Janet, Ann Cvetkovich, and Ann Reynolds, eds. *Political Emotions: New Agendas in Communications:* London: Routledge, 2010. Print.

Steenman-Marcuse, Conny, ed. *The Rhetoric of Canadian Writing*. Amsterdam: Rodophi, 2002. Print.

Theweleit, Klaus. *Male Fantasies*. 2 vols. Trans. Erica Carter and Chris Turner. Minneapolis: U of Minnesota P, 1987 and 1989. Print.

Williams, Raymond. *The Long Revolution*. London: Chatto and Windus, 1961. Print.

———. *Modern Tragedy*. Ed. and intro. Pamela McCallum. Peterborough: Broadview, 2006. Print.

Young, Robert J.C. "Fanon and the Turn to Armed Struggle in Africa." *Wasafiri* 44 (Spring 2005): 33–41. Print.

Chapter 3
Language and Interdisciplinarity: (Re-)contextualizing Nicole Brossard's *Picture Theory*

KARL E. JIRGENS

Part One: A Short Historical Perspective on Language and Interdisciplinary Performance in Canada

Canada has a strong history of language-based inter-media expression. In particular, electronically enhanced, language-based performance is traceable to artists and groups such as the Automatistes, Norman McLaren, Herman Voaden, Hugh Lecaine, and James Reaney. In the meantime, there has been an explosion of contemporary, digitally influenced, language-engaged expression by artists such as Nicole Brossard, Janet Cardiff and George Büres Miller, Arthur Kroker, Vera Frenkel, and Robert Lepage, among others. In a global village bristling with digital communications, it serves us well to turn our attention to those who initiated and extended the field of language in response to electronic media.

The 1948 Automatiste manifesto *Refus global* (*Total Refusal*) established an unprecedented artistic and political position in Canadian art. Automatiste member Claude Gauvreau wrote twenty-six short performative intermedia pieces between 1944 and 1946, which responded to non-figurative paintings created by the group. In *Egregore* Ray Ellenwood comments on Gauvreau's performance *Bien-être être* (*The Good Life*):

> Thus, the audience watching Gauvreau's *Bien-être* were confronted with scraps of dialogue which seemed to have no connection, punctuated by long monologues made up of apparently random images and accompanying actions which seemed to depict some kind of temporal and spiritual progression from marriage to old age and death, but with many unexplained elements. (102)

Ellenwood informs us that Automatiste collaborators on *Bien-être* included Muriel Guilbaut and Claude Gauvreau, with sets by Pierre Gauvreau, costumes by Magdeleine Arbour, as well as lighting effects by Maurice Perron. Beginning with, but moving beyond French Surrealist techniques, Gauvreau sought ruptured form and mixed elements of language to create "explorational images" whose meaning would be immediately apparent, if only on an intuitive level. The performance features a newlywed couple setting up house, speaking in disconnected monologues. The play ends with the woman falling dead, leaving the man alone, while a green light troubles him and prevents him from entering an adjacent room, where someone is playing a five-note theme obsessively on the piano. The man eventually forces his way into the room, and emerges blinded and without hands. The piano is removed for his monologue. Ellenwood observes that the performance evokes the conventions of boulevard comedy while simultaneously denying them, noting an aesthetic of disconnection and psychic disorientation (144). Such disjunctive and nightmarish performances can be read as types of "rebus," or as syncretist puzzles that invite audiences to decipher them after the fact.

Inspired by the Group of Seven, Herman Voaden studied drama at Queen's University and developed an appreciation of theatre that synthesized the performing arts. He developed inter-media theatre, combining unique lighting effects, music, dance, innovative sets, and over-laying voices. His productions include *Rocks and Earth Song* (1932), *Hill-Land* (1934), *Murder Pattern* (1936), and *Ascend as the Sun* (1942). Voaden's inter-media symphonic expressionism is extended by Gilles Maheu, founder of the Québec-based group Carbone 14, recognized internationally for its productions of *Hamlet Machine* and, in particular, rapid montage sequences of *Le Dortoir*.

Outside of Québec, James Reaney offered an early integration of electronic media within a performative context. Mixing visuals, vocals, and sound, *Colours in the Dark*, which deployed electronic lighting and rapid-fire scene changes to depict alternating scenes of local history, changed our perception of theatre. In his "Author's Note" Reaney explains that the play's inter-media mosaic of acoustic and visual elements involves a quest for identity:

> I happen to have a play box and it's filled with not only toys and school relics, but also deedboxes, ancestral coffin plates—in short, a whole life. When you sort through the play box you eventually see your whole life—as well as all of life—things like Sunday School albums which show Elijah being fed by ravens,

St. Stephen being stoned. The theatrical experience in front of you now is designed to give you that mosaic—that all-things-happening-at-the-same-time-galaxy-higgledy-piggledy feeling that rummaging through a play box can give you. (8)

Reaney's performance as mosaic creates a rebus puzzle of thoughts and memories. The disjunctive stylistics abandon any conventional sense of continuity and invite a reassembly of elements in the mind of the audience in order to generate meaning. Such syncretist stylistics recur in contemporary expression.

Presently, we are in the midst of neo-baroque cultural developments that demand fresh critical responses. The January 2009 issue of the *PMLA* is devoted to Latin American neo-baroque but excludes North American proponents. Critics in that issue note that the neo-baroque reacts against earlier imperialist models, while critic William Egginton claims that the neo-baroque engages incompleteness in pursuit of illusory depth (141).

Gilles Deleuze's study, *The Fold*, pursues related viewpoints and speaks of the baroque tendency to engage vision as it decentres or shifts perspectives (21). Enfoldment of interior and exterior spaces accompanies subsequent unfoldings. Leibniz's view that space can never be void, but always includes matter anticipates post-relativity theories on physics. Manipulations of space-time typify the neo-baroque, which has affinities with the "postmodern" and is typically ironic and parodic (not necessarily in the disparaging sense). Post-Einsteinian views, including relativity, the uncertainty principle, probability theory, fuzzy logic, chaos and fractal theory, are evident in neo-baroque expression.

Samuel Beckett's *Krapp's Last Tape* marks a milestone integrating electronic media with performance, while earlier futurist experiments explored wide possibilities. Neo-baroque inter-media performance has deep roots in the Renaissance art of Gianlorenzo Bernini and performance installations of Leonardo da Vinci. In "Renaissance Performance: Notes on Prototypical Artistic Actions in the Age of Platonic Princes," Attanasio di Felice speaks of precedents and confirms that da Vinci pioneered syncretist, inter-media performance, while noting that the later baroque impulse was adopted by futurists, who added Bergsonian absurdities, irony, and Einsteinian perspectives on physics (9).

Critical views useful in interpreting neo-baroque expression include Iserian "gaps," Deleuzian oscillations of "difference and repetition," Baudrillardian simulacra, Blanchot's views on gaze and silence, and Kristeva's applications of semiotics and paragrammatics (i.e., pattern recognition of conceptual networks with ambivalent or polysemous interpretations). The emergence of new interdisciplinary digital forms results in the partial obsolescence of established aesthetic and theoretical models, inviting critical perspectives not confined to texts solely rendered on the page.

As with the baroque, so with the neo-baroque, we are faced with a *syncretic* breadth of vision and a multiplicity of expressive forms. So, to add to both the *PMLA* coverage and to Deleuze, I find that digitally enhanced, language-based inter-media performances frequently feature the following elements: spectacle, *trompe l'oeil*, anamorphosis, *mise en abyme* (i.e., into the abyss, infinite regression, dream within a dream), manifold layers of sensory stimuli, polyvalent meaning, multi-stable perceptions, self-similarity, reiterative patterns, multiple surfacing, inclusion of the quotidian, refusals of a metaphysics of depth, convolutions of interior and exterior space, and plays of often ritualistic simulacra. In addition, such expressions feature disjunction, fragmentation, fractalization, chaos patterns, aporia, electronic prostheses, technological self-replications, and what Espen Aarseth in *Cybertext: Perspectives on Ergodic Literature* has dubbed "ergodic" qualities—that is, qualities demanding direct audience engagement to generate meaning. Although space does not permit a detailed explication, virtually all of the above elements are evident in varying degrees in *Picture Theory* and other texts by Nicole Brossard. I qualify my view of the neo-baroque in agreement with Gregg Lambert, who, in *The Return of the Baroque in Modern Culture*, notes that there may not be one but rather many "Baroques" (139).

Neo-baroque features are evident in works of artists such as Robert Lepage, Vera Frenkel, Janet Cardiff, and George Büres Miller. Robert Lepage's performances share affinities with earlier artists such as Laurie Anderson or Robert Wilson. Lepage's productions, including *Tectonic Plates*, *Polygraph*, *Zulu Time*, *Geometry of Miracles*, *Far Side of the Moon*, *Ka*, and his production of Berlioz's *Damnation of Faust* feature multi-layered physical actions, multiple voices, kinetic actors and props, interplays of slides, cycloramas, robotics, synthesized and musical sounds, including vocal, instrumental, and digital, abrupt and disjunctive scene changes, ellipses, visual ambiguities, overt uses of *trompe l'oeil*, and reiterations generating an emergent and beautiful chaos in a multi-sensory barrage akin to a three-ring electric circus.

Vera Frenkel's performative works also adopt neo-baroque configurations. Her looped ten-minute parodic, inter-media performance/installation *This Is Your Messiah Speaking* uses public audio address systems and large-format video screens strategically placed around shopping malls to convey

(Re-)contextualizing Nicole Brossard's *Picture Theory* 63

Figures 3.1–3.3 *The Messiah with the Right Credentials*, the most recent work in Frenkel's ongoing Messiah Project, traces the collusive connections between consumerism, fundamentalism, and romance. Commissioned for the 2011 McLuhan 100 Festival, this nine-episode series of interventions for the three-hundred-screen network of the Toronto subway system features interwoven modes of narrative and representation, from handwriting to American Sign Language, revealing through distilled texts and compelling images the psychic engines of the culture. Images courtesy of the artist and V-Tape (Toronto).

several modes of communication and representation, including text, recorded speech, and American Sign Language, to trace and disclose the bond between messianism and consumerism as two conflicting romances of rescue. The following is a portion of the voice-over from Frenkel's installation documented in *Rampike*:

I KNOW (FOR EXAMPLE) THAT PEOPLE MUST SHOP
FOR THE RIGHT MESSIAH AT THE RIGHT PRICE.
WHERE REDEEMERS ARE CONCERNED,
COMPARE GUARANTEES. (27)

Using guerrilla-art tactics with a digital interface, Frenkel co-opts and "theatricalizes" public space while deconstructing consumerist public address systems with her parodic, libertarian challenge featuring ambivalent language, interval, and multi-stable perceptions (that is, for shoppers, the performance is interrupted by daily events in the mall). The resulting subtle but multiple and enfolded layers of stimuli comingle higher spiritual and quotidian commercial values. The arrhythmic shopping experience, mixed with the rhythmic audio-video presentation, result in an appropriately disjunctive neo-baroque contrapuntality as Frenkel questions individual and socio-cultural mores.

Neo-baroque stylistics are integral to the language-based performative installations of Janet Cardiff and George Büres Miller. *Paradise Institute* established their reputations at the Venice Bienalle, while their *Forty-Part Motet* features forty digitally recorded voices, channelled through forty small speakers set within a single space. Walking through that space, one gets the uncanny audio-illusion of moving through a live group of people. Cardiff and Miller's forty-five-minute piece *The Missing Voice* offers one of the best examples of inter-media multi-sensory experience. Using sophisticated bi-aural microphone systems that mimic exactly sound reception by human ears, Cardiff and Miller prepared a walking tour through London with a pre-recorded audio track on CD with headphones starting at Whitechapel Library, past Liverpool Street train station, and ending at a quiet spot off Commercial Street. The audio track features street sounds along the route, overlaid with the narrator-tour guide's comments on landmarks, as well as the guide's unexpected comments on the user's anticipated questions, giving the effect that the guide's voice is actually inside one's head. Atop that, the disc features multiple layers of audio, including the narrator's own footsteps, and a stream of consciousness, subtly poetic interior monologue

Figure 3.4 Janet Cardiff and George Büres Miller, *The Forty-Part Motet*, Rideau Chapel, National Gallery of Canada, Ottawa (2012). Image courtesy of the artists, Luhring Augustine, New York, and Galerie Barbara Weiss, Berlin.

Figure 3.5 Janet Cardiff and George Büres Miller, *Paradise Institute*, Venice Biennale (2001). Mixed media, duration: 13 min. Dimensions: 5.1 m × 11 m × 3m high. Image courtesy of the artists, Luhring Augustine, New York, and Galerie Barbara Weiss, Berlin.

narrated by a female voice, which includes the embedded voices of male interlopers in a film noir plot. The female voice evokes a desire to simply "get lost." Atop this layer, one experiences one's own interior monologue, plus actual sounds of people and automobiles on the street that are difficult to distinguish from pre-recorded "virtual" street sounds. Surreal situations arise. For example, one hears a revving motor, rushing air, and is warned by the guide of a rapidly approaching automobile, but there is no car—it is a virtual audio-illusion. The city provides the setting for this inter-media performance featuring architectural sights, music by street bands, smells of restaurants, tactile contact with park benches, and the ambient sounds of trains as one walks past Liverpool station. This piece does not loop home like other walking tours by Cardiff and Miller, but deliberately stops in

Figure 3.6 Janet Cardiff and George Büres Miller, *The Missing Voice: Case Study B* (1999). Audio walk, 50 minutes. Commissioned and produced by Artangel (London, UK). Presented via CD Discman, taking individuals on a walking tour through the Spitalfields district of East London, an area once frequented by Jack the Ripper. Image courtesy of the artists, Luhring Augustine, New York, and Galerie Barbara Weiss, Berlin. Available online at: <http://www.cardiffmiller.com/artworks/walks/missing_voice.html>.

midtown London, leaving the audience "lost" to find its own way back. In Deleuzian fashion, Cardiff and Miller's three-dimensional, interactive, total sensory performance generates a polyvalent *aporia* between virtuality and actuality, between interior and exterior spaces, or what Lacan calls *Innenwelt* and *Umwelt*.

Part Two: Barbara Godard: Interpreting Nicole Brossard's *Picture Theory*

The neo-baroque aesthetics and multi-layered elements evident in syncretist performances such as those above help to (re-)contextualize the structural innovations in Nicole Brossard's texts. For years, Brossard's writing has drawn inspiration from electronically based media, including audio, video, virtual reality, and holography so as to extend the literary frontier. Brossard's application of neo-baroque technique is apparent in her novel *Baroque at Dawn*, and neo-baroque features are manifest throughout *Picture Theory*.

Brossard's choreography of diegesis through language features shifts in scene, perspective, variegated textualities, and multiple literary forms. It moves beyond conventions of the novel and integrates with principles of performance and digital culture. A textual composition by Brossard can be read as notation for an inter-media "thought" performance. As her novel *Baroque at Dawn* hints, Brossard adopts neo-baroque aesthetics, inviting readers to interpret her texts as rebus by interacting and reassembling the manifold jigsaw-like layers. Brossard is primarily a text artist. In addition she has produced several CDs in conjunction with her novels, including *Mauve Desert*. Brossard's *Picture Theory* (translated recently by Barbara Godard) pursues an alter/native feminist utopia while employing digital and holographic principles, as well as neo-baroque and neo-cubist arrangements inspired by Wittgenstein.

In "'Grammar in Use': Wittgenstein/Gertrude Stein/Marinetti" (Chapter 3 of *Wittgenstein's Ladder*) Marjorie Perloff identifies direct links between Wittgenstein's views and Gertrude Stein's stylistics:

> In both cases [Wittgenstein and Stein] accordingly, grammar, taken for granted by most writers who are "at home" in their own language and hence are likely to pay more attention to image and metaphor, to figures of heightening, embellishment, and transformation, becomes a contested site. (87)

Perloff's observation on the "contested site" of grammar resonates with what Brossard identifies as a holographic view of text. In her essay "The Textured Angle of Desire," Brossard discusses influences of digital culture and holography on her writing:

> I have always been interested in everything that has to do with the eye and the gaze. —I started to read about holography and was totally taken by some of the vocabulary relating to it: real image, virtual image, reflection, wave length, holographic brain. Also by the fact that all the information about the image is contained in every fragment of the holographic plate. I related that information to the fact that sentences might also contain the whole of what is at stake in a novel. For me, the hologram became the perfect metaphor to project the intuitive synthesis that I had in mind of a woman who could be real, virtual and symbolic. (117)

Brossard's holographic technique features multiple perspectives, split images, and mirrored visions, generating a seemingly three-dimensional, yet virtual reality purportedly predicated upon an actuality. In keeping with holographic principles, characters and events in the novel are portrayed as transitional waves of light moving through shifting mnemonic planes. Such depictions serve doubly well when one recalls that holography, like writing, is an often variable extension of human memory. Brossard's writing presents images of the self (as author), with several layers of fictionalized selves, including characters portrayed in novels within the novel, all presented through disjunctive perspectives that keep returning to individual events. Apart from holography, the novel depicts a self-reflexive narrator/author/character as she engages with digital media, including computer technology, thereby rendering porous the border between virtuality and actuality. In holographic form, Brossard's expression on lexical and clausal levels echoes larger patterns of the novel, supporting "intuitive synthesis" between "real, virtual, and symbolic." Lynne Huffer discusses Brossard's writing as a subject-less space of dissolution. This definition of literature concurs with Blanchot's *The Gaze of Orpheus*, where he posits a *metonymic* understanding of literature as a spatial realm where language negates or displaces the world in order to preserve it. Brossard's texts are multi-layered, polyvalent, paragrammatic, and reiterative, all true to neo-baroque form. Nicole Brossard's formal innovations exemplify the discussion of self-reflexivity in Linda Hutcheon's study *Narcissistic Narrative: The Metafictional Paradox*. Brossard uses of language as ruptured and recursive fractal, replete with multiple diegetic layers (flux of thought), *mise en abyme*, and enfolding of internal and external space indicate the importance of "double-time" or cubist-like, multiple spatio-temporal references points (re-)presented contiguously.

Long aware of "double-time" engagements between author, narrator, and protagonist, Brossard spoke with Lynne Huffer years ago about these engagements in "An Interview with Nicole Brossard Montreal, October 1993":

> I now feel that besides the creative tension of being *une fille en combat dans la cité*, there is also another tension ... a double-time where the sensation of slowness of the act of writing and the sensation of speeding among images (virtual, fractal, or numeric) mix in such a way that the writer wonders with a sudden disquietude to what world she belongs; if she is drifting away from the shore or heading back toward the idea of a future, another shore. (121)

Brossard's alter/native view features a kinetic environment of language that is indeterminate, fluctuating, and unpredictable. Her engagement with this multi-layered experience is complete, so that it is pointless to divide the self (including the self-as-author) from characters in the narrative. In her interview with Huffer, Brossard says:

> Very early on, I said that I saw myself as an explorer in language and that I was writing to comprehend the society in which I live and the civilization to which I belong. Actually, understanding what goes on means trying to process the double-time in which I feel I am living: on the one hand, a historical linear time-space with familiar patriarchal scenarios such as war, rape, and violence; on the other, a polysemic, polymorphic, polymoral time where the speed and volume of information erase depth of meaning, where science proposes itself as an alternative to nature, where reality and fiction manage *exaequo* to offer proof of our ordeals and of the most dreadful fantasies. (115)

Picture Theory emerges as a rebus, a highly disjunctive and holographic text that demands an intuitive or phenomenological response to generate meaning. In her preface to the novel, Barbara Godard comments:

> This is a book of light of clair-voyance, about perception and the wave interaction of light through which is realized the virtuality of writing: "Today a white light made them real." Holography, or writing, is transformed in the whiteout of the scene of production/seduction where desire, time, memory "flow as information in optical fibres," into the Hologram, a combinatory through which a potential woman is modelled: "At the ultimate equation, I would loom into view." "... she had come to the point in full fiction abundant(ly) to re/cite herself perfectly readable." This is a move into abstraction, into specular fiction in the future anterior by a character/writer who will never be able to narrate, to make causal connections, but only to recombine signs in endlessly variable sets that generate varying pictures. (7)

The "endlessly variable sets that generate varying pictures" identified by Godard indicate manifold neo-baroque layerings, and cubist stylistics informed by Wittgenstein's "picture theory." The "future anterior" occurs when a past participle is combined with an auxiliary verb conjugated as if it were in the future indicative, as in "We will have arrived by that time." The future anterior projects hypothetically into the future *as if one already knows* what will happen, thus emphasizing the sense of "double-time."

Brossard's post-Einsteinian and self-reflexive portrayal of "double-time" or multiply layered time/space permits introductions of alternate selves and alter egos underscoring the artificiality of textual constructs. Brossard fragments and integrates versions of self, author, narrator, and protagonist into ever-expanding reiterative patterns representing the diegetic *flux* of a mind in action as indicated by the name of the protagonist Florence Dérive, who both questions and exists within the text, even as she derives it.

Brossard's paragrammatic, dynamic, reiterative, bifurcated, curvilinear, and extravagant text montages thought in action. In her preface, Godard comments on the connections with cubism and Wittgenstein:

> Pursuing Gertrude Stein's investigation of predictive logic and "sentences," Brossard connects through the metonymic chain "Stein" to the "Picture Theory" of Wittgenstein with its propositional logic, its concern with the rules of syntax that discriminate sense and nonsense, its statement that a picture or model is itself a fact. (8)

Godard's statement gestures to Lacan's notion of a metonymic chain of signifiers, which helps trace the "imaginary" or patterns of the unconscious. The metonymic chain of montaged memory is inherently cubist, juxtaposing multiple viewpoints. Gertrude Stein's development of cubist technique in literary form includes cutting up and repeating elements of language on lexical, clausal, and conceptual levels. In his study, *Cubism and Twentieth-Century Art*, Robert Rosenblum comments on a brief incident involving Picasso and Stein and the emergence of cubism:

> The artist need no longer accept the data of reality as fixed and irrevocable. And the spectator himself, like the artist, becomes a creator who reconstructs the new world in infinite ways. Again a Joycean analogy may be apt. Not the least remarkable thing about *Ulysses* is that it has been subject to an infinite number of interpretations, all partial, some contradictory, and none absolute. And on a more prosaic level, the complex, concealed identities of Cubist art found a surprising parallel in the military art of camouflage, developed largely by the French during the First World War. Gertrude Stein, in fact, recounts in her biography of Picasso how amazed he was to see the first camouflaged truck pass down the Boulevard Raspail and how he cried out, "Yes, it is we who made it; that is Cubism." (48)

In *Picture Theory* Brossard camouflages the differences between author, narrator, and character, even while presenting a disjunctive montage and ruptured "double-time" or multi-temporal depictions of space/time. The convolution of "actual," "virtual" and "symbolic" echoes holography while it alludes to Wittgenstein's views. A picture may be a representation or "proposition" of something else, but a proposition also constitutes an aspect of actuality as a "thing" with a presence. In his *Tractatus*, Wittgenstein says in proposition 4.003 that:

> Most of the propositions and questions to be found in philosophical works are not false but nonsensical. Consequently, we cannot give any answer to questions of this kind, but can only point out that they are nonsensical. Most of the propositions and questions of philosophers arise from our failure to understand the logic of our language. (23)

Concluding that language is propositional, Wittgenstein states that "A proposition is a picture of reality" (4.01) and exemplifies by saying: "Propositions *show* the logical form of reality. They display it" (4.121). An astute writer can apply these principles so that a proposition can indicate forms and patterns of *thought* (as subject) that simultaneously represent the thing observed, and the (often self-conscious) deliberations of the observer. This diegetic double proposition in language coincides with Brossard's holographic "double-time."

Cubism presents "propositions" or representations of objects observed from several perspectives simultaneously. Such multiple perspectives allude to memory and the kinetic position of the observer or artist. Admittedly, there is a difference between paint and words. A cubist painting permits representation of several spatio-temporal *loci* simultaneously, but text is a plastic medium that unfolds through time, word by word, sentence by sentence. Nonetheless, a single scene can be depicted and re-depicted textually from several perspectives, as is the "White Scene" in the novel, which appears and reappears throughout *Picture Theory* with changing perspectives. Brossard's first White Scene and its subsequent manifestations all involve the "double-time" of the narrator, both "present" and "absent," self-consciously and self-reflexively depicting the scene while aware of herself in the present, looking to a hypothetical future when she will recall and recreate the event in words:

> To reconstitute would be the avowal of what could only in fiction be transformed by time. Still, there we were, the horizon. I will never know how to narrate. Here on the carpet, intertwined women. Visible. This is how I tried to understand the effect of the scene. And then without ever later having to nuance it. Imperative grammar incendiary. I think of this scene like the seaside, energy has no secret. She added: "The instant is rough and senseless." In relief, I tell about its intensity, the vital force like a cliché: click, photo, the repercussion.
> the other scene: I wait for her to come back with the book. I am waiting for the book. The book is there between her hands, lips are ready to speak in an unexpected way. (23)

The author/narrator/protagonist's situation in this first rendition of the "White Scene" represents several complex spatio-temporal *loci*, including a present rendered into the past ("Here on the carpet"), a future anterior ("I will never know how to narrate"), and an alternate and implied "present" sometime *after* the event ("I think of this scene like the seaside"). The linguistic "proposition" here then indicates "thought" as an unfixed and multi-temporal movement. The scene implicitly acknowledges that the "proposal" is provisional and potentially incomplete. The narrator focuses on one aspect, implicitly excluding others ("In relief, I tell about its intensity").

Even a cursory tracing of some focal points in following depictions of the "White Scene" as a "metonymic chain" reveals recurring concerns: "I will never know how to narrate" (23); "Rivetted to each other as though suspended by writing, we exist in the laborious creation of desire of which we can conceive no idea. Or the Idea, everything that manages to transform mental space" (26); "Conjugated with the lighting, the pleasure of audacity dangerously clothes the body of the other with an existenshe'll film from which arises, condensed in an image, the harmony that makes sense" (31); "Imperative grammar incendiary, baroque eyes, I close them in profusion, traversed by the hypothesis that on the carpet, we have barely moved" (36).

Points of attention range from the self-consciousness author/narrator/protagonist and her concern about how to narrate the scene, to an awareness of how experience shifts to memory, to an intuitive and conceivable harmony of meaning, to an imperative yet baroque grammar that conveys intense sexuality and an awareness of language as "hypothesis" or in Wittgensteinian terms as "proposition." There are numerous shorter references to the "White Scene" throughout the novel, but in all cases, the revisited scene indicates a provisionality, confirming language as proposition while depicting layered fugue-like, paragrammatic movements of overlapping thoughts as a kind of diegetic performance.

Wittgenstein's views resonate throughout *Picture Theory*, which adapts principles from the *Tractatus*. Brossard's *Picture Theory* can be considered a "thought novel" or "thought performance" replete with layers of presence and absence, memory and observation, language and silence. These and other binaries embody the principles of language as holography and flux of thought within an intuitive synthesis of real and virtual, where the author as active agent (re-)shapes linguistic proposals. Her multi-temporal narrative form permits Brossard to (re-)invent the idea of woman, to embrace womanhood, and to perform freely as both creator and subject in language. Throughout her preface to *Picture Theory*, Barbara Godard acknowledges a range of binaries within the novel, including self/other, author/translator, francophone/anglophone, artist/model, representation/actuality, past/future, words/pictures, linearity/laterality. But she also notes that Brossard challenges the Aristotelian logic of binary oppositions that situate "woman" in discourse as a "lack" or "token of exchange" (8).

In addition, Godard appears to be fully aware that her engagement with Brossard's text is both a creative act and a form of socio-cultural and political activism. In *The Postcolonial Critic: Interviews, Strategies, Dialogues* (1990), Gayatri Chakravorty Spivak reminds us that Derrida and Lyotard have established that *language itself* is a condition of a cultural and political situation that responds to and forwards psycho-sexual-socio and other influences (25). Susan Holbrook comments on the *jouissant* intimacy of translation in her essay, "Mauve Arrows and the Erotics of Translation." Additionally, in *The Ear of the Other: Otobiography, Transference, Translation*, Jacques Derrida notes that translation constitutes a rewriting of a text, and not just the transference of ideas:

> Is this our situation? Is it a question of the same ear, a borrowed ear, the one that you are lending me or that I lend myself in speaking? Or rather, do we hear, do we understand each other already with another ear? (35).

Attending with "another ear," Barbara Godard asserts that Brossard's language constitutes an act of subversion, transgression, and vision, allowing Brossard to assert her lesbian and feminist views in bypassing conventions of the masculine text or patriarchal "master" narratives. Godard's adept translation extends this act of subversion.

In her preface, Godard "inhabits" Brossard's style and "jams" with the language, much like a jazz musician joining in with another artist. Further study could pursue a close comparative reading of Brossard's original French text and Godard's translation. In her interpretation of the novel, Godard explores a broad range of linguistic registers, including neologisms, puns, compound words, interjections, and complex clausal structures that leap across manifold cultural world views while refusing forced closure. In her essay, "Relational Logic: Of Linguistic and Other Transactions in the Americas," Godard states: "Fiction participates along with cultural discourses in the articulation of a spatial imaginary expanding in narrative form the implications of this rhetoric of relation as a mode of identification" (344). Godard identifies an intercontinental imaginary that renders geopolitical and conceptual borders porous through several effects, including parallax, borderblur, transformation, and inter-semiotics, as they transcend landscapes, langscapes, and mindscapes. In translating the novel, Barbara Godard interprets it. For years, Godard has been aware of the cultural politics of translating from French to English for a Canadian audience. In her essay "Structuralism/Post-Structuralism: Language, Reality, and Canadian Literature," she concludes that to be Canadian is to inhabit a colonial space from which one perceives discourse as a form of power and desire (46). And in her preface to *Picture Theory*, Godard notes that what I have been calling a neo-baroque aesthetic characterized by disjunctive narrative form is driven by metonymic chains of signification:

> In the absence of narrative connections holding the text together, or of leitmotifs, *Picture Theory* is linked by networks of signifiers. The translator must remember what combinations she used previously for the same sets of phonemes and confront the complexities of change in semantic field necessitated by the different nuances in register of meaning in the French term and the English translated term. As a theory of sign activity as combinatory, of the text as paragram, in Julia Kristeva's terms, *Picture Theory* foregrounds a theory of the signifier as continuous difference, of a network of sliding signs which entails a theory of the transformativity of the translation effect. This theory is developed in the network of *dérive*, which is simultaneously the surrealist associative "drift" of the sign, linguistic "derivation" productive of language change and the mathematical function, the "derivative." Characters and issues are derived from the Steins—Gertrude and Ludwig—but are set adrift on the play of the signifier. (10)

As "thought novel," diegetic performance, and paragrammatic rebus, Brossard's *Picture Theory* emerges as a watermark in the progression of intermedia expression. Godard's translation captures the novel's neo-baroque, cubist, holographic, Wittgensteinian, and post-relativity nuances, simultaneously adding her own interpretation. Arguably, every act of translation is a creative act, and Godard's rich understanding of the subtleties of sociopolitical, gender, literary, stylistic, and aesthetic elements engages with Brossard's text to generate an expression that confirms a feminism identifying itself on its own terms, so that, in its own words, it "had come to the point in full fiction abundant(ly) to re/cite herself perfectly readable" (195).

Works Cited

Aarseth, Espen. *Cybertext: Perspectives on Ergodic Literature*. Baltimore/London: Johns Hopkins UP, 1997. Print.
Baudrillard, Jean. *Jean Baudrillard: Selected Writings*. Ed. Mark Poster. Stanford: Polity, 1988. Print.

Beckett, Samuel. *Krapp's Last Tape: and Other Dramatic Pieces.* New York: Grove, 1958. Print.
Blanchot, Maurice. *The Gaze of Orpheus and Other Literary Essays.* Trans. Lydia Davis. Barrytown, NY: Station Hill, 1981. Print.
Brossard, Nicole. *Baroque at Dawn.* Trans. Patricia Claxton. Toronto: McClelland and Stewart, 1997. Print.
———. *Le Désert mauve.* Montreal: Hexagone, 1987. Print.
———. *Picture Theory.* Trans. Barbara Godard. Toronto/Buffalo/Lancaster: Guernica Editions, 2006. Print.
———. *Picture Theory.* French version. Montreal: Les Éditions de l'Hexagone: Typo, 1991. Print.
———. "The Textured Angle of Desire." Trans. Barbara Godard. *Yale French Studies* 87 (1995): 105–14. Trans. of "L'Angle tramé du désir." *La Théorie, le dimanche.* Ed. Louky Bersianik, Nicole Brossard, Louise Cotnoir, Louise Dupré, Gail Scott, and France Théoret. Montreal: Editions du Remue-Ménage, 1988. 13–26. Print.
Cardiff, Janet, and George Büres Miller. Web. January 12, 2011. <http://www.cardiff-miller.com/>.
Deleuze, Gilles. *The Fold: Leibniz and the Baroque.* Trans. Tom Conley. Minneapolis: U of Minneapolis P, 1993. Print.
Derrida, Jacques. *The Ear of the Other: Otobiography, Transference, Translation.* Ed. Christie McDonald. Lincoln: U of Nebraska P, 1988. Print.
di Felice, Attanasio. "Renaissance Performance: Notes on Prototypical Artistic Actions in the Age of Platonic Princes." *The Art of Performance: A Critical Anthology.* Ed. Gregory Battcock and Robert Nickas. New York: E.P. Dutton, 1984. Print.
Ellenwood, Ray. *Egregore: A History of the Montréal Automatist Movement.* Toronto: Exile Editions, 1992. Print.
Frenkel, Vera. "This Is Your Messiah Speaking." Documentation of exhibition at Art Gallery of Sudbury, September 2000, curated by Bill Huffman. *Rampike* 12.1 (2001): 26–27. Print.
Godard, Barbara. *Canadian Literature at the Crossroads of Language and Culture.* Ed. Smaro Kamboureli. Edmonton: NeWest, 2008. Print.
———. "Structuralism/Post-Structuralism: Language, Reality, and Canadian Literature." *Future Indicative.* Ed. John Moss. Ottawa: U of Ottawa P, 1987. Print.
Holbrook, Susan. "Mauve Arrows and the Erotics of Translation." *Essays on Canadian Writing* 61 (Spring 1997): 1–16. Print.
Huffer, Lynne. "From Lesbos to Montreal: Nicole Brossard's Urban Fictions." *Yale French Studies* 90 (1996): 95–114. Print.
———. "An Interview with Nicole Brossard Montreal, October 1993." Trans. David Dean. *Yale French Studies* 87 (1995): 115–21. Print.
Hutcheon, Linda. *Narcissistic Narrative: The Metafictional Paradox.* New York: Methuen, 1980. Print.

Lacan, Jacques. *Écrits*. Trans. Alan Sheridan. New York: W.W. Norton, 1977. Print.
Lambert, Gregg. *The Return of the Baroque in Modern Culture*. New York: Continuum, 2004. Print.
Lepage, Robert, and Marie Brassard. *Polygraph*. Trans. Gyllian Raby. London: Methuen, 1997. Print.
Lepage, Robert, et al. *Tectonic Plates*. Working ed. Québec: Ex Machina, 1990. Print.
Maheu, Gilles. *Encyclopedia of Canadian Theatre*. n. pag. Web. January 12, 2011. <http://www.canadiantheatre.com/dict.pl?term=Maheu%2C%20Gilles>.
Perloff, Marjorie. *Wittgenstein's Ladder*. Chicago/London: U of Chicago P, 1996. Print.
PMLA. 124.1 (January 2009). Print.
Reaney, James. *Colours in the Dark*. Vancouver: Talonbooks, 1969. Print.
Rosenblum, Robert. *Cubism and Twentieth-Century Art*. New York: Prentice-Hall, 1976. Print.
Spivak, Gayatri Chakravorty. *The Postcolonial Critic: Interviews, Strategies, Dialogues*. New York: Routledge, 1990. Print.
Voaden, Herman. *Canadian Theatre Encyclopedia*. n. pag. Web. January 12, 2011. <http://www.canadiantheatre.com/dict.pl?term=Voaden%2C%20Herman>.
———. *Hill-Land*. *Major Canadian Plays of the Canadian Theatre, 1934–1984*. Ed. Richard Perkyns. Toronto: Irwin, 1984. Print.
Wittgenstein, Ludwig. *Tractatus Logico-Philosophicus*. Trans. D.F. Pears and B.F. McGuinness. Intro. Bertrand Russell. London/New York: Routledge, 2008. Print.
———. *Tractatus Logico-Philosophicus*. Web. January 12, 2011. <http://www.gutenberg.org/catalog/world/readfile?fk_files=1288493>.
———. *Wittgenstein's Lectures Cambridge, 1930–32*. Chicago: U of Chicago P, 1989. Print.

Chapter 4
Writing the Museum: Visual Art and Literature: Denise Desautels and Louise Warren

CLAUDINE POTVIN

The art object, the *atelier* or studio, as much as the literary text, belong to a certain degree, in terms of space, to the myth of Babel, "a figure stressing the chaos of relations in light of incommensurability of languages and the incompleteness of understanding," as Barbara Godard defines it in *Canadian Literature at the Crossroads of Language and Culture* (331). Paradoxically, Babel tends to show how discourses strive to recreate contemporary forms of textual anti-utopias. Babel implies not only the incompleteness but equally the otherness and the difference, and a profound desire to rethink territoriality, rupture, encounter, and seduction, inverting fictions of imperfection, unfitness, and uniformity symbolized by the unfinished or demolished tower. When they meet, visual art and literature reconstruct Babel as "a contemporary hieroglyph for translation" (Godard 337). What the Babel narrative introduces is then the possibility of collective communication, in which each in his own tongue speaks to his fellow human being (Zumthor 195).

Through postmodernist rhetoric and writing modes focused on subversion and transgression of traditional linguistic and semantic codes, many Québec women writers from the 1970s on have deconstructed the concepts of unity, representation, masterpiece, and authority, particularly in what I consider the text-museum, as they rewrite the body, voice, and the artist's canvas. I am referring here to a textual practice where visual art (or the allusion to it) finds itself as part of the narrative through the narrator, a character, a series of motifs, or is described/located within the "story" as a reference, a form of explanation, a meaning. As feminist critics have argued in the last decades, visual forms underlying fiction (painting, drawing, photograph, sculpture, reproduction, frame, installation, exhibition, etc.) can be effective in questioning the politics as well as the semantics and the aesthetics of the "official" gaze that has viewed and evaluated women's works through history. Actually, writing the museum narrative (artist, image, art history, etc.) allows the writer to redefine a new aesthetics or a new textual effect as the image speaks to the text or emerges between lines/words or vice versa—that is, as *tableau* effect inscribed within the text. By extension, the museum (the image) is seen here as an open space or program (Paquin 97), an architectural and ideological construct, an (anti)-utopia capable of transforming text and image into ex-position, installation, performance, movement. Institution or literary representation, exclusion or confinement, the museum proposes a constant dialogism between images and thoughts (words); it invests, becomes, the book, a text-museum.

This study examines the relation between the literary and the visual arts in two specific works: a poetic collection by Denise Desautels (*Leçons de Venise*, 1990)[1] and a novel by Louise Warren (*Tableaux d'Aurélie*, 1989).[2] Rather than a simple illustration or a gloss, the work of art is conceived in these two books as structural element, allusion, or principle of composition. In other words, the interpretation of a specific image (real or imaginary) present or suggested by the text, as well as the creative process, rests essentially on the narrator's auto-fiction or the artist's voice and gaze. Now, to read a story through and with the image supposes a certain contemplation of forms, shapes, and colours evoked between the lines. Although the literary relations to the visual in Desautels's and Warren's texts belong to very different registers, in both cases, the exploration of the museal image supposes on one side a perception of the visual as an object or work of art and on the other the image's *locus* of exposition, which suggests that the museum figure as the image tends to become language. Both writers show in their writings a constant preoccupation with the visual, either through the inclusion of visual representations of artworks within the book and a dialogue between words and images (*Leçons de Venise*)[3] or through the insertion of the visual dimension within the narrative (*Tableaux d'Aurélie*).

Desautels and Warren explore in these writings a museal experience as a new form of rapport between the reader/spectator/*voyeur* and the text. In that context, the visual, the image, permeates the writing in order to establish a possible link between a given visual aesthetics, some literary practices, and a contemporary feminist epistemology. Desautels's and Warren's fictions belong to what I have called the text-museum[4] because they create a pictorial effect, a visual trace, as the image challenges the author and the reader, as art finds itself inscribed/described within the text. As the fiction becomes a translation of art into words, the image signifies through written language, through the displacement of desire, and through the narcissistic transfer of desire to the subject. The object of my analysis is not exclusively centred on the image or illustration per se, but rather metaphorically. I consider its significance in relation to the processes of production and perception themselves that generate the text through a plurality of optical devices. In the case of a written representation of the image, the pseudo-transparency of the visual model is recuperated by the complexity of language. Obviously, the image does not remit to a realistic field of representation, nor can it be perceived as a reproduction of reality or a copy of the same. In this sense, my reading of Desautels and Warren situates itself within the verbal field, within the *ekphrasis*, since I examine the visual as a narrative form interpreted by a narrator who recreates her own creative process.[5] Ultimately, the sculpture, the picture, the past images, the performance, the photograph, etc., exist through the words and the reader receives them already framed. Object, commentary, description, fiction by turns, the image belongs to or is part of the story, the same way the word frames the picture. In this context, the glossary attached to museum, art, canvas, ruins (in an archaeological sense) are to be equally seen here in a broad sense, as writing and art include each other.

Preparatory Classes in Venice

Denise Desautels is a very prolific writer, recognized nationally and internationally. She has published more than thirty poetic collections and a number of artist books; she has received various literary prizes, among them the Governor General's Award and the prestigious Prix Athanase-David. She is known for her multiple collaborations with visual artists (painters, sculptors, lithographers, designers, photographers, etc.). Most of her books are accompanied by an artist's productions; she has also largely contributed to exposition catalogues and artist books. She admits that the visual arts from artists with whom she has worked have allowed her to displace her imaginary and forced her to cross frontiers, which she might not have been able to if left alone.[6] By choosing to include works of art in her writings, she sees herself as capable of bypassing fear and opening her memory, her intimacy. She situates her own work within a land already metamorphosed by art and artists. Pierre Ouellet captures this collaboration or this relation (self/other); in his terms, "*je*" is part of a community (in the case of Desautels, an artistic community) and works *comme* and not only *avec* "*l'autre*": "faire de ce *comme* le lieu d'un *avec*, transformer une ressemblance en une «rassemblance», une manière d'*être-comme* en une façon d'*être-ensemble*, seule métaphore à quoi la poésie puisse encore tenir" (269).

At the beginning, because their universe seemed so close to hers, Desautels would present a completed manuscript to some artists and ask them for a couple of images for a given book. Obviously, in time, the writer modified her approach. She would instead contact an artist before finishing her book and think in terms of true collaboration rather than independent contributions. For example, as she was preparing *Leçons de Venise* in 1988, she made a point to meet Michel Goulet, who was presenting his sculptures at the Venice Biennale. In her interview for *Voix et images* she mentioned: "Sans doute y avait-il beaucoup d'inconscience dans l'enthousiasme qui me portait vers cet univers masculin autour duquel j'allais articuler le mien. Pourtant je ne l'ai jamais regretté. *Leçons de Venise* m'a donné la chance de mettre en écriture—ce qui n'avait peut-être été jusque-là qu'une intuition—les liens troublants et pourtant subtils qui existent entre l'image et le politique" (Dupré, "D'abord l'intime" 230). For Desautels, this type of experience will mean erasing her writer's obsessions or coming back to them with a different perspective.

Denise Desautels wrote *Leçons de Venise* around three sculptures by Michel Goulet[7] presented at the *Biennale di Venezia* 1988; a coloured and detached photograph of the sculptures/installations is placed at the beginning of the three sections of the book composed of twenty-three numbered fragments each. The titles of these three groups of compositions correspond to the names given to his pieces by the sculptor. Written as prose poems, these fragments follow, comment, and describe to a certain degree, not necessarily in linear order, Goulet's visions. His work is not inserted in the book to illustrate the text, no more than the poem's function is to literally comment or reproduce verbally the visualized image. Furthermore, if the work of art questions the politics of aesthetic conventions, so does the text in its own way. The three sculptures inserted in *Leçons de Venise* support more than inspiration; they constitute postmodern manifestations echoed in the text through the spatial (Venice, *Giardini di Castello, Ca' D'Oro, Piazza San Marco*, Paris/*Centre Georges-Pompidou*, etc.) and temporal (March, June, July 1988, "*les années 50*," February, December 1989, January, March 1990, "*Deux ans déjà*," etc.) fragments and details suggested by the past and the circulation of the gallery's *promeneuse*. In both cases, space and time become museological memory.[8] Obviously Desautels's text does not constitute a simple or naive companion to the exhibition or illustration but rather the elaboration of an intimate reflection. As the narrator walks through the gallery, intrigued by the art object, the image becomes her voice. Louise Dupré points out about another text, *Ce fauve, le Bonheur*, that visual arts trigger the narrative, which ends with the narrator's visit to the Musée des Beaux-Arts to see a Van Gogh exposition ("Déplier le temps" 313). Returning to this moment, and in particular to the narrator's interest in *La chambre à Arles*, Barbara Havercroft shows how Van Gogh's painting contributed to the discovery of Desautels's own voice: "C'est donc l'espace de la chambre *masculine*, celle du peintre, et le «cri» de chacune de ses toiles qui lui permettent de faire les premier [*sic*] pas vers la découverte de sa vraie voix" (56).

In the first segment of *Leçons de Venise* called "*Motifs/mobiles*," the *locus* of the poem (from *Piazza San Marco* to the *Centre Georges-Pompidou*) suggests a theatre, an archaeological site, ruins, a museum. It is only in the sixth stanza (stop or station) that the narrator alludes to Goulet's sculpture, which she describes in these terms: "Un lit vide, décomposé. Les montants, tête et pied désaxés, dessinent des lignes et des formes aériennes. Ce lit est embarassé de chaises insoutenables où je ne peux pas m'asseoir, où je ne peux penser à m'asseoir, car je ne suis pas invitée" (*LV*, "*Motifs/mobiles*" 6). Impossible to sleep in this bed, impossible to sit on these chairs; the usefulness of the familiar object is denied by the absence on the one hand (no mattress, no sheets) and the accumulation of chairs and tables in the middle of the bed on the other, as much as by the fact that the head of the iron bed is suspended against the wall, placing the whole apparatus in a very uncomfortable angular position. The angle is repeated in an empty drawing table placed at a certain distance, which seems to authorize the insertion of the narrator's I/eye, which simultaneously observes and allows the chairs to speak: "Je ferai parler les chaises, d'une manière ou d'une autre" (*LV*, "*Motifs/mobiles*" 9). As her eye walks through these objects (bed, chairs, tables, artist's work desk), the narrator becomes aware that, if these tangled lines suggest an inhabited room, "ces oeuvres s'ouvrent et consentent à m'inquiéter; puis à me consoler" since the forms allow her to seek "les mots qui vivifieront, les sons fougueux qui redonneront à l'oeuvre sa mobilité" (*LV*, "*Motifs/mobiles*" 10). As she later remembers these objects "déformés et détournés de leur utilité première," she admits that for her, "il n'y aura toujours que des mots et des histoires ambigües, aux origines souvent inexpliquées, qui se trament entre eux" (*LV*, "*Motifs/mobiles*" 13). Of course, the empty bed, nonetheless mobile, "sans rien en lui qui entrave le mouvement de la vie vers la mort (*LV*, "*Motifs/mobiles*" 19), brings back childhood memories of absence: another untidy bed, reminiscent of the slow motion of death, ancient love stories, ruins resisting the erosion of language, a motive to write.

In the second group of poems, "*Faction factice*," the sculptor's proposition exposes a reality fiction as well as the invention of falseness. Goulet's installation is composed of ten erect rifles posed at equidistance against a white wall. At ground level, the guns' shoulders, slightly separated from the wall, seem to be held in place by small objects: sponge, binoculars, candlestick, brush, cup, a minute paper umbrella, etc. At the top, the guns sustain (or are sustained by) a series of identically shaped books identified in the text as dictionaries "dans lesquels sont ordonnés le sens des mots" (*LV*, "*Faction factice*" 1), ses mots à elle—also maintained by different objects.[9] The books block the bullets, the exit of violence in a way, and suggest simultaneously the possible end or destruction of civilization and knowledge. As a matter of fact, if these guns seem innocent at first sight in this gallery, they do nevertheless occupy a space and remind us of the existence of real objects. This time, Desautels describes the scene at the very beginning: "Dix fusils, des vrais, sont alignés contre un mur. Dix canons verticaux, parallèles, pointent vers le haut. Dix crosses glissent, s'éloignent du mur et semblent retenues au dernier instant par une tasse, une brosse, une éponge ou un chandelier qui se trouvaient là par hazard" (*LV*, "*Faction factice*" 1). The forms bring back another visual instance, the contemplation of *Femmes de Venise* by Giacometti, nine vertical forms as dark as the guns, as static as the chairs, or "à une armée de femmes en marche au moment de la pose" (*LV*, "*Faction factice*" 6). The verticality reminds us of the repetition of acts of war, the tragedy of the Montreal Massacre,[10] the gesture of a man condemning women to horizontality, decoy, utopia, and death.

As François Paré has shown, the figure of repetition, psychic and scriptural, defines all of Desautels's poetic work. The word "repetition" not only appears in the title of an eponym collection (1986), but we also find numerous mentions of the word itself in *Leçons de Venise*. According to Paré, repetition implies also exclusion in its relation to time (death/past—writing/present). The "fusil à répétition" (*LV*, "*Faction factice*" 10), the repetition of the image in Goulet (the gun and the book) disturbs the narrator/author, creating a malaise between reality and the imaginary, between sculptor and writer, between fact and representation, between image and word. As the narrator leafs through the catalogue *Canada XLIII Biennale di Venezia 1988*, two years later, the re/production of *Faction factice* blinds her momentarily. She then writes:

> Nature? Culture? Je n'y arrive plus. La violence n'est ni fausse ni lointaine. J'aurais dû me méfier des coïncidences [...] Installée naïvement dans la protection de l'art, du simulacre, j'ai évoqué le péril comme s'il était impossible qu'il ait lieu maintenant, comme si tous les fusils du monde avaient été dépourvus de leurs terribles marteaux [...] oubliant que j'étais une femme / sur la ligne de feu. (*LV*, "*Faction factice*" 18)

Hence, the necessity for the body, at the end of this second viewing, to "reprendre son souffle," since "il hésite entre l'objet d'art et la réalité" (*LV*, "*Faction factice*" 23). The woman-subject is definitely "fracture de l'histoire et institution de la mémoire (Paré 280) and the sculptor will learn that she is "dans l'histoire" (*LV*, "*Faction factice*" 21). In this context, works of art are pre/text(s); between art and life, writing inserts itself as an autonomous interval, betweenness, renewed transgression.

The third instalment of *Leçons de Venise*, "*Table du travail*," features a low rectangular table made of metal, depicted by Desautels as "encombrée d'objets qui renvoient à d'autres objets qu'on prétend connaître, autrement peut-être, alors qu'on ne les connaît pas; à d'autres univers, à d'autres sens" (*LV*, "*Table du travail*" 1). Other universes, other meanings are inscribed in the narrator's silence: "Il n'y a que le silence qui marque une place vide" (*LV*, "*Table du travail*" 2). In contraposition, the museum visitor witnesses the presence of two chairs (an armchair with a round seat and the other one square, without arms) placed or inverted one on top of the other. Again, there is not a living soul in the decor. Again, Goulet resorts to the book motif to fill the otherwise almost empty space. Three volumes are resting on the floor under the chairs, half hidden by one of the chair's bars. What appears to be a sculpture, a ceramic, or a metal plate rests on top of this scaffolding. The heteroclite selection of miniatures found on the table—"le fouillis évident des objets, parmi les dés, l'écrou à oreilles, la bobine de fil, le compas, le taille-crayons, la gomme, le pince-notes, les caractères d'imprimerie, le mètre à ruban, la boussole, la clé à molette, le revolver ..." (*LV*, "*Table du travail*" 3)—as well as the inverted chairs, may suggest chaos (abundance of details). However, the apparent disconnection constitutes *clins d'oeil* to another kind of fiction (fabrication/dressmaking, orientation/geography, letters/writing); the meticulous position of objects on the table (making it possible, at more or less close view, to identify each one of them), the absolute regularity of the lines, and the impeccable positioning of the chairs contradict this idea of disorder, which is confirmed by the narrator: "la position des objets nie le désordre sur la petite table." At the most, "'[C]'est comme un nouvel ordre,' dit le sculpteur quand on l'interroge" (*LV*, "*Table du travail*" 17 and 4). Order is reinforced by the presence of books perceived by the narrator as encyclopedias:

> De plus près, apparaît la fausseté de la substitution. L'évidence du mensonge trahit le livre manquant. Le premier tome de l'encyclopédie n'est qu'un volume, que des couches superposées, que des pièces d'un puzzle. Le premier tome est une forme exacte sans image du monde, une présence physique, matérielle, sans mots. (*LV*, "*Table du travail*" 5)

Encyclopedias, culture, order, meaning, above all classification, accumulation, erudition; the images and books give a false (or different) replica of the world, as the first tome itself is an exact form of an empty narration to be recuperated by the sculptor and the writer's hand: "La *Table du travail* est celle du sculpteur comme elle est la mienne" (*LV*, "*Table du travail*" 20) reaffirms the narrator's voice. Ultimately, the narrator's gaze always meets art in its own words in order to find life.

Writing under the Influence

Louise Warren is also a prolific writer. She has published more than fifteen poetry collections, a dozen of essays on creation and art, and two short novels (*récits*); she often writes for expositions, and has produced numerous *livres d'artistes*. Like many Québec women writers (Nicole Brossard, Madeleine Gagnon, Anne-Marie Alonzo, Monique Proulx, France Théoret, Madeleine Monette, and others), Warren explores a museal culture in the feminine in which the image, the museum (artist, painting, creation), invests the narration. This is the case in her first novel *Tableaux d'Aurélie*.

Tableaux d'Aurélie could be read as a family narrative centred on memory, dream, and death of family members. Louise Warren situates her novel within an intimate or autobiographical register, although the narrator, named Aurélie, is never identified with the author. The association with Warren comes from the pictorial motive that dominates the text and the writer's reflection on art. Painting as the narrator's profession is divided into three poles: studio, the act of painting per se, and the *tableau* or *toile* (color, brush, scene, odour). On the one hand, the studio's weight, to use Aurélie's expression, on the other, the quest for a position (place, look, mood, time) where her artistic practice will become palpable, transparent:

> Je fais de l'ordre dans l'atelier pour donner de l'espace à cette foudre que je sens battre au fond de moi. Les pinceaux nettoyés, souples, prêts à être trempés dans la couleur onctueuse. Les larges pots de verre, alignés sous une couverture délavée, tachée, qui me suit partout comme un talisman. Les livres et les catalogues d'exposition s'amplifient dans une grande malle, le cahier du croquis s'ouvre sur la table à dessin. (*TA* 55)

As the artist prepares her tools, the canvas becomes textuality: "Les toiles ont été montées, reccouvertes d'enduit pendant la nuit. Me voilà à mon deuxième café du matin, prête à commencer cette série de visages d'Aurélie (literary and pictural) qui ne cesse de m'obséder" (*TA* 56). The memory of the grandmother, whose name is also Aurélie, leaves on the page as well as on the painting textual and visual traces of subjectivity and voice of the first signs of life within the mother's womb. The act of painting echoes the gesture of writing and the picture brings back the family's gaze. In this context, the work of art is an image drawn by the reader as he or she receives the text. It is also "un visage *qui nous regarde*, un tissu vivant," writes Louise Warren in her essay *Interroger l'intensité*,[11] and she adds that "[L]'oeuvre d'art agit sur nous avec la même intensité quand nous nous laissons regarder par elle et quand nous fermons les yeux pour mieux en être absorbés" (*II* 111). So, Aurélie's *tableaux* (words or images, stories or paintings) do not need a "mode d'emploi pas plus qu'un poème ou un roman ne nécessite le support de l'illustration. Dans un cas comme dans l'autre, cette surenchère du langage peut tuer une oeuvre" (*II* 101–2). The image does not illustrate, any more than the text describes or comments. It is rather a question of dialogue between two gazes, two languages, and two bodies searching for the sublime. In the case of the protagonist, it is a question of painting everything (canvas, walls, fabric, furniture) incessantly, with fury, drawing "des flèches qui ne vont nulle part" (*TA* 101), the same way she writes.

"Je rêve d'une peinture nomade" (*TA* 85), writes the narrator/painter of *Tableaux d'Aurélie*. According to Rosi Braidotti, the nomadic mode implies a form of creativity, a performative metaphor, a plurality of traces, an interaction of experiences and knowledge (6). The postmodern subject will be seen in terms of location (atelier/studio). In other words, where does the narrator situate herself when she speaks and when she declares wanting to be loved as a woman and as a painter? This woman who writes and paints constructs her identity precisely in-between, within a double picture.

Consequently, the frame is shattered, given as a form of higher bid. In the fifth chapter of *Interrroger l'intensité*, titled "Maintenant je suis une lettre," Warren remembers a displaced picture and a frame constructed by the father: "[U]n jour, le tableau fut déplacé, accroché à un autre mur, non loin d'une fenêtre. Le midi, les rayons du soleil vacillaient sur les pourtours de bois blond, encadrement que mon père avait fabriqué pour éclairer, adoucir le portrait" (67). As Derrida argues in *La vérité en peinture*, the *parergon* (frame) is a surplus, against, beside, and on top of the completed work, outside but simultaneously inside, "contre, à côté et en plus de l'*ergon*, du travail fait, du fait, de l'oeuvre mais il ne tombe pas à côté, il touche et coopère, depuis un certain dehors, simplement dedans" (63). The fact that the father built the first framework for the first painting shows to what degree the frame (beside/*à-côté de*), if it serves to box the picture, equally allows the narrative to exit the field of representation.

Apparently at the centre of *Tableaux d'Aurélie*, at the origin, the painting's subject (the two Aurélies, the unknown ancestor and the narrator/painter) is connected to a marginal or outside dimension (from colour to brushes, from smell to cloth), to action (gesture and movement), and to memory (the family scene itself). Most fragments or chapters' subtitles confirm the intimate rapport between subject ("Les cheveux d'Aurélie"), family ("Sous verre"), fiction ("Mon carnet de rêves"), daily life ("Foulure à la cheville"), and "*tableau*" ("Peinture naïve," "Scène champêtre," "Coloriages"). The last subtitles allude to a rural milieu and a childhood activity situating the narrator in a process of learning, by opposition to professional. For her fourteenth birthday, Aurélie received a paintbox from her father and an easel from her mother. As another gift, the mother registered her daughter in an intensive oil painting course. These courses will immediately project the teenager outside the artistic institution: "je reproduisais fidèlement les affreuses compositions qui nous étaient imposées [...] Rapidement dégoûtée de ces cours, il me semblait que j'allais étouffer [...] La peinture prit alors une odeur d'éther et des années d'anesthésie m'ont poursuivie avant que je sente le goût de peindre à nouveau" (*TA* 68–69).

In the last part of her novel, *Croquis*, a kind of appendix, Warren puts the accent exclusively on visual art. From the point of view of style and content, this section is totally disconnected from the previous one and entirely located within the iconographic order. Just a few pages (six), a few paragraphs (between one and eight lines), some of them precisely subtitled

"Esquisse ...," "Matisse," "Gravure sur bois," "Fusain," "Toile de fond (ou Décor?)," "Portrait ...," "La signature," "Modèle vivant," "Les statues," "Papier japon" (the bold emphasis unique to this section suggests its importance in the writer's mind). Despite the descriptive perspectives of some of the other subtitles of the same fragment ("Jeanne," "Hiver," "Parc," "La couleur rouge," "Midi," "Insomnie," etc.), the final section represents a form of "figurative abstraction" as reality is represented most of the time with a blurred and displaced connotation (non-referential).

As form, material, topic, and insomnia, art becomes periodically slippery, a sort of blockage, until the obsession takes over; then the narrator spends "[T]rois jours à peindre sans arrêt" (135). For Warren, to open oneself to creation implies more an attitude of *dessaisissement* rather than fascination or obsession (*II* 73). *Se dessaisir* or to relinquish is the antithesis of grabbing hold of: it is to abandon, to free oneself in order to recreate word and image. The art object (the idea of art) constantly challenges language. For the encounter to be possible, language must appropriate art, "et l'écriture, tout comme l'image, se réfléchit autant dans le silence que dans la parole" (*II* 102). There are no illustrations in Warren's novel. However, the allusions to art, painting, canvas, ruins, and memory, frame the text as a museum, where the protagonist observes, paints, and writes her own story, her own perception of herself and reality, her own image.[12] Writing and art include each other in the narrative.

Traditionally, the art museum was considered an enterprise of consecration (masterpiece, patrimony, cultural goods), a tool of education (aesthetic norm, service to the community), and a research institution (knowledge). *Tableaux d'Aurélie* abolishes this concept and replaces it with the notion of process. In "A Museum and Its Memory: The Art of Recovering History," Michael Fehr notes that "most museums are in fact representation machines that point via the material stored inside them to something outside themselves; that is, they function like pictures through which one looks, almost as if through a window, into an illusory room, into history, the history of art." According to Fehr, it is therefore possible to design museums as "spaces that present the fiction we require to find our bearings in the world, as fiction, and as rooms that comprehend the viewer as a historical subject" (59) and allow the spectator/reader to see what is within their walls. The text-museum precisely aims at making this kind of connection possible.

***

The conversation between art and literature is obviously present within the narrator's desire; as a matter of fact, the narrators of *Tableaux d'Aurélie* and

Leçons de Venise aspire to "être aimée comme femme et peintre" (*TA*, 96), and I would add, as writer, and wish to be the hand "qui sculpte les mots" (*LV*, Table de travail 5). In Aurélie's story, art is all together theme, search, and quest. In her prelude to *La poésie mémoire de l'art*, Warren points out that each poem in her collection contributes to the construction of an imaginary museum and that all voices create a vast polyphony condensed in the voice of "[C]elle qui entre dans l'atelier, celle qui habite la couleur, [...] enfin celle qui, d'un seul instant ou d'une lente coulée, unit le poète à l'artiste, l'art à la poésie" (7). For Desautels, the image becomes vivid memory and the writer installs it literally within her fiction, within the word. If the hand sculpts the word, the image speaks to the narrator whose answers bounce back like waves, operating new meanings in "translation."[13] In both cases though, visual forms construct the textual.

Interestingly enough, W.J.T. Mitchell questions the gender or desire of the image: "As for the gender of pictures, it's clear that the 'default' position of images is feminine, 'constructing spectatorship' in art historian Norman Bryson's words, 'around an opposition between women as images and man as bearer of the look'—not images of women, but images *as* women" (35). For that matter, Mitchell contends, to ask what images want would be asking oneself what women want. In the end, we could say that images do not want anything at all. Does that mean once again that women's desire is still inscribed within absence or lack (always objectified through the other's gaze)? Does feminine desire not belong to the symbolic order? Or is it precisely these "absences" or memories that fill the popular or erudite textual museums? "[T]he paintings desire in short," continues Mitchell, "is to change places with the beholder, to transfix or paralyze the beholder, turning him or her into an image for the gaze of the picture in what might be called the 'Medusa effect'" (36), or the Warren and Desautels/Goulet effect.

In conclusion, outlining the emergence of the image within the writing enlightens the relation between visual aesthetic, writing strategies, and production/reception of the text. Be it as a form of illusion, illustration, reproduction, or motive, the textual emerges from the visual as the image becomes the narrative (*tableau* effect); otherwise, the literary seems to use the visual and tries to define it, speak it, frame it as monument or archaeology, discourse of its own representation (art as *parole*/voice, word). Articulating their project around the visual, Desautels and Warren favour the museographic experience as a new form of relation between reader/spectator and text. The text-museum tends to abolish or transgress the boundaries between presentation and representation, reproduction and myth, illusion and reality, between performance and literature. A link word/image transpires between book/literature and art, body/text and text/museum, textual and visual experimentation. Desautels's and Warren's literary practices rethink and reposition the visual within the textual not as a patch but as a linguistic key, a signifier of the narrative and lyrical codes.

Notes

1 The book has no pagination. For all references to this book, I will indicate between brackets the abbreviation *LV*, followed by the title of the section and the number of the fragment.
2 For all references to this book, I will indicate between brackets the abbreviation *TA*, followed by the folio.
3 Visual representations are present in almost all of Denise Desautels's publications: drawings, photographs, sculptures, art objects, etc. She has collaborated with numerous artists, among them (to name only a few) Léon Bellefleur, Francine Simonin, Jocelyne Alloucherie, Ariane Thézé, Alain Laframboise, Martha Townsend, Monique Bertrand, and Michel Goulet.
4 This commentary on Desautels and Warren is part of a book in preparation (*Clins d'oeil de la littérature au musée*). I have developed the "text-museum" notion in previous publications around works by several writers, among them France Daigle, Madeleine Gagnon, Madeleine Monette, and Nicole Brossard (see Potvin 2005, 2006, 2009, 2010).
5 Desautels has dedicated herself mainly to poetry. But as Louise Dupré has noted, the reader recognizes in her lyrical voice various narrative elements, a desire to tell her own story, particularly present in writings of contemporary Québec women poets (see *Présentation* 225). *Leçons de Venise* is written in poetic prose; it actually contains a strong narrative line around the usual topics privileged by the author (childhood, death, loss, pain, ruins, memory, voice, and words). Warren herself is above all a poet and an essayist; however, *Tableaux d'Aurélie* is a family narrative constructed around the creative process itself (writing/painting). I therefore use the terminology narrative, story, *récit*, not in the strict sense of plot or intrigue, traditionally used for novel criticism, but in a wider perspective of "fragmented storyline."
6 See her conversation with Louise Dupré in the special issue of *Voix et images* dedicated to her work. The poet says: "En choisissant d'aller vers des oeuvres d'art, souvent exigeantes, porteuses des grandes inquietudes humaines, je choisis d'une certaine manière de ne pas fuir, de contourner cette fois non pas le péril lui-même mais la peur du péril, et d'ouvrir ainsi ma petite mémoire à d'autres memoires ..." (Dupré, "D'abord l'intime" 229).
7 Artist-sculptor Michel Goulet lives and works in Montreal. Considered by many as one of the prominent sculptors of his generation, his work has been

shown in numerous prestigious group exhibitions. He has exhibited in major institutions and museums. In 1988, he represented Canada at the Venice Biennale. In 1990, he received the *Prix Paul-Émile Borduas*.

8   Desautels's fiction installs a problematic modernism (recycled as "*modernité*") as the author rethinks art as discursive, personal, cultural, and historical fields. Bridget Elliot and Jo-Ann Wallace argue in *Women Artists and Writers: Modernist (im)positionings* that modernism is not simply a series of discrete texts and images, but a discourse. Produced by various cultural agents, it is itself productive of meaning (1–6). Marie Carani situates the origins of the Québec modernist movement around the end of the 1930s and the beginning of the 1950s when an important renewal of the traditional collective values would take place. Art would then open to new themes—urban life, nude, contemporary life, etc.—and new formal approaches (lines, colours, textures, positions, structures) (76–77). Later on, literature will follow the same evolution (from linearity to deconstruction).

9   Unfortunately, the small photograph does not allow me to identify clearly these objects. We can see their disparate and unexpected nature, though, similar to the ones found on the floor at the end of the gun's shoulders.

10 The fragments 12 to 14 of "*Faction factice*" relate the murder of fourteen women at the École polytechnique of the Université de Montréal on December 6, 1989. The need to repeat the verse "Se border les unes les autres" *ad infinitum* (nine times in the fourteenth passage) when only one gun (and one moment to separate men from women) sufficed to eliminate fourteen bodies—"un amoncellement de petites mortes" (*LV*, "*Faction factice*" 12)—situates the woman subject in a historical trajectory marked by women's disappearance and assassination. The systematic rape and elimination of thousands of Mexican women (Ciudad Juarez) and Native women in Canada (Highway of Tears) perpetuate an identical (numerically more dramatic) "histoire-spectacle" (*LV*, "*Faction factice*" 12). See the 2009 film *Backyard* (original title: *El traspatio*), directed by Carlos Carrera.

11 My reading of *Tableaux d'Aurélie* owes a lot to this wonderful essay in which Warren writes about her writing practice, different artists' works, and their common aesthetic experience. For all references to this book, I will indicate between brackets the abbreviation *II*, followed by the folio. In reality, all of Warren's essays are pertinent to my discussion of art and literature, particularly her trilogy (*Objets du monde: Archives du vivant; Bleu de Delft: Archives de solitude; La Forme et le deuil: Archives du lac*) on creativity, loss, mourning, act of reading/writing/painting, art, poetry, etc.

12 Regarding the poetics of look, see Lucie Lequin's article, "Elle écrit la lumière: Louise Warren et l'écriture de l'oeil."

13 I am using the term "translation" with prudence. As Rose-Marie Arbour mentions in *L'art qui nous est contemporain*, "ce que le langage peut nommer de

l'oeuvre, de son contexte artistique et culturel, des intentions de l'artiste, de la réception par les spectateurs (and writers obviously), n'équivaut pas à une *traduction* de l'oeuvre" (20). Translation does not mean to replace a sign by another but a reading process.

Works Cited

Arbour, Rose-Marie. *L'Art qui nous est contemporain.* Montreal: Éditions Artextes, 1999. Print.

Braidotti, Rosi. *Nomadic Subjects: Embodiment and Sexual Difference in ContemporaryFeminist Theory.* New York: Columbia UP, 1994. Print.

Carani, Marie. "L'Idée du *refus* comme mémoire et comme identité chez les artistes visuels contemporains québécois." *Des lieux de mémoire: Identité et culture modernes au Québec 1930-1960.* Ed. Marie Carani. Ottawa: Les Presses de l'Université d'Ottawa, 1995. 75–90. Print.

Derrida, Jacques. *La Vérité en peinture.* Paris: Flammarion, 1978. Print.

Desautels, Denise. *Ce fauve, le Bonheur.* Montreal: l'Hexagone, 1998. Print.

———. *Leçons de Venise.* Saint-Lambert: Éditions du Noroît, 1990. Print.

———. *La Répétition* (with photographs from *La Sale de classe.* Installation by Irene F. Whittome). Montreal: Éditions de La nouvelle barre du jour, 1986. Print.

Dupré, Louise. "D'abord l'intime: Entretien avec Denise Desautels." *Voix et images* XXVI.2.77 (Winter 2001): 227–40). Print.

———. "Déplier le temps: Mémoire et temporalité dans *La promeneuse et l'oiseau et Ce fauve, le Bonheur* de Denise Desautels." *Voix et images* XXVI.2.77 (Winter 2001): 302–16. Print.

———. "Présentation." *Voix et images* XXVI.2.77 (Winter 2001): 224–26. Print.

Elliot, Bridget, and Jo-Ann Wallace. *Women Artists and Writers: Modernist (im)positionings.* London/New York: Routledge, 1994. Print.

Fehr, Michael. "A Museum and Its Memory: The Art of Recovering History." *Museums and Memory.* Ed. Susan A. Crane. Stanford: Stanford UP, 2000. 35–59. Print.

Godard, Barbara. *Canadian Literature at the Crossroads of Language and Culture. Selected Essays by Barbara Godard 1987–2005.* Ed. Smaro Kamboureli. Edmonton: NeWest, 2008. Print.

Havercroft, Barbara. "Espace autofictif, sexuation et deuil chez Denise Desautels et Paul Chanel Malenfant." *Sexuation, espace, écriture: La literature québécoise en transformation.* Ed. Louise Dupré, Jaap Lintvelt, and Janet M. Paterson. Québec: Éditions Nota bene, Coll. Littérature(s), 2002. 43–65. Print.

Lequin, Lucie. "Elle écrit la lumière: Louise Warren et l'écriture de l'oeil." *Dalhousie French Studies* 31 (Summer 1995): 113–25. Print.

Mitchell, W.J.T. *What Do Pictures Want? The Lives and Loves of Images.* Chicago/London: U of Chicago P, 2005. Print.

Ouellet, Pierre. "L'une comme l'autre: Compassion et coénonciation dans *Cimetières: La Rage muette*." *Voix et images* XXVI.2.77 (Winter 2001): 264–74. Print.

Paquin, Nycole. "Corps-à-corps: L'Objet d'art et son récepteur." *Travaux sémiotiques*. Ed. Jacques Allard. Montreal: Les Cahiers du département d'études littéraires, UQÀM, 1984. 97–118. Print.

Paré, François. "La Figure de la répétition dans l'oeuvre de Denise Desautels." *Voix et images* XXVI.2.77 (Winter 2001): 275–87. Print.

Potvin, Claudine. "L'Écriture et la toile: l'acte textuel et l'acte pictural chez Madeleine Gagnon." Spec. issue: "Figures de l'artiste." Ed. Kirsty Bell. *Dalhousie French Studies* 87 (Summer 2009): 7–15. Print.

———. "L'Épaisseur de l'art: Art et écriture chez France Daigle." *Entre textes et images: Constructions identitaires en Acadie et au Québec*. Ed. Monika Boehringer, Kisty Bell, and Hans R. Runte. Edmonton/Moncton/Shippagan: Institut d'études canadiennes/Université de Moncton, 2010. 207–20. Print.

———. "Flirting with the Museum Narrative: From *Picture Theory* to *Hier*." *Nicole Brossard: Essays on Her Works*. Toronto/Buffalo/Chicago/Lancaster: Guernica. Coll. Writers Series, 2005. 101–22. Print.

———. "La Rhétorique du visuel: *Amandes et melon* de Madeleine Monette." *La Rhétorique au feminine*. Ed. Annette Hayward. Québec: Éditions nota bene, 2006. 381–400. Print.

Warren, Louise. *Bleu de Delft: Archives de solitude*. Montreal: Trait d'union, Coll. Spirale, 2003. New ed. Montreal: Éditions Typo, 2006. Print.

———. *La Forme et le deuil: Archives du lac*. Montreal: l'Hexagone, 2010.

———. *Interroger l'intensité*. Laval: Trois, 1999. New ed. Montreal: Éditions Typo, 2009. Print.

———. *Objets du monde: Archives du vivant*. Montreal: VLB éditeur, Coll. Le soi et l'autre. 2005. Print.

———. *La Poésie mémoire de l'art: Anthologie*. Trois-Rivières: Art Le Sabord, 2003. Print.

———. *Tableaux d'Aurélie*. Montreal: VLB éditeur, 1989. Print.

Zumthor, Paul. *Babel ou l'inachèvement*. Paris: Seuiil, 1997. Print.

PART TWO

Culture/Policy/Institutions

Chapter 5
Negotiating Literatures in Contiguity: France Daigle in/and Québec

LIANNE MOYES AND CATHERINE LECLERC

Barbara Godard was one of a handful of Canadianists who know, and base their analyses on, literary texts and critical discourses published both in French and English within Canada. Since the 1980s, most scholars of Canadian literature have characterized their object of study as "English Canadian" and have distinguished that object from Québec literature out of respect for the historical and cultural specificity of the latter, for its hard-won autonomy.[1] Godard, however, did not limit the scope of her analysis to English Canada. She continued to turn her literary critical ear to Québec and very often brought modes of analysis current in Québec letters to bear upon Canadian literature. Godard's scholarship played a key role, for example, in bringing literary institutional questions to the attention of those in the field of Canadian literature. In her essay "A Literature in the Making: Rewriting and the Dynamism of the Cultural Field" from *Canadian Literature at the Crossroads*, Godard discussed the mechanisms by which Canadian letters imported and consecrated Québec writers in translation. Focusing primarily on women writers Gabrielle Roy, Marie-Claire Blais, and Anne Hébert, Godard was especially attentive to subversive elements in their writing that are lost when that writing is removed from its original field of cultural production and made to serve a Canadian national narrative. Keeping ever within her critical horizons the possibility of an ethical relation between Canadian and Québec letters, her feminist "field analysis" invited scholars to take into account "the differences between two habituses, between those contexts of everyday life where power exerts itself" (*Canadian Literature* 294).

Godard worked to realize the possibility of such an ethical relation in a number of projects, among them the bilingual feminist magazine *Tessera* (1984–2005), of which she was a co-founder and long-standing co-editor. *Tessera* was part of a network of small magazines and small publishers that, in Godard's terms, "transmit a different representation of Quebec literature" (*Canadian Literature* 284). Circulating without cultural consecration in a marginal field of production, the magazine opened creative and critical spaces for conversations that did not resolve to a single voice or language, and fictions of identity in excess of prevailing paradigms of nation and gender. *Tessera* was a space in which women writers mediated for themselves the relations among fields of literary production, including relations of translation. This measure of agency allowed writers to take risks across languages and to reimagine the role of the translator beyond the confines of fidelity and betrayal. This agency also stood in sharp contrast to the traffic in francophone women writers carried out by the English Canadian literary field, that is, in sharp contrast to the forms of exchange through which francophone women writers were appropriated as symbols of cultural difference.[2]

Our preoccupation in this chapter is with the relations between Québec letters and Acadian letters, relations brought sharply into focus by a relatively minor incident: the Canada Council for the Arts' rejection of an application from the Université de Montréal to make Acadian author France Daigle writer in residence for the 2008–9 academic year. Since the 1960s, the Québec literary institution has constructed itself as the centre of French-language literary culture in North America and has paid relatively little attention to Franco-Canadian writers outside its borders (Doyon-Gosselin, "(In)(ter)dépendance" 55; Boudreau, "Les Rapports Acadie/Québec" 10; Levasseur). So this gesture of invitation on the part of the Centre de recherche interuniversitaire sur la littérature et la culture québécoises (CRILCQ) at the Université de Montréal was important both for what it suggests about shifts in the relation of the Québec literary institution to French-language writing outside its borders and about the terms of integration into Québec letters for an Acadian writer. Our essay, insofar as it focuses on a woman writer integrated into a literature to which she is something of an outsider, raises questions of the kind Godard addresses in "A Literature in the Making." However, as we hope to demonstrate, the stakes of the Acadie–Québec relation are not necessarily comparable to those of the Québec–Canada relation. Whereas the Québec–Canada relation is routinely figured as a disintegrating heterosexual marriage in which Québec holds the position of dissatisfied woman (Probyn 80–1), the Acadie–Québec relation is more likely to be figured as a relation of siblings in which gender difference plays a less decisive role.

Whereas Godard's engagement with critical discourse in and on Québec was considerable, she published little on French Canadian literatures outside Québec. There are, of course, several exceptions. Her essay "A Literature in the Making" acknowledges the French *Canadian* background[3] of Québec-based literary figures such as Franco-Manitoban Gabrielle Roy (285, 296) and Franco-Ontarian Jean Éthier-Blais (309); and her issue of *Tessera* "Talking Pictures/Lire le visuel," co-edited with Louise Cotnoir, features the poems of France Daigle (64–73).[4] Godard's most sustained treatment of the work of a francophone from outside Québec is her discussion of the writing of Lola Lemire Tostevin, alongside that of Mary di Michele and Smaro Kamboureli, in the 1990 article "The Discourse of the Other: Canadian Literature and the Question of Ethnicity," an article to which we return below.

"Canadian literature," in Godard's critical mapping, cohabits with Québec literature and is inhabited by French-language writing, whether that writing is Franco-Ontarian, Franco-Manitoban, or Acadian. Such a critical mapping is facilitated by her attention to the category of "women's writing," which intersects with and disrupts those of "Canadian literature" and "Québec literature." "Québec literature," on the other hand, is generally constructed in Godard's work as a French-language corpus. Her oeuvre is relatively circumspect about the implications of Québec's territorialization of its literature for writing in French outside Québec or for writing in English inside Québec.[5] In this sense, the reading of textual practices and institutional relationships we are undertaking here, at the junction of Québec and Acadian literatures, exceeds Godard's mappings of Canadian and Québec letters. What our approach nonetheless draws from Godard is her attention to power relationships, both in their symbolic violence and in their concrete effects on the functioning of institutions: what actions can be taken, what discourses can be uttered, and how they will be received. Our approach shares Godard's conception of the cultural field as a tense and stratified terrain, with multiple, contending, and contested delimitations. And it partakes of her refusal of the totalizing and homogenizing narratives often used to account for it. In other words, Godard's interest in "(op)positions taken within a complex terrain" (*Canadian Literature* 270) is what guides us.

Although she covered both Canadian and Québec literatures, and with the same in-depth knowledge, Godard's critical eye was sharper toward English Canada (where she situated herself) than it was toward francophone Québec. As a result, the critical stance we take in our analysis also falls outside her scope. By interrogating the institutional (dis)connections between Québec and Acadian literatures, our essay displaces Godard's preoccupation with interactions between Canada's and Québec's cultural fields. Or, perhaps, it adds a layer to Godard's frame of analysis for such interactions. Indeed, in studying the interaction between Québec and Acadian letters, we are moving toward smaller interfaces than the ones studied by Godard. We are subdividing the maps she drew. In doing so, we are inspired by her capacity to identify the appropriative effects of gestures of inclusion in circumstances where asymmetrical relations of power prevail. Our analysis of the CRILCQ's application to bring Daigle to the Université de Montréal leads us to believe that such appropriative effects can be found in the treatment of Acadian literature by the Québec literary institution. Godard's assessment that "The partial inclusion of Quebec literary works within the field of English-Canadian cultural production decontextualizes and refracts them" (*Canadian Literature* 294) can also be said of the partial inclusion of Acadian literary works within the field of Québec cultural production. Similarly, Godard's interest in forms of dissension *within* the loosely bound Canadian cultural field can be transplanted to Québec.

But *caveat lector*: such a comparison must itself be read in terms of the asymmetrical relations of power to which Godard so often drew our attention. Noticing the reproduction of similar appropriative gestures on a smaller scale does not amount to saying that Québec's hegemony over French Canadian letters is the same as English Canada's position toward Québec literature. For the relationship between Acadian and Québec letters is *also* imbricated within the relationship between Québec and English Canada's literary institutions. A French Canadian literary text, for example, is more likely to be discussed by a scholar of Québec letters than by a scholar of Canadian letters.[6] At the same time, it is significant that *Tessera*, a feminist journal, published Daigle alongside Barbara Sternberg, and that Godard, a feminist scholar, read Tostevin alongside di Michele and Kamboureli. Godard's feminist mappings exceed the divisions among Canadian, French Canadian, and Québec literatures, and raise important questions about the interactions between gender and minority language positions. Our goal in this essay is to open up the latter category and to interrogate the relations between positions—Acadian and Québécois—that are minoritized by, and with regard to, Canada. It matters, for example, that the three feminists from different minority backgrounds juxtaposed in Godard's article all write and publish primarily in English. It also matters that Daigle and Sternberg do not usually work in the same language: Daigle is a French-language writer. The relations between Acadian and Québec literatures, we argue, may be studied in terms of their relationship to Canadian literature, but they must also, and crucially, be analyzed for the specificity of their own interactions.

In this essay, we examine the ways in which relations of power express themselves and how different interconnected systems end up disadvantaging both France Daigle and the CRILCQ. We hope to underline the multi-layered context in which power relations take place, a context where the layers at play (be they institutional goals, personal interests, or the form and content of literary texts) are all imbricated in one another. Within this context, we try to discern which "(op)positions [were] taken," while keeping in mind that such (op)positions always depend on partial narratives, even as these narratives have potentially far-reaching effects of refraction. In this sense, our study can be seen not only as a displacement, but also as an extension of Barbara Godard's work.

Before turning to the case of France Daigle, it is worth pausing over Godard's 1990 discussion of Tostevin's writing in "The Discourse of the Other: Canadian Literature and the Question of Ethnicity." This article, which focuses on Tostevin's poetics, nonetheless affords insight into the complex interactions among English Canadian, French Canadian, and Québec letters, and the value of institutional analysis for understanding those interactions. Godard is interested in writers who complicate the routine association of English with Canada and French with Québec by writing in a language other than French or English, or by writing in more than one language. Tostevin, whose work is published with English-language presses in Canada, writes in French and English.[7] Her poetic practice, Godard explains, records the speaker's process of losing or "unspeaking" French and negotiating the contradictions of her relationship to English, a language she finds enabling as well as violating. Godard's article presents Tostevin as "a Franco-Ontarian, who has had an objective experience of colonization" (160). At the same time, it makes Québec literature (and not Franco-Ontarian literature) the cultural and geographical point of reference for Tostevin's writing. Godard compares Tostevin's "attention to the material signifier" to that of Québec writers Hubert Aquin and Réjean Ducharme, and she explains Tostevin's textual strategies in terms of a desire for re-territorialization, which is thwarted by her location "as a French-Canadian writer *outside* Quebec" (160, Godard's emphasis).[8]

The tendency in "The Discourse of the Other" to frame linguistic alterity in terms of, or with reference to, Québec is all the more significant if we consider that Godard does not take up the question of Tostevin's relation to the field of Franco-Ontarian literature. The latter question is one that preoccupies François Paré. Tostevin's name, he points out, does not appear in anthologies or accounts of Franco-Ontarian literature (*La Distance* 215). For Paré, Tostevin's practice of writing primarily in English and publishing with English-language presses has implications for the production and reception of her work.[9] Her writing community, her audience, and her literary institutional location, he argues, are English Canadian more than Franco-Ontarian (*La Distance* 216–17). Paré's argument is supported by the subtitle of Godard's article, "Canadian Literature and the Question of Ethnicity." In other words, Lola Lemire Tostevin is a Franco-Ontarian, but she is not read as a Franco-Ontarian writer.[10] If, in Godard and Paré, Tostevin's writing is associated with different literatures, this variability is symptomatic of the troubled institutional location of French-language writing outside Québec, and of bilingual writing in any context.

Godard's gesture of connecting Tostevin to Québec is not inaccurate. After all, Tostevin draws from Québec writers as well as from French writers in the French-language sections of her work. But the omission in Godard's article of the Franco-Ontarian literary and institutional connection has the effect of reinterpreting Tostevin within the terms of the linguistic division between (English) Canada and (French) Québec. Tostevin's bilingual writing practice, which stands in a position of unruliness to both Canadian and Québec literatures, has the potential to destabilize the habitual linguistic divide, but not if the field of Franco-Ontarian literature and Tostevin's tenuous relationship to it are removed from the discussion. As Godard argues throughout "A Literature in the Making," Canadian literature tends to overlook difference—the language in which the text is written as well as the language politics raised by the text—when it integrates French-language writers (*Canadian Literature* 300). In associating Tostevin's writing with Québec letters, Godard is in effect acknowledging Tostevin's use of the French language. At the same time, it is relatively easy for anglophone readers of Godard's article to forget that Tostevin's texts are written more in English than in French, and that this predominance of English is part of what has allowed Canadian letters to take Tostevin into its fold, bilingual writing and all. As we suggest in this essay, there are several contradictory ways of overlooking difference, and they are not exclusive to English Canadian letters.

Federal Mediations

In June 2008, the Centre de recherche interuniversitaire sur la littérature et la culture québécoises (CRILCQ) at the Université de Montréal learned that its request to the Canada Council for support to bring France Daigle from New Brunswick as writer in residence had been declined. When the CRILCQ phoned the council, the program officer explained that the application had not adequately addressed or justified the role of an *Acadian* writer at a research centre devoted to *Québécois* literature and culture. The CRILCQ found the decision surprising given that they had offered the same level of detail and description for their collaboration with France Daigle as they had for previous successful applications involving other writers, albeit Québec-based. Was this explanation on the part of an information officer simply a convenient rationale for justifying a decision determined by limited funds? It is possible that there were more convincing applications and that among the applicants were writers or institutions that had not benefited from council funds as often as the CRILCQ. Given that the council does not send applicants a written report, we do not know in any detail the grounds for the jury's decision. All we know is that in justifying the council's decision, the officer chose to focus on the role and relevance of an Acadian writer for a Québec studies centre. In such a context, it makes no sense to pass judgments or make pronouncements. Our purpose here is not to critique the CRILCQ or the Canada Council but to offer a critical reading of the incident. The challenge of such a reading lies in the number of possible positions from which to analyze the literary institutional relations as well as the contradictions that structure them.

What makes this instance of non-funding especially interesting is the involvement of three parties—a federal jury, a Québec research centre, and an Acadian writer—all of whom are French-speaking. The classic conflict between Canada and Québec is interrupted and transformed by the fact that the writer in question is Acadian. The CRILCQ's invitation to France Daigle requires but does not receive federal sanction. Funding is denied on the grounds that the CRILCQ, a part of the Québec literary institution, has not adequately acknowledged that Daigle is part of the field of Acadian letters. Why did the council place such emphasis on the specificity of an Acadian writer and on the need to explain her relevance to a Québec studies centre? One possible response is that the Canada Council was holding the Québec literary institution to its own national and geographical definitions, definitions that would not include the writing of Acadians. Such a response raises further questions: Is the Canada Council out of sync with the field of Québec letters? The latter had certainly defined itself territorially, but here was an example of an interuniversity centre for research on Québec culture placing pressure on that definition, looking beyond questions of identity and territoriality to broader linkages among francophone writers. Indeed, the gesture of the CRILCQ can be read as one of listening to the edges of the field, even if this is not explained in the application. Incidentally, the CRILCQ's gesture is in keeping with the aims of the Author Residencies program, which, according to the Canada Council website, encourages innovative residencies involving writers from outside the host's city ("Literary Readings and Author Residencies Program").

What stake does a federal institution such as the Canada Council have in maintaining a distinction between French Canada and Québec, and what happens when Acadian and Québécois literatures come together—that is, when the Québec literary institution opens its borders to Acadian writers or when Acadian writers find publishers and readers in Québec? Many Acadian writers have publicly complained about Québec's view of Acadian literature as primarily folkloric, about its traditional ignorance of their urban-based literature, or about the need for Acadian writers to establish themselves in Québec in order to gain recognition from the Québec literary institution. They have done so in interviews and essays as well as in their fiction. Herménégilde Chiasson, for instance, criticizes Québec's "anthropological view" of Acadie, where Acadians, depicted by writers who have long left their native region, are seen as old-fashioned fishermen who talk funny.[11] Similarly, Gérald Leblanc, in his novel *Moncton Mantra*, depicts an argument that takes place in Montreal between his narrator and a "nationalist brute in a lumberjack shirt," who tells him: "Acadie? Doesn't exist anymore. It's folklore. Finished, man" (95).[12] The CRILCQ's invitation to Daigle, a writer who lives in Moncton and writes about a contemporary, urban-based Acadie, is therefore an important one—and this makes it even more pressing to inquire into the mediating role of the Canada Council and what it means to foreclose the possibilities opened by such a gesture. In immediate terms, both the CRILCQ and Daigle suffered, Daigle in particular because she had made concrete plans to move to Montreal for the year. The CRILCQ found that the Canada Council had defined them instead of allowing them to define themselves and had imposed its ideas about what constitutes Québec culture instead of allowing them to explore their own borders. They were extremely frustrated. They experienced the refusal as a reminder that, even though Québec literature is independent from Canadian literature in terms of teaching and criticism, it still falls within its fold and has to bend to its categories when it comes to grant money.

In evaluating the mediating role of the Canada Council, it is important to consider the latter's decision-making practices. According to the council's website, the council makes its decisions based on the recommendation of juries composed of "practising artists and other professionals working in the arts" ("Peer Assessment"). In other words, writers are judged by their peers. Particularly significant for our research is the fact that French-language applications are assessed by a French-speaking jury. This jury, in keeping with the council's guidelines, includes francophones from minority as well as majority communities.[13] On the one hand, Québec literature has no special status within the council's system, whose dividing line is between English and French Canada rather than between (English) Canada and (French) Québec. On the other hand, francophone members of the council's juries are predominantly from Québec. As a result, the views of Quebecers are given more weight than those of other francophone jurors.[14] Considering the heterogeneity of juries and the fact that they change from year to year, it would be difficult to paint the Canada Council with a single ideological brush, to characterize the council's decision, for example, as that of a federal body in any unitary sense. In fact, the composition of the jury accentuates the multiple and contradictory perspectives to which we alluded above. It is possible to imagine some members of the jury seeking to reinforce the boundary between Acadian and Québécois letters, others seeking to render it more porous and, within each of these tendencies, having different reasons for doing so.

What is more, the jury's decision may have had *nothing to do* with the members' perspectives on relations between the two literatures. Similarly, the explanation given to the CRILCQ by the council's information officer may or may not have been an accurate account of the jury's consensus. We do not know why the jury made the decision it did. Although the list of juries is now available (the Canada Council publishes the names of winners once the residency is completed and those of jurors a year later), we have no intention of contacting them or of drawing conclusions from the composition of a specific jury. Our argument is concerned less with the individuals involved than with the institutional relations brought to light by the CRILCQ's invitation to Daigle and by the Canada Council's refusal of the CRILCQ's application.

Québec–Acadie Relations

The council's decision also invites reflection about the CRILCQ's relation to France Daigle. Why was the CRILCQ interested in working with Daigle? The application expresses a keen interest in Daigle's writing for the theatre and for film as well as in her novels. Presenting Daigle as a writer preoccupied by philosophical or conceptual questions related to language and writing, it anticipates visits to graduate and research seminars as well as writing workshops for students. Except in a biographical note, the application does not identify Daigle as an Acadian writer, an identification Daigle complicates in her writing, but nonetheless embraces. In other words, the application approaches Daigle as it would a Québec-based writer. There are some signs in the discourse of the application that she is not Québec-based: the use, for example, of the category "écrivains francophones" instead of "écrivains québécois" and the reference to Daigle's work as news writer for "Radio-Canada, région Atlantique." But these points of cultural reference and geographical location outside Québec are not foregrounded or discussed.

In choosing Daigle among other possible Acadian writers, the CRILCQ went for a renowned and well-established writer, but also for one whose specific location could be minimized. Indeed, France Daigle started her career as a writer preoccupied primarily by questions of form. She belongs to a generation of women writers who set themselves apart from the Acadian neo-nationalist poetry of their time and who tried to reinvent Acadie's national memory differently. According to Paré, her modernity is tied to a jamming of collective values, which are not disavowed but deliberately fractured and opened up (*La Distance* 206). Daigle's early work, which is highly euphemistic, barely mentions Acadie and does not use the Acadian vernacular.[15] And while Moncton and Chiac (Moncton's Acadian bilingual slang) are at the heart of her recent work, they never take precedence over the formal questions at the foundations of her writing trajectory. By basing its application on these questions, the CRILCQ privileges the element that unites Daigle's work in all its diversity and that makes it resonate beyond the borders of Acadie.

This is not to say that the relations between Acadie and Québec are of no interest to members of the CRILCQ. Élizabeth Nardout-Lafarge, director of the CRILCQ at the time of the application, is co-author of the 2007 volume *Histoire de la littérature québécoise*, a literary history that includes a chapter on "La Nouvelle francophonie canadienne." In the latter chapter, the authors signal the effects of Québec's "indépendance littéraire" (Biron, Dumont, and Nardout-Lafarge 568) on French-language literatures outside Québec and the historical differences between Franco-Ontarian writing (which invented itself in the 1970s) and Acadian writing (which had existed as such before Québec literature). They also note the engagement in Daigle's writing with the problematic of legitimacy for Acadian writers (570). Nonetheless, this knowledge of Daigle's active participation in Acadian letters does not translate into the application itself, which passes over her Acadianness.

Members of the CRILCQ, in our brief conversations with them, were aware of their relatively seamless integration of Daigle into the field of Québec letters. Given her explicit links to the field, they considered it unnecessary to treat the application for Daigle's residency differently from previous ones. A quick look at Daigle's publishing history shows that seven of her eleven books have been either published or co-published in Québec. Yet it is also true that Daigle was, by choice, very loyal to les Éditions d'Acadie until the Acadian publisher went out of business in 2000. In any case, Boréal, her current publisher and one of the most important in Québec, refused *La Vraie vie* in the 1990s before taking Daigle under its wing from 2001 onward. Since then all of France Daigle's novels have been published with Boréal. And being recognized by and integrated into the Québec literary institution has meant an increase in Québec readers, reviewers, and distributors, which makes her a better known writer than she was previously.[16] In this respect, the cultural work carried out by the coordinator, research assistants, and researchers of centres such as the CRILCQ plays a role in this process of legitimization. This is not to say that Daigle's writing does not also enjoy a popular as well as a critical reception among readers outside Québec[17] or that circles of readers outside Québec are entirely separate from those inside.[18] In fact, Daigle has used the new Québec base that Boréal provides her to publish the four most "Acadian" of her novels, both in theme and in language. And these four novels have been her most popular so far, not only in Québec[19] and in Acadie, but also elsewhere in francophone Canada, where Daigle is among the most frequently studied writers.

In light of the support and cultural recognition the Québec literary institution has been able to provide a writer such as Daigle, it makes sense to the CRILCQ to integrate her within Québec letters. Daigle's oeuvre is a part of the latter field, albeit non-exclusively. And, importantly, taken as part of Québec letters, Daigle's oeuvre is a sign of how Québec literature operates as a sphere of influence for francophone culture outside as well as inside

Québec. A centre for research into Québec culture such as the CRILCQ does not see the need to explain to a federal funding body its status as sphere of francophone cultural and literary influence. Nor does it see the need to justify an Acadian writer's presence at the centre. The CRILCQ expects the Canada Council to understand and recognize its status as sphere of influence and its capacity to judge the relevance of a given writer for the projects of its research centre. Reluctant to folklorize Daigle's contribution to Québec letters or to "reduce" her to the specificities of her Acadian identity, it chooses to insist on her "universal" appeal—her ideas about writing and her engagement with different genres, for example. These, then, are some of the grounds on which the CRILCQ might have written its application to the Canada Council in the way it did. In a cultural space that others take to be differentiated and tension-filled, in a cultural space of encounter and negotiation, the CRILCQ proceeded with a sense of relative entitlement. The field of Québec letters has worked to organize and conceptualize itself as the literature of a majority, and it has largely succeeded. Perhaps because of this, it has difficulty imagining that a writer such as Daigle would be willing to associate herself with minority status or that an explanation of her minority status would be necessary to secure funding for her residency. In constructing her as a francophone writer, not as an Acadian writer, the CRILCQ gives her majority status. It extends to its guest writers the gains Québec literature has made for itself in the past few decades of its modernity and its establishment as a national literature capable of moving beyond national concerns.

Acadie–Québec Relations

The CRILCQ's invitation to Daigle makes sense in light of her links to the Québec literary institution, but these links are not necessarily well known to all potential jurors. Where the CRILCQ favoured straightforward integration, the Canada Council jury was looking for more recognition of the specificity of Daigle's location. Without participating in discourses and practices of "Québec bashing,"[20] we would like to turn to alternative perspectives, notably those suggested by Daigle's recent novels. What are, for an Acadian writer, the terms of integration into the Québec literary institution? What are the different attitudes toward "passing by way of Québec"? We have thus far emphasized the continuities or links that structure Daigle's relation to Québec letters, but there are also discontinuities that need to be taken into account.

It must be remembered that Québec created its national literature by rejecting its minority status as French Canadian. Concentrating on a territory where francophones could be a majority, it excluded French Canadian minorities from its own boundaries, except as warning signs of the dangers to be expected by linguistic minorities.[21] And it is true that both the French language and the literary institution are in a much more precarious state outside these boundaries. On a linguistic level, the relationship Québec francophones have developed with the French language in the past few decades is quite different from that of francophones outside its borders.[22] Francophones in Québec have a somewhat majoritarian relation to French, whereas Acadians, like other francophones across Canada, have a minoritarian relation to French. The latter's francophone identity is not entirely dissociated from their relationship to English as well as French. On a literary level, even though Acadie has developed its own literary institution since the 1970s, "this institution is by no means entirely autonomous, and relies on Québec for an important part of the production, distribution, reception and consecration of Acadian literary texts," to the point that "even today, it is impossible to imagine the existence of Acadian literature without the assistance of the Québec literary institution" (Boudreau, "Les Rapports Acadie/Québec" 7–8).[23] The result of such disparities is not always harmonious. Acadians have been resentful of Quebecers' alarmist depiction of their situation, as well as of their monopolization of the federal resources devoted to French Canada. Quebecers, on the other hand, have at times accused Acadians of playing into the hands of the federal government. Whereas the Canadian ideology of official bilingualism is seen in Québec as a method for containing and restricting the use of French, it has been successfully used by Acadians to increase the profile of French in New Brunswick.[24]

Unlike some of her Acadian male colleagues, Daigle has been discreet about the complicated relationship between Acadian writers and Québec. When asked about it, she emphasizes the potential for collaboration. In her work, Québec is not given a significant place as a source of legitimization. Daigle's narrators, aiming bigger, tend to bypass it in favour of Paris. In *Pas pire* [*Just Fine*], for instance, where the narrator is a writer named France Daigle, like the novel's author, we find the assertion that "everything's a matter of legitimization" (*Just Fine* 93).[25] At the time of the action, the narrator's novel, titled *Pas pire*, has already been published and the narrator is invited to discuss this publication on France's most popular literary TV show, Bernard Pivot's *Bouillon de culture*. Of course, apart from the existence of *Pas pire* as a novel, everything in this storyline is pure fiction. Outside the world of fiction, such an invitation would be unlikely, and did not indeed happen. And while allowing it to take place, the text itself is careful enough to describe it as "a wild notion" (*Just Fine* 91), an "extravagant fantas[y]" (39) "[of] a kind we don't get too much of in these parts" (91).[26] After all, *Pas pire* is a novel according to which "death, or at least nonexistence, is inscribed in our [Acadian] genes" (93).[27] The novel strikes a delicate balance between fostering a sense of vitality in the French-language cultural milieu of Moncton—with the help of fantasy and the occasional utopian impulse—and signalling the fragility of that milieu. Fictitious as it is, the invitation to *Bouillon de culture* is nonetheless the trigger for a reflection on legitimacy and recognition that involves France primarily, but does not leave out Québec. When she receives the message left on her answering machine by "the cultural attaché of the provincial intergovernmental affairs minister" (*Just Fine* 39), the fictional France Daigle starts imagining "opportunities [she] had never dared to imagine" (39) and her first hypothesis is the following: "Maybe a Québec author had expressed interest in my work and wanted to come work with me in Moncton as part of a cultural exchange between the two provinces" (39).[28]

In a way, the CRILCQ's invitation to the real France Daigle is a clear sign of interest from the Québec literary institution. It is partly fulfilling France Daigle the character's fantasy of interprovincial exchange and dream of recognition. It is also, however, a far cry from that fantasy and that dream in the sense that the exchange was never to take place in Moncton, on Daigle's turf, and never to extend the recognition of an individual Acadian writer to the environment that had nourished her. Instead, the exchange follows the usual direction of literary exchanges between Québec and Acadie, whereby an Acadian writer has to move to Québec—whether in person or in publication—and become part of its system to be acclaimed there. The gesture made by the CRILCQ is one of connection and recognition, but is also potentially one of appropriation. Commenting on Daigle's move to Boréal with the publication of *Un fin passage* in 2001, Québec journalist Mélanie Saint-Hilaire wrote in *L'Actualité*: "By bringing France Daigle from her native Acadie to Québec, *Un fin passage* confirmed that she has, is worthy of, a place amongst writers" (68).[29] In this respect, Daigle's focus on legitimization via France more than via Québec, in her fiction, might be understood as her way of complicating, indeed relativizing, Québec's status as a cultural centre.

Then again, *Petites difficultés d'existence* [*Life's Little Difficulties*], Daigle's 2002 and latest novel, offers a scene where help does come from Québec in the project at the heart of the novel, the project of putting Moncton, Daigle's hometown and that of her main characters, on the international map. Sitting with friends and acquaintances at a table in a Moncton café, Terry, one of France Daigle's recurring characters, tells the story of Québec singer Mara Tremblay mentioning Moncton on French television:

> "The other night, on TV-France, there was a québécoise singer talking about just this song. She said she'd met a guy from Moncton who told her his grand-mère used to sing it to him."
> "So?"
> "Well, she never said Moncton en Acadie or Moncton, New Brunswick, or any such thing. As if everybody and his uncle knew where Moncton was.… As though we were une grande ville or some well-known place." (*Life's Little Difficulties* 111)[30]

In this passage, where the usual hierarchy between France, Québec, and Acadie is perfectly maintained, Terry expresses his surprise at, and appreciation of, the unlikely notion of Moncton being mentioned without requiring any extra explanation.[31] Of course, by doing so, he also provides his readers with the very information whose absence he was celebrating. Such an absence is so unlikely to Daigle's characters that they conclude from Tremblay's gesture that she is an eccentric: "Mara Tremblay. You don't forget a name like that.… Come to think of it, you wouldn't really forget the girl non plus" (112).[32] And they are quick to bring Moncton back to its small-town size, that of a city where everybody knows everybody: "I'm wondering who the fellow was she met" (112).[33] Yet the possibility of naming a place without having to specify where it is is a significant sign of legitimization in their eyes. It turns Moncton into a big cosmopolitan city, what Daigle's character calls "une place *right* connue" (*Petites difficultés* 137).

Which leaves open the question: In presenting France Daigle as a writer worthy of interest without stressing her Acadian origin and the Acadian setting of her work, did the CRILCQ ignore this Acadianness and try to appropriate her, simply claiming her as a Quebecer? Or did it take it for granted, as something obvious and obviously known, the way Mara Tremblay does with Moncton in *Petites difficultés d'existence*, therefore treating her as "une grande auteure ou une personne right connue"?

Having begun with the question of federal mediations in the relations between Acadie and Québec, we conclude with these passages from France Daigle's novels, passages that anticipate the institutional questions under discussion here. Daigle's novels speak eloquently of the will on the part of the Acadian writer to mediate for herself the interprovincial relations brought to the fore by the Canada Council's non-funding of the CRILCQ's 2008 application. Critics have not been insensitive to the thematization of the writer–audience relation in Daigle's work. The writer-character's fantasy in *Pas Pire*, of being invited to France to participate in *Bouillon de culture*, is well cited and routinely read as emblematic of the struggle for legitimacy on the part of the Acadian writer.[34] It is only recently, however, that attention has been given to the phone message from the provincial intergovernmental affairs office that launches the fantasy or to the rapid shift in desired audience from Québec to France.[35] The latter shift is important. It suggests, as does the thwarted attempt on the part of the CRILCQ to bring Daigle to Montreal, just how high the stakes are in the relations between Acadie and Québec.

The regulation of borders between contiguous literatures is a further symptom of these high stakes. In times and places where borders are uncontested, this regulatory process is hardly noticed. In times of redefinition, however, the border guards become more exigent. Contradictory pressures meet and clash. Québec literature seems to be undergoing such a redefinition at the moment, as is indicated by the recent inclusion of Anglo-Québec writing *within* its borders.[36] Similarly, Québec's relationship with Franco-Canadian minority literatures is no longer limited to ignorance or selective absorption, although traces of these practices remain. Power relationships between the two literatures have not disappeared, but they can no longer be read the same way. In 2010, Benoît Doyon-Gosselin goes as far as to argue that "Québec literature would be less important if it were the only francophone literature in North America" and that, as a result, it "*needs* to continue to open itself to Canada's francophone literatures in order to act as a leader, as a meeting point" ("(In)(ter)dépendance" 55; emphasis ours).[37]

Literary institutions in many places are moving away from a strong national model. This is certainly true of Québec's, which, according to *Histoire de la littérature québécoise*, now privileges practices of "decentring" [*décentrement*] (Biron, Dumont, and Nardout-Lafarge 529). How this transformation affects the modes of interaction between Québec and Acadian letters remains to be evaluated. One can hypothesize that for the CRILCQ, France Daigle's work provided a model for decentring, and that ignoring borders made the model more effective. Others in the various fields with a stake in the literary border between Acadie and Québec, however, had many different reasons to stand in the way of a smooth crossing.

Notes

1 Not all critics would characterize the relation of English Canadian literature to Québec literature in these terms. Rather than respect for hard-won autonomy, Frank Davey finds impatience and a "desire to get on with defining a Canada in which Francophone Quebec political/cultural aspirations are not major elements" (6). The latter project, he argues, subtends anglophone Canadian literary critical discourse and practice throughout the twentieth century.
2 See Godard's comments regarding the "'ethnographic' impulse of the dominant discourse on translation in English Canada," an impulse she characterizes as "self-knowledge through an encounter with the other" (*Canadian Literature* 288).
3 In English, (Franco-)Québécois and French Canadian are often used synonymously, whereas in French the two terms differentiate francophones from Québec and francophones from other Canadian provinces.
4 Inspired by the project notes of filmmaker Barbara Sternberg and intercut with Daigle's letters to Sternberg, these poems, "Tending Towards the Horizontal: Text," are written in English. That Daigle generally writes in French is nonetheless clear from an interview in the same issue in which Sternberg explains to Godard that she has a long history of reading Daigle, but that, unable to understand French, she usually gets a friend to read to her and to translate (Godard, "Shifting Realities: An Interview" 44). For a brief discussion of Daigle's poems published in *Tessera*, see Paré (*La Distance* 209).
5 An exception is her work on Gail Scott, where Scott's internal connections with Québec are made abundantly clear (see "Writing from the Border").
6 Acadian and French Canadian literary texts are rarely studied by anglophone scholars working in Canadian studies. For instance, out of the vast diversity of papers presented at the three TransCanada conferences (2005, 2007, and 2009), and despite the fact that François Paré gave a keynote address in Sackville in 2009 on "Systems of Tradition and Pluralism in Contemporary Acadia," no paper other than our own focused on francophone literatures outside Québec.
7 One of her novels, the bilingual *Frog Moon*, has been translated into (bilingual) French as *Kaki* by Robert Dickson. Interestingly, Dickson is a poet who, like Tostevin, wrote in French and English. Unlike her, however, he chose to publish his work in French with the Franco-Ontarian press Prise de parole. His gesture of publishing *Kaki* in French can be read as an attempt to reintegrate Tostevin's work within the Franco-Ontarian literary horizon.
8 Godard's construction of Tostevin's textual strategies as both akin to that of specific Québec writers *and* the result of her position outside Québec is not in itself contradictory. Aquin and Ducharme are themselves struggling to inhabit French from outside the centre of French-language culture.
9 On this point, see Paré's observation that Lianne Moyes's reading of Tostevin's bilingual writing practice underestimates the scriptural importance of English

in Tostevin's oeuvre and the precarity of Franco-Ontarian culture it suggests (Moyes, "To bite"; Paré, *La Distance* 217).

10 Catherine Leclerc reads Lola Lemire Tostevin as a Franco-Ontarian writer who speaks back to a field of literature from which she has taken a certain feminist distance (*Des langues* 332–39). For Leclerc, Tostevin becomes a kind of Patrice Desbiens character talking back to him.

11 Chiasson's take on Québec's "anthropological view" of Acadie, presented in several unpublished essays, can be found in Boudreau's "Les Rapports Acadie/Québec."

12 Translation Jo-Anne Elder. In the original: "brute nationaliste en chemise de bûcheron," and "L'Acadie, ça existe pu. C'est du folklore. C'est fini, bonhomme!" (Leblanc 110). Our text uses the available English translations of Acadian works in the body of the text, and the original in footnotes. All other translations are Leclerc's.

13 According to the Canada Council website, committees are selected with a concern to take equitable account of a number of factors, one of which is listed as "Language—artists and arts professionals from the two official language communities of Canada, as well as the official-language communities in minority situations such as Anglophones living in Quebec and Francophones living outside Quebec" ("Peer Assessment"). In 2007–8, for example, there was one member from Ontario (Ottawa) and two from Québec; in 2008–9, there was one member from New Brunswick and two from Québec ("Annual Reports").

14 In her own experience of a Canada Council jury, France Daigle felt that her perspective was at times different from that of her Québec co-jurors. In one instance in particular, she was unable to persuade a co-juror of the value of a Franco-Manitoban project that would have led to important literary developments in the region. The co-juror favoured a Québec project whose quality was no better in Daigle's view (Personal interview with Catherine Leclerc).

15 Daigle describes her early euphemistic and formalist style as being influenced by Marguerite Duras, but also as reproducing what she perceives to be a typically Acadian restraint. (See Boudreau, "Le Rapport à la langue," 36 and 38.)

16 In 2001, after the publication of *Un fin passage* by Boréal, Daigle was featured in Montreal's daily *La Presse* (Guy), as well as in Québec's widely read magazine *L'Actualité* (Saint-Hilaire). (See also Levasseur 254.)

17 In addition to *Histoire de la littérature québécoise*, Daigle's commentators in Québec include Lise Gauvin and Catherine Leclerc. In Acadie, Raoul Boudreau, François Giroux, and Chantal G. Richard, among others, have analyzed her work. Monika Boehringer, who obtained her Ph.D. at University of Toronto, writes on Daigle from Mount Allison University in Sackville (near Moncton), New Brunswick. In Ontario, commentators include François Paré and Kathleen Kellett-Betsos. Janet Den Toonder writes on Daigle from the Netherlands, and Margareta Gyurcsik from Romania.

18 Jean Morency, a professor at Université de Moncton who directed an issue of the journal *Voix et images* on France Daigle, is originally from Québec;

Pénélope Cormier, originally from Moncton, recently presented a paper on Daigle at McGill University; Benoît Doyon-Gosselin, now a professor at Université Laval, wrote his thesis on France Daigle and Franco-Manitoban writer J.R. Léveillé at Université de Moncton, and did his previous studies in Manitoba; Cecilia W. Francis writes on Daigle from St. Thomas University in Fredericton, New Brunswick, and holds her Ph.D. from Université Laval.

19 Boréal started publishing France Daigle with *Un fin passage* (*A Fine Passage*) and then went on to publish *Petites difficultés d'existence* (*Life's Little Difficulties*) and *Pour sûr* It also republished *Pas pire* (*Just Fine*). All of these novels except *Pour sûr*, the most recent, have been translated into English by a (then) Québec-based translator and writer, Robert Majzels.

20 Confronted with Québec's gains as a majority culture, the Québec-basher turns those gains against Québec by accusing it of not being as good or open-minded a majority as the English Canadian one. Québec-bashing is in part a remnant of British colonialism, a regime that worked to consolidate a sense of the moral superiority of English over French, while its contemporary manifestations often use cultural diversity as a focal point. The gesture of Québec-bashing fails to take into account the possibility that English-speaking Canadians are also potentially authors of racism. It overlooks efforts on the part of Quebecers to expose, analyze, and counter discourses and practices of racism, or judges those efforts without taking into account the specificity of the Québec situation and strategies regarding racism and other forms of discrimination.

21 See Paré (*Les littératures de l'exiguïté* 31, 41–42; *La Distance* 8); for an extra-literary perspective, see Heller (*Linguistic Minorities* 69).

22 The relationship of Québec anglophones to French is also different. That the only significant population of anglophones fluent in French in Canada exists in Québec is a sign of the vitality of French in that province.

23 "Cette institution n'est certes pas entièrement autonome et elle se repose sur le Québec pour une partie importante de la production, la diffusion, la réception, et la consécration des ouvrages de littérature acadienne.... aujourd'hui encore, on ne peut guère imaginer l'existence d'une littérature acadienne sans le concours de l'institution littéraire québécoise."

24 Official monolingualism was introduced in Québec with the Charter of the French language (Law 101) in 1977. Official bilingualism was introduced in the province of New Brunswick in 1984. For an Acadian take on these questions, see Boudreau ("Les Rapports Acadie/Québec") and Beaulieu. Québec interpretations are rarer, but Beaumier's is telling: "With the redefinition of Canada since the Trudeau era, Acadians have benefitted much more than Québécois" ("avec la redéfinition du Canada depuis l'ère Trudeau, les Acadiens ont trouvé leur compte beaucoup plus que les Québécois") (B4). Despite the polarization described above, it is possible to find examples of collaboration and understanding. Québec writer Claude Beausoleil and Acadian writer

Gérald Leblanc, for instance, collaborated on an anthology of Acadian poetry, co-published by Éditions Perce-Neige in New Brunswick and Écrits des Forges in Québec. See also Denault and Cardinal.

25 Translation Robert Majzels. In the original: "tout est affaire de légitimation" (*Pas pire* 107).

26 In the original: "une hypothèse délirante" (*Pas pire* 105); "les fabulations les plus extravagantes" (49); "ce genre de fantaisie qui ne passe pas souvent par ici" (105).

27 In the original: "la mort, ou tout au moins l'inexistence, est inscrite dans nos gènes [acadiens]" (*Pas pire* 107). It is precisely this non-existence that many Acadian literary texts seek to contest. Often, as in Gérald Leblanc's *Moncton Mantra*, such a contestation is presented in connection to Québec. Daigle's Acadian nationalism, however, is more circumspect than that of her male counterparts, and is not presented as a conflict with Québec.

28 In the original: "l'attaché de presse du ministre des Affaires intergouvernementales de la province" (*Pas pire* 49); "les occasions les plus inespérées" (49); "Peut-être qu'un auteur du Québec avait manifesté de l'intérêt pour mon travail, au point de vouloir venir travailler avec moi à Moncton, dans le cadre d'une entente culturelle conclue entre les deux provinces" (49). Note the French "au point de," which, more than the English translation, stresses the extreme represented by this possibility.

29 "En menant France Daigle de son Acadie natale au Québec, *Un fin passage* lui a confirmé qu'elle avait sa place parmi les écrivains."

30 In the original: " — L'autre soir, à TV5, y'a une chanteuse québécoise qui parlait de c'te chanson-icitte. A disait qu'à l'avait rencontré un gars de Moncton qui y'avait dit que sa grand-mère y chantait ça. — *So?* — Ben, a l'a pas dit Moncton en Acadie, ou Moncton au Nouveau-Brunswick ni rien de même. Comme si tout le monde savait où c'est qu'est Moncton.... Comme si on était une grande ville ou une place *right* connue" (*Petites difficultés* 137).

31 As Benoît Doyon-Gosselin and Jean Morency remarked in 2004, the utopian acknowledgement here is double: that a Québec performer is compelled to mention Moncton on French television proves the symbolic importance of the city; that her French interlocutor does not need to ask about the city confirms its influence (80).

32 In the original: "Mara Tremblay. Tu peux pas vraiment oublier un nom de même.... Ben, tant qu'à ça, tu peux pas vraiment oublier la fille non plus" (*Petites difficultés* 138).

33 In the original: "Je me demande qui c'qu'est le gars qu'a l'a rencontré" (*Petites difficultés* 138).

34 See Biron, Dumont, and Nardout-Lafarge (570); Boudreau and Boudreau (177); Cécilia W. Francis (127); Gauvin (25–26); Giroux (46–47 and 52); Leclerc ("L'Acadie rayonne" 90–91).

35 See Benoît Doyon-Gosselin's "(In)(ter)dépendance" (48).

36 The most recent review of works originating from Québec on Anglo-Québec writing can be found in Moyes's "Conflicts in Contiguity." Following its chapter on "La nouvelle francophonie canadienne," *Histoire de la littérature québécoise* has a chapter on "La traduction de la littérature anglo-québécoise" (573–80).

37 "Si la littérature québécoise était la seule littérature francophone en Amérique, son importance serait moindre ... le Québec doit continuer de s'ouvrir aux littératures francophones du Canada pour agir comme chef de file, comme point de rencontre ..."

Works Cited

Beaulieu, Gérard. "Le Québec et la question québécoise dans les quotidiens du Nouveau-Brunswick 1960–1998." *Les relations entre le Québec et L'Acadie: de la tradition à la modernité*. Ed. Fernand Harvey and Gérard Beaulieu. Québec/Moncton: Éditions de l'IQRC (Presses de l'Université Laval)/Éditions d'Acadie, 2000. 97–125. Print.

Beaumier, Jacques. "Qu'est l'Acadie devenue?" *Le Devoir* July 30 and 31, 2005: B4. Print.

Biron, Michel, François Dumont, and Élizabeth Nardout-Lafarge. *Histoire de la littérature québécoise*. 2007. Montreal: Boréal, 2010. Print.

Boehringer, Monika. "'A Private Open Space': Crossing Boundaries and Constructing Identities in France Daigle's Auto/Fictions." *Zeitschrift für Kanada-Studien* 27.2 (2007): 30–42. Print.

Boudreau, Annette, and Raoul Boudreau. "La littérature comme moyen de reconquête de la parole. L'exemple de l'Acadie." *Glottopol* 3 (January 2004): 165–80. Web. December 10, 2010. <http://www.univ-rouen.fr/dyalang/glottopol/telecharger/numero_3/gpl313boudreau.pdf>.

Boudreau, Raoul. "Le Rapport à la langue dans les romans de France Daigle: du refoulement à l'ironie." *Voix et images* 29.3.87 (Spring 2004): 31–45. Print.

———. "Les Rapports Acadie/Québec dans les essais d'Herménégilde Chiasson." *Contemporary Acadian Literature*. Ed. Raoul Boudreau. Spec. issue of *Québec Studies* 43 (Spring/Summer 2007): 3–21. Print.

Canada Council for the Arts. "Annual Reports & List of Peer Assessment Committee Members." 2007–8, 2008–9. Web. December 21, 2010. <http://www.canadacouncil.ca/aboutus/organization/annualreports/default.htm>.

———. "Literary Readings and Author Residencies Program: Author Residencies." February 2010. Web. December 21, 2010. <http://www.canadacouncil.ca/grants/writing/wb128792870370822784.htm>.

———. "Peer Assessment." September 2009. Web. December 21, 2010. <http://www.canadacouncil.ca/aboutus/Governance/PeerAssessment/gq127234205403281250.htm>.

Centre de recherche interuniversitaire sur la littérature et la culture québécoises (CRILCQ)/Site Université de Montréal. "Sommaire du projet et documents d'appui—Résidences d'écrivains." Unpublished grant application. April 2008. Print.

Cormier, Pénélope. "Les contraintes créatrices dans l'œuvre de France Daigle: déplacement, dépassement." 41st Anniversary Convention—Northeast Modern Language Association (NeMLA), McGill University. April 8, 2010. Conference presentation. Print.

Daigle, France. *A Fine Passage*. Trans. Robert Majzels. 2001. Toronto: Anansi, 2002. Print.

———. *La beauté de l'affaire. Fiction autobiographique à plusieurs voix sur son rapport tortueux au langage*. Outremont/Moncton: Éditions nbj/Éditions d'Acadie, 1991. Print.

———. *L'été avant la mort*. With Hélène Harbec. Montreal: Éditions du remue-ménage, 1986. Print.

———. *Film d'amour et de dépendance. Chef-d'oeuvre obscur*. Moncton: Éditions d'Acadie, 1984. Print.

———. *Histoire de la maison qui brûle. Vaguement suivi d'un dernier regard sur la maison qui brûle*. Moncton: Éditions d'Acadie, 1985. Print.

———. *Just Fine*. Trans. Robert Majzels. 1998. Toronto: Anansi, 1999. Print.

———. *Life's Little Difficulties*. Trans. Robert Majzels. 2002. Toronto: Anansi, 2004. Print.

———. *1953: Chronicle of a Birth Foretold*. Trans. Robert Majzels. 1995. Toronto: Anansi, 1997. Print.

———. *1953: Chronique d'une naissance annoncée*. Moncton: Éditions d'Acadie, 1995. Print.

———. *Pas pire*. Moncton: Éditions d'Acadie, 1998. Print.

———. *Pas pire*, 2nd ed. Montreal: Boréal Compact, 2002. Print.

———. *Petites difficultés d'existence*. Montreal: Boréal, 2002. Print.

———. *Real Life*. Trans. Sally Ross. 1993. Don Mills: Anansi, 1995. Print.

———. *Sans jamais parler du vent. Roman de crainte et d'espoir que la mort arrive à temps*. Moncton: Éditions d'Acadie, 1983. Print.

———. "Tending Towards the Horizontal: Text." *Tessera* 13 (Winter 1992): 64–73. Print.

———. *Un fin passage*. Montreal: Boréal, 2001. Print.

———. *Variations en B et K. Plans, devis, et contrat pour l'infrastructure d'un pont*. Outremont: Éditions nbj, 1985. Print.

———. *La Vraie vie*. Montreal/Moncton: L'Hexagone/Éditions d'Acadie, 1993. Print.

Davey, Frank. "'And Quebec': Canadian Literature and Its Quebec Questions." *Canadian Poetry* 40 (Spring/Summer 1997): 6–26. Print.

Denault, Anne-Andrée, and Linda Cardinal. "Rupture et continuité: Une relecture des représentations des effets de la Révolution tranquille sur les rapports entre les sociétés acadienne et québécoise." *Québec Studies* 43 (Spring/Summer 2007): 67–81. Print.

Doyon-Gosselin, Benoît. "(In)(ter)dépendance des littératures francophones du Canada." *La littérature québécoise en regard des autres littératures francophones.* Ed. Lise Gauvin. Spec. issue of *Québec Studies* 49 (Spring/Summer 2010): 47–58. Print.

———. *Pour une herméneutique de l'espace. L'œuvre romanesque de J.R. Léveillé et France Daigle.* Québec: Nota Bene, 2010. Print.

Doyon-Gosselin, Benoît, and Jean Morency. "Le monde de Moncton, Moncton ville du monde: l'inscription de la ville dans les romans récents de France Daigle." *France Daigle.* Ed. Jean Morency. Spec. issue of *Voix et images* 29.3.87 (Spring 2004): 69–83. Print.

Francis, Cécilia W. "L'autofiction de France Daigle: Identité, perception visuelle, et réinvention de soi. *Voix et images* 28.3.84 (Spring 2003): 114–38. Print.

Gauvin, Lise. "Petites difficultés d'existence: la relation écrivain-lecteur dans les romans de France Daigle." *Contemporary Acadian Literature.* Spec. issue of *Québec Studies* 43 (Spring/Summer 2007): 23–28. Print.

Giroux, François. "Sémiologie du personnage autofictif dans *Pas pire* de France Daigle." *Francophonies d'Amérique* 17 (Spring 2004): 45–54. Web. December 10, 2010. <http://muse.jhu.edu/journals/fda/summary/v017/17.1giroux01.html>.

Godard, Barbara. *Canadian Literature at the Crossroads of Language and Culture: Selected Essays by Barbara Godard, 1987–2005.* Ed. Smaro Kamboreli. Edmonton: NeWest, 2008. Print.

———. "The Discourse of the Other: Canadian Literature and the Question of Ethnicity." *Massachusetts Review* 31.1/2 (Spring 1990): 153–84. Print.

———. "Shifting Realities: An Interview." With Barbara Sternberg. *Tessera* 13 (Winter 1992): 43–63. Print.

———. "Writing from the Border: Gail Scott on 'The Main.'" *Gail Scott: Essays on Her Works.* Ed. Lianne Moyes. Toronto: Guernica, 2002. 117–41. Print.

Godard, Barbara, and Louise Cotnoir, eds. *Tessera* 13 (Winter 1992). Print.

Guy, Chantal. "Le monde à dos Daigle." Rev. of *Un fin passage. La Presse* September 23, 2001: B3. Print.

Gyurcsik, Margareta. "Regards croisés sur l'Europe et l'Acadie: *1953* de France Daigle." *L'émergence et la reconnaissance des études acadiennes: à la rencontre de soi et de l'autre.* Ed. Marie-Linda Lord (with the collaboration of Mélanie Le Blanc). Moncton: Association internationale des études acadiennes, 2004. 59–70. Print.

Heller, Monica. *Linguistic Minorities and Modernity: A Sociolinguistic Ethnography.* London: Longman, 1999. Print.

Kellett-Betsos, Kathleen. "Histoire et quête identitaire dans *1953: Chronique d'une naissance annoncée* de France Daigle." *Métamorphoses et avatars littéraires dans la francophonie canadienne.* Ed. Louis Bélanger. Vanier: L'Interligne, 2000. 35–47. Print.

Leblanc, Gérald. *Moncton Mantra.* Moncton: Perce-Neige, 1997. Print.
———. *Moncton Mantra.* Trans. Jo-Anne Elder. Toronto: Guernica, 2001. Print.
Leblanc, Gérald, and Claude Beausoleil. *La poésie acadienne.* 1988. Moncton/ Trois-Rivières: Perce-Neige/Écrits de Forges, 1999. Print.
Leclerc, Catherine. "L'Acadie rayonne. Lire France Daigle à travers sa traduction." *France Daigle.* Ed. Jean Morency. Spec. issue of *Voix et images* 29.3.87 (Spring 2004): 85–100. Print.
———. *Des langues en partage? Cohabitation du français et de l'anglais en littérature contemporaine.* Montreal: XYZ, 2010. Print.
———. Interview with France Daigle, July 2009.
Levasseur, Jean. "La réception de la littérature acadienne au Québec depuis 1970." *Les relations entre le Québec et l'Acadie. De la tradition à la modernité.* Ed. Fernand Harvey and Gérard Beaulieu. Québec/Moncton: Éditions de l'IQRC (Presses de l'Université Laval)/Éditions d'Acadie, 2000. 237–59. Print.
Morency, Jean, ed. *France Daigle.* Spec. issue of *Voix et images* 29.3.87 (Spring 2004). Print.
Moyes, Lianne. "Conflict in Contiguity: An Update." *Textes, territoires, traduction: (dé)localisations/dislocations de la littérature anglo-québécoise.* Ed. Lianne Moyes and Gillian Lane-Mercier. Spec. issue of *Québec Studies* 44 (Fall 2007/ Winter 2008): 1–20. Print.
———. Interview with Élisabeth Nardout-Lafarge and Patrick Poirier, spring 2009.
———. "'To bite the bit between the teeth': Lola Lemire Tostevin's Bilingual Writing Practice." *Translation Studies in Canada* 5 (1994): 75–83. Print.
Paré, François. "La distance d'ici à Québec." *Revue de l'Université de Moncton* 30.1 (1997): 5–17. Print.
———. *La distance habitée.* Ottawa: Nordir, 2003. Print.
———. *Les littératures de l'exiguïté.* Ottawa: Nordir, 1992. Print.
———. "Systems of Tradition and Pluralism in Contemporary Acadia." TransCanada 3. Mount Allison University. July 17, 2009. Keynote address.
Probyn, Elspeth. *Outside Belongings.* New York: Routledge, 1996. Print.
Richard, Chantal G. "Déconstruction de la langue ou construction d'une norme chiaque? La langue inachevée dans les romans de Jean Babineau et France Daigle." *L'œuvre littéraire et ses inachèvements.* Ed. Janine Gallant, Hélène Destrempes, and Jean Morency. Montreal: Groupéditions, 2007. 239–48. Print.
Saint-Hilaire, Mélanie. "Je suis manière de *proud* de toi." *L'Actualité* 27.3 (March 1, 2002): 66–68. Print.
Toonder, Janet Den. "L'acte créateur et l'espace littéraire dans l'autofiction de France Daigle (*La beauté de l'affaire, 1953* et *Pas pire*)." *Relief* 3.1 (2009): 77–94. Web. December 10, 2010. <http://www.revue-relief.org/index.php/relief/article/view/411/548>.
Tostevin, Lola Lemire. *Frog Moon.* Toronto: Cormorant Books, 1994. Print.
———. *Kaki.* Trans. Robert Dickson. Sudbury: Prise de parole, 1997. Print.

Chapter 6
A Lack of Public Memory: A Public Memory of Lack

PHANUEL ANTWI

(For Robert Nii Odarty Lamptey: 1920–2010)

In the summer of 2008, while sitting in the archives at the Hamilton Public Library, slowly sifting through the folders I had requested on textile companies in Canada West during 1830 to 1860, I happened upon a folder that was disturbingly out of place.[1] The archivist had mistakenly brought me a folder containing newspaper clippings of KKK demonstrations in the vicinity at a later period, from the 1920s to 1950s. This archive of images—newspaper clippings of Klansmen marching through Hamilton's James Street North on horses (Figure 6.1); again, on foot, marching through Hamilton's King Street West (Figure 6.2); a gathering of two-hundred-plus Hamiltonians watching a cross burn on the mountain (Figure 6.3); and a record of newspaper clippings with headings such as "KKK May Be Wooing High School Students"—shocked me out of my daze. My skin jumped. I flexed my spine to sit upright. Gathering myself, I wore a smile to press down any discomfort.

This experience of "archival jolt" (Bishop 36) was a reminder of the importance of remaining alert to serendipity, to chance associations in research. What archival logic would catalogue textile companies and the KKK together? What was this unwanted fortune, this "terrible gift" (Simon 187) bestowed on me in this arbitrary way? But if the jolt was to become what Ted Bishop calls "a portal to knowledge and ... an assurance that [one has] connected with something real" (36), it seemed to me it would also require

Figure 6.1: Members of the Ku Klux Klan marching south on James Street past the Lister Building, around 1930. (*Source:* Hamilton Public Library, Local History & Archives)

me to consider my own shock and discomfort, and hence the availability of the affective, of *feeling*, as another such "portal to knowledge." As I held a photocopy of the images with my sweaty palms, I felt anxious, energized; I spun in different directions; I wondered how to move beyond this mixture of shock-disgust-voyeuristic pleasure. What should I do with my bodily sensations, these affective entanglements, and how could they become the basis for theorizing out from "accident," from apparent "exception," toward an exploration of the wider "structure of feeling" that this KKK activity may have been part of?

In this essay, I take these traces of KKK activity in southern Ontario as my starting point and attempt to move across what has been constituted as a negative space, a public memory of relative absence or lack, in order to gesture at how a history of anti-black feeling in southern Ontario might need to proceed. I do not claim to be illuminating negative space; the archive does not yield a coherent body of "evidence" for this history of affect. Connections must be drawn against the grain of pedagogies of public memory, which distance Ontario from such excessive performances of hatred and denigration, and against the grain of disciplined knowledges that

Figure 6.2: Members of the Ku Klux Klan marching west on King Street West, sometime about 1930. (*Source:* Hamilton Public Library, Local History & Archives)

determine legitimate comparisons and relationalities, so not every stage of my argument is ratified by the archive and the memory that it makes available through its evidence. I move through a public memory of lack by examining materials around its edges, which do not so much overturn the truth of this memory as point to some of the means by which this truth has been produced and maintained. Drawing connections between the documented KKK demonstrations and other rituals of racial abuse in Ontario history, including the performances of the Loyal Orange Lodge (commonly referred to as the Orange Order), and the tradition of blackface minstrelsy at two elite educational institutions, I recast feeling as a portal to knowledge, as a different order of archival truth claims, and examine what that means in terms of documentation, linkages, by looking at traces, testimonies, of different kinds around the edges of this negative space of public memory. Here lies the paradox in my essay. On the one hand, I have the accident of the file coming to me in the archive, which leads me down a path of working with other archival documents, part of a positive history of documentation. On the other hand, I have to follow the lead of something quite other, something that is not necessarily available in this positive, material form, and that is affect. It seems, then, that I am doing a history of feeling, which is also a history of how a negative space/public memory of lack came to be constructed.

Figure 6.3: Ku Klux Klan burn a fiery cross on the mountain in Hamilton. (Source: Hamilton Public Library, Local History & Archives)

In my bringing together affect and archival material as a way to understand the immediate and the historical feelings of anti-blackness, I have been inspired by the new scholarship on affect to explore these feelings as products of unfinished work. Scholars like Sara Ahmed, Ann Cvetkovich, Lauren Berlant, Raymond Williams, Elizabeth Povinelli, José Esteban Muñoz, Heather Love, and many others working in the field of affect studies have convincingly drawn connections between individual feelings and social structures such as racism, diaspora, homophobia, highlighting the "affective elements of consciousness and relationships: not feelings against thought, but thought as felt and feeling as thought: practical consciousness of a present kind, in a living and interrelating continuity" (Williams 132). For example, in his study *Marxism and Literature*, Raymond Williams introduces the concept "structure of feeling" to explain the connections and coalitions between working-class groups, generated by shared values and practices that are "in process" yet, at the same time, historically situated. As Williams explains, the concept is chiefly "concerned with meanings and values as they are actively lived and felt" (132). As such, these structures are "social experiences in solution, as distinct from other social semantic formations which have been precipitated and are more evidently and more immediately available" (134).

Barbara Godard's insistence that we always work comparatively, that we position local cultural production in relation to a geopolitical space, suggests an answer to why, in this essay, these cultural practices would be grouped together. Over the years, Godard called on literary critics in the Canadian contexts to, first, move the work of comparative Canadian studies from literatures to a broader sense of cultural production, but also from the intra-national (Canadian) comparison to hemispheric comparisons. What this methodology unsettles is our habits of "intra-national" comparison in Canadian literary criticism, even in Canadian historiography—and, as my essay will suggest, the interprovincial comparisons can serve self-congratulatory histories, can construct alibis or "worse cases," just as the cultural habit of comparing Canada to the United States, in terms of race politics, constructs an aura of relative Canadian innocence. Therefore, instead of comparing/contrasting Ontario and the "West," I am focusing on the filament that links them; instead of comparing Canada to the United States (abolitionist Ontario to the slave-owning, racist United States or to the American South—those kinds of comparisons), I am looking at Ontario as a node in a wider imperial field of the Americas.

Relational logic, as Godard demonstrates, is "a project to relate" ("Relational Logics" 357). In laying out her argument, she recalls the Summit of the Americas and the North American Free Trade Agreement (NAFTA) as examples of mediations that shape the scope of cross-border contacts and transnational economic and political agreements. Certainly, Godard remarks, these transnational quasi-judicial mechanisms go "beyond those of commodity exchange," inevitably serving as opportunities for "new forms of hemispheric governance" and foregrounding ways in which "exchanges are also taking place in cultural fields where the work of symbolic mediation gives shape to verbal and visual representations of these new economic and social relations" (319). What interests me is the way in which the logic of relationality champions a mode of relatedness that "foreground[s] troubled relations to community, the uncertainty of social cohesiveness, in terms of ethical or psychical disturbances" (325), and, as a result, offers "different logics of cultural contact through which to give symbolic force to the 'territorial stretch' of a hemispheric imaginary" (357). While the logic of comparison carries denotation of contrast and plays up difference, the logic of relationality "propose[s] different forms of identification for subjects and favour[s] different axes of relations" (326). In other words, one finds in the relational logic that there is a "clash over how to represent the social imaginary" (325). Drawing, for example, on the metaphors of "borderline, Babel, or anthropophagy" as they are used to manage diversity in art productions in Canada and Brazil, Godard "abandons such binary relations between centre and periphery" to argue that the relational logic in "the Americas" demands a "search for different grounds for comparison." These comparisons must, on the one hand, be "in favour of transversal or horizontal relations among the peripheral literatures of the Americas," and, on the other, be in favour of "analysis of the processes of mediation at work in such *trans-actions*" (317; emphasis in the original). The claim made by Godard is that we look more closely at the ways in which the Americas, "a new transnational order[,] proposes greater integration among the nations of the Americas" (318). By this Godard declares, in effect, a study of culture and cultural products—including, but not limited to, literature, art, media, language, etc.—that engage in contextual and relational analytical constructions. This study, in her view, must carry out a de-stratified analysis with a range of methods and approaches.

Godard's articulation prepares us to think on a scale of affective charges across the Americas, driving us to record this geographical location as a method, even a geographical heuristic model, a "field of interpretation" ("Relational Logics" 320) that highlights the interconnected and violent foundational histories and informs the "representations of contact and exchange that circulate in the Americas" (318). In this elastic configuration of the Americas, difference and relationality announce "a new hemispheric imaginary," "in part a tightening of continental ties" (318, 321), reminding us of how people, ideas, organizations, and commodities move across borders quickly, if not always easily. Within this interpretive field of the Americas, these movements "propos[e] differential logics and politics of exogamic relations" (318), which, Godard notes, are "key to the discursive formation of the Americas" (322).[2] Indeed, then, my appeal to connect the Orange Order, the KKK, and blackface minstrelsy is not simply a belated response or a causal argument, but mainly a way to argue that the racial feelings generated by these disparate groups and cultural practices co-produce and co-shape each other in the Americas. As I work to think through "the power/knowledge nexus" that, as Godard argues in another essay about "realigning geopolitical identities," "cut[s] and mark[s] the boundaries of inside and outside" ("Deterritorializing" 171, 161, 171), my central argument is that these disparate groups and practices manifest deployments of racial sensation and affect and that it is these feelings that tie the KKK, the Orange Order, and blackface minstrelsy together in a common (micropolitical) strategy of power or organization of power relations.

A useful way to begin, then, is to outline the transnational reach of my three objects of analysis. In sight and sound, minstrelsy forms part of the culture of industry of the transatlantic imaginary; the Orange Order has been described as spreading through the British Empire; and the KKK has been described as an "Invisible Empire." In addition to the global mobility and sociality of these cultural groups and practices, they also circulate (uncomfortable) emotions, and the emotional work that they collectively shape and produce can be read, following Sara Ahmed's work on emotion as economy, as a form of capital (45). As raw materials (capital), these racial feelings circulate to integrate the Americas. In this essay, I explore the negative affect of anti-black feelings in relation to these cultural practices; that is to say, I explore blackness within the sites of "negative" affective economies, sites where the racial fantasy and racial hatred, and their resulting violence, are performed. I do so because I have come to understand that racial "feeling calls attention to a real social experience and a certain kind of historical truth" (Ngai 5); that black "[c]ultural knowledge is stored in a variety of institutional forms" (Freedgood 23); that the very representational formulas that degenerate blackness or render it invisible or unintelligible, that deny black historicity, yield black history.

Historian Alan Bartley draws attention to a prevalent short-sightedness in KKK scholarship in Canada, which has neglected to examine Ontario's chapter of the Klan. He begins by asking why the Klan became a political force in Saskatchewan but not in Ontario and offers this "hypothesi[s]": "the robust Imperial, British and Orange culture of 1920s Ontario was a barrier to political action the Klan could not overcome" (157). According to Bartley, the Orange Order and its sensibility took the place of the KKK in Ontario, or the kind of sentiment mobilized by the Orange Order might otherwise have found expression in the form of KKK rituals. In other words, the local political conditions in Ontario stood in the way of the Klan. In a passing hint in a footnote, Bartley writes that both Martin Robin and Julian Sher, in their important studies of the formation of the KKK in Canada, fail to "examine in any depth the reasons for the Klan's lack of success in Ontario" (170f).[3] I take up Bartley's phrase, "the Klan's lack of success in Ontario," as a worthwhile provocation for at least two reasons. First, given the Klan's campaign of intimidation toward racialized groups, the language of lack not only flattens out its fascistic history, but it also blocks reflection on and investigation of the material evidence of the Klan's success. Second, the language of lack is symptomatic of the hegemonic explanatory formulas of concealment, omission, and derision, which continue to consign blackness in Canada to a field of oblivion. Because this expression of lack is located within the hegemonic common sense of what Antonio Gramsci terms "the national popular," it submerges and tidies away the perplexities of racial terror out of the provincial and national popular and, for this reason, produces an attitude and a history of black lack, of black absence, and relatedly of the absence of anti-black feeling. But in this essay, I am more interested in the history of black presence in Canada and in the history of derision, of feeling, and that as *part of* black history, *part of* what sketches the contours of black existence in Canada historically.

Notwithstanding the local insights that Bartley's situated readings offer regarding the joint grip of the Conservative Party and the Orange Order on the political and social life of Ontario, understanding that restraint is a respectable, culturally valued emotional state, one that is in accordance with the greater sense of order of Ontario society, allows us to engage the KKK documentations, the Orange Order, and blackface minstrelsy as infrastructures of anti-black feelings in Ontario and to highlight them as civilizing processes marked by emotional restraint. The privileging of such restraint is a crucial move within the system of distinction, one that allows for Ontario decorum, or civility, explains the absence of a history of showy, embarrassing racism like that in Saskatchewan, or the southern United States, as the story goes (in the strategic comparisons). And, while my feelings in the archive and the archival documentations all go against the controlling perception of Ontario civility, restraint is also linked, through inversion, to another thread in my essay and that is the theatricality, ritualism, performative nature of my object of analysis: KKK rituals, the Orange tradition of parades, and minstrelsy as a stage tradition.

Telling in Bartley's assertion of lack is a tension between the "knowledge [that] is produced" in the body of his essay and "what escapes in the unfolding" of his argument (Cixous 527). The articulation of the Klan's lack of success in Ontario, through a "narrative of analogy," "re-cover[s]" the racial abuse and hatred of Ontario's past (Godard, "Deterritorializing" 163). The sequence in Bartley's analogy, the one concerning the Orange Order explaining the Klan's failure to succeed, undermines the (con)sequences in that failure. The language of lack conceals, even contains, the violence of the Klan's mere presence—that is to say, it explains away the affective aspects of what might be called an aesthetic politics of race. If we adopt a materialist reading and assert that the white cotton hoods bear stains of racial atrocity, and, as Paul Gilroy suggests about the glamour of fascism, that as visual markers of communication (commercializing intimidation and anti-black feelings) they articulate a form of "'aestheticization' and 'theatricalization' of politics" (150), then what aesthetic perceptions might emerge when we invite hermeneutic attention to the racial feelings elicited by the swastikas, the white cotton hoods, and the burnt cork? The public practices of the theatrical shows, the Klan marches, and the Orange parades? How do these iconographies and forms of theatricality of race secure the links between aesthetic and anti-black feelings? The key point I want to make is that the KKK, the Orange Order, and blackface minstrelsy are all public performances; they have to do with different kinds of public space, demarcating it, staking claim to it for white Ontarians. As a result, the apparent "lack of success" of a particular group, the KKK, measured in quantitative terms by historians like Bartley, comes up against a different kind of evidence, the traces of these public practices that shaped spaces, identities, territories of belonging, entitlement, fear.

This idiom of lack argues along two official and legitimate pathways of comparison that must be critically examined: on the one hand, morally superior Canada versus a United States contaminated by racist violence and, on the other, restrained Ontario versus a redneck "West." This celebration, at once mediated by the binary of Canada with the United States, *and*, in the context of this essay, Ontario with Saskatchewan, is, following Eva Mackey, "[t]he constant attempt to construct an authentic, differentiated, and bounded identity [that] has been central to the project of Canadian nation-building, and is often shaped through comparison with, and demonisation of, the United States" (145). According to Mackey, this is a "kind of 'strategic essentialism' based upon particular images of Canada as victim" (12). Though Mackey is accurate in saying that the "[t]he construction of Canada as a gendered body, victimized by external and more powerful others, creates a fiction of a homogenous and unified body, an image that elides the way the Canadian nation can victimize internal 'others' on the basis of race, culture, gender or class" (12), Bartley's argument, which is shaped through comparison, underscores an asymmetry between Ontario and Saskatchewan KKK chapters, introducing the long tradition of regionalist resentment within Canada, which is as powerful a fiction as is national homogeneity. The imagining of this lack gains support from the way Ontario, as part of its provincial attractions,[4] marks the "Underground Railway" as a sign of its abolitionist past, its morally superior past, framing Ontario as a place to seek refuge.[5]

On Ontario's lack, Robin writes, "[f]or the most part, Ontario Klansmen restricted themselves to practicing queer rituals, burning an occasional cross, staging an odd meeting in odd dress, and spreading, through the spoken and written word, the gospel of white, Protestant, gentile, Canada" (13). On the surface, the attribution of restraint to Ontario Klansmen supports Bartley's argument "that Klan organizers were up against leading members of the Ontario legal and police establishment" (162). However, Robin's adjectives—"queer," "odd," signifying in its repetition strange and exceptional, i.e., rare, did not happen here—are also saying the KKK did spread its "gospel," whereas Bartley has said the KKK was not "successful" in doing so. Here lies the contradiction in Robin's statement. He seems to begin by emphasizing "restricted," "odd," uncommon rituals, but his statement ends by suggesting a wide dispersal. If they were so odd, why did they have the capacity to spread the gospel? Is Robin laying the emphasis on the fact that the spreading happened through the spoken and written word rather than the rituals? He seems to emphasize the oddness and excess of the KKK rituals, and one might argue that his language here performs the Ontarian "restraint" that he is describing.

While the bizarre rituals of the Klan are in a sense a parody of blackness (as "tribal," "primitive," Big Other), the distance between Ontario and Saskatchewan is used to mark difference at the same time that it is used as a marker of lack. Consequently, the over-there workings of the Klan are also used to determine what constitutes success here. To put it simply, lack of success becomes the work of numbers, a quantitative historical analysis, as suggested by Bartley's question at the end of his essay: "What was there in the Klan's political agenda which was not already within reach of the Tory-Orange axis? In truth very little" (170). Bartley seems to be suggesting that if the Orange Order was a "barrier" to KKK "success," it is because of their similar values—that is why they were competitors, why it was one or the other that would "succeed." For Bartley, the Orange culture took hold more than the KKK not because the values were different but because the expressive style was. Orange culture in Ontario, he writes, "offered something the Klan could not—legitimacy." Continuing, "the Lodge was a bastion of respectability in 1920s Ontario. The KKK was not, and it offered no prospects of ever coming close. The whiff of criminality associated with the Klan ensured that it would run afoul of the established order and prevailing prejudices" (158). Bartley notes that the Orange Order did not need the Klan to institutionalize xenophobia, anti-black, and anti-Catholic sentiments.

Aside from Bartley assuming a certain affective code in Ontario that is different from Saskatchewan, also notice that lack is created in parallel to other narratives (the Orange Order's success). And yet, what escapes and/ or is at work in this discourse of lack is the political desire and power that the Klan attempts to harness, namely, white supremacy and one of its main constitutional principles, anti-blackness. From this perspective, what is overlooked or, to use Cixous's words, what is negligible in the argument of "lack," by which failure is attributed to the Klan's political actions in Ontario, is a produced forgetfulness of the fact that the Klan is itself a political system, one that publicly exercises terror (Figure 6.2).

Critical attempts to reason away how local politics affected the Klan's supposed "lack of success" in Ontario underscore questions of methodology. It is also noteworthy that Saskatchewan is *the* selected province to which Ontario is compared because, again and again, the diverse academic disciplines conducting scholarship on the KKK in Canada depict Saskatchewan (in the 1920s) as the place where the Klan reached the height of its influence (Backhouse; Bartley; Robin; Sher; Walker). Why, on the question of the Klan, does one engage in an interprovincial comparison when the KKK is an empire committed to extending its invisible filaments beyond the borders of law and order? And what else do we learn from this comparison? In contrast to the interprovincial comparative history of Bartley and other critics, a more revealing comparison might require attention to the incorporation (i.e., affiliations, location-inclusions, and inscriptions) of Klan culture and domination into what might be called the North American quadrant of the Americas, with South America, Central America, and the Caribbean as the remaining geographical quadrants of the Americas. Other kinds of comparisons can include an examination of how Klansmen moved with the western frontiers of North America, first primarily across the United States and eventually into the western plains of Canada. This means that while examining the transnational dynamics that enable KKK migration and the national forces that militate against it, one might also notice how Ontario's chapter of the Klan illuminates the trans-regional formations across the Americas. In this light, I propose Godard's concept of "relational logic," a formulation used to examine "the re-invention of the Americas," as a useful rubric for rethinking the racial transactions that these critics cross-compare. In fact, it allows us to see these disparate political formations as tapping into a common strategy of power.

Stamped in a second edition of the *Kloran: Knights of the Ku Klux Klan*, the KKK's handbook, a revealing apologetic/justificatory note (dated March 1, 1928) shows how the over-determined difference that Bartley's comparative logic engenders overlooks the Klan's unmappable *ripple effect/affect*. The note, signed by the "Imperial Wizard" in Regina, Saskatchewan, reads:

> To Exalted Cyclops and all Klansmen: —
>
> This is the Official Kloran of the Invisible Knights of the Ku Klux Klan. To avoid delay these books were ordered from Toronto from the same printer who had the order for the Klan in the East. The order as originally given did not domicile headquarters of the Klan and the name was not to be printed but when the proof was checked this was put in and when we purchased the books we did not know of said change. (6)

This note highlights an economic exchange across provinces *from* Toronto, Ontario, *to* Regina, Saskatchewan, and affirms the inseparability of ideology and politics in economics (the Klan chapters of "the East," i.e., southern Ontario, all use the same Toronto printer). The exchange, given its direction, is as much a trade, a commodity exchange, as a political one. The Klan in Toronto, at the very least, succeeds politically and economically in printing these books, acting as the Canadian source for the dissemination of KKK ideology. Fulfilling an "order" not only marks an ability to succeed, but also suggests that the Klan in Ontario played a role (however in/significant) in Saskatchewan's success.[6] The point is that relational logic serves as an effective approach to seek nuanced methods not only to foreground the Klan chapters in Ontario with their distinctive regional patterns and as part of overlapping social movements in the Americas, but also to note that the printer, as a powerful engine for disseminating Klan ideas, served as a colonial administrator, a vital link to the world, spreading the ideological, political, and administrative purpose of the Invisible Empire. I liken the printer to a colonial administrator to emphasize that each seeded and sold an image of the empire as, in the case of the KKK, "Not for self but for others" (*Kloran* 46), and achieved this by exercising control over the circulation of people and ideas. Hence, to say that imagining the Klan in Ontario is connected to other geopolitical spaces in the broader Americas is to think of Ontario as one province in a hemispheric imaginary. In other words, I seek to position Ontario with its racial feelings as a concern and a participant in the shared affective exchange *with/in* the Americas.

To appreciate this move to include Ontario in hemispheric conversations, and to position it as a province of transcontinental proportion, it might help to turn to the very organization that Bartley and other critics say blocked the Klan's success in Ontario, the Orange Order. Given that the Orange Order spread along with the British Empire (as a way to legitimize its political integrity), the social history of Orange culture insists on its transnational character (Akenson; Bartley; Houston and Smyth; Jenkins;

Kaufmann; Wilson). In fact, taking stock of this insistent collaboration, the mobility and settlement of Orange culture in Ontario underscores processes of encounters, competition, and solidarity, together with the circulation of emotions and ideas. As it circulates through the Atlantic world, the Orange culture of some Irish immigrants exports into Ontario the ideology of conservatism and anti-Catholic sentiments at the same time as it focuses on creating a pro-British and pro-Empire Protestant association or institution. This is to say that the circulation of Orange culture through the colonies makes the Orange Order a diaspora that is as concerned with religion and politics as it is with embedding racial fear in the spaces it impacts.

Pierre Bourdieu's influential work *Distinction: A Social Critique of the Judgement of Taste* (1984), the work on the sociological account of aesthetics, is helpful in articulating the Orange Order's capacity for affecting the racial feelings in Ontario. I note that a disarticulation of the Orange Order and the negative racial feelings it effected in Ontario establishes a system of "distinction" between the elite cultural field of the Order and non-elitist cultural organizations such as the KKK, giving weight to the claim that class distinction provides an alibi that Ontario was too refined to be a terrain for the KKK. Of course the social capital of Ontario as a significant station of the Underground Railway encourages many to see Ontario as different from other provinces and to distinguish the Order from the KKK. However, the aesthetics of the parades that each group mobilized questions this strategy of distinction and points to their relational cultural capital. The KKK and the Orange Order rituals are, in both cases, performative rituals that intimidate, provoke, and stake claims to space, to ownership of space. Their public, theatrical aspect is a really good way of insisting on their *in*distinctness. As popular public events, the parades animate a field of social relations and become occasions for inclusivity. They rarely fail to attract a crowd and to evoke a host of emotions in that crowd (see Figure 6.1). However, where they allow for play-acting and masked performance, where the large gatherings offer an effective façade of cohesion thus augmenting, anonymously, the power of the collective, where one can overturn or do without many sanctioned behaviours, the Orange parade (with its Protestant background) and Klan marches are occasions for legitimizing white exclusivity. In this relational logic of exclusion, of mutually supporting and operating within the same fields of affect, of ripple affects, the KKK and the Order operate with a divisive force, threatening the lives of Catholics, French, and racialized people. Understanding that this extra-legal activity forms part of Orange memory in Ontario is also to understand that the

Orange Order operated in an extra-legal space, one that afforded it the authority to impose its own kind of morality and bring its own kind of order to unconnected events.

Racial hatred was not limited to lower-class street parades orchestrated by the Orange Order, but went on in the halls of the most elite, exclusive institutions, like St Andrew's College and Upper Canada College (UCC), where the upper class sent their sons to be properly trained to take on leadership roles in society. And just as the Orange Order was a transnational institution, so was minstrel performance. Some of these undertones may perhaps be located in the historical reality of blackface minstrel performances at St. Andrew's and UCC, "the school [that] serves as a powerful beacon of the Canadian Establishment" (FitzGerald xvii). Both St. Andrew's College and UCC are cultural sites that work to expand the cultural references for the anti-black feelings that are etched in the cultural space of Ontario. The October 1889 issue of *The College Times*, UCC's yearbook, ran an editorial gladly endorsing "a letter from one of the old boys" who was protesting the cancellation[7] of its annual minstrel show, the entertainment that "has taken place for such a number of years that its origin cannot be traced," and that has provided "so many pleasurable associations." The Old Boy urges that "with a little restraint it could still be made into a really first class entertainment, and in every respect worthy of the name of the U.C.C. Minstrels" (12). The editorial note that accompanied the letter cries: "It seems too bad that we cannot have some enjoyment at Christmas" (11). What is involved in this publicly performative citing of a cherished, even fetishized past is not only an anxious process of linking enjoyment and identity to justify the complicity of a ritualized memory but also a governing logic of entertainment on which to link minstrel performance to the wider terrain of anti-black feeling in Ontario. In one way, the valuation used to bolster the appeal for its continuation hinges on a kind of unknowability—"its origins cannot be traced"—suggesting that the nostalgic tone, masked as an "ingrained habituation" (Weber 25), reaches beyond habituation to reproduce an unequal field of social relations. I contend that the Old Boy's suggestion to promote "restraint" in the face of impending racial conflicts not only supports a climate of anti-black sentiments, but also drives us to note how whites are marked by it, how they enjoy through it.

In the December 1889 issue, a second editorial, from another Old Boy denouncing the cancellation of UCC's annual minstrel show, appeared under the headline "The Merry Minstrels." He writes, "[i]t seems too bad that so many of the old customs have been abolished. This goes to show that the old spirit of the College, that College which has built up such a reputation for herself, appears to be dying out. Old boys will remember," he goes on to write, "the minstrels, in which every boy felt himself interested *with a longing desire to hear the jokes upon the other boys*" (20; emphasis added). Worth noting here is how displacement, disguise, permits the unsayable, permits transgressive speech. And the enjoyment of intimacy between the boys is linked through this citation, this mask of otherness. Later he remembers:

> After the minstrels we all retired with the feeling that we had [spent] a most enjoyable evening. Now, what have the present pupils to look forward to on that evening? Nothing! I hear that some objection was made to some parts of last year's minstrels. Could not the parts to which objection is made at the rehearsals be omitted? I think that with proper management the minstrels could be made into a very fine entertainment and would again be looked forward to with as much pleasure by the present pupils as they were by the boys in my time. (Old Boy, 20)

Stephen Johnson has pointed out that "without question, minstrel show was the entertainment of choice in North America from the 1840s through the 1870s" (58). Given the popularity of minstrelsy in this quadrant of the Americas, of the desires and feelings of experiences of spectators at nineteenth-century minstrel shows, Eric Lott astutely notes that this theatrical form "captured an antebellum structure of racial feeling" (6). In Canada West, Patrick O'Neill notes performances of *Uncle Tom's Cabin* at Toronto's Royal Lyceum in 1853, 1854, 1856, and 1860 (qtd. in Johnson 56). As a result, minstrelsy "increasingly routinized white familiarity with black culture" (Lott 48), and it is these experiences of minstrel pleasure and identification that, I believe, motivate the Old Boys to bother to write. But from what affectations do they fear the prohibition will distance "the [new] boys"? As I concern myself with the role the minstrel shows played in the socialization of these Boys, especially in how they got their enjoyment, I also concern myself with the racial entitlement that reinforces *and* preserves a commodified blackness, not to mention a white racial consciousness. While the editors and the Old Boys avoid (disavow) responsibility for the racialized representations that caricature blackness by minimizing the cultural work of the objectionable parts, and while it is worth noting again that we do not actually know what was objectionable, these Boys, at the same time, depend on such representations for their personal enjoyment, suggesting the minstrel show is not so different from the KKK march and the Orange parade. The disavowal opens space for an escape from responsibility, situating the letters as expressing more than mere denials. In fact, what each of the Old Boys sees as a denial of enjoyment portrays a series of attachments to the object of enjoyment (blackface minstrel shows), illuminating a link between transnational commodity and Ontario as a place of white masculine subject formation. The cultural practice of blackface minstrelsy is part of the social relations that support the formation of this intersubjective identity.

In a 1907 cartoon for the *College Times*, we experience how race organizes visual pleasure in the form of a blackfaced/minstrelized cartoon (Figure 6.4). Taking the illustration to be advertising a show at the college, it is an advertisement for a promise of a certain kind of affect, of intimacy. Moreover, as advertisement, this illustration creates an aura of desirability around the minstrel show, the product. And, of course, the illustration is itself a commodity that, in this instance, enhances forms of social exchange. Therefore, presented to be looked at, dressed in black jacket, black pants, white long-sleeved shirt, and an oversized necktie, the blackfaced cartoon is experienced through a mediation of structures of representation, including the structure of the orchestra, of entertainment, of advertisement, of audience, of visual art, of culture. I emphasize the word "structure" by way of indicating the breadth of services provided by the allegorical representations of the cartoon. The visual rhetoric of the minstrelized cartoon, with its ability to condense and compress black culture into a fetishized commodity, instantiates the genre of cartoon as an aid and medium for caricature and, as a result, draws our attention to the minstrelized cartoon as a *mise en abyme*. A visual medium for caricaturing (cartoon) is used to represent a caricatured culture (blackface minstrelsy). This mirroring or doubling underlines the pivotal role that the illustrated caricature played in normalizing the putting on of "race," as in the blackening of the face, which we come to observe being forcefully protected by the Old Boys in their letters. Therefore the cessation of the UCC minstrel shows disrupts the normalization of blackface minstrelsy, and the Old Boys' protests ground their identity formation in an intimate, long-term relationship with minstrel shows. At UCC, blackface minstrelsy seems to have provided a justification for transgressive speech acts, for a lifting of decorum and restraint that seem to have been deemed to have gone too far.

In the cartoon, the audience's encounter with minstrel spectacle also foregrounds its encounter with blackness as caricatured otherness, as associated with the promise of pleasure, of transgressive humour. Appearing

Figure 6.4: A blackfaced/minstrelized cartoon advertising a show at Upper Canada College (*Source:* Upper Canada College Special Archive)

still on the stage, with legs crossed, arms outstretched with fingers in white gloves, the facial expression on the blackfaced cartoon (widened eyes, downcast smile) accents an animation that, according to the write-up for the show, will "delight multitudes," including "theatre-goers." In the visual animation of the illustration, graphically signified by the sounds that the laughing audience makes, delight articulates a physical pleasure with bodily manifestation. This manifestation, the animation of the audiences' laughing heads, suggests minstrel sounds (and the sounds that the audience makes) matter.[8] So, far from being merely a visual encounter of caricatured blackness, the very soundings of popular minstrel songs activate and organize the psychic formations and drives of Ontario.

In 1920, K.B. Carson, a student of St. Andrew's College, invited his Uncle Josh, "a middle-aged, married-man and a church elder," to his school's first staged minstrel show. After the show, Uncle Josh, according to Carson's report in the *St. Andrew's College Review*, opined the following review: "The show's fine except there were too darn many niggers in it; the song 'Buy Low' should put the kibosh on the H.C.L., nobody could 'Buy High' after that" (21). For Carson's contemporary audience, the phrase "H.C.L." (high cost of living) carried meanings within the context of the Great War. That Uncle Josh draws on economic language to critique the show bears highlighting. Carson writes, "Uncle thought the minstrels were bricklayers with their white trousers, and even when I enlightened him, persisted in saying out loud to my great confusion, 'Well, they ought to be bricklayers anyways'" (20–21). Here Uncle implies that the minstrel show is a degrading spectacle that will affect taste, a crucial point since St. Andrew's College is an engine of class distinction and the enjoyment of "low" minstrelsy risks diminishing this class distinction, i.e., the ability to withstand a "high cost of living." It also thereby reduces class to a matter of buying power when the implication is that it should be about more solid sources of distinction, like good breeding. Notwithstanding, Uncle Josh, we learn from Carson, was "pleased and bestowed a dime upon [him] all at once" (21).

Given that the boys in St. Andrew's College Literary Society were, as far as I have been able to ascertain, all white, Uncle Josh's articulations of excess—"there were too darn many niggers in the show"—expresses a desire to escape the simulation of blackness. Here, the excess of black people is rather their very emptiness on stage. That is to say, the presence in the form of mimicry is also a statement about the impossibility of their real presence. And is it not the case that the mimicry, which distances, at the same time acknowledges a proximity that has to be managed? In fact, the UCC Old Boy claims that "with proper management the minstrels could be made into a very fine entertainment"—as if the problem is not one of racism but of mismanagement. He is not willing to sacrifice the minstrel show precisely because it enables the white management of race relations in Ontario, but it appears that the management techniques need fine-tuning. This moment of inversion, the presencing of absence, withdraws from the events of the present—from a group of white boys denigrating black culture and people—to enter a field of discourse that has long monitored black migration into Canada, as far back as the fugitive slaves who fled from south of the border, particularly in growing numbers after the passage of the Fugitive Slave Act of 1850. Uncle Josh's reading of emptiness as excess, then, needs to be thought together with Upper Canadian Chief Justice Sir John Beverly Robinson's 1837 fear "that Canada might become a refuge for criminal blacks" if fugitive slaves are not surrendered on legal grounds. To his belief, "there were already too many Negroes in Canada" (qtd. in Reinders 76). (How ironic that this later on, in the twentieth century, becomes the basis for cosmopolitan Ontario's self-promotion in terms of its "heritage of tolerance.") In addition to the repetitive anti-black tone held in common across generations, these quite similar expressions of white fear hauntingly bring to the fore a pattern of reducing racial proximity to a panic over space. While some may contend that the space of the nation and that of minstrel shows are quite different, I suggest we remove the protective capsule around each production to register how, as sites of culture, both narrate and calculate the place and space of blackness.

As a means of bringing the connection between these two realms into focus, let me turn again to the blackfaced cartoon. The cartoonist, J. (Joseph) Sheard, was a student at Upper Canada College from 1903 to 1907. According to the records, the *Roll of Pupils of Upper Canada College*, Joseph Sheard lived at the same address as another UCC alumni (from 1869 to 1870), Charles Sheard. Given the years each attended UCC, it is probable that Joseph Sheard, the cartoonist, was the son of Charles Sheard, the Orangeman. It is worth noting that Charles Sheard was also the son of another Joseph Sheard, the man who served as mayor of Toronto in 1871 and 1872. My genealogical tracings here use the object of the blackfaced cartoon to connect family ties and rely on kinship linkages to construct a relationship between the Orange Order and blackface minstrelsy. My interest is not to judge Charles Sheard's participation in the Orange Order. Rather, my point is first of all to underline the transnational flows in this geography of relations and, in so doing, to connect anti-black sentiment with both the Orange Order and the political establishment of Ontario.

Moreover, Joseph Sheard's illustration points to the affective and physical effort it takes to collapse distance, borders, limits, including bodies, between the audience and the commodity of minstrelsy. In this collapse lies a problem of excess requiring elimination, not address. The economies of reproduction, whereby "too darn many niggers" is continually re-articulated, function to regiment a house of memory (Ontario) that seeks to maintain itself in disposing of an excess that no longer has a place, and this is a response to the immanent pressures of the material world. A common concern that all of these groups seem so invested in is panic over space. The Orange Order is interested in policing neighbourhoods—separating Catholics and Protestants—in the same way that the Klan would seek to determine racial division of living space. This poetics of control is, in a sociological reality, what Michel Foucault, in tracing a genealogy of racism as an instrument of management for the state, characterizes a bio-political organization of space.

In my analysis so far, I have refused the illusion of discursive separability that works to structure disciplinary narratives. I have refused because the disciplined comparisons of Ontario versus the West, Upper Canada versus the United Kingdom, Canada versus the United States, provide alibis, habits of comparison that have to do with nationalist history, central Canadian memory, the idea of multicultural Canada emerging out of a history of tolerance. I maintain that discursive regimes, on their own, create epistemological gaps, thus it is important for those of us concerned with articulating the perplexities of life through modalities of race to rethink the connections between knowing and not knowing and, in rethinking this relation, to ask not only *what* we know about the racial violence in Ontario's past, but also *how* we have come to know this past.[9] These simple questions treat the past as a problematic site of query—problematic in the literal sense of the word: "that a state of affairs is possible rather than actual or necessarily so" (*OED*). This definition of problematic insists that the past is not as knowable and/or even a known quantity in itself. Rather, what we know and what we do not know are both regimes of knowing, explaining the importance of examining the conditions that make both possible.

Exactly how much political force the Klan exerted on the daily texture of social life in Ontario is, of course, a difficult empirical question. Therefore, to mark this force as "a failure, lack" overlooks the vulnerabilities to which we are differently subject. As an example, I turn to a living memory narrated by a black man in Dionne Brand and Krisantha Sri Bhaggiyadatta's *Rivers Have Sources* (1986), a book that archives, through oral narratives, the "random and institutional" ways in which racial oppression, as always present, always threatening, shape a "culture of everyday" racism that pervades the daily lives of racialized people in Canada (3, 8):

> We did not live that close together, we still lived separately. Blacks always lived separately. It was safer that way, you could disappear. If you had a community you could not disappear. We were always scared of the Ku Klux Klan. There was organized racist activity at the time. You had Orangemen, Masons, all of them.
>
> But they did not really need the Klan in those days. There was racism in the streets. It was just there. When we went to school we went through back streets and empty houses to get there and back. We did not go onto the main drag. We used to play in the rain. They would call us crazy. But it was safe in the rain, nobody else was out in the street. (151–52)

To be sure, the official absence of Jim Crow laws in Ontario in the1920s, 1930s, 1940s, and 1950s[10] did not mean black people were not *kept in their place*, nor did it mean that they were ignorant of the segregating and monitoring practices and institutions that governed their lives. In fact, from living under these governing practices, with their rituals of social control, of learning to avoid passing through visible zones of public spaces, of having to walk through *back streets* and *empty houses* in order to get to school and back, this particular respondent, born in 1918 in Toronto, is attuned to the socio-spatial dynamic at the heart of racial difference and, as a result, tunes us in on his everyday insecurities and the regimes of fear that shaped his life and the lives of many other black people around him.

Although the respondent's claim that "the Klan in those days [was] not really needed" sounds similar to Bartley noting the parallel values and principles of the Orange Order and the KKK, I maintain it is a different statement from Bartley's that the Klan was not successful because the fact that "there was racism in the streets" flags the emotionally charged space of the street for black people in the 1920s. This racist climate was a result of a synthesis of political forces, including "the Ku Klux Klan, the Orangemen, Masons, all of them" (to which I would add practices of blackface minstrelsy). My sense in this context is that the suturing of different political forces embedded the main drag with racial fear, in turn, patterning the scale of mobility through space for black bodies. This fear, as a mobilizing force, must then be acknowledged as a way of knowing and being in the physical space of the street. In fact, the geographical space of Ontario must be recognized as being made with racial fear, driving me to maintain that the fear felt by black people on the "main drag" is connected to the street as the parade ground for Orangemen and the KKK, and is thus irreducible to one political force.

It might be interesting to note a difference between Bartley's statement and the black respondent's, even where it seems they are making a similar observation about the Orange Order providing the fearful enforcement function in Ontario. Both locate this terrorizing affect in the precincts of a broadly legitimated and respected Ontario institution and, acknowledging a parallel between these institutions, insist that these racist principles (and their affects) were institutionalized in broadly accepted and admired and influential social organizations in Ontario. And yet, I have focused on the emotional geography of the street to demonstrate that the Klan was a political force and, as a result, to indicate how and why Bartley's assertion that "the Loyal Orange Lodge in Ontario's political culture was a major impediment to the growth of the Klan as a political force" (168) might be understood in another way. A difference worth noting in Bartley's and the black respondent's account of the relationship between the Klan and the Orange Order is how Bartley characterizes the relations as one of competition while the black respondent experienced them as working together. How, then, does this lived and remembered experience of fear amount to lack? I take cultural presence of the fear engendered by the KKK as further evidence of success. In this light, the language of lack is further understood as a language of racial silence, as white silence, silences *made*. Because Bartley's statement is ambiguous, it is possible for a "Canadian reader" who believes in a history of Klan absence in Ontario to read this as a positive affirmation of the racial history of the province. Also, the continued established place of the Orange Order in Ontario is not positioned on a par with the Klan, whereas the black respondent statement is less ambiguous in the parallel it draws between these institutions. This ambiguity can be strategic, reifying a public memory of lack as a doing, even a feeling ignored, not accounted for, making a public memory of lack a learned ignorance. What the autobiographical accounts of articulations between the Orange Order and the KKK by Brand and Sri Bhaggiyadatta's respondent allow is a moment of public visibility, of learning about lives and accounts that are otherwise inaccessible in the historical record.

Using the Orange Lodge and the Tory government of the 1920s as comparative referent points works as a strategy of official nationalist narratives to set Ontario apart from the work of hate and to suggest that that work is always brought into the province, not of the province. It reasserts and lends support to the national discourse of relegating black histories as happening elsewhere (Walcott 35). These comparing referents, therefore, overshadow the Klan's achievements by marking off its associations and, as a result, flattening out a set of intervening and cross-cutting points of reference. It is in this light that the Klan's political agenda alone cannot determine its lack of success nor mark its failure to succeed. As such, the political system of white supremacy is crucial, in particular the capacity to exercise dominance over others on the basis of difference, whether racial or religious. If we return to Bartley's contention that we should "not overstate the presence and impact of the Klan in Ontario," what grounds of inquiry does his warning steer us away from or to? Instead of being concerned with any overstatement, especially since overstatement gets us back to the calculus of quantity, positivist history, it might be time to think in more nuanced ways about that presence, and ask not only what political actions it achieved but also contend with the emotions that its presence elicited and, thereby, circulated.

By now it is fair to take us back to the archive, to remind us of the fact that the file came to me by accident, and the fact that it takes these accidents of archival research to get beyond the self-congratulatory kind of comparative history (official memory) to the kind of disruptive linkages I draw. So "accident" has some kind of relation to accessing affect and the history of affect. It gets us to feel where we really live. A public memory of lack averts our analytical gaze from recognizing the work that practices of anti-black feeling left behind. In addition to the affectively charged spaces, it leaves behind a cultural and discursive space of absence, of forgetfulness, of structural silence. This becomes a malleable cultural and spatial container in which to actively etch the racial and social violence in the remaking of Ontario. In other words, it leaves behind a public memory of lack. The paradox of lack is its memorializing apparatus. The phrase "a public memory of lack" highlights itself as a mechanism, a manager of memory. At the same time, it calls attention to the technocratic endeavour produced in the name of lack and the links between oblivion and commemoration. There is a way in which commemorative naming practices that aim to "correct" earlier mistakes have the effect of erasing historical identities through repetition, creating what anthropologist Evans-Pritchard terms a "structural amnesia," where the social order and memory correspond at the level of the provincial discourse, and obliterate other histories, in the name of a common course toward a national name. Therefore, memorializing lack by positioning the Klan, this invisible empire, as a failed empire, is an attempt to cohere public memory around Ontario's conservatism at the time, with its regressive attitude and policies toward race and, through this work of coherence, mediate the provincial inscription of its origin story.

Keeping in mind the role that this violent narrative plays in the civic memory, what happens to memories marginal to popular culture, excluded from the valued, usable past of the nation or, in this case, of the province? Turning again to the archival folder, you will remember that it is the Klansmen, the horses, and the white people who are archived. What is not represented is the *black* fear, the *black* anger, and the *black* resistance. Is there not an almost affective violence of history that remains to be accounted for and engaged with in the experience of the black Torontonian? Or, for that matter, does not my affective experience allow us to speak, as it were, to the lack, or to make the lack speak to us? I want to end by suggesting that there is a remnant of the lack that is actually materially present in the affective experience of many black Canadians, in my experience. In other words, it is less a question of the lack of success and more one concerning a lack of the lack of awareness of the affective makeup of this supposed lack. In some sense, my visceral reaction in the archive was a way of accessing this absence, this lack. Perhaps, my present-day feelings are somehow filling in the gap—*signifying the archive*—representing the unrepresented.

Notes

Though I take full responsibility for any mistakes and errors contained in this chapter, I am indebted to Riisa Walden, Amber Dean, Mauricio Martinez, Ron Cummings, Daniel Coleman, and Don Goellnicht for their invaluable insights and help on an earlier draft. I thank Eva C. Karpinski and Jennifer Henderson for their constructive editorial suggestions. I also thank Jennifer Henderson in particular for her continuing interest in and support of my work. My warmest thanks to the archivists I met while working on this piece for their professional help and generosity, especially Margaret Houghton and Laura Lamb at the Hamilton Public Library Local History & Archives, and Martha Tuff, the main archivist at Upper Canada College. Finally, I gratefully acknowledge the financial support of the Institute on Globalization and the Human Condition, which provided a grant for research and the writing of this chapter.

1   This essay was already completed when news unfolded of a former police officer, Blair Crowley, who, at a Halloween costume party organized by the Royal Canadian Legion in Campbellford, Ontario, dressed up in a "Ku Klux Klan outfit, trailing a noose-necked man in blackface" to "win first prize" at the party (Reinhart). In addition to the jarring correspondence between my essay and this current event, it is worth noting Mr. Crowley's understanding of the event. He says, "my outfit wasn't meant to be anything racist. I apologize if I offended anybody." According to the reporter, Mr. Crowley goes on to describe "the practice of Klan lynchings of black people" as a practice "'gone for years and years and years ...,'" a practice that he believes "'is so past-tense.'" Also worth noting are the descriptions of this event by Tad Seaborn, a former resident of Campbellford, who now lives in Toronto. He describes the incident as "'some rural, institutionalized ignorance, lack of education and life experience outside the local culture bubble'" (Reinhart). My point is to remind us that the dynamics of blackface minstrelsy and the work of the KKK are not events of the past; they continue to function as central organizing forces in the racial politics of Ontario.

2   Godard's hemispheric approach has a long-standing history. See José Julián Martí Pérez's "Our America" (1891); Hortense Spillers's edited collection, *Comparative American Identities: Race, Sex, and Nationality in the Modern Text* (1991), and particularly Spillers's introductory essay, "Who Cuts the Border? Some Readings on 'America.'" Although this volume deals with the United States in relation to the Caribbean and Central America, there is no mention of Canada. Godard's voice in this hemispheric conversation is important because Canada and Brazil, the two largest geographical territories in the Americas, remain peripheral in the literatures of hemispheric studies. So, when in "Relational Logic" she reads visual and textual representations by Brazilian and Canadian artists and writers, Godard is not only engaging in an inter-Americas study, she is also responding to under-examined localities and relations in the literature. Recently, see the work of Claudia Sadowski-Smith, *Globalization on the Line: Culture, Capital, and Citizenship at U.S. Borders* (2002) and *Border Fictions* (2008), which does take Canada into account.

3   His footnote brings to mind Hélène Cixous's comment on footnoting as "a typographical metaphor of repression which is always too near but nevertheless negligible" (537). The salience of race, which is overlooked by Bartley's measure of political action, forms part of this repression. I maintain that what is "too near but nevertheless negligible" is the success of white racism in wiping clean the historical-cultural slate upon which this work of lack is written, and through this gesture creating its own social space by avoiding the racial feelings that make up or organize Ontario. In this context, one can argue, lack is "colour-blind."

4   The following is how the online website of Ontario Tourism describes Ontario: "This area also figured prominently in the heroic story of the 'Underground Railroad.' Beginning in the 1820s, after the War of 1812 and before the American Civil War, thousands of refugee slaves made their way to this area seeking safety and a new life. Following 'The Road That Led to Freedom' will lead you to many historical sites in this area that commemorate this important period in North American history."

5   In an article on the Media Centre section on the website of Canadian Tourism Commission (CTC), a national tourism organization that, "in collaboration with the tourism industry, the governments of Canada, the provinces and the territories," is dedicated to promoting the Canadian tourism industry by "marketing" Canada as a desirable travel destination as well as providing accurate information to the industry, Cathy Stapells writes: "Underground Railroad communities exist throughout southern Ontario, extending from Windsor to Toronto and north from Fort Erie to Owen Sound, Thornbury and Barrie. Visitors can explore this dramatic aspect of Canada's past at 29 sites around the province, seven of which lie along Niagara's Freedom Trail in the Niagara/St. Catharines area."

I highlight the above quotation not to impugn CTC for generating an aura of tourism cachet around Ontario through an association with the Underground Railway, but to raise the structural relationship between the fastest-growing international industry of tourism, its commemorative language, and the work of recuperating history in Ontario.

6   It might be interesting to examine to what extent Toronto's version of the *Kloran* influenced the rituals and dogma of Regina's KKK chapters.
7   At this stage in my research, I have no idea why the show was cancelled other than to guess that there must have been protests from the neighbouring black communities.
8   It is possible to consider the signified laughter as tears. In other words, the distance between pleasure and pain in the minstrel performance is collapsed. I am motivated along this line of thought because of how the cartoon denies us the facial markers of the audience. That we see only the back of their heads yet are expected to infer enjoyment and delight (through the emoticon utilized) suggests we acknowledge the degree to which to laugh is sometimes to be caught in both pleasant and unpleasant emotion.
9   For more on how ignorance is central to our structures of knowing, particularly as they pertain to discourses of race, to ways we are taught how to know and what to know, see Shannon Sullivan and Nancy Tuana's edited collection, *Race and Epistemologies of Ignorance*.
10 Because the black male respondent was born in 1918 in Toronto, I am assuming the description of the Klan, Orangemen, Mason, etc., applies for the 1920s, 1930s, 1940s, and 1950s.

Works Cited

Ahmed, Sara. *The Cultural Politics of Emotion*. New York: Routledge, 2004. Print.
Akenson, Donald Harman. *The Orangeman: The Life & Times of Ogle Gowan*. Toronto: James Lorimer and Company, Publishers, 1983. Print.
Backhouse, Constance. *Colour-Coded: A Legal History of Racism in Canada, 1900–1950*. Toronto: U of Toronto P, 1999. Print.
Bartley, Allan. "A Public Nuisance: The Ku Klux Klan in Ontario 1923–27." *Journal of Canadian Studies* 30.3 (1995): 156–70. Print.
Bishop, Ted. *Riding with Rilke: Reflections on Motorcycles and Books*. New York: W.W. Norton and Company, 2006. Print.
Bourdieu, Pierre. *Distinction: A Social Critique of the Judgement of Taste*. Trans. and ed. New York: Routledge and Kegan Paul, 1984. Print.
Brand, Dionne, and Krisantha Sri Bhaggiyadatta. *Rivers Have Sources, Trees Have Roots: Speaking of Racism*. Toronto: Cross Cultural Communication Centre, 1986. Print.

Cixous, Hélène. "Fiction and Its Phantoms: A Reading of Freud's *Das Unheimliche* (The 'uncanny')." *New Literary History* 7.3 (Spring 1976): 525–48, 619–45. Print.

"Editorial Notes." *The College Times* October 1889: 11–12. Upper Canada College Archives, Toronto. Print.

Evans-Pritchard, Edward Evan. *The Nuer: A Description of the Modes of Livelihood and Political Institutions of a Nolotic People.* New York: Oxford UP, 1969. Print.

FitzGerald, James. *Old Boys: The Powerful Legacy of Upper Canada College.* Toronto: Macfarlane Walter and Ross, 1994. Print.

Freedgood, Elaine. *The Ideas in Things: Fugitive Meaning in the Victorian Novel.* Chicago: U of Chicago P, 2006. Print.

Gilroy, Paul. *Against Race: Imagining Political Culture Beyond the Color Line.* Cambridge, MA: Harvard UP, 2000. Print.

Godard, Barbara. "Deterritorializing Strategies: Nourbese Philip as Caucasianist Ethnographer." *Canadian Literature at the Crossroads of Language and Culture.* Ed. Smaro Kamboureli. Edmonton: NeWest, 2008. Print.

———. "Relational Logics: Of Linguistic and Other Transactions in the Americas." *Canadian Literature at the Crossroads of Language and Culture.* Ed. Smaro Kamboureli. Edmonton: NeWest, 2008. 315–57. Print.

Gramsci, Antonio. *The Modern Prince and Other Writings.* New York: International Publishers, 1959. Print.

Houston, Cecil J., and William J. Smyth. *The Sash Canada Wore: A Historical Geography of the Orange Order in Canada.* Toronto: U of Toronto P, 1980. Print.

Jenkins, William. "Views from 'the Hub of the Empire': Loyal Orange Lodges in Early Twentieth-Century Toronto." *The Orange Order in Canada.* Ed. David A. Wilson. Portland: Four Courts, 2007. 128–45. Print.

Johnson, Stephen. "Uncle Tom and the Minstrels: Seeing Black and White on Stage in Canada West Prior to the American Civil War." *(Post)Colonial Stages: Critical and Creative Views on Drama, Theatre, and Performance.* Ed. Helene Gilbert. Hebden Bridge, Yorkshire: Dangaroo, 1999. 55–63. Print.

Kaufmann, Eric. "The Orange Order in Ontario, Newfoundland, Scotland, and Northern Ireland: A Macro-social Analysis." *The Orange Order in Canada.* Ed. David A. Wilson. Portland: Four Courts, 2007. 32–68. Print.

Kloran: Knights of the Ku Klux Klan. 2nd ed. Toronto, 1928. Clara Thomas Archives and Special Collections, York University. CPC 1928-0074. Print.

Lott, Eric. *Love and Theft: Blackface Minstrelsy and the American Working Class.* New York: Oxford UP, 1993. Print.

Mackey, Eva. *The House of Difference: Cultural Politics and National Identity in Canada.* New York: Routledge, 1999. Print.

Martí José. "Our America." *The Jose Marti Reader.* Ed. Deborah Shnookal and Mirta Muniz. New York: Ocean Press, 1891. Print.
Ngai, Sianne. *Ugly Feelings.* Cambridge: Harvard UP, 2005. Print.
Old Boy. "The Merry Minstrels." *The College Times* December 1889: 20. Upper Canada College Archives, Toronto. Print.
———. "To the Editors of the College Times." *The College Times* October 1889: 12. Upper Canada College Archives, Toronto. Print.
Reinders, Robert C. "Anglo-Canadian Abolitionism: The John Anderson Case, 1860–1861." *Renaissance and Modern Studies* 21 (1975): 72–97. Print.
Reinhart, Anthony. "Ontario Legion Branch Shut Down after KKK Halloween Costume Debacle." *Globe and Mail* November 3, 2010. Web. November 3, 2010. <http://www.theglobeandmail.com/news/national/ontario/ontario-legion-branch-shut-down-after-kkk-halloween-costume-debacle/article1784812/>.
Robin, Martin. *Shades of Right: Nativist and Fascist Politics in Canada, 1920–1940.* Toronto: U of Toronto P, 1992. Print.
Sadowski-Smith, Claudia. *Border Fictions: Globalization, Empire, and Writing at the Boundaries of the United States.* Virginia: U of Virginia P, 2008. Print.
———. *Globalization on the Line: Culture, Capital, and Citizenship at U.S. Borders.* New York: Palgrave Macmillan, 2002. Print.
Sher, Julian. *White Hoods: Canada's Ku Klux Klan.* Vancouver: New Star Books, 1983. Print.
Simon, Roger. "Terrible Gift: Museums and the Possibility of Hope Without Consolation." *Journal of Museum Management and Curatorship* 21.3 (2006): 187–204. Print.
Stapells, Cathy. "Follow the North Star to Freedom." Media Centre for the Canadian Tourism Commission. March 15, 2007. Web. January 10, 2011. <http://mediacentre.canada.travel/content/travel_story_ideas/underground_railroad>.
———. "Lest we forget, follow the Freedom Trail." December 10, 2010. Web. January 10, 2011. <http://www.ego4u.com/en/read-on/countries/canada/underground-railroad>.
Sullivan, Shannon, and Nancy Tuana, eds. *Race and Epistemologies of Ignorance.* New York: State U of New York P, 2007. Print.
"Uncle Josh, Dramatic Critic." *St. Andrew's College Review* (Midsummer 1920): 21. St. Andrew's College Archive, Aurora. Print.
Walcott, Rinaldo. *Black Like Who? Writing Black Canada.* 2nd rev. ed. Toronto: Insomniac, 2003. Print.
Walker, James W. St.G. *"Race," Rights, and the Law in the Supreme Court of Canada: Historical Case Studies.* Waterloo: Wilfrid Laurier UP, 1997. Print.
Weber, Max. *Economy and Society: An Outline of Interpretive Sociology.* New York: Bedminster, 1968. Print.

Williams, Raymond. *Marxism and Literature*. Oxford: Oxford UP, 1977. Print.
Wilson, David. "Introduction: 'Who Are These People?'" *The Orange Order in Canada*. Ed. David A. Wilson. Portland: Four Courts, 2007. 9–24. Print.
Young, Archibald Hope. *Roll of Pupils of Upper Canada College: Toronto, January 1830 to June 1916*. Kingston: Hanson, Crozier, and Edgar, 1917. The William Ready Division of Archives and Research Collections, McMaster University. Print.

Chapter 7

"The Toil and Spoil of Translation": A Godardian Reading of the *Study-Guide: Discover Canada/Guide d'étude: Découvrir le Canada* (2010)

LEN M. FINDLAY

One of Barbara Godard's most accomplished and suggestive essays is "Writing Between Cultures" (1997). This essay, rightly reprinted in Smaro Kamboureli's 2008 collection of some of Barbara's most important pieces, deserves to be better known for its exemplary mix of difficulty, intellectual range, cultural openness, and political engagement. It also needs to be better known because of its continuing utility for the effective analysis of social, cultural, and literary texts and the practices they legitimate and promote. In this chapter I will first assess the main arguments of "Writing Between Cultures," paying special attention to its account of translation and "non-translation," and of the ways in which "normative grammar[s]" help produce "relations of ruling" (202). I will then offer a comparative analysis of the English and French texts of the new *Guide*'s depiction of "The Rights and Responsibilities of Citizenship." From this predominantly textualist view of translation from one of Canada's two official languages into the other, I will then shift to a broader sense of textuality and translation in order to more fully decode and restate the current political moment into priorities and imperatives of the federal government, one of whose key policy documents is the *Guide*.[1] I will conclude by connecting my textual and contextual analysis to the activity of translation as an enduring and invaluable instrument of the engaged and indigenous humanities, an activity that can continue to offer, as Barbara's work so often offers, a critical portrait of the nation through a literary humanist lens and possible pathways toward writing and communicating more justly *among* as well as "between" cultures.

Writing Between Cultures (1997)

In her interview with Smaro Kamboureli, begun in 2007, Barbara Godard offers a compelling account of how she came to translation in response to the Official Languages Act of 1969, the subsequent funding of literary translation through the Canada Council, and her heavy involvement in Coach House Press's translation series from its inception in 1973. She also sought, through translation, to provide texts for her teaching, to share experimental Québécois fiction with anglophone readers, and to develop her own linguistic proficiency and cultural politics via the major challenges posed, for instance, by Antonine Maillet's "innovative written version of Acadian oral speech" in *The Tale of Don L'orignal* (42) and by the poetry of Nicole Brossard. As usual, Godard's reflections on her practice are robustly contextualist:

> Participating on the jury for the Canada Council [now Governor General's] translation prize launched me into writing about translation theory, at first through the annual translation review for the "Letters in Canada" section of the *University of Toronto Quarterly*. The first time I attended the meeting to select the prize-winning book, I was dumbfounded that my shortlist bore no relation to anybody else's. The best translation was being determined on the placement of the commas in the English text, not on the challenges posed by the French text and the translator's creative response to them. This concept of value did not match my theory of translation, but I did not know how to argue my case. In the intervening year I set out to read everything I could on translation theory and found much to inspire me in the work of Henri Meschonnic and Antoine Berman, writing from a post-structuralistic approach. This helped me clarify a difference between "domesticating" and "foreignizing" translation strategies, as Lawrence Venuti would later adapt Berman's terminology, the domesticating strategy which had troubled me with its understanding that the translated text should be totally naturalized so that it appeared as if it had been written in English. (*Canadian Literature* 42–43)

We encounter here some of the most important and enduring features and themes of Godard's work. Her willingness to participate in new cultural structures in unglamorous, often unsung ways speaks to her intellectual generosity and commitment to the collective good. At the same time, and as on many occasions before and since, she finds herself the outsider on the inside, out of step with dominant assumptions and as yet incapable of persuading others to think differently. However, her response to this predicament is not to abandon a practitioner's sense of things but to turn instead to theory to help improve and justify her practice. This mix of diligence and determination gives her work allusive as well as analytical and political distinctiveness, all the while eschewing pedantry and condescension. She takes on the daunting prose of two French theorists who were already having an influence in Québec,[2] and she uses them to nuance her own understanding, but also to problematize "the concept of value" and expose power relations underlying translators' notions of fidelity and equivalence. Her willingness to use an awkward term, "foreignizing," encourages the reader to think about connections between otherness and violence. Meanwhile, she uncovers the patriarchal implications of "domesticating," extending and redirecting the ideas of two foreign male mentors so as to make a difference in Canada. By the time of the first meeting of the Canadian Association of Translation Studies in 1987, she was ready to deliver a boldly feminist account of "the dynamic interactions between hegemonic systems and subaltern subversions of them" (43). And this intervention leads in turn to a special issue of *Tessera* (1989) whose "reflections on 'womanhandling' the text in translation have been identified as a distinctive contribution of a 'Canadian school of translation theory,' which has introduced a new cultural paradigm of translation that exposes the political implications of intercultural transfer fundamental to any comparative activity" (43). This is not academic bragging by Godard but the honesty of a remarkably empowering role model whose affirmations are habitually more unsettling than congratulatory, and are so for herself as much as for her auditors and readers.

"Writing Between Cultures," published in *TTR* in 1997, shows Godard at the height of her powers, and is an effort that ranks in my view with essays such as Derrida's "Signature, Event, Context" and Spivak's "Can the Subaltern Speak?" In more than thirty pages of dense argument, bolstered by forty notes, some of which are as challenging as the main text they attempt to clarify, Godard unpacks the complexities of two particular "moments" in Canadian history via the correspondence of a seventeeth-century, French-born Ursuline nun and a play by a Canadian Aboriginal writer and scholar. The essay is organized in two main parts and in a broadly chronological way, starting with events in New France and then turning to the present in order to clarify what it means for translation studies to be taking "a cultural turn" in the 1990s. After setting her agenda, Godard turns to Mère Marie de l'Incarnation and "Con/version" as the creation of a scene of instruction shaped by one kind of harmonist translation theory. Godard then turns to Daniel David Moses and "Re/version" as the creation of a "scene of insurrection" shaped by a very different translation theory. The epigraphs to this essay link the two texts to be analyzed through the notions of "stones rolling around in my head" and "stones in your mouth, "a gesture toward literary echo or allusion that prepares for a much more concerted connection of two writers who may seem at first blush to have little in common. The third epigraph is one that Moses himself uses as an epigraph to his play and that Godard chooses to repeat and gloss: "A nation is not defeated until the hearts of its women are on the ground." This Cheyenne proverb, like the two excerpts that precede it, is intended by Godard to "highlight the toil and spoil of translation" while inspiring her "to examine systematic interference between languages at two different moments in the wake of imperialism" (201).

In the first of her two chosen moments, Godard strives to demonstrate how "first contact between Europeans and Amerindians" led to "Canadian concepts [being] translated vertically into European vernaculars and produced as Europe's other in a systematic erasure of horizontal translation among Amerindian languages that effects cultural and political hegemony" (201). Godard moves from Latin as the *lingua franca* of early modern Europe Englished from Stephen Parmenius by Richard Hakluyt in a way designed to promote a *terra nullius* into which European subjects could most expeditiously insert themselves physically and imaginatively (210).[3] The vertical/horizontal binary dear to structuralists is now politically coded by Godard while the indigene as absence in Newfoundland is supplemented by the Indian as the target of exploitation and conversion in New France. An "imperial alibi" (207) is derived from "non-translation," according to which "*intracultural* competence" is strategically misprized as "a problem in *intercultural* competence" by means of which the indigenous subject is split into unintelligible savage and conscripted Native informant. The indigene must be intimidated into subjection or educated into compliance. Between elimination and assimilation, silence and "appended glossaries" to Cartier's voyages, interpellated as the subject and imitator of colonial writing between cultures, the indigene lives the contradictions of an enforced shift from relationship and gift economies to private ownership and imperial title (209).

Within a broader repertoire of relations of ruling, the "womanhandling" of translation by Mère Marie allows for correction and rewriting of foundational elisions and illusions stemming from male sources and authorities. Marie is constrained and empowered by her religious vows. Eager to convert and recruit young Aboriginal women to the Ursuline order, she translates a more encompassing contradiction into a feminized discourse of "split subjectivity" weighted more heavily toward "female submission" (212).

Disavowing the eloquence and linguistic erudition of the male priests in New France, she attributes her own learning of "Algonkian, Montagnais, Huron, and Iroquois" to "divine inspiration": "I spoke lovingly to our Lord about it, and he came to my aid to such a degree that in a short time I had such a great facility in the language so that the activity of my interior life was neither hindered nor interrupted" (213). From a prodigious archive Godard cites (in her own translation) and comments in detail on a passage of symptomatic overdetermination. Mère Marie's gendered abjection combines with a linguistically authorized sovereign subjectivity, so that, in Canada's interior, she can preserve her own Franco-Canadian Catholic interiority. Her acquisition of indigenous languages, first described by her as "humanly impossible" (213), becomes possible through divine intercession that preserves a colonial hierarchy among living languages and their native speakers while using a quasi-dead language, Latin, as the privileged, "universal" Catholic access to the Word beyond all human languages and their politically stratified imperfections. Indigenous women posed a particular difficulty to colonization, as the Cheyenne proverb had attested. To make such women tractable, bilingual Native informants is Mère Marie's duty within an "instrumental hierarchy" (215) divinely ordained and (in) humanly enforced. Within this "traffic in languages" (217), success breeds success in two forms: the more efficient assimilation of the indigene, and increased investment in settling New France. Translation has already taken an acculturating turn in the service of God and King. In this "politics of translation," "[g]estures are read with infallible certainty: the potentially disruptive logic of the Algonkian languages is e-rased in the trope that turns them into Latin, the language of imperial truth" (219).

After this performance of incriminating exegesis, Godard turns to an indigenous subject who practises translation to anti-imperial ends. The "theory of equivalence" that had translated indigenous difference into deficiency and deference is now inverted by Daniel David Moses in *Almighty Voice and His Wife* (1992), a two-part staging and racist rewriting of the life of a young Cree man who provoked the full violence of the state (both physical and ideological) after he killed a government cow in Saskatchewan in the 1890s and resisted arrest. Here we see "translation as creative difference" (220) with an insurrectionist understanding and distribution of its "toil and spoil." The seventeenth-century co-optation of indigenous subjects like Marie Amiskouevan (214–16) did not effect the complete disappearance of such subjects. The plenitude of events cannot be reduced to the instrumentalities of any language of domination and delegitimation.

The move from colonial regulation-through-representation to indigenous agency and the ambiguities and excess of performance, from colonial duplicity to creative redoubling, is a key modal shift that uses and abuses the "language of the master" (220). In Godard's reading, "Moses develops a horizontal model of translation between aboriginal cultures privileging creative borrowing" (220) outside and against individual ownership and the sanctity of private property. A Delaware dramatist stages Cree and Sioux ritual across indigenous difference while disrupting dominant assumptions and hierarchies through the "palimpsestic overwriting" that translates (into English) indigenous relations of misruling and unruling. We have shifted from Catholic patriarchy to "feminine power of cultural creation" (221). Trickery and transparency are re-inflected as defiant humour and the visibility of ghosts, escaping the self-serving solemnities of the dominant, and their anxieties about heresy and miracle, into a zone of shadows and shape-changing and an optic that eludes surveillance while exposing the colonial state's panoptic urges and instruments. In this revisionary reordering, "If the epistolary genre constitutes Marie de l'Incarnation's translator as subjected to the higher authority of the divine addressee, the combination of story and performance in Moses's play reconfigures the enunciation of the translating subject as polyvalent within the play of social forces" (225).

Godard is especially attentive to complexity when she considers performance in relation to orality and theatricality, ethnographic authenticity and Euro-Canadian high culture. Writing between cultures, she sees Moses not as attempting to convert the other to indigenous views but as authorizing "aboriginal playwrights to produce cross-over works, intersemiotically translating traditional storytelling techniques with their enigmatic teaching form into the agonistic model of dramatic conflict of aesthetic texts" (226). The syncretic refusal by the Ghost Dance (229) of the demand that its adherents conform or disappear, and the vertiginous excesses of a Trickster aesthetic and hermeneutic, are welcomed equally by Godard as highly distinctive and much needed practices:

> Tracing localized economies of damage and neglect in writing as resistance challenges the monopoly of discursive practices and articulates different conditions of possibility which make visible the limits of dominant fictions of the real. Translation as resistance, then, would be a tactic of intervention in what constitutes the basis of "linguistic" as well "national" identity in Canada. (232)

Like disembodied devotion, performative embodiment is construed to implicate willy-nilly a much broader range of insurgent, decolonizing practices. A lateralist and multilateralist exchange of languages and value systems redeems economy from reduction to profit and loss. Evincing a characteristic bravura of convergence, Godard uses her two key examples to articulate "translation of language but not culture [Mère Marie] and the translation of culture but not language [Moses]" (233). This provocative chiasmus hearkens back to the protracted theoretical preliminaries that bring her slowly and circuitously to engagement with her two examples of translation. It brings us back also to one of the key Godardian frames here and elsewhere, the frame within which all state simplifications, including those promoted in government publications, are interrogated:

> Within the Canadian context, under official bilingualism, there has been a tendency to conceptualize linguistic and cultural relations in binary terms. Canada's policy of official "multiculturalism" encourages first nations peoples and immigrants to retain their cultures though not their languages which remain unofficial. Multiculturalism, as culture without language(s) and authority, or voices reconcilable in one voice, figures an end of translation in a fiction of unanimity. Against this, I want to argue, Canadian literature discourse has developed within contradiction, between cultures, between languages. (203)

What others consider the exception, interference, or surmountable obstacle, Godard embraces as the constitutive rule, and as generative rather than degenerative.

A Godardian Reading of the *Guide*

In concluding her essay, Godard admits that her "contention that translation theories are constituted in a particular historical instance of enunciation from within a dynamic field of variation will necessitate further analysis of other moments in the history of translation in Canada" (234). And it is to one such moment that I now turn. As we have seen, a Godardian reading proceeds with an expanded sense of textuality, semiotics, and power relations. It can engage as readily and productively with a non-literary text as with a self-consciously aesthetic one. It tracks the toil and spoil of translation in highly particular as well as ambitiously contextualist ways so as to retrieve—as constitutive rather than aberrant—aporia, indeterminacy, or violence; tendentious elements and telling absences; the discrete and the interrelated that come before us or are interpreted for us as harmonious, redemptive, natural, or inevitable.

On the matter of citizenship, the state has a clear incentive to create the impression of the nation talking to itself in an act of collective, discreetly instructive, patriotic musing about "rights and responsibilities." The national brand can thus be tinkered with, but without bruising or otherwise blemishing it. As an officially bilingual and multicultural country with a tradition of Royal Commissions to deal with abrasive differences, Canada is represented to itself as able to solve its problems, those problems being relatively minor compared to the challenges facing other countries and compared to the array of successes and opportunities to which Canada can point. Canada can translate itself to itself in the orderly, just, and productive management of diversity. If indeed "our fundamentals are sound," as Finance Minister Flaherty keeps on saying, then all our deliberations will continue to entail "recalibration" and strategic "stimulus," not radical reimagining and change. Accordingly, the official imbrication of language and culture aspires to the condition of embrocation, soothing wounds and readying muscles for the next great national effort, whether economic or military or both (as the Harper government shifts from peacekeeping to peacemaking as part of a broader re-militarization of the national imaginary). Within this frame of cautious self-satisfaction discreetly laced with fear, the new "study guide" is a self-declared scene of instruction calculated to help educate Canadians about their own country while attracting to it the right sort of new Canadians. But can the *Guide* be overwritten or culturally turned to reveal a scene of insurrection as well as instruction?

The *Guide* begins by extending an invitation to discover/*découvrir* Canada inside and beyond this text. The virtual synonymy of the English and French verbs suggests a unanimity further buttressed by the imperial and colonial history of "discovery," a common history sanitized bilingually and ignoring any post-colonial embarrassments incurred by Eurocentric presumption and self-absorption. The strong sense of bilingual equivalence and domestication continues with the Oath (Serment) of Citizenship, a script to be performed orally in officially ordained circumstances in either English or French in texts almost identical to each other. The text of the Oath is given in both languages in both versions of the *Guide*, laid out in parallel columns at the outset to reinforce the sense of full and faithful translatability and hence identical undertakings and senses of commitment. However, these parallel texts are immediately followed by an interpretative aid to "Understanding the Oath," a gloss that begins to subvert state-sponsored fictions of unity and harmony even as it seeks to confirm them:

> In Canada, we profess our loyalty to a person who represents all Canadians and not to a document such as a constitution, a banner such as a flag, or a geopolit-

ical entity such as a country. In our constitutional monarchy, these elements are encompassed by the sovereign (Queen or King). It is a remarkably simple yet powerful principle: Canada is personified by the Sovereign just as the sovereign is personified by Canada.

Au Canada, nous jurons notre fidelité à une personne humaine qui nous représente tous, plutôt que de nous engager à servir un document, une oriflamme ou un territoire. Dans notre monarchie constitutionnelle, la souveraine (reine ou roi) symbolise à la fois notre constitution, notre drapeau et notre pays. C'est un principe d'une remarquable simplicité, mais également d'une grande signification: la Souveraine personnifie le Canada et le Canada personnifie la Souveraine.

Unlike with the parallel texts of the Oath and the National Anthem (40), the two commentaries on the Oath are not designed to be read together, and a Godardian reader can quickly see why. The *Guide* becomes bilingual in both unilingual versions when its authors think the domestication effect of untroubled equivalence is virtually guaranteed. At other points, there is an adjustment or "reasonable accommodation" of the linguistic distinctiveness of each official language and the particular history that informs it. Constitutional monarchy, historically and currently, plays very differently in France than in the United Kingdom of Great Britain and Northern Ireland. The pledge to the sovereign in English is deemed an act of professing while the French swearing seems slightly stronger (picking up on the extra "solenellement" in the French Oath). The English version mentions "all Canadians" while the French is more vague, a species of non-translation favoured to avoid memories of nineteenth-century patriots and rebellion that attend the term "Canadien."[4] In English the sovereign is claimed to "encompass" constitution, banner, and country, while in French she is thought rather to "symbolize'" them, thus replacing Durhamesque spectres of physical surrounding and swamping with notions of recognition and interpretation. The fussiness of "a geopolitical entity such as a country" is reduced in translation to the more assured, colloquial, and politically nondescript "'territoire." After such sensitivity, the commentary becomes more plainly directive in both languages, urging all readers to see the relation between sovereign and citizenry as "simple but powerful," though the French version, still straining to avoid any hint of earlier conquest or the War Measures Act, replaces power with meaningfulness or portentousness ("grande signification"). The sovereign person is also a personification of Canada, and Canada of the sovereign. A chiasmic construction emphasizes readily intelligible and desirable translatability in both languages, implying an Anglo-French normative grammar that expresses relations of ruling across foundational conflict and its iterative resolution. Domestication can produce domestic violence unless one prudently keeps the parties separate from each other when the conversation threatens to take an awkward turn. Personification emerges as the master trope of allegiance and responsiveness, allowing the reciprocal exchange of agency and identity. The sovereign may have other and more important realms to head or impersonate, and not "all Canadians" or "Canadiens et Canadiennes" may be equally happy with this arrangement of unity in diversity, or with the later pre-eminence of the "Canadian Crown" in the section on Canadian symbols (38–40). But the *Guide*, in parallel performative tracks and then divergent interpretative tracks, tries to keep the state apparatus both endearing and intact.

As in the Ursuline articulation discussed earlier, linguistic equivalence and hierarchy function within historically specific vectors of power. English and French are bearers of "Christian civilizations" (11), underwritten by the Latinity of Magna Carta, Habeas corpus, and A Mare Usque Ad Mare. The first of these three, "also known [translated] as the Great Charter of Freedoms" (8), privileges evolutionary English liberty over its revolutionary and republican French analogue, though it fails to mention the attendant Carta de Foresta, an apt enough omission in a country whose environmental record is so appalling. Magna Carta is characterized as beginning a process that leads more or less directly over time to the "summariz[ing] of fundamental freedoms" and "setting out of additional rights" in the Canadian Charter of Rights and Freedoms (Part I of the Constitution Act of 1982). Democratic governance has displaced the divine providence on which Marie de l'Incarnation relied, accommodating the Protestant/ Catholic divide along largely linguistic lines in the Quebec Act of 1774, and recognizing Canada's two official languages as communicative peers partnering horizontally from above in the vertical maintenance of the bilingual nation, but also as "important symbols of identity" within unity. After all, anglophones and francophones have "lived together in partnership and creative tension for more than 300 years" (39).

However, there is a major problem with this scenario. On the one hand, and thanks to advice provided by John Ralston Saul to the authors of the *Guide*,[5] there is a commitment to the notion of Canada's *three* founding peoples: "Aboriginal, French, and British" (10). So how can there be only two official languages into which every other indigenous or immigrant/ heritage language must be translated in compliance with Canadian law? Part of the answer to this derives from the illusion (critiqued by Godard) that Aboriginal peoples historically had no forms of writing but only the unreliable medium of orality. Part derives from the selective Euro-Canadian esteeming of orality, as in the demand that a person swear the Oath of Citizenship in public before a citizenship judge after passing a written exam. The formalities of such a situation are viewed as the most compelling proof of knowledge and commitment, whereas the making of glossaries via catechizing Native informants and the ceremonious making of treaty with the Canadian Crown too often resulted in the inadvertent or deliberate mistranslation of Aboriginal speech into French and English so as to advance a colonial agenda. And yet another part of the perceived problem is that the Aboriginal languages are too many, too different from each other, too localized, too primitive, and mostly doomed anyway. There is neither point nor practicality to even considering giving any of them official federal status. Aboriginal peoples are welcome to their cultural distinctiveness, but not to using their cultures in conjunction with their respective languages in politically instrumental ways as real equivalents to English and French.

The hegemony of English and French is asserted in the face of what the *Guide* terms "Non-official languages widely spoken in Canadian homes" (13). What this designation means is immigrant languages like Chinese. Home, it is implied, is a place for the non-threatening performance of linguistic difference. But home seems not to be associated with Aboriginal peoples, whether they live on or off reserve. And their languages are not mentioned at all here: they are, it seems, neither official nor unofficial, spoken and written in some unspecified region between hegemonic and immigrant cultures, in the dwindling interstice between assimilation and irreversible decline. It is an erasure or evasion that would not have surprised Godard or Daniel David Moses. The *Guide* allows that "Diverse, vibrant First Nations cultures" preceded European settlement in North America, but such commendation occurs in the past tense and is described as "rooted in religious beliefs about their relationship to the Creator, the natural environment and each other." That rootedness implies vulnerability to the juggernaut of progress, and a primitiveness foreshadowed in the preceding section on "The Rights and Responsibilities of Citizenship," where it is claimed: "Canadian law has several sources, including laws passed by Parliament and the provincial legislatures, English common law, the civil code of France, and the unwritten constitution we have inherited from Great Britain" (8). Amidst the prestige of the written and unwritten, the legal tradition that dare not speak its name here is Aboriginal legal tradition that scholars like Sakej Henderson, Taiaiake Alfred, and Trish Monture have been documenting and animating for two decades or more in ways that have changed the thinking of Canada's highest courts though not, it would seem, the thinking and representational politics of the Government of Canada. This unforgiveable silence on Aboriginal law is repeated in the later section on "The Justice System" (36–37). Given how disproportionately the justice system impacts on Aboriginal peoples, especially young people, and how the *Guide* seems at other points intent on respecting the accomplishments and values of all three founding peoples, it is extremely disappointing to encounter the culpably uninformed or unacceptably deliberate effort to write out a plenary and persistent Aboriginal presence from the inter-translations of Canada's two hegemonic languages and knowledge systems.

A Godardian sense of the non-coincidence of subaltern Canadian languages and cultures gets to the mendacious heart of socially and politically conservative re-inscriptions of citizenship as internally respectful and externally inclusive. We could readily extend this to the more general characterization of culture in the *Guide*, or to the individualizing of environmental responsibility, or to family values talk, or to broader patterns of coding and evasion unwilling to accept gay marriage as part of the pitch to potential immigrants, or to the Harper government's political base at home. Or one could turn (as Barbara Godard undoubtedly would) to gender critique and "discover" that gender is a proxy for equality and thus for democracy (9). But, as usual, there is a hidden agenda too:

> In Canada, men and women are equal under the law. Canada's openness and generosity do not extend to barbaric cultural practices that tolerate spousal abuse, "honour killings," female genital mutilation or other gender-based violence. Those guilty of these crimes are severely punished under Canada's criminal laws.

> Au Canada, hommes et femmes sont égaux devant la loi. L'ouverture et la générosité du Canada excluent les pratiques culturelles barbares qui tolèrent la violence conjugale, les meurtres d'honneur, la mutilation sexuelle des femmes, les mariages forcés ou d'autres actes de violence sur le sexe. Les personnes coupables de tels crimes fondée sont sévèrement punies par les lois canadiennes.

The discourse of barbarity, like the discourse of discovery, has much to live down in the construction of the other. Here it is put to work by a socially conservative government endlessly "tough on crime," fervently defending "traditional" family values, yet attempting to align itself with gender equality and "civilized" precepts and behaviour. The presumption of a common

Christian civilization is expressed in what seems like an untroubled translation from one official language into its only peer, though one may wonder about the quotes around "honour killings" in English and their absence in French. Is this meant to suggest something about reasonable accommodation in Quebec or about the capacity of the French language to disparage without diacritical aids? The ironies and ambiguities proliferate, as the mention of honour makes one think, for example, of the Honour of the Crown as key to the fulfillment of treaty obligations with Aboriginal peoples. Or when commitment to the safety and equality of women calls to mind the numbers of Aboriginal women missing in our major cities, and official indifference to them, their grieving families, and those who march in solidarity with them. Or when one thinks of a government that concertedly withdraws funding from women's groups across Canada (see, e.g., Neve and Gergin, and the particularly telling case of Sisters in Spirit, <http://www.nac.ca/programs/sisters-spirit>). The *Guide*'s selective silence about gender politics and gender justice at home is of a piece with the cheap righteousness directed abroad to oppose violence against the person and rights of women in countries like Sudan and Pakistan.

Feeling the need for further clarification of what is being promoted and refused in the name of gender equality, the English and French texts discussed above are each followed by the same egalitarian triptych, which apparently translates the spirit of these statements. In the first "stock image" of the triptych, a young white woman is giving blood while being attended by a black male health care worker. Caring is redistributed across the genders, and across a racialized difference too, in a scene of respectful and beneficial incursion into the female body. The third image, again a stock one, shows a white, middle-aged married couple in leisure attire, holding hands against a mountain background, their broad smiles radiating happiness in support of the notion that their marriage is strong as a rock because they are equal partners in it. The middle image is not from stock but from Debbie Farnand, a communications analyst with Citizenship and Immigration Canada. The photo is entitled "Children's Program" according to the list of credits at the end of the *Guide* (58). It depicts a young female teacher assisting two girls in hijabs with their school work. Here, as in the justification of the Canadian mission in Afghanistan, education is promoted as the avenue to equality and a fuller liberty. But this image, like the other two visual translations of a luridly alarmist text, seems embarrassingly bland. Another version of non-translation is at work here, inter-semiotically, between graphic words and apparently illustrative images inoculated against violence and injustice at home and barbaric practices in remote, mostly Islamic places. However, a fiction of equity cannot suppress the difference between Canadian law and justice, and the fact that potential citizens of a certain sort must make cultural concessions as well as linguistic acquisitions in order to become good Canadians.

In sum, written between cultures, the *Guide* demonstrates and distributes the toil and spoil of translation: from language to language, medium to medium, and culture to culture (as, for example, in the preference of the Riel rebellion to Riel resistance, an action that spurns current academic usage as well as cultural mobilization by Métis activists). It strives to be authoritative, as is evident in the list of acknowledgements with which it concludes. But this list is itself inadvertently revealing. Of the twenty-six individuals named as sources of advice, only five are women. There are no Aboriginal political leaders on the list, nor a scholar of Aboriginal *sui generis* citizenship like Sakej Henderson. A pro-military historian like Jack Granatstein, an emphatically Anglocentric one like Margaret MacMillan, or one who favours the Native-newcomer lens like Jim Miller,[6] were sure to have supplied sound scholarly advice to the government officials (not all of which may have been acted on). But the document could be a great deal better than it is by being more self-critical and more honest about persistent and emergent injustices that have attended the recent rise of "the ugly Canadian" (see Findlay, "Citizenship and the University"). The *Guide* desperately needed (and still needs) a less embedded set of advisers.

Naming Between Cultures

Under pressure from various groups and the media, the Harper government has made changes in later iterations of the *Guide*. However, it seems to have learned little from the process of critique and response. The minister responsible for this initiative, Jason Kenney, made only too clear during the run-up to the May 2011 federal election that his portfolio includes abusing his powers to help target and secure "the" immigrant vote, especially in what he and/or his underlings termed "very ethnic ridings" (an expression that translates into French in a way that leads directly to Jacques Parizeau's disastrous remark about "la monnaie et les votes ethniques"). Kenney apologized for the fundraising letter sent from his office and threw yet another political aide (de Souza) under the Harper bus. However, a micro-cultural targeting undertaken in English, and aimed primarily at Hindi, Punjabi, and Chinese language speakers in the Greater Toronto Area, scarcely seems to accord with most of the letter and spirit of the *Guide* in the cynical homogenizing and tracking of minorities. The naming of these Canadians in such crude terms, combined with the apprehensions felt by voters whose family members are still being considered for immigration to Canada, brought calls for Kenney's resignation. His strategy seemed to work at first, and he was hailed as a "star" of the new federal cabinet, but one who could not be elevated from his current portfolio because he is too effective there. However, academic analysis of the election results now suggests that immigrants did not move to the Conservatives in massive numbers, and that Kenney may be confined to his current ministry because his "work is far from done" (Delacourt). In a world of targeting, both ethically and pragmatically questionable, what *will* the next iteration of the *Guide* look like?

When the new federal cabinet was announced, it included not only new faces but a new name for a crucially important department. Indian and Northern Affairs Canada is now to be known as Aboriginal Affairs and Northern Development Canada. It was a unilateral move on the Harper government's part, a "rebrand[ing]" "out of the blue" that "has received mixed reviews, and rightly so" (Cuthand). The substitution of "Aboriginal" for "Indian" is translated between dominant cultures as the change from "Indiennes" to "Autochtones," terms described on the official website by Minister Duncan, who is continuing in this portfolio, as "more up to date and inclusive"; "plus actuel et plus englobant." All above board and straightforward, one might say, if one ignored the vectors of power, the historical context, and the failure to consult those peoples in whose name and interests one is purporting to act. With Godardian caveats about the *Guide* in mind, the neo-colonial arrogance and menace of this move becomes clear. As Bill Curry remarked in the *Globe and Mail* (1, 4), "there is power in the naming ... the semantic shift could have all sorts of consequences for native people from the laws governing their treatment, the services they get, and even their identities." Why so surprised? And why the ascription of passivity to Aboriginal peoples? Perhaps the most pointed, insurrectionist response came from Patrick Madahbee, leader of the Anishinabek Nation. "We are not Aboriginal, we are Anishnabek.... Trying to lump First Nations, Metis and Inuit peoples together might save space on the minister's business card, but it is disrespectful of the truly distinct nature of the communities with whom he needs to establish better relationships" (APTN National News). Defining linguistic modernity and the scope of inclusiveness, as Minister Duncan feels entitled to do, suggests that Indian Affairs, in the toxically colonial sense, is alive and well despite *its* voluntary name change. However, the same cannot be said with any certainty for Canada's First peoples and Métis on whom a new designation has been imposed. They remain as in-between as ever, relying on humour, irony, solidarity, and resolve to try to shame and serially litigate the federal government into embracing the Duty to Consult and the Honour of the Crown. Once again, normative grammars are attempting to dictate the relations of ruling. But all my relations of unruling remain in place too. Toil and spoil, toil and spoil, continue to translate as injustice and misprision. Meanwhile, the labour of official legitimation and theft demand a Godardian vigilance, foreignizing, and womanhandling, in order to call them more effectively to account. May this situation inspire collaborations.

Notes

1 One of the keys to the Harper government's progress from successive minorities to a majority in May 2011 has been its wooing of immigrants' votes away from the federal Liberals. Despite regular controversies, some of which will be discussed later in this chapter, Minister Kenney succeeded remarkably in this endeavour and is currently considered a "star" in the Harper Cabinet.
2 Meschonnic and Berman show how broad and provisional the notion of poststructuralism was at this time for Godard, and how she identified the power of translation via its connections to broader intellectual and political movements. Meschonnic combines theory and practice in a distinctive mix of poetry and erudition, wary of appeals to origin and claims of transparency. He discerns mixture and hierarchy where others claim purity and parity, doing so by connecting the sign to multiple genres, to its own unconscious, and insisting that "la force du signe cache une faiblesse: tout le rapport entre le langage et le corps, entre une langue et une littérature, une langue et une culture, lui échappe" (299; see also, e.g., 8, 22, 53, 56). The slightly younger Berman comes at the sign's rationality and unconscious via Heidegger's reading of Hölderlin's translation of Sophocles, exposing "the system of deformation that operates in every translation and prevents it from being 'a trial of the foreign' [une épreuve de l'étranger; Die Erfahrung des Fremden]" (Berman, "Translation" 286). Berman made an especially powerful impact on Annie Brisset.
3 Godard's thoroughness and acuity are clear in how she engages with an early text and connects it to the circulation of discovery discourse and the translation of that discourse into national vernaculars in ways both deferential and acquisitive. In her comments and extended note on Parmenius's Latin text, and how Hakluyt chooses to translate it, she reads the power relations between the two male friends convincingly, and also the different ways in which they diminish and disfigure that which they purport to represent in language.

Parmenius sees Newfoundland through lenses both sumptuary and weakly self-critical, while Hakluyt pushes this invaluable eyewitness account from reportage toward recruitment of settlers. Parmenius's quandary is captured with intense pathos when he feels forced to report nothing but desolation (*praeter solitudinem nihil video*). This emptiness, the desert the Romans had created in Britain and called peace, refers to inhabitants as well as customs and territories. A nullity is both observed and imagined, and then softened in translation, the shift from imperial Latin to proto-imperial English still silencing those indigenes who could refute both versions. For bilingual texts of the letter, and some excellent contextualizing of the expedition that occasioned it, see Quinn and Cheshire. That said, Godard's is a remarkably distinctive and insightful reading.

4   See, e.g., the 1830s agenda of *Le Canadien* newspaper discussed in Findlay ("Towards Canada"). Later in the *Guide* it is noted that "The House of Commons recognized in 2006 that Quebecois form a nation within a united Canada" (12). The French version more evocatively locates the Québec nation in geography and history "au sein d'un Canada uni."

5   Saul is cited among the individuals whose advice is acknowledged at the end of the *Guide* (57). Saul's argument for three founding peoples is made compellingly in *A Fair Country*.

6   In contrast to an expression like "invader–settler," Native–newcomer relations threatens to substitute a quasi-neutral temporal category for one that insists on the violence of colonialism. Native–newcomer also tends to mask the fact that the newcomer precedes the Native cognitively and linguistically, thereby recentring the white European colonizing subject. At the very least we should change the expression to newcomer–Native relations.

Works Cited

APTN National News. "Aboriginal Affairs Name Change 'Disrespectful.'" Web. <http://aptn.ca/news/2011/05/18/aboriginal-affairs-name-change>.

Berman, Antoine. "Préface." Annie Brisset. *Sociocritique de la traduction: Théâtre et altérité au Québec (1968–1988)*. Longueuil: Les Éditions du Préambule, 1990. 9–19. Print.

———. "Translation and the Trials of the Foreign." Trans. Lawrence Venuti. *The Translation Studies Reader*. London: Routledge, 2000. 284–97. Print.

Citizenship and Immigration Canada/Citoyenneté et Immigration Canada. *Study Guide—Discover Canada: The Rights and Responsibilities of Citizenship. Guide d'étude—Découvrir le Canada: Les Droits et responsabilités liés à la citoyenneté*. 2010 ed. [The most recent update was published March 14, 2011.] Web. <http://www.cic.gc.ca/english/resources/publications/discover/section11.asp>.

Curry, Bill. "Aboriginal Affairs: Simple Name Change, Historic Consequence." *Globe and Mail* May 19, 2011: A1, 4. Print.
Cuthand, Doug. "Name Change Portends Trouble for First Nations." *Saskatoon StarPhoenix* May 20, 2011: A13. Print.
Delacourt, Susan. "The Ethnic Conservative Myth." *Toronto Star* May 24, 2011. Web. <http://www.thestar.com/news/canada/2011/05/20/the_ethnic_conservative_myth.html>.
de Souza, Mike. "Jason Kenney Apologizes, Staffer Quits over Fundraising Letter." *Montreal Gazette* March 3, 2011: 1. Print.
Findlay, L.M. "Citizenship and the University: Beyond the Ugly Canadian and the Semiotic Stockade." *Contours: Journal of the Humanities Institute* 1 (Spring/Summer, 2012): n.p. Print.
———. "Towards Canada as Aesthetic State: François-Xavier Garneau's *Canadien* Poetics." *Studies in Canadian Literature* 32.2 (2007): 28–42. Print.
"From Symbols to Hope." Editorial. *Globe and Mail* May 19, 2011: A16. Print.
Gergin, Maria. "Freedom of Speech Restricted, Discouraged by Harper Government." *CCPA Monitor* 17.10 (April 2011): 21–24. Print.
Godard, Barbara. *Canadian Literature at the Crossroads of Language and Culture. Selected Essays 1987–2005*. Ed. Smaro Kamboureli. Edmonton: NeWest, 2008. Print.
Meschonnic, Henri. *De la langue française: Essai sur une clarté obscure*. Paris: Hachette, 1997. Print.
Neve, Alex. "The Big Chill: Basic Freedoms of Speech and Advocacy Are Now under Siege." *CCPA Monitor* 17.7 (March 2011): 1, 6–7. Print.
Quinn, David B., and Neil M. Cheshire, eds. *The New Found Land of Stephen Parmenius: The Life and Writings of a Hungarian Poet, Drowned on a Voyage from Newfoundland, 1583*. Toronto: U of Toronto P, 1972. Print.
Saul, John Ralston. *A Fair Country: Telling Truths about Canada*. Toronto: Viking Canada, 2008. Print.
Sisters in Spirit. <http://www.nac.ca/programs/sisters-spirit>.

Chapter 8

Notes Toward Thinking Transsexual Institutional Poetics

TRISH SALAH

While transgender figures have enjoyed a prominent place in the imaginative and rhetorical vocabulary of feminism, transsexuality has long been an object of disapprobation, if not outright censure, within feminist discourses.[1] Asking the question of the difference transsexuality makes to feminist theorizing and oppositional practices of sexual difference, this essay argues that transsexual cultural work both reiterates and displaces feminist analysis of sexual difference as an embodied situation/site of enunciation and symbolic inscription.

This essay takes its inspiration from several movements in the work of Barbara Godard, extending her analysis of gendered practices of inscription and cultural economy into the field of transsexual cultural production. Further, it interrogates that cultural field as structured by counter-hegemonic—yet locally dominant—formations such as liberal post-feminism and gay and lesbian film festivals. These formations have operated as regulatory discourses on gender that have authorized, contoured, censured, inspired, prefigured, and been contested by transgender discourses. Situating transsexual discourse as the discourse of "the other of the other,"[2] this essay investigates how, in our post-feminist moment, liberal feminisms and LGBTQ organizations arrogate to themselves the purview of interpreting and governing dissident sex and gender minority expression and politics for the societal mainstream. In naming this moment post-feminist, I draw upon those thinkers who articulate that *post-*, not in the sense of being against feminism, but rather "after" the selective integration of elements of feminist rhetoric into common sense and increased access to the social apparatuses of power has been granted to some of those who deploy such rhetorics (both women and men).³

More broadly, I draw upon an understanding of this discourse of "the other of the other" as operating within a cultural field, wherein culture is viewed as "an autonomous and self-regulating field of social reproduction and value positioned asymmetrically ... within an all encompassing economy to whose ends it is subordinate" (Godard, "Notes from the Cultural Field" 237). Godard's reworking of Pierre Bourdieu's thinking around cultural capital to theorize the differential valuation of gendered cultural labour is particularly pertinent to my discussion, especially regarding what I see as a constitutive elision of the value of trans sex worker labour even within LGBTQ discourses. There is also a question of how the somatechnics of crossing sex, as well as recombining gender, sexuality, and sex in both subjective and symbolic locales, causes trans subjects to enter into and disappear from gendered economies of cultural value.

The 1993 video *Gender Troublemakers: Transsexuals in the Gay Community* functions in the first instance as a critical response to and refusal of uninformed representations of transsexual lives and sexualities—that is, as an intervention into the politics of representation. It was produced by two Toronto transsexual artist-activists, Xanthra McKay and Jeanne B. (a.k.a. Mirha-Soleil Ross), who concerned themselves with speaking first and foremost to transsexuals, but not to the exclusion of speaking to members of other communities. Ironically, however, as Ross has said, the film was "not transgender enough" for gay and lesbian film festivals. Ross and McKay submitted the film to numerous gay and lesbian film festivals unsuccessfully, though the film was later screened as part of the Queer Sites academic conference.⁴ Made with a "8mm home video camera ... [and] ... their last two hundred bucks," *Gender Troublemakers* is quite literally a home movie, set in the kitchen, bedroom, and living room of a Toronto apartment.⁵ The film combines elements of "talking head" documentary and soft-core erotic film, intercutting footage of Ross and McKay interviewing one another in a question-and-answer discussion format, and footage of McKay and Ross rolling around in bed and making love to one another in other domestic spaces. Centrally concerned with the invisibility and silence of transsexuals in discussions of transsexuality, Ross and McKay initiate a conversation between transsexuals, on transsexual terms, while attempting to insert that conversation into a network of circulation that will speak "to other sexual communities as well as our own."

Both re-appropriating and reproaching the academic uptake of transgender, the video opens with a text still that frames what is to come for the viewer: "We are two 'gender queers,' 'gender outlaws,' 'trans dykes,' 'gender troublemakers' who don't look like Tula." Along with the video's title—"gender troublemakers"—this opening indexes Ross and McKay's familiarity with, and critical distance from, queer (and mainstream media) discourses on and of transgender. The two women self-designate through a list of portmanteau terms that hitch together or align queer and transgender signifiers, which are in turn qualified by their placement in scare quotes, on text stills, and by the reference to Tula. Tula, or Caroline Cossey, is a well-known transsexual model and actress who at various times has been a Bond girl, a Playboy Bunny, and commercial model. By marking their distance from both queer theory and the stereotypically beautiful and heterosexual transsexual model, McKay and Ross claim divergent and specific forms of transsexual embodiment and gendered belonging:

> We made this video spontaneously to make our bodies, our sexualities, our lives visible to other sexual communities as well as our own.
>
> Because transsexuals' backgrounds are all unique, this video does not pretend (nor can any other) to be a universal statement for transsexuals' experiences and issues.
>
> We have our own culture, language, stories and thus it is time for us and only us to document ourselves.

The word "trans-dyke" is worth lingering over in this regard: rather than simply referencing a transsexual lesbian identity of the sort claimed by Kate Bornstein or Beth Elliot, who lay claim to the queer possibility of transsexual women being lesbians, in McKay and Ross's usage, trans-dyke describes the sexual orientation of a transsexual woman desiring other transsexual women. The erotic footage of Ross and McKay together gives flesh to their discussions of trans-dyke erotic and emotional intimacy, which begin and close the video. This literal embodiment of their discourse is affectively emphatic, bringing what is sweet, playful, and sentimental to the fore, as well as making graphic the ordinary loveliness and awkwardness of sexuality. The resultant affect is bawdy, comic, and hopeful, even as it is complicatedly counterpoised to their narratives of violence and exclusion from the gay male community; Ross and McKay's erotic narrative is one of loss and rediscovery, and it is with a complex mixture of seriousness and irreverence that it approaches its avowedly romantic, almost utopian, horizon.

Perhaps a bawdy, at times irreverently comic mode is a necessary bridge between the utopian and romantic frame and the stark contrast with most of the conversations Ross and McKay have, which address the difficulties of living in the gay community as effeminate gay men during transition, and afterward, as transsexual women. Ross speaks of the difficulty of finding partners, of experiences of gay male repulsion toward her femininity, even when she lived as a man in Montreal, and of the unwillingness of gay men who had known her as a man to acknowledge or respect her identification as a woman during transition and after. McKay remarks on the verbal and physical harassment she routinely suffered at the hands of gay men during transition and states that as soon as she started to "assert (her) visual identity (her) sex life dropped to zero" and that she was given a choice between having sex and living her gender. Of course there is a complex of embodied, social, experiential, and not entirely conscious determinations at work within any person's shifting sense of one's self as a sexually attractive being, but McKay's account is corroborated by narratives of other trans women (Stryker, "Transgender Rage"; Salah, "Trans-fixed"). At the same time, when thinking about how one negotiates matters of body image when one is adopting an embodiment that is pathologized and marked as monstrous, even unintelligible, it is difficult not to recall the meaning given by Jones to aphanisis.[6] What's more, McKay here evokes a history of transsexuality's clinical management, in which homophobia intersected with gender normativity in the protocols that adjudicated suitability for sex reassignment.[7] Both at the clinic and in the "gay ghetto," toleration of transsexual difference has been secured through defensive desexualization of the transsexual as desiring subject.

The narratives McKay and Ross give do more than suggest the tremendous gulf separating the valorization of transgressive gender in queer transgender academic and activist discourses from the social circumstances facing transsexuals living in gay male communities. They also constitute a challenge to the naturalized status of erotic orientation, a challenge to (queer) identifications and disidentifications with genetic bodies, an ethical challenge to the obviousness of our own desires, and to the possibly necessary task of rendering political solidarity in the register of erotic recognition and affectional attachment.

The force of these quite radical challenges emerges in the disjunction between the claims of queer theory, invoked by Ross and McKay's appropriation of its rhetoric, and the "on the ground" experiences of two transsexuals living in gay communities. This disjunction suggests that both in its putative function as a more inclusive, open-ended rubric for the LGBTQ community and in terms of destabilizing identitarian logics, and celebrating fluid desires and identifications, the effects of queer are, after all, merely figural; that is, they are spectacular rather than performative and affective transformations of gay and lesbian practices and identities.

So while Ross and McKay's video obviously has important affirmative dimensions in terms of sexualizing and aestheticizing transsexual bodies in a context of ongoing social negation, it also puts negation to work in significant ways. The centring of trans-dyke, gender-queer bodies here mobilizes an aesthetic and erotic economy that does not require non-transsexual bodies as a positive point of reference. The political and sexual affective economy of (non-transsexual) lesbian separatism is redoubled even as it is unmoored from reference to non-transsexual bodies and subjects. As with its earlier, non-transsexual (anti-transsexual) lesbian formation, separatism seems to work by repudiation and consolidation in the projective making of self. Transvaluing experiences of transphobic social negation is achieved through the process of recounting and naming violence as violence in a public speech act (however small that public might have initially been); similarly, performing an alternative economy of desire, producing the body as desiring and desirable in a way that puts that body into circulation is as much a libidinal act as it is one of representation. Of course for such acts to be efficacious, they must draw their force from somewhere, and while the embodied and desiring self is one resource, another is the representational codes of sexual outsider, "gender outlaw," or "troublemaker," which the film's opening text stills initially cited with a measure of satiric distance.

At the same time, separatism is redeployed to critique "femmephobia" and misogyny as well as transphobia in gay male communities; necessarily, this transsexual separatism also retains a relationship to prior separatist formations. This relationship of redoubled reference operates both analogically, in terms of enabling the possible meanings of trans-dyke and/or transsexual separatisms, and critically, in light of lesbian separatist transphobia.[8]

It may seem redundant to modify the political signifier "lesbian separatist" with the designation "non-transsexual." As Henry Rubin and others have argued, the refusal of both FTM and MTF transsexuality was a key dimension in the constitution of the lesbian separatist subject (*Self-Made Men*). This question of definitional exclusion within identity formation draws together the Foucauldian concern with governmental aspects of identity management, normative values in new social movements, and the "self-organizing," if ultimately interminable, work of affect in making the self intelligible and acceptable to itself.

Gender Troublemakers asked questions that were—in 1993, at least—seemingly too troubling for many queer communities to entertain. Ross and McKay submitted the film to numerous gay and lesbian film festivals unsuccessfully, though the film was later screened as part of the Queer Sites[9] academic conference. It was the ongoing experience of being unable to see transsexual artworks, poetry, film, or video presented in queer, "alternative," or mainstream venues that led Mirha-Soleil Ross, with the aid of Xanthra McKay, to conceive of and coordinate the second community text I want to discuss, Counting Past 2.

The fall of 1997 was a boom time for transsexual and transgender representation, featuring the debut, on November 22, of TrannyFest, the first transgender film festival in the United States, the debut of the International Transgender Film and Video Festival in London, UK, over four days in October that year, and, on September 12, the launch of the first such event in North America, Counting Past 2: Performance-Film-Video-Spoken Word with Transsexual Nerve! in Toronto.[10] All three festivals consciously centred transsexual and transgender representation, though they made different curatorial choices about what that meant. These choices in turn represented and produced their own affective and identificatory organizations.

For instance, with the most substantial set of offerings, the International Transgender Film and Video Festival, organized and curated by Zachary Nataf, foregrounded a global selection of films, combining biographical feature-length films about transgender and transsexual people such as *You Don't Know Dick*, autobiographical shorts by trans people, anthropologically minded documentaries such as *Shinjuku Boys* and *Paris Is Burning*, and historical and commercial representations of trans people. With both global and historical aspirations the International Festival organizers clearly privileged rubrics of inclusion, globality, diversity, and difference, particularly attending to and articulating national, racial, and cultural difference as they smoothed over the axes of sexuality and gender identity political differences within and across trans and queer communities.

Trannyfest and Counting Past 2 were more modest in scale, but not necessarily in other ways; for example, in Trannyfest's first year, its directors Christopher Lee and Al Austin featured a single day of film programs, with a thematic emphasis on sexuality and erotica, sex work, and continuities between lesbian and gay, punk, gender-bending, and transsexual representations. Like the London International festival, Trannyfest has been strongly committed to fostering ties between transsexual, transgender, and queer constituencies, and did not restrict its programming to work produced by self-identified transgender and transsexual film and video makers.

Sharing some thematic and stylistic affinities with Trannyfest, Counting Past 2, which during its inaugural year took place over only a single evening, articulated a curatorial commitment to *exclusively* programming film and video work produced by transsexual and transgender people. The following curatorial statement from the Counting Past 2 website outlines why Ross felt such a stance was necessary:

> I decided to put together *Counting Past 2* in 1997 after almost a decade of struggling with *the* big wigs at queer film festivals either not showing any interest in my work (which is concerned mainly with transsexual sexual representation) or telling me that my films were not "transgender" enough to fit in their queer programs.... Every decade has its own wave of fascination, exoticization, sensationalization, economic exploitation, and misrepresentation of transsexuals. The 90's are no exception with more and more academics, writers, film makers, and activists making a hobby or a lucrative project out of deconstructing, reconstructing, redeconstructing, and re-reconstructing gender or of attacking "old fashioned" and "deluded" transsexuals under the guise of "dismantling the binary gender system...." (Counting Past 2, Background and Objectives)

Ross locates her own impulse to develop a separate space for transsexual representation "on transsexual terms" as a response to what she sees as a persistent pattern of queer festival programming that celebrates trans-themed programs by non-trans filmmakers, including films that she and many other transsexuals find irrelevant, appropriative, exploitative, and frequently offensive. The flip side of this process is evidenced in the unwillingness of queer film programmers to screen work by transsexuals, or at least by transsexuals who are not queer-identified or operating within the expectations of a queer cinema well on its way to establishing its own aesthetic conventions.[11] As with her earlier work in *Gender Troublemakers*, there is explicit, if snarkily satirical, reference made to queer theoretical norms she takes as at least locally dominant within sexual minority contexts. Though mobilizing identity rhetoric, Ross's critique is less concerned with questions of authenticity, essence, or positive representation than it is with the discursive, material, and institutional conditions of possibility for the production of transsexual art and culture, as well as for its circulation, and reception within different public and sexual minority counter-public forums. Further, in recognition of the economic requirements of artistic production (such as the cost of film stock) and the marginal economic situation of many trans people, Counting Past 2 combined its screenings with spoken word, performance, live music, and audio art. Ross made explicit the intention behind these curatorial decisions:

> Making a commitment to maintaining a festival that is not thematic (i.e.: showing work made by TS/TG/intersex people as opposed to showing work about TS/TG/intersex lives) and one that includes TG/intersex artists while focusing on TS work poses some challenges: One: There is very little circulating annually and most of it comes from the same (albeit talented!!) handful of queer-identified TS/TG film makers who have made it in Queer Film Fest circuits. Two: A large percentage of transsexual & transgendered people live way, way below the poverty line and making films is just not a realistic project for them. Therefore, right from the beginning, a multi-disciplinary festival which was going to validate dance, music, spoken word, and embrace artists who do not have the resources or the connections for making movies became imperative. (Counting Past 2, Background and Objectives)

Thus the event drew equally upon the traditions of bawdy burlesque and Brechtian cabaret, at times in a scathingly satirical tone and confrontational address. Ross herself hosted the cabaret/filmfest, and her speech moved animatedly from effusive welcomes and "thank yous" to those who attended the events, to the details and logistics of the events, to spontaneous and often hilarious stories to fill time around the inevitable technical glitches, and to critical enunciations of the curatorial position outlined above.

Evaluative criteria are always inflected with social values even as they are lived as preference, affective response, and "taste." In *Distinction*, Pierre Bourdieu argues not only the class-based (and thus constructed) character of taste, but its animation through "unconscious" belief and subjectively inhabited "dispositions." Such internalized practices of perception, affective response, and social action (elements of what Bourdieu names as habitus [4]) provide one way to think the "affirmative experience," if coercive dimension, of normative values, though clearly such inhabited values also take up objects in negation. Recalling Bourdieu's model of habitus brings together the inherited attributes of social class with experiential history, allowing us to think about the ways in which "low class," earnest, or identity political transsexual art might suffer not only in the judgment of art world snobbery, but how the production and content norms of lesbian and gay film festivals might become naturalized as "standard criteria" for interesting cultural work by members of sexual minorities, and finally how personal histories in feminist and queer debate might translate into demographic or generational postures of exhaustion or boredom in response to identity political work. Indeed, the work of affective distinction might also manifest as middle-class discomfort at the felt presence of poor, sex-working, substance-using, or otherwise marginal others.

It is crucial to read Counting Past 2's eschewal of production values and thematic codes geared at drawing in a potentially lucrative lesbian and gay or, more broadly, non-transsexual audience through and beyond the relational process outlined by Pierre Bourdieu, by which cultural prestige accrues to elite forms in dialectical tension with the commercial productivity of mass forms. As Barbara Godard demonstrates in her reading of gender's difference and displacement of the terms of this dialectic, Bourdieu neglects to consider in his thinking the devaluation of women's "anti-economic" cultural labour. Godard contests both elite "disinterestedness" and the imperatives of the market; in her reading, "feminists bring with them no accumulation of capital, either economic, which might be reconverted into support for their cultural productions. Nor through their labour are feminist producers brought into the cycle of consecration, so that the investment of their work accumulates the 'authority' and convertibility of a recognized name" ("Feminist Periodicals" 211).[12] If this is true of feminist editorial collectives in relationship to elite and market fields of cultural production and circulation, it is not necessarily the case where feminist formations have entered into articulation with state and interstate bodies, such as the UN and the transnational NGO industrial complex. Regardless, the situation is more acute in terms of transsexual community-based production, which has suffered, as Namaste has demonstrated, from a routine refusal on the part of mainstream and alternative media to mention, let alone cover, such events:

> Festival organizer Mirha-Soleil Ross sent out press releases, faxes, and telephone calls to all the major mainstream and lesbian/gay media in and around the greater Toronto area ... including mainstream newspapers such as the *Toronto Star* and the *Globe and Mail*, as well as alternative publications like *Eye* and *Now Magazine*. Local television stations were also contacted. Incredibly, CP2 received only one mention in the Arts section of the *Globe and Mail*. (*Sex Change* 44)

Despite these obstacles, Counting Past 2 expanded rapidly in the next two years from an evening-length cabaret to a four-day event by dramatically increasing its film and video programs, growing its cabaret, and incorporating panel discussions with cultural producers and community activists, theatrical and musical programs, lectures, slide shows, and a book launch. In large part because of its multidisciplinary and activist mandate, in addition to creating a forum for socially marginal artists, Counting Past 2 performed several key functions in making transsexual/transgender community.

First, Counting Past 2 facilitated the sharing of information among transsexual and transgender people as to the particularities of our bodies and our lives. As Sandy Stone has noted, "It is difficult to articulate a counter-discourse if one is programmed to disappear" ("The Empire" 295). This is as true if one is operating a medicalized narrative that requires the concealment and re-description of a pre-transition history, as if one is engaging the vanguardism of a queer feminism that makes self-description in its idiom a precondition for political speech or legitimacy.

Second, Counting Past 2 inaugurated a transsexual-centred space of cultural production; it occupied and re-territorialized queer and straight bars, cultural and academic zones, such as Buddies in Bad Times Theatre, The Bloor Cinema, the University of Toronto campus as spaces for transsexual, transgender, and intersex folk, and, what's more, as spaces for prostitutes, drug users, people on welfare and disability benefits. Bringing poor and economically marginal trans constituencies into spaces usually marked as middle class, whether queer, feminist or straight, may have been as challenging as the screening of works whose production values did not meet the expectations of screening committees or audiences attached to the formal and content conventions validated at queer film and video festivals.

A third key function was that, in recognizing that transgender representations and cultural producers were, relative to transsexual artists, privileged in their access to the queer film festival circuit, curator Mirha-Soleil Ross attempted to develop a context that was transgender and intersex inclusive but transsexual-centred. This choice obviously produced its own asymmetries of representation, but it is important to recall that Ross did consistently program works by trans people working within queer paradigms (such as Del La Grace Volcano and Christopher Lee) who were receiving play in queer/transgender contexts; she simply did not limit her programming to, or privilege, works or aesthetic criteria from those contexts. Despite this, Ross's decision did have obvious consequences, as keynotes by Aiyyana Maracle, Max Wolfe Valerio, and Viviane Namaste, though relatively well attended, and "successful," did not draw the audiences in the numbers generated by U.S. queer-trans celebrities Leslie Feinberg, Kate Bornstein, or Judith Halberstam, with their significant queer community crossover appeal. As well, the centring of transsexual artists often drew accusations of exclusivity, "naive" identity politics, and bad (parochial) art. Perhaps this is an understandable reaction in a context that is more concerned with creating spaces where in transsexual, transgender, and intersex audiences, artists and representations could come together rather than playing to expectations that privilege "insider" queer viewing pleasure over the production of knowledges, narratives, and image repertoires that open the space for transsexual lives and politics.

That is not to say there were not less rational and more affective dynamics at work. Bourdieu is helpful for tracking the ways in which subordinate and oppositional groups negotiate the negation of their own "good taste:" "[i]t must never be forgotten that the working-class 'aesthetic' is a dominated 'aesthetic' which is constantly obliged to define itself in terms of the dominant aesthetics ..." (41). Certainly, in Ross's commitment to and celebration of works that did not accord with the dominant content and production norms, there was a kind of Rabelaisian exuberance and unapologetic "fuck you" to the "good taste" of the large LGBTQ filmfests that at times exceeded but perhaps fell into the problematic agon to which any counter-discourse is heir.

The unapologetic inclusion of work by subjects visibly marked by poverty and criminality, as well as the embrace of crude production values, reliance upon experiential knowledge, or strident political critique may be easily dismissed as courting the distasteful and uninteresting. Audience and media responses to community-based transsexual cultural productions such as Counting Past 2 may be overdetermined by an affective resistance, registered viscerally as well at the level of aesthetic and intellectual judgment, to cultural forms embodying and representing "knowledges that have been disqualified as nonconceptual knowledges, as insufficiently elaborated knowledges, naïve knowledges, hierarchically inferior knowledges ..." (Foucault, qtd. in Stryker, *(De)Subjugated Knowledges* 13).

Working with, but complicating, the class-based categories allocating "distinction" and cultural prestige in Bourdieu's work, Barbara Godard draws attention to the gender bias operative as symbolic value that accrues to aesthetic production, which is marked as outside of a "generalized field" whose coordinates are plotted in relation to the market ("Feminist Periodicals" 211). As she says, "value is the effect of many operations of differentiation that establish a work's pertinence within a socially stratified field" (210). Godard discusses the ways in which women's unpaid cultural production is not recognized and not valued within an economy of aesthetic prestige (i.e., within the "'restricted field' of 'high art'" [211]). This, of course, coheres with the more general devaluation of women's labour, the failure to recognize the gendered work of social reproduction.

Regarding the labour of transsexual and transgender subjects, it seems that there is, again, a crisis of classification wherein a suspicion as to the ontological (sexed) status of the trans subject may preclude the assignment of value; certainly, non-passing trans people's difficulty in accessing paid employment within the legal economy is directly tied to transphobic repudiation of not only trans people's sex of identification, but of their value as people within the sex of assignment. Conversely, transsexual women's most consistently lucrative form of employment, sex work, constitutes a social and legal scandal, in as much as sex work puts on the market women's participation in an economy of exchange that operates through its opacity as exchange (i.e., sexual and emotional labour within heterosexual marriage) (Irigaray 185). It is perhaps this scandal that requires that women, including transsexual women, who engage in sex work be symbolically abjected, without value beyond their sexual labour, and treated as disposable in relation to it, and simultaneously barred from recognition as producers of value or culture. There is also the question of "the other of the other": the feminist engaging the public remains haunted by that *other* public woman, the prostitute (Bell 2, 3).

If, as Godard argues, "feminists have been conscious of the ease with which feminist discourse can be manipulated to turn an emancipatory discourse for women into an oppressive discourse on woman" ("Feminist Periodicals" 213), this is a consciousness both transsexuals and sex workers have also had regarding feminist and queer uptakes of their discourses. Particularly at issue then are those moments when trans discourses seek currency, articulation, or recognition within feminist and queerly animated counter-hegemonic formations. Hence it seems urgent to emphasize the importance of Counting Past 2 and festivals of its kind as emergent counter-public spaces, contiguous to but not subsumed within queer and feminist formations; hence as sites wherein "the other of the other"—transsexual, transgender, and intersex audiences—could engage one another as well as representations and artists from their own communities. A few examples will suggest their range: *Shadmith Manzo Performance* was a video short by Boyd Kodak and Cat Grant, documenting the then recent deportation from Canada of Mexican transsexual activist Shadmith Manzo. Grant and Kodak's grainy, eight-minute documentary told the story of Manzo's efforts to claim refugee status, and of immigration officials' refusal to acknowledge her transsexual status. It also shared glimpses of her life in Toronto's community and with her partner, Crystal, and showcased Manzo's volunteer work as the coordinator of the Transition Support Group at the 519 Community Centre. Finally, it detailed the circumstances and brutal, if routine, manner of her deportation. Beyond documenting the injustice to and suffering of Shadmith Manzo and her partner, *Shadmith Manzo Performance* was used to educate broader communities about Manzo's situation and that of other trans people immigrating to escape persecution and violence. It also functioned as a tool to raise funds to fight for her return to Canada.

Another documentary, *Trappings of Transhood*, by Christopher Lee and Elise Hurwitz, featured interviews with a diverse sampling of "pre-op," "post-op," and "no-op" trans men that gave some at that time difficult to obtain information on the particulars of FTM transition, as well as engaging in frank and controversial discussions on questions of male privilege, homophobia and queerness, sexuality and racial segregation within trans communities. Lee has referred to the film as his "community service" before moving onto more "fun stuff."[13] Certainly, it was a "service" that was otherwise lacking from sites of public life, one providing symbolic, affective, and practical resources to a still emergent community. Lee's subsequent production, *Alley of the Tranny Boys*, was equally groundbreaking as the first feature-length porno starring a full cast of trans men, in a retro 1970s porn style, with trans men inhabiting and enjoying, only somewhat ironically, their sexily macho roles. *Alley* screened at Counting Past 2 the following year.

Live performances by festival keynotes such as Aiyyana Maracle and Max Wolf Valerio gave Counting Past 2 audiences more immediate contact with innovative work by established performance artists and writers who, notwithstanding successful careers prior to transition, were having difficulty circulating their work after. Maracle's one-woman show, *Chronicle of a Transformed Woman*, incorporated elements of First Nations medicine ritual and detailed her use of Native/traditional technologies for transitioning genders, imbricating personal history, cultural archive and narratives of collective suffering, and struggle under colonial rule. Max Wolf Valerio read from what would eventually be published as his *The Testosterone Files*, an archival documentation of changing physicality, sexuality, affective orientation, and social perception during his first few years on testosterone. And as suggested in Ross's curatorial statement, the inclusion of a cabaret element allowed for the participation of a more socially and economically diverse group of trans artists than might be involved in straight film and video festival.[14]

Counting Past 2 also provided a forum for conversations among trans artists, one of the crucial conditions for generating a critical and aesthetic discourse grounded in the experiences of transsexual and transgender people, and facilitating discussions among transgender/transsexual communities across national borders. Over the years the festival featured work by intersexuals, transgenders, butch lesbians, and both male-to-female and female-to-male transsexuals, and new work from artists based in Canada, Germany, Japan, the Caribbean, Latin America, New Zealand, Australia, Québec, the United States, and the United Kingdom.

As knowledge production by "the other of the other" for "the other of the other" that worked to enable survival and desirable, desiring lives, the work showcased at Counting Past 2 mobilized, albeit through radically different contents and media, a generation of value through an economy of the gift. This value-generating labour[15] is identified by Elena Basile ("Love's Interests") and highlighted by Barbara Godard in discussions of collectively run feminist periodicals ("Feminist Periodicals" 212). Godard cautions, however, that preferring the economy of the gift over that of accumulation entails a deepening risk of devaluation in a public sphere reconstituted as economic privatization.

The festival's growth was not uncomplicated; as Namaste has documented, transsexuals' access to the mainstream media was and remains fraught. Repeated approaches to both alternative and lesbian and gay media were ambivalently successful at best, and occasionally the tabloids proved better venues for promotion. That is not to say that there was no progress made; over three years the festival generated an audience, and garnered some institutional and financial support from the Maggie's Toronto Prostitutes' Community Service Project, the Toronto Women's Bookstore, the Sexual Diversity Studies Program at the University of Toronto, the 519 Community Centre, and other arts festivals such as Desh Pardesh, the Inside Out Lesbian and Gay Film Festival, and Rights on Reel: the Toronto Human Rights Film Festival. Despite those gains, however, the festival was largely driven by the volunteer labour of Ross and a close cohort of friends and allies, and financed by Ross and her partner Mark Karbusicky. After three years, Ross retired Counting Past 2, though under the stewardship of Boyd Kodak and Cat Grant, the festival was resurrected for a final year in 2002.

Other trans film festivals also had difficulty maintaining themselves as annual events. By 1999 *Trannyfest* was a week-long event, and its expanded format included artists' panels, performance events, etc., but it also went into hiatus that year, re-emerging in 2001, under Christopher Lee's sole directorship, as a biannual event. Similarly, the London-based International Festival had switched hands from Nataf to Kam Wai Kui after 1998 and enjoyed its final year in 1999. The London festival was replaced by the Amsterdam-based Nederlands Transgender Film Festival in 2001, also under Kam Wai Kui's directorship, and has operated biannually since that time (Kui, "History").

I want to note that while all three film festivals saw tough times, it is significant that two of three festivals have survived and grown (if not as annual events), and that one did not. There are various factors one might invoke to account for this situation: differing municipal, even national, cultural contexts; differing degrees of institutional and/or community support; questions of legibility to mainstream and straight alternative press; varying interpretations of mandates to represent, involve, and/or respond to the needs of economically as well as socially and sexually marginal constituencies; personal burnout on the part of charismatic, visionary, entrepreneurial, and hard-working founding curators with greater or lesser ability or inclination to cultivate their own successors. All of these have undoubtedly played a role, but the curatorial distinctions between Counting Past 2 and the other two festivals, the International Transgender Film and Video Festival and San Francisco's TrannyFest, which I've highlighted, strike me as particularly relevant in this regard with implications for festival programming, funding, audience, and community involvement—in short, with implications for the festivals' capacity to be sustainable as counter-public spaces.[16]

I conclude by observing that without practising separatism, Counting Past 2 did not court legitimation through the adoption of queer or feminist economies of prestige. This difficulty returns us again to the question of the value of transgendered, transsexual, and sex worker labour, and of how "the other of the other" might sustain herself without being subsumed in, or perhaps precisely negated by, the more successful counter-hegemonic productions of queer and feminist cultures. This question becomes more acute still if we mark ways in which queer and feminist liberalism have entered post-feminist and homo-normative accommodation with neo-liberal economics and cultural governance.

Notes

This chapter reworks and extends arguments originally presented in my doctoral dissertation, "An Inquiry into Transsexual and Transgender Rhetorics, Affects, and Politics," undertaken under the inspired and generous supervision of Dr. Barbara Godard.

The terms "transgender" and "transsexual" have been the subject of considerable debate internal to trans and queer communities. Transsexuality emerged as a clinical term in the mid-twentieth century for people who wished to alter their physical sex to correspond to their gender of identification. The language of transgender is rooted in a rejection of transsexuality, and was posed as alternative nomenclature for those who identified across sex, but did not necessarily wish to alter their physical embodiment. In the work of Leslie Feinberg and Gordene Olga MacKenzie, it was launched as an umbrella term for all those who disidentified with either their sex of assignment and/or the gendered presentations and behaviours conventionally associated with it. Subsequently many transsexual and intersex activists and theorists have objected to the subsuming of transsexuality and intersex under a "transgender umbrella," claiming the term "transgender" is inaccurate, anti-transsexual, and obscures distinct and at times conflicting political agendas. At the same time, many have come to use the term "transgender" interchangeably with the term "transsexual." For representative critiques, see Namaste's *Invisible Lives*, Rubin's "Phenomenology as Method in Trans Studies," and Herndon's "FAQ." Both transsexual and transgender people employ the shorthand of MTF and FTM to designate "male-to-female" and "female-to-male" transitions respectively.

1   The significance of transgender figures for feminist discourses has generated a large body of scholarly work and is too large a topic to substantively engage here. Briefly, Janice Raymond's 1979 *The Transsexual Empire: The Making of the She-Male* is the canonical radical feminist text on transsexuality and, as many have argued, its vitriolic repudiation of transsexuality stood as the dominant, if not uncontested, feminist position on transsexuality for over a decade. Drawing uncritically upon the worst stereotypes of the psychiatric literature, Raymond's book denounced MTF transsexuals as rapists and enforcers of conservative gender norms as well as victims of patriarchal medical hubris, while largely glossing over the existence of FTM transsexuals, dismissing them as women employing misguided means to survive patriarchal oppression. Though challenged by Stone, Namaste, and others in the early 1990s, transphobia remains a significant tendency within some feminist thought and organizing. While contemporary queer feminist discourses generally condemn Raymond's text, there are at times curious parallels. Trans men (FTM transsexuals) are often celebrated and welcomed within women's spaces, but paradoxically may be refused recognition as men; trans women (MTF transsexuals) appear most palatable to queer feminism when they claim to embody queer gender, forgoing their identification as women.

In this essay I focus on the ways in which trans women are constructed as the "other of the other" in ways that intensify and extend the misogynist devaluation of women's labour. The erasure of trans men is an effect of a somewhat different dynamic, one that turns upon the denial of their status as men, but also values them, in a non-consensual way, as "special men" who are "not quite, not like" men. Henry Rubin has done some important preliminary work in theorizing and challenging this phenomenon. For some representative transsexual and transgender readings of trans figuration in feminism, see Stone's "The Empire," Namaste's "Tragic Misreadings" and *Invisible Lives*, Prosser's *Second Skins*, Rubin's "Reading Like a (Transsexual) Man," and Salah's "Writing Trans Genre."

2   I am drawing upon Shannon Bell's use of this phrase to describe the situation of the prostitute in relationship to feminist discourses. I do so both because I believe transsexuals are positioned analogously to sex workers within many feminist discourses, and because for many MTF transsexuals, sex work is a source of income and a site of individual and communal self-fashioning *and* politicization. Further, I would suggest that there is a rhetorical and affective bleed between transphobic and anti-sex worker feminist discourses (Bell, *Reading, Writing, and Rewriting*; Namaste, *Sex Change*).

3   By post-feminism, I intend three tendencies that mark feminist gains, losses, and complicities with common sense and social power. First, since the late 1960s we've seen explicitly feminist interventions to both critique the state and claim a place at the table in governance: in the Canadian context, Barbara Godard has documented and analyzed the rising and falling fortunes of feminist ventures into lobbying, policy-making, and state-sponsored cultural production, charting especially the consequences for explicitly feminist projects (such as activist lobbying bodies like NAC and feminist periodicals) subjected to an ongoing process of de-funding and delegitimization since the late 1980s ("Feminist Periodicals"). Second, we have seen concomitant, if selective, integration of elements of feminist projects within mainstream institutions (the corporate media, the state, the UN and the NGO industrial complex, universities, as well as U.S. presidential tickets and "feminist" justifications for imperialist war, i.e., "we're doing it for the women") (Halley, *Split Decisions*). While it would be tempting to read these as either appropriations that can be resisted from the site of a pure and oppositional authentic feminism or the legacy of a weak, always already suspect, white, middle-class "liberal" feminist project—which, again, could be denounced from the site of a more authentically radical camp—my contention is that the problem is deeper and broader. Whether we are discussing the intellectual vanguardism of queer, post-colonial, and post-structuralist feminisms, the anti-oppression and anti-authoritarian militancy of transnational feminist projects, or the grassroots radical feminism of violence against women organizing in the shelter movements, feminist endeavours broadly intervene in and do their work through the material and symbolic culture of the neo-liberal university, state, and social movements. It seems that in order to make such interventions there needs to be an other woman, an insistently silenced or silent woman whom these feminist projects speak for and

often against (prostitutes, transsexuals, veiled women). Spivak has discussed this as the problem of subaltern speech ("Subaltern"). Finally, post-feminism can be seen as manifest in the popular resuscitation of the cult of femininity, reinvigorated by some combination of postmodern/queer irony, selective feminist consciousness (in the liberal individualist/consumerist mode), and "generationally coded" refusal of what are perceived as the normativities of second wave feminist practices (Hallows and Moseley).

4 Speaking particularly to the Toronto context, Namaste points out that the Inside/Out: Lesbian and Gay Film Festival's decision to not screen *Gender Troublemakers* was particularly troubling given that the festival that year programmed a "gender bending" film night, featuring "drag queens, chicks with dicks and other sexual anomalies" [*sic*]. Namaste situates this event in terms of an interplay between selective deployment of trans "image content" and the systemic exclusion of transsexual cultural production, in lesbian and gay, as well as straight, media (*Sex Change* 43).

5 These details are from the promotional copy for the video, available on the website of its distributor, VTape: <http://www.vtape.org/catalogue.htm>. In the time since 1993, *Gender Troublemakers* has in fact been screened at a few film festivals, including Vancouver's Out on Screen in 1994, and San Francisco's TrannyFest in 1998.

6 In Laplanche and Pontalis's summary aphanisis is a fear of "the disappearance of sexual desire. According to Jones, aphanisis is the object, in both sexes, of a fear more profound than the fear of castration" (*The Language of Psychoanalysis* 40).

7 See Stone's "Empire"; Namaste's *Invisible Lives* (202–5).

8 The differences between trans-dyke and transsexual women's separatisms can be understood on the model of the distinction between lesbian separatist and woman-only spaces afforded by Kate Bornstein. The trans-dyke space charted in *Gender Troublemakers* symbolically re-territorializes desiring pathways for trans-dyke eroticism, and actively distinguishes itself against (separates from) social space seen to be transphobic and hegemonic (gay male and lesbian separatist); transsexual separatist spaces, such as the New Woman Conference, constitute woman-only space for post-operative transsexual women who have "completed" a social-surgical transition. That is, the latter articulates a positive and restrictive criteria for admission to the category "woman," albeit one specific to transsexual women. For more on the New Women's Conference and controversies surrounding its identity politics, see Riki Ann Wilchins's "Transsexual Separatism? or Is Anyone Out There Listening?"

9 For another account of the systemic exclusion of transsexual cultural production from lesbian and gay as well as straight media, see Namaste's "Beyond Image Content: Examining Transsexuals' Access to the Media" in *Sex Change, Social Change*.

10 Unfortunately, the websites for both the now defunct International Transgender Film Festival and Counting Past 2 have gone off-line. However, as of this writing in February 2011, much of their content is still accessible through The Way Back Machine, a search engine that accesses "snapshots" of cached files of the entire web from 1996 to the present. The Way Back Machine does not produce a perfect copy, however, as some graphics, flash, links, etc., are non-operational, and content on The Way Back Machine is sometimes removed at the request of copyright holders or for other reasons. The Way Back Machine is part of a dynamic archival project of the International School of Information Science of the Bibliotheca Alexandrina. For more on The Way Back Machine, visit <http://www.bibalex.org/ISIS/archive_web.htm>. For more on the International Transgender Film Festival, listen to Nancy Nangeroni and Gordene McKenzie's "Interview with Zach Nataf" (2003).

11 Ross is not alone in articulating this critique. On a panel discussion at the Trans Canada: Crossing Gender Borders event, "a celebratory evening of spoken word, performance and video art created by transgendered and transsexual artists," writer Max Wolfe Valerio described the difficulty of going from being a sought-after performer at spoken-word events in the San Francisco Bay Area to being unable to find performance and publishing venues during and after his transition in the mid-1980s and early 1990s. This shift corresponded to his transition from butch to FTM identification and presentation and was, on Valerio's account, an effect of a lesbian feminist culture that is indifferent to men at best and hostile to them at worst, as well as reflecting a more specific, if widespread, anti-transsexual sentiment in that context. For more on Valerio's account of the challenges of transitioning out of a lesbian feminist cultural milieu, see his memoir, *The Testosterone Files*.

12 Corroborating Godard's insights, Rita Felski's articulation of the para-aesthetic work of feminist poetics helps us think about how these impasses have played out in other scenes. Felski enumerates the barriers that have traditional barred most women's access to the aesthetic, both material (money, time, education) and symbolic (the gendered norms governing what is considered great art, as well as the sexism of the institutional practices of the art world, routinely diminishing or erasing the accomplishments of women artists, etc.). Further, she suggests that in the context of feminist art, which is not at all the same thing as women's art, there has traditionally been a questioning of the relation between aesthetic and social practices, focusing on women's sexuality, embodiment, and subjectivity. Hence it can be consider para-aesthetic in aim as well as effect (*Doing Time*)

Trans artists have similarly encountered specific, if not absolute, barriers to cultural production. Poverty and truncated access to university or even high school education are common to those who transition young, whereas those who postpone transitioning have had to grapple with loss of employment,

pre-transition work experience, contacts, and artistic productions; traditionally this was due to the treatment protocols for transsexuality, which emphasized the retroactive production of a pre-transition history congruent with one's post-transition sex, though as that clinical protocol has lost force, other factors have come to seem more pressing.
13 Personal communication.
14 Namaste has observed that "the cabaret showcases a much more ethnically diverse group of people than that comprising the filmmakers.... Mister Cool presented an energetic Soca dance from Trinidad while Maury Mariana delighted participants with a flamenco dance" (*Sex Change* 55). The cabaret context also plays homage to, and creates continuity with, the long history of transsexuals working as showgirls and "impersonators" in burlesque reviews and drag shows. As Namaste notes, there is substantial crossover between prostitute and show queen milieu, and Counting Past 2 grounded itself in those milieux as much as it did in academic and arts contexts, ensuring that prostitutes and performers could be comfortable within its environs (55–56).
15 While capitalist economics understand value in the registers of labour (production) and use (consumption), feminist critics have highlighted the invisible and unvalued labour of social reproduction. Basile extends feminist psychoanalytic articulations of maternal labour and love as a foundational gift that is unpayable and incalculable, and anthropological theorizations of gift-giving practices as precursors to any possible economy of circulation or exchange, in order to make explicit the contradictory value of love's labour in constituting (feminist) cultural production as gift economy ("Love's Interest").
16 Of course this may not be unrelated to other distinctions: for example, Ross, Counting Past 2's curator for three years, is a transsexual woman situated within sex-working and street-active communities. Zachary Nataf, Kam Wai Kui, and Christopher Lee are FTM transsexuals with strong ties to lesbian and queer arts milieux and resources.

Works Cited

Basile, Elena, "Love's Interests." *Tessera* 22 (1997): 56–61. Print.
Bell, Shannon. *Reading, Writing, and Rewriting the Prostitute Body*. Bloomington/Indianapolis: Indiana UP, 1994. Print.
Bourdieu, Pierre. *Distinction: A Social Critique of the Judgment of Taste*. Trans. Richard Nice. Cambridge: Harvard UP, 2007. Print.
Feinberg, Leslie. "Transgender Liberation: A Movement Whose Time Has Come." *Materialist Feminism: A Reader in Class*. Ed. Rosemary and Chrys Ingraham. New York: Routledge, 1997. Print.
Felski, Rita. *Doing Time: Feminist Theory and Postmodern Culture*. New York: New York UP, 2000. Print.

Gender Troublemakers: Transsexuals in the Gay Community. Dir. Mirha-Soleil Ross and Xanthra McKay. Perf. Mirha-Soleil Ross and Xanthra McKay. Toronto, 1993. Video.
Godard, Barbara. "Culture at the Crossroads." *Resources for Feminist Research/Documentation sur la recherche féministe* 32.3–4 (2007): 13–28. Print.
———. "Feminist Periodicals and the Production of Cultural Value: The Canadian Context." *Women's Studies International Forum* 25.2 (2002): 209–23. Print.
———. "Notes from the Cultural Field." *Canadian Literature at the Crossroads of Language and Culture*. Ed. Smaro Kamboureli. Edmonton: NeWest, 2008. Print.
Halley, Janet. *Split Decisions: How and Why to Take a Break from Feminism*. Princeton: Princeton UP, 2006. Print.
Hallows, Joanne, and Rachel Moseley. "Popularity Contests: The Meanings of Popular Feminism." *Feminism and Popular Culture*. Ed. Hollows and Moseley. London/New York: Berg, 2006. 1–22. Print.
Herndon, April. "FAQ: Why Doesn't ISNA Want to Eradicate Gender?" The Intersex Society of North America. Web. September 9, 2006. <http://www.isna.org/faq/not_eradicating_gender>.
Irigaray, Luce. "Women on the Market. *This Sex Which Is Not One*. Trans. Catherine Porter. Ithaca: Cornell UP, 1985. Print.
Kodak, Boyd, and Cat Grant. *The Shadmith Manzo Performance*. Toronto, 1997. Video.
Kui, Kam Wai. "History of the International and Netherlands Transgender Film Festivals." Gender/Transgender Dynamics: Then and Now Panel. Image+Nation: Montreal International LGBT Film Festival, 20th Anniversary Symposium. Concordia University, Montreal, November 16, 2007.
Laplanche, J., and J.B. Pontalis. *The Language of Psychoanalysis*. Trans. Donald Nicholson-Smith. New York/London: W.W. Norton and Company, 1973. Print.
Lee, Christopher. *Alley of the Trannyboys*. U.S., 1998. Video.
Lee, Christopher, and Elise Hurwitz. *Trappings of Transhood*. U.S., 1997. Video.
MacKenzie, Gordene Olga. *Transgender Nation*. Bowling Green, OH: Bowling Green State U Popular P, 1994. Print.
Maracle, Aiyyanna. "Chronicle of a Transformed Woman." Reading at Counting Past 2: Performance-Film-Video-Spoken Word with Transsexual Nerve! Curated by Mirha-Soleil Ross. University of Toronto, Toronto, September 1999.
Namaste, Ki. "Tragic Misreadings: Queer Theory's Erasure of Transgender Subjectivity." *Queer Studies: A Lesbian, Gay, Bisexual, and Transgender Anthology*. Ed. Brett Beemyn and Mickey Eliason. New York: New York UP, 1996. 183–203. Print.
Namaste, Viviane K. *Invisible Lives: The Erasure of Transsexual and Transgendered People*. Chicago: U of Chicago P, 2000. Print.

———. *Sex Change, Social Change: Reflections on Identity, Institutions, and Imperialism*. Toronto: Woman's Press, 2005. Print.

Nataf, Zach. Interview by Nancy Nangeroni and Gordene McKenzie. "Representations of Transgenderism in the Media." *GenderTalk Web Radio*. Program no. 395, January 20, 2003. Web. April 17, 2008. <http://www.gendertalk.com/radio/programs/350/gt395.shtml>.

Prosser, Jay. *Second Skins: The Body Narratives of Transsexuality*. New York: Columbia UP, 1998. Print.

Raymond, Janice. *The Transsexual Empire: The Making of the She-Male*. Boston: Beacon, 1979. Print.

Ross, Mirha-Soleil. "Counting Past 2: Background and Objectives." Counting Past 2: Performance-Film-Video-Spoken Word with Transsexual Nerve! <www.countingpast2.com>. Web. November 12, 2007. Currently off-line, archived at: <http://web.archive.org/web/20001202160700/>. www.countingpast2.com/background.html>.

———. "Prostitution as Financially, Sexually, and Culturally Validating for French Working Class Transsexuals." Sex Trade 101: A Panel Discussion on Sex Worker's Rights, Toronto, 2000.

———. *Yapping Outloud: Contagious Thoughts from an Unrepentant Whore*. Written and performed by Mirha-Soleil Ross. Assoc. dir.: Nicola Stamp. Dist.: V-Tape, Toronto, 2002. Video.

Rubin, Henry. "Phenomenology as Method in Trans Studies." The Transgender Issue. Spec. issue of *GLQ* 4.2 (1998): 263–81. Print.

———. "Reading Like a (Transsexual) Man." *Men Doing Feminism*. Ed. Tom Digby. New York: Routledge, 1998. 305–24. Print.

———. *Self-Made Men: Identity and Embodiment among Transsexual Men*. Nashville: Vanderbilt UP, 2003. Print.

Salah, Trish. "Trans-fixed in Lesbian Paradise: Reflections on the Toronto Women's Bathhouse." *Sexy Feminisms*. Ed. Susannah Luhmann and Rachel Warburton. Spec. issue of *Atlantis: A Women's Studies Journal* 31.2 (Autumn 2007): 24–29. Print.

———. "What's All the Yap? Reading Mirha-Soleil Ross' Performance of Activist Pedagogy." *Spoken Word Performance*. Ed. Theresa Cowan and Ric Knowles. Spec. issue of *Canadian Theatre Review* 130 (Spring 2007): 64–71. Print.

———. "Writing Trans Genre: An Inquiry into Transsexual and Transgender Rhetorics, Affects, and Politics." Unpublished Ph.D. dissertation, York University, Toronto, 2009. Print.

Spivak, Gayatri. "Can the Subaltern Speak?" *Marxism and the Interpretation of Culture*. Ed. Cary Nelson and Lawrence Grossberg. Basingstoke: Macmillan Education, 1988. 271–313. Print.

Stone, Sandy. "The Empire Strikes Back: A Posttranssexual Manifesto." *Body Guards: The Cultural Politics of Gender Ambiguity*. Ed. Julia Epstein and Kristina Straub. New York/London: Routledge, 1991. 280–304. Print.

Stryker, Susan. "(De)Subjugated Knowledges: An Introduction to Transgender Studies." *The Transgender Studies Reader.* Ed. Susan Stryker and Stephen Whittle. New York: Routledge, 2006. 1–17. Print.

———. "My Words to Victor Frankenstein above the Village of Chamounix—Performing Transgender Rage." *GLQ* 1.3 (1994): 227–54. Print.

Valerio, Max Wolf. "The Joker Is Wild! Changing Sex and Other Crimes of Passion: A Reading." Counting Past 2: Performance-Film-Video-Spoken Word with Transsexual Nerve! Curated by Mirha-Soleil Ross. Tallulah's Cabaret, Buddies in Bad Times Theater, Toronto, September 12, 1998.

———. *The Testosterone Files.* Emeryville: Seal Press, 2006. Print.

Wilchins, Riki Ann. "Transexual Separatism? or Is Anyone Out There Listening?" *Twenty: The Official Newsletter of the XX Club.* May/June 1996. Web. November 12, 2007. <http://www.twentyclub.org/news/july96.html>.

PART THREE

Translation/Transculturation

Chapter 9

Voyage autour de la traduction:
The Translator as Writer and Theorist

ALESSANDRA CAPPERDONI

> You've chosen the difficult task of reading backwards in your language what in mine flows from source.
> Reality is what we invent.
>
> —Nicole Brossard, *Mauve Desert*

The title of this essay owes something to Susanne Lamy's playful discussion of *écriture au féminin* in "Voyage autour d'une écriture" (*D'elles* 53–60). The labyrinthine circularity of Lamy's writing, performing theory as poetics, is perhaps apropos to begin a discussion of Barbara Godard's work on translation as theory interweaving praxis and thought.[1] *Écriture au féminin* and feminist translation share not only a figuration of language as a site of meaning production rather than communication, but also a creative process working through the slippages and displacement of language, and transforming the relation of textuality to the corporeal and the imaginary. They also move in complex and ambiguous ways in-between dominant, marginal, or silenced discourses to produce knowledges of difference (*différance* and *déplacement*) from within dominant thought. By producing knowledges rather than reproducing existing knowledge, *écriture au féminin* and feminist translation perform an ethics of intervention that defies coding and categorization. If Jakobson had already noted this process of displacement in inter-lingual and inter-semiotic translation, feminist writers read it through the framework of psychoanalysis and insist this is a condition of phallic language (the repetition of the sliding signifier), yet one that can be used against itself: "Une éthique exigeante sous-tend l'audace de celles qui osent dire: *je ne répète pas, j'inaugure*" (56). Both, therefore, can best be understood as feminist *poiesis*, unhinging received notions of knowledge production by shifting the attention to the transformative and performative aspects of language, which, in effect, interweaves their practices and theories.

Rather than a relation of equivalence between languages, based on the assumption of the transparency of linguistic systems, the movement between *écriture* and translation reworks dominant systems of thought by foregrounding the encounter between asymmetrical systems (author and reader/translator or production and representation) in which gender plays a determining role. Not surprisingly, then, it would be difficult to separate the strains of Godard's work as discursively contained "areas" of research. Her unceasing efforts to carve an institutional and societal space for feminist thought meant bringing together theories of writing informed by semiotics and post-structuralism, theories of gender, and theories of translation. As a key figure in the production and dissemination of feminist writing and theory in Canada and internationally, Barbara Godard has contributed in significant ways to the shaping of a feminist theory and practice of translation as feminist *poiesis*, crossing the boundaries of writing and theory and drawing attention not only to the "translational" aspect of all feminist writing but also to the visibility of the translator's intervention into the text. Indeed, her work has become synonymous with the specificity of Canadian feminist theory and translational practice, as shown in her many interventions at Canadian and international conferences and poetic colloquia, as well as in academic and non-academic publications.

This essay discusses Barbara Godard's feminist translations of works by Nicole Brossard, France Théoret, and Antonine Maillet as trajectories of reading and writing women's texts. Infused by her theoretical work on gender and feminist thought, Godard's theories and practice of translation are necessarily marked by the double movement of women's writing "as re/reading and re/writing" (Godard, "Theorizing Feminist Discourse/Translation" 46). Reading, in that the relationship of the translator to the author's text is marked by the displacement effect of entering the language of the other and the encounter with the affective relations produced by the linguistic and social context of the author's work. Writing, in that by drawing attention to the translator's (feminist) intervention in the text, all feminist translation breaks down the illusion of transparency of the text and foregrounds the production of knowledge that the translation brings forth.

Feminist translation is *poiesis*, therefore, in that by blurring the boundaries between writing and theory, the translation engenders a new subject retracing the unwritten of women's words, the corporeal, the feminine, and exposes the "fiction of gender" as being discursively produced. My discussion aims to bring to light the interrelationship in Godard's work between feminist translation as praxis, feminist theory of translation, and feminist thought as *poiesis*. But it also reads this important work in the context of the discourse of the nation, marked by the institutionalization of bilingualism, the asymmetrical position of the "other" culture(s) in relation to English Canada, and the challenge of feminist cultural labour to dominant notions of nation and culture throughout the 1970s, 1980s, and 1990s. As I hope to demonstrate, Barbara Godard's translation practice, her theorization on feminist *poiesis* and translation, and cultural activism were central to the shaping of both a Canadian feminist theory of translation and a Canadian feminist poetics.

In a key essay published in the first issue of the feminist journal *Tessera* in 1984, "Ex-centriques, Eccentric, Avant-Garde: Women and Modernism in the Literatures of Canada," Godard makes a powerful argument about the significance of women's writing in the formation of Canadian letters, while highlighting their marginalized position as an effect of the "problematics of established literary discourse" (58).[2] This decentralization is captured through the figuration of the ex-centric, a folding of the inside and the outside into the structures of knowledge production, a "madness" of discourse exposing the ways in which women are excluded from systems of thought and gender is produced through that very exclusion. In a bold move, Godard critiques not only the silencing of women's voices and culture throughout a Canadian (and Western) literary tradition but the power of language and discourse in producing "the fiction of gender." By bringing to light the doubleness of women's language within patriarchal discourse, the ambiguous reworking of memory as retroactive gesture mediated by language, and the relation of women's cultural production to the body of the mother tongue, the article is in conversation with the many contributions to the issue, from Louise Dupré's "La mémoire complice, doublement" and Louise Cotnoir's "S'écrire avec, dans et contre le langage" to Daphne Marlatt's "Musing with Mothertongue" and Gail Scott's "Red Tin + White Tulle." Women's relation to language, then, is one already marked by translation, an insight that Madeleine Gagnon had developed in addressing the alienation of women in language and culture, and the double alienation of women from colonized Québec.[3] The translation efforts in the issue, where articles by Québécois writers appear both in French and in English, also mark the creation of a space of knowledge produced through the collaboration among women from Québec and English Canada—an economy of gift working against the logic of proprietorship and commodification of culture reproduced by the literary establishment.[4] But it also highlights the cultural nexus of language, translation, and politics as a central preoccupation of *Tessera*'s cultural activism—to which Godard contributed, together with the co-editors Daphne Marlatt, Kathy Mezei, and Gail Scott, closely argued articles on feminist theory, writing, and translation.

Writing as reading, which became the title of the next issue of *Tessera* 2 in 1985, was already part of Godard's preoccupations with the politics of the aesthetics and culture.[5] Her translation of experimental poetic works from Québec during the 1970s had positioned her not only as a privileged interlocutor of both Québec and English Canada, but also made her more alert to the politics of language and nation and the affective relations it brings to bear on the social. As Kathy Mezei illustrates in her discussion of Godard's contribution to translation studies in Canada, this work would also prompt her collaboration with Frank Davey on the Coach House Press Translation Series from 1972 to 1978, when she translated poetical and political manifestoes by Québec writers and nationalists for *Open Letter*, at a time when "an animated discussion about translation with the Toronto Research Group (bpNichol, Steve McCaffery, and Barbara Caruso)" was also taking place (Mezei 206).[6] Through her editorial work for the series, gendered differences in response to translation also became apparent. Work on translation, at this time, also included her participation in the MLA Women's Caucus project on translations of women's texts with a bibliography of Québec women writers in translation, which noted gendered differences.[7] These projects prepared the ground for the elaboration of a theory of women's ex-centric relation to language and culture. Indeed, prior to the publication of the article in *Tessera*, she had also worked on the translation of two important, though very different, texts by women—*Don L'Orignal* and *L'Amèr*.

In 1974 Godard began working on the translation of Antonine Maillet's *Don L'Orignal* (1972), a highly original novel that won the author the Governor General's Award for fiction.[8] A text recuperating the sixteenth-century Acadian language of Maillet's native country and adapting it to a modern readership, *Don L'Orignal* combines the genre of the fantastic with a narrative about land and culture steeped in a tradition of oral history, vernacular, and gossip. Godard's creative solutions are not meant to reproduce a supposedly "original" Acadian language or even attempt to convey

Maillet's recreation in English. Instead, she emphasizes the translational nature of Maillet's text, which, in its original form, is already, to echo Octavio Paz, "a translation of a translation of a translation" (9). In the polyphony of voices, gestures, and signs that characterize the oral/folktale structure of Maillet's text, Godard inscribes translation as a further layer of signification, a double moment between oral and literary language, which, as she would point out in her essay on Maillet, "has particular relevance in Canada where both English and French writers have been aware of 'translated' language—standard British or American, international French—dominating literature" ("The Tale of a Narrative" 53). Her use of dialects and language tonalities drawing from the linguistic patrimony of the American South, for example, would immediately be captured by the reader as "out of place" in the context of an Acadian tale. But this dissonant quality is precisely the point: the concreteness of La Sagouine's utterance foregrounds the individuality of the speaking subject (rather than the representativeness of a people's distinctive culture), the diversity marking oral language, and the manipulation of the linguistic sign through a translational process drawing attention to language itself. Language, as Bakhtin indicated in "The Problem of Speech Genres," is always borrowed language, for its individual use is at once singular, social, and other: "an other's word, which belongs to another person and is filled with echoes of the other's utterance" (88). This process of borrowing, which Jacques Lacan would later articulate as the notion of language being always the language of the Other (*l'Autre du langage*), points to the translational process underlying any speech act: to speak is to translate our imaginary and experiential world (a world already shaped by the signifier) into a language that belongs to the social, of which our words are also to become part. All language, therefore, is translation, though the stakes are different with respect to social relations. In the context of 1970s feminist politics, in "Mon corps est mots," Madeleine Gagnon will best express the specificity of women's words and bodies in relation to the phallic orders of language as a condition of "foreignness in language," yet one that can be subverted from within: "I am a foreigner to myself in my own language and I translate myself by quoting all the others" (*New French Feminisms* 180).

In *The Tale of Don L'Orignal* markers of otherness abound and should be read in the context of writing as translation, rather than the translator's instrumental solutions to convey the author's intent. The translator writes alongside the author in doing justice to a genre that is both novelistic dialogism (in the sense discussed by Bakhtin in his theory of the novel) and live speech, which, through its tall tale, deconstructs the notion of referentiality of language. But Godard's rereading of Maillet's work also emphasizes the marginalization of oral culture through the institutionalization of knowledge. To what effect? As feminist historians have repeatedly pointed out, the rise of institutionalized knowledge meant the exclusion of women's knowledge from the domain of the intelligible; their words and other knowledges are confined to gossip and wise women's tales and thus excluded from Truth. Maillet's work recuperates this knowledge without any pretension of "going back" to an originary moment. It is the eccentricity of her protagonist, the flow of her accented speech, and the earthy quality of her language that mark her excess in relation to established (literary) cultural forms and her foreignness to culture. And it is precisely this quality that Godard captures and brings to light in her translation as seen, for example, in La Sagouine's invective against the mainlanders toward the end of the novel. Godard's translation foregrounds the inflection of live speech and the sputtering anger of La Sagouine's body while the original text retains a stronger echo of the narrator's native language:

> Woe to ya, whitewashed city of rotten people! Woe to ya fine men, letting widows and orphans die sooner than buy their cod that stinks of fisherman's sweat! Woe to ya skinflints who don't wanna marry yer daughters to our guys so yer blood'll stay pale and ya'll look like Holy Jesus of Prague! Woe to ya sons of bitchees who burns our islands so as to wash yer eyeballs cause ya don't wanna look at the shacks o us poor fold! Woe to ya others, ya church mice, ya Tartuffes, ya Holier-than-Thous, ya toads in holy water who deported us from our land so ya could clear yer conscience that's tired of puttin up with us and our dirty feet and rottin teeth! But listen closely to me, La Sagouine, daughter of Jos à Pit à Boy Thomas Picoté, who's talkin to ya. There'll come a day when ya'll crawl on all fours, pickin up the shit ya flung at us and that day ya'll know the bomination of desolation, I prophesy that fer ya. (102)

> Malheur à toi, ville de bourgeois pourris, blanchie à la chaux ! Malheur à vous autres, becs-fins, qui laissez corver les veuves et les orphelins plutôt que de leur acheter leur morue qui sent la sueur des pêcheux ! Malheur à vous autres, fesses-tordues, qui voulez pas marier vos filles à nos gars pour conserver votre sang pâle qui vous donne des airs de Saint-Jésus-de-Prague ! Malheur à vous autres, salauds, qui nour brûlez nos îles pour vous laver la peau de l'œil qui veut pas voir les cabanes des pauvres genses ! Malheur à vous autres, rats d'église, mangeux de baluster, saintes nitouches, fripeux de bénitier, qui nous déportez de nos terres pour vous nettoyer la conscience qui se fatigue de nous porter avec nos pieds

sales et nos dents gâtées ! Mais écoutez-moi ben, moi, la Sagouine qui vous parle, fille à Jos à Pit à Boy à Thomas Picoté ; y viendra un jour où c'est que vous ramasserez à quatre pattes les crottes que vous nous avez garrochées, et vous connaîtrez ce jour-là votre bomination de la désolation, c'est moi qui vous le prédis. (164)

This rereading of Maillet's text through the ex-centricity of La Sagouine to language, culture, and memory contributes to the translator's exploratory work on the question of language and gender in women's writing, which was to become more visible in *These Our Mothers, Or: The Disintegrating Chapter*. Published in 1983, the translation of Nicole Brossard's *L'Amèr, ou le Chapitre effrité* (1977) marks a turning point in feminist cultural production in anglophone Canada. The preface to the translation briefly highlights the difficulty of working on a text that takes language as its primary site of deconstruction of gender (how to translate the silent *e* of the French feminine?) and, foremost, a text that is imbued with the author's readings of Derrida and Deleuze, yet other translations of theory and writing. No cues are offered to the reader in dealing with a text that explodes, literally, the concept of literature and representation. Godard's solutions to the "problem" of the original are inventive, showing her intervention into the text as an amorous reading relationship. The layered meanings and threads of signification in the title, *L'Amèr*, pointing to the mother (*mère*), the fluidity and engulfing feeling of her life-giving embrace, like the embrace of the sea (*la mer*), and the sourness of the mother–daughter relationship (*l'amer*), are unravelled through the English title that weaves "theseourmothers," "The Sea Our Mother," "Sea (S)mothers," and "(S)our Mothers," into a synthesis in the graphic play of "TheSe our mothers," where the S embraces both "our" and "mothers." The drift of words and their wealth of connotations disrupt the normative understanding of meaning and referentiality. To what do these terms refer? What reality do they represent? What happens to "meaning" when words call each other up and the translation can follow multiple directions, with different solutions? Translation from French into English, therefore, calls into question the unproblematic passage from one language to another, one system of representation to another, as if language were a self-contained system *re*-presenting the factuality of *reality*. There is no easy passage, for translation is already part of the act of writing and speaking. All language is translational, and Brossard's work aims to show the ways in which translational writing makes visible the processes of inter-lingual and inter-semiotic translation as part of all linguistic systems of communication, meaning formation, and human interaction. *La realité de la fiction*. In some instances, such translation requires a condensation and different twist to Brossard's words, so that the shocking first line of the poem, "J'ai tué le ventre. Moi ma vie en été la lune. Moi ma mort" (11), playing on the splits between *je*, *moi*, and *ma*, becomes "I killed the womb. *My* life in summer the moon. *My* death" (13), a different tonality required in the act of pronouncing *my*, yet one that does not betray the *moi/ma* play. Elsewhere, different layers and echoes of words become necessary, so that Brossard's "Ma mère, ma fille. Mamelle, une seule vie, la mienne. Réseau clandestin de reproduction. Matrice et matière anonymes" (11), tracing a line of correspondences along the movement of the *m*, the *m* of generation or "alphabet of origin" as she will say later, becomes "My mother, my daughter. Mamma, Mam*elle*, Mamilla, a single life, mine. Clandestine system of reproduction. Anonymous matrix and matter" (13). This strategy brings a richer connotation to the "mother" through its different folds—maternal speech, she (*elle*), affection, relationship, bodily encounter, literary and social construction.

Godard's translation proves to be attentive reading of the radical practice of Brossard's writing—a text that deconstructs the idea of the book and takes to task the fictions of patriarchal discourse. It is also an intimate reading, for who could best dance through the richness of this text if not she who has followed the unfolding of *écriture au féminin* in Québec women's writing and worked on their texts in earlier translations? At no moment does the translation become a burden or an obstacle to the reader. Instead, the labour of reading is filled with pleasure and the excitement of discovery. One by one, the codes enclosing the perceptions of reality and trapping women's bodies through the appropriation of matter (the social, economic, biological, historical, legal, logical, representational, and literary codes that Godard dissects in her essay "*L'Amèr*, or, the Exploding Chapter: Nicole Brossard at the Site of Feminist Deconstruction") fall apart and show themselves for what they are: codes, not reality. The delirious walk within the language of the other thus produces a double effect. As "she breaks the contract binding her to figuration" (Brossard, *These Our Mothers* 62), the translator can unleash the differential relations in language onto an/other scene of writing, ready to meet the words of anglophone feminist writers.[9]

Yet this translation should not be read as an isolated enterprise. Readings, conferences, and translations of avant-garde work become important sites for Godard's articulation of a feminist theory of translation inflected by the specificity of Canadian writing. I want to flesh out briefly these different yet interwoven moments and spaces. The avant-garde Québécois journal *La Barre du jour*,[10] where experimental work on feminist poetics was published, is perhaps the earliest of these sites.[11] In 1978, Godard had worked with Josée M. LeBlond on the translation of nine pieces from the special issue of *La Barre du jour* 56–57 ("*le corps, les mots, l'imaginaire*" 1977) for *Room of One's Own* 4.1.[12] The importance of the journal for the creation of feminist theorization of writing would also be highlighted by Godard in her essay "The Avant-Garde in Canada: *Open Letter* and *La Barre du jour*," published in a special issue of *Ellipse* in 1979. It is on the base of Godard's essay that Larry Shouldice, the editor of the issue, chose which texts to translate. The experimental feminist work of Nicole Brossard and the Québécois writers of this decade would indeed become an important source of exchanges and collaboration. In 1981, Brossard asked Godard to translate a section of *Amantes* for her to read together with Adrienne Rich during the third event of the Writers in Dialogue in Toronto, organized by Betsy Warland.[13] The reading was directed to an audience not attuned to the work of experimental Québécois writers in French. In her essay "The Translator as Ventriloquist," published in *Prism* in 1982, Godard discusses the double movement of language and sound in gendered translation and explains her translational process as one of "ventriloquism." In her preface to *Lovhers*, she further notes: "In these circumstances, I opted to be a ventriloquist, to make the poems sound like Brossard's poems, and let the meaning take care of itself. To a certain degree, Brossard's text invites this type of transformation, since it is the associative drift of the sound of words that generates sequences" (10). This is also the time Godard began working on the translation of Nicole Brossard's *L'Amèr* and presented on Brossard's work at conferences for APFUCC (Association des Professeurs de Français des Universités et Collèges Canadiens) and AACS/CAAS (a joint meeting of the American Association of Canadian Studies and the Canadian Association of American Studies) in 1982.[14] In 1984, at the Conference on Literary Translation organized by Sherry Simon in Montreal, where Godard delivered a paper on "The Translator as She," Brossard and Godard did a joint reading from *Journal intime* with the "original" text following the translation, a reverse gesture toward the translational aspect of all writing practices. The double voices of the texts and the interweaving materiality of sound and writing had a powerful effect on both writer and translator.[15] In a personal exchange, Godard notes that the 1984 event had a profound impact on Susanne Lamy and her feminist work on gender and translation and, foremost, it is by being translated that Brossard "became alert to translation."[16] Thus she places translation at the very heart of a feminist experimental practice at the intersection of *écriture*, translation, and gender.

Alongside her work on Québécois feminists from *La Barre du jour*, this is also a time of groundbreaking conferences that brought the question of gender, subjectivity, and writing to the very centre of critical enquiry. Godard organized the first of these, The Dialogue Conference at York University in 1981, the proceedings of which were to be published as *Gynocritics: Feminist Approaches to Writing by Canadian and Québécois Women/ Gynocritiques: Démarches féministes à l'écriture des canadiennes et québécoises* in 1987. The "theoretical energy" that arose from this encounter of feminist writers, artists, critics, and cultural workers at large, which West Coast writer Daphne Marlatt recalls as "a major turning point" (9), would result in the collective idea shared by Godard, Marlatt, Kathy Mezei, and Gail Scott to create a magazine dedicated to women's culture and feminist writing. It was the beginning of *Tessera*, which would push the exploration of the semiotics of language and translation as a practice of reading and writing, and in 1989 would also devote the entire issue 6 to writing and translation. This productive encounter was channelled into a second conference, Women and Words, to take place in Vancouver, BC, in 1983, at the time of the publication of Godard's translation of *L'Amèr*. Organized by Daphne Marlatt and Betsy Warland as part of the West Coast women's collective, the conference brought together women artists, writers, translators, and cultural workers from across Canada in unprecedented numbers.[17] Godard participated in the seminar "Translation: Relationship Between Writer and Translator," and spoke on "The Writer and the Translator."[18] The wealth of contributions to *In the Feminine: Women and Words/Les femmes et les mots* (1985), edited by the collective and including Godard's essay "The Translator as She" and her translation of Louise Cotnoir's "The Marked Gender," testifies to the richness of the event. This web of relations and movement in-between practices and discourses, therefore, locates her theorization on gender and feminist work on translation at the centre of Canadian cultural production of these years—an important moment for feminist work and women's writing in Canada.

Godard's fertile collaboration with Nicole Brossard would extend through the years to come with the translation of *Amantes* (*Lovhers* 1986), *Picture Theory* (*Picture Theory* 1991, revised edition in 2006), and *Journal intime* (*Intimate Journal* 2004), further inflecting her translation practice with her theorization on the body of writing and *écriture au féminin*. All editions will be introduced by prefaces/articles providing key theorizations of translation as praxis of writing as well as a reading of writing. In *Lovhers*, Godard foregrounds the author's work on the materiality of language, enumerates the challenges that the play on the polyvalence of signifiers and vertigoes of language presents to the translator, and stresses the notion that every reading act is an act of translation. Brossard's recurrent line "JE N'ARRÊTE PAS DE LIRE" is translated by Godard through the double evocation of the homophonic line dé/lire, "I DON'T STOP READING/DELIRING," a gesture that intersects the material act of page turning and the immersion into the world of other women's words of both poetic voice/character and translator—a differential reading ("lire *dans le différé*" 164) brought forth by the translational act. In the Preface to *Picture Theory*, Godard notes that the act of interpretation requires a momentary freezing of meaning of the author's text, the realization that "the reading subject becomes the writing subject, a subject con-figured in/by the encounter with the textual object" (10). This encounter between reading and writing also effects a process of displacement and an epistemological transformation at the level of subjectivity and knowledge formation.[19] But she also notes how the text cannot be isolated from a context of Canadian bilingualism in which reading French and English acquires a different signification and brings to light the different power dynamics at stake. In its movement in-between languages (of body, thought, the erotic, women's lives, the social, city, time, and the orders of discourse), translation destabilizes identity and meaning and rewrites memory and the "great modernist books of the night" (7), especially Djuna Barnes's *Nightwood*, through the drift of the sign of Claire Dérive's text/goings.

These concerns will be further elaborated in Godard's "Translating Translating Translation" and "The Moving Intimacy of Language," introductions to France Théoret's *The Tangible Word* (1991) and Brossard's *Intimate Journal* (2004). Subjectivity is the key word here, as the authors' work on the materiality of language (the "tangible" word) focuses more specifically on the problem of enunciation for the female subject, woman's coming to voice (and to writing), and the effects that the decentring of the self in the encounter with the other have on the relational codes of languages, bodies, and cultures. For Godard, this practice represents an economy of translation that opens up to radical possibilities of writing, a performative translation that enacts a new kind of subjectivity. In *The Tangible Word* (1991), Godard brings together four texts of a writer central to the emergence of *écriture au féminin* in Québec yet little translated: France Théoret's *Bloody Mary, A Voice for Odile, Vertigoes*, and *Of Necessity a Whore* (published respectively in 1970, 1978, 1979, and 1980).[20] The writer's concern with unspeaking the knots of language to give voice to the unspoken is writing praxis, ethics, and politics. Such voicing interrogates the margins of representation, the frame of discourse, and the values that code women as signs of exchange. But the stumbling effect of language, its uncertainties and contradictions, turn this strategy against itself. As the circulation of knowledge is blocked, the restricted economy (desires and social relations under hierarchical orders) is disrupted. Difference emerges in language and produces a shift in relations as the "inarticulate" and the "unnameable" become agents in the discursive field. Godard notes that "this 'deterritorialization,' a transformative project of articulating the in/articulate(d), is an encounter with alterity and transcoding that Théoret terms translation" (9). The task of the feminist translator, then, is to allow translation to act rather than reproduce. How to render the labour of coming into voice without re-enacting the violence of translation as imposition of a linguistic and cultural framework, a symbolic language "already there"? How to do justice to the vertigo of "unspeaking" and the emergence into articulation in a foreign language, when that language is also the translator's own language of dominant culture? Godard recalls her difficulty as she was looking for a flowing sentence while "stumbling against the infinitive, the sentence that refused to move forward, that hesitated, repeated itself." It is in reading to an audience at the University of Calgary that Godard as translator realizes how she had to "submit" herself to the "knots" imposed by the text and work alongside Théoret in using language against itself "to imagine, to invent, the unknown" (12). Indeed, she notes, "in these circumstances, language unravels itself, turns back on itself, rattling off nonsense, running off at the mouth in its unspeaking" (13). The "transformative effect" of the "endless slippage" and "recombination of signifiers" (13) writes translation as writing.

Similarly, in Brossard's *Intimate Journal* the play of repetition and fragmentary writing, Godard notes, "stages the scene of translation from the perspective of the translated, but it also performs acts of translation in its self-reflexive meditation on representation as repetition with a difference" ("The Moving" 14). This poses not a few problems to the translator's work: How to translate a text that stages its own translation? How to render heteroglossia into an/other language—language of the dominant in Canadian culture? Like reading and writing, translation is also research, and in uncovering the multiplication of meaning of Brossard's language by retracing the many experimental works with which she is in conversation, she decides to participate in the creative process, inventing or inserting words and back-translating citations "to emphasize their performative over pedagogic function," thus becoming co-agent with Brossard's textual production, rather than follower or imitator. The result is indeed compelling—like all of her work.

Perhaps Godard's preface title to Théoret's *The Tangible Word*, "Translating Translating Translation," best resonates with her lifelong commitment to exploring the intimate relationship of writing and translation, the indeterminate space between the author's and reader-translator's worlds, and the different horizons produced by the performative work *on* and *with* language. This work is in itself a *voyage autour de la traduction* if, by *autour* we understand the indeterminacy of writing tending toward a never-achieved goal, *jouissance*, rather than mastery. Not restricted to a *topoi* or a figure of writing, feminist translation indeed becomes, in Godard's work, a *re-écriture*, bringing to fruition Derrida's notion that "the only complete reading is the one which transforms the book into a simultaneous network of reciprocal relationships" (24). But these "reciprocal relationships," in Godard's hands, expand even further to bring together women's voices from across borders of nation, language, and politics to engender a Canadian-inflected theory of translation *au féminin*.

Notes

1 Lamy presented the paper at the Conference of Inter-American Women Writers in Ottawa in May 1978. It was later included as a chapter in *D'elles*, published by L'Hexagone in 1979. Lamy muses on the significance of *écriture au féminin* as writing practice that simultaneously inscribes women's words in the language system of dominant discourse and transgresses the borders of language by reorienting it toward desire and the body, what Nicole Brossard would later conceptualize as *le corps/texte*.
2 *Tessera* 1, published as a guest issue of *Room of One's Own* 8.4 (1984). A first version of this paper was presented at the 4th Interamerican Woman Writers Conference in Mexico, June 4, 1981. The paper was also discussed in the Mexican daily *Excelsior*, Literary Section June 5: 1.
3 Madeleine Gagnon, "Mon corps est mots," in Hélène Cixous, Madeleine Gagnon, et Annie Leclerc, *La venue à l'écriture* (Paris: Union générale d'éditions 10/18, 1977), 69. Trans. in *New French Feminisms*.
4 After the publication in *Room of One's Own*, the following three issues of *Tessera* appeared as special issues of established journals in *La Nouvelle Barre du jour*, *CV2*, and *Canadian Fiction Magazine*.
5 "L'écriture comme lecture." Guest issue of *NBJ: Nouvelle Barre du jour*, 1985.
6 Translations would include Paul Chamberland, Jacques Brault, and Michèle Lalonde.

7   This work was presented at a panel in San Francisco in 1979, and was later published under the editorship of Marjorie Resnick and Isabelle Coutivron.
8   *The Tale of Don L'Orignal* was not to be published until 1978 due to the original publisher's misgivings.
9   In *Readings from the Labyrinth*, Daphne Marlatt notes that "Musing with Mothertongue" was her "first attempt to illuminate poetics with feminist theory" (1). The first draft of the essay was written in 1982, when she was also writing the poem "Touch to My Tongue," and it was stimulated by a range of events that had rapidly changed her relationship to writing. The Dialogue Conference, organized by Barbara Godard at York in 1981, was definitely one of the events. Marlatt had first encountered the writing of Nicole Brossard (her essay "l'e muet mutant") in a special issue of *Ellipse* dedicated to *Tish* and *La Nouvelle Barre du jour* in 1979. As Marlatt further notes, during both The Dialogue Conference and Women and Words, many anglophone writers were eager to establish closer relations to Québécois feminist writers. By the time of Godard's translation in 1983, the cultural environment was therefore ripe for an exchange between anglophone and Québécois feminist poetics.
10 In the 1970s, Godard wrote several essays on gender and language in relation to Canadian women authors, such as Sheila Watson, Audrey Thomas, and Antonine Maillet, which attended, albeit indirectly, to questions of translation and preceded the more prolific production on women's writings, gender, and translation throughout the 1980s.
11 The avant-garde magazines *La Barre du jour* (1965–77), followed by *La Nouvelle Barre du jour* (1977–90), and *Les Têtes de pioches*, co-founded by Nicole Brossard and France Théoret, contributed in a significant way to the formation of a radical culture in Québec. In particular, *NBJ* created a space for groundbreaking theoretical and creative feminist work throughout the 1970s. In 1985, the journal hosted the second issue of *Tessera*.
12 Godard translated poetry by Louky Bersianik ("Noli mi tangere"), Yolande Villemaire ("My Heart Beat Like a Bolo"), and Mireille Lanctôt ("The Claybaker").
13 Godard translated thirty pages from *Amantes* for the reading, which took place on May 1, 1981. The translation of "The Temptation" was published with a critical introduction in *Prism International* XX.3 (Spring 1982): 30–34, and "My Continent" later appeared in *Fireweed* 13 (1982): 105–7.
14 "La Langue maternelle: *La Nouvelle barre du jour*, vers une poétique féministe" and "*L'Amèr*, or, the Exploding Chapter."
15 Sections of *Intimate Journal* later appeared in the Canadian Women Writer's Engagement Calender, edited by Adele Wiseman, in 1986.
16 Email from Godard, March 31, 2009.
17 The West Coast Women and Words Society.

18 The seminar was moderated by Kathy Mezei and included, together with Barbara Godard, translators Claudette Branchard and Danielle Thaler, poet and translator Gwladys Downes, and poet Cécile Cloutier. Godard also presented at a panel on "Difference Between French and English Canadian Women Writers Since 1950."
19 Godard elaborated on this notion in her paper "Essay/ons traduction/translation: The Subject in/of Translation," read at the department of Women's Studies, University of Calgary, February 15, 1990, and Feminist Theory, An International Debate, University of Glasgow, July 13, 1991.
20 Her translated work includes her contribution to the issue of *La Barre du jour*, "*les femmes, les mots, l'imaginaire*" (no. 65–67, 1977) and the performance piece *La Nef des sorcières*, translated for a production in Toronto.

Works Cited

Bakhtin, M.M. "The Problem of Speech Genres." *Speech Genres and Other Late Essays*. Trans. Vern W. McGee. Ed. Garyl Emerson and Michael Holquist. Austin: U of Texas P, 1986. 60–102. Print.

Barnes, Djuna. *Nightwood*. New York: Harcourt, Brace, 1937.

Bersianik, Louky. "Noli mi tangere." Trans. Barbara Godard. *Room of One's Own* IV.1 (September 1978): 98–110. Print.

Brossard, Nicole. *Intimate Journal, or, Here's a Manuscript*. Trans. Barbara Godard. Toronto: Mercury, 2004. Print.

———. "L'e muet mutant." *Ellipse* 23/24 (1979): 44–63.

———. *Lovhers*. Trans. Barbara Godard. Montreal: Guernica, 1986. Print.

——— *Mauve Desert*. Trans. Susanne de Lotbinière-Harwood. Toronto: Coach House, 1990. Print.

———. *Picture Theory*. Trans. Barbara Godard. Montreal: Guernica, 1991. Print.

———. *These Our Mothers, Or: The Disintegrating Chapter*. Trans. Barbara Godard. Toronto: Coach House, 1983. Print.

Cotnoir, Louise. "S'écrire avec, dans et contre le langage." *Tessera* 1 (Winter/Hiver). Guest issue of *Room of One's Own* 8.4 (1984): 47–49. Print.

Derrida, Jacques. *Writing and Difference*. Trans. Alan Bass. Chicago: U of Chicago P, 1978. Print.

Dupré, Louise. "La mémoire complice, doublement." *Tessera* 1 (Winter/Hiver). Guest issue of *Room of One's Own* 8.4 (1984): 25–32. Print.

Gagnon, Madeleine. "Body I." *New French Feminisms*. Ed. Elaine Marks and Isabelle de Courtivron. New York: Schocken Books, 1980. Print.

Godard, Barbara. "Annotated Bibliography of the Writings of French-Canadian Women Writers in English Translation." *Women Writers in Translation: An Annotated Bibliography*. Ed. Marjorie Resnick and Isabelle Courtivron. Boston: Garland, 1984. 93–112. Print.

———. "*L'Amèr* or the Exploding Chapter: Nicole Brossard at the Site of Feminist Deconstruction." *Atlantis* 9.2 (Spring 1984): 23–34. Print.
———. "The Avant-Garde in Canada: *Open Letter* and *La Barre du jour*." Spec. issue of *Ellipse* 23/24 (1979): 98–113. Print.
———. "Ex-centriques, Eccentric, Avant-Garde: Women and Modernism in the Literatures of Canada." *Tessera* 1 (Winter/Hiver). Guest issue of *Room of One's Own* 8.4 (1984): 57–75. Print.
———, ed. *Gynocritics: Feminist Approaches to Writing by Canadian and Québécois Women/Gynocritiques: Démarches féministes à l'écriture des canadiennes et québécoises*. Toronto: ECW, 1987. Print.
———. "The Moving Intimacy of Language." Introduction to Nicole Brossard, *Intimate Journal, or, Here's a Manuscript*. Trans. Barbara Godard. Toronto: Mercury, 2004. Print.
———. "Preface." Nicole Brossard, *Lovhers*. Trans. Barbara Godard. Montreal: Guernica, 1986. Print.
———. "Preface." Nicole Brossard, *Picture Theory*. New York: Roof, 1990. 7–12. Print.
———. "The Tale of a Narrative: Antonine Maillet's *Don l'Orignal*." *Atlantis* 5.1 (Autumn 1979): 51–69. Print.
———. "Theorizing Feminist Discourse/Translation." *Tessera* 6 (1989): 42–53. Print.
———. "Translating Translating Translation." Preface to France Théoret, *The Tangible Word*. Trans. Barbara Godard. Montreal: Guernica, 1991. 7–14. Print.
———. "The Translator as She." *In the Feminine: Women and Words/Les Femmes et les mots*. Edmonton: Longspoon, 1985. 193–98. Print.
———. "The Translator as Ventriloquist." *Prism International* 20.3 (Spring 1982): 35–36. Print.
Jakobson, Roman. "On Linguistic Aspects of Translation." 1959. *The Translation Studies Reader*. Ed. Lawrence Venuti. London: Routledge, 2000. 113–19. Print.
Lacan, Jacques. "Fonction et champ de la parole et du langage." *Écrits I*. Paris: Seuil, 1966. 123–43. Print.
———. "L'insistence de la letter dans l'inconscient (ou la raison depuis Freud)." *Écrits I*. Paris: Seuil, 1966. 249–89. Print.
Lamy, Susanne. "Voyage autour d'une écriture." *D'elles*. Montreal: L'Hexagone, 1979. Print.
Lanctôt, Mireille. "The Claybaker." Trans. Barbara Godard. *Room of One's Own* IV.1 (September 1978): 87–91. Print.
Maillet, Antonine. *Don l'Orignal*. Trans. Barbara Godard. Toronto: Clarke, Irwin, 1978. Print.

Marlatt, Daphne. "Musing with Mothertongue." *Tessera* 1 (Winter/Hiver). Guest issue of *Room of One's Own* 8.4 (1984): 53–56. Print.

———. *Readings from the Labyrinth*. Edmonton: NeWest, 1998. Print.

Mezei, Kathy. "Transformations of Barbara Godard." *Writing Between the Lines: Portraits of Canadian Anglophone Translators*. Ed. and intro. Agnes Whitfield. Waterloo, ON: Wilfrid Laurier UP, 2006. Print.

Paz, Octavio. *Traducción: Literatura y Literalidad*. Barcelona: Tusquets Editor, 1971. Print.

Scott, Gail. "Red Tin + White Tulle." *Tessera* 1 (Winter/Hiver). Guest issue of *Room of One's Own* 8.4 (1984): 123–29. Print.

Théoret, France. *The Tangible Word*. Trans. Barbara Godard. Montreal: Guernica, 1991. Print.

Villemaire, Yolande. "My Heart Beats Like a Bolo." Trans. Barbara Godard. *Room of One's Own* IV.1 (September 1978): 111–28. Print.

Women and Words Collective. *In the Feminine: Women and Words/Les Femmes et les mots*. Edmonton: Longspoon, 1985. Print.

Chapter 10

Taking Deleuze in the Middle, or Doing Intellectual History by the Letter

JASON DEMERS

In her two essays on Deleuze and translation, Barbara Godard not only provides an account of the disciplinary and geopolitical relations that have had a determining effect on the way that Deleuze is taken up in translation, she also develops a Deleuzian theory of translation. Although Deleuze had little to say about translation specifically, Godard focalizes Deleuze's work on the fold, the event, and transcreation through the question of translation in order to develop a model that takes both Deleuze and the field of translation studies in novel and productive directions.

Godard elaborates a Deleuzian theory of translation by, as she puts it, "taking [Deleuze] in the middle" (rather than from behind, as Deleuze himself did with philosophy). When Deleuze took philosophy from behind, his goal was to create a monster in the philosopher's image through an act of philosophical buggery, which was an act of faithful betrayal (Deleuze, *Negotiations* 6). When Godard takes Deleuze in the middle, she is "taking him at his word but making it ramify in a 'becoming-other' to create a theory of translation as productive transformation by expansion rather than as instrumental communication" ("Deleuze and Translation" 60). Godard *expands* Deleuze's theory by making him say something that he did not. She does so by taking him in the middle that he celebrated—the plateau, intermezzo—as the place where things pick up speed and break free from dualisms. When Godard articulates what a conjunction between Deleuze *and* translation might look like, her work on the topic installs an "and" between them. And (this) is how translation works.

Below I explain and expand Godard's Deleuzian theory of translation in two sections. In the first section I collect the terms and practices that Godard employs to operationalize an associative theory of translation. Beyond the fold, transcreation, and event from "Deleuze and Translation," I consider Godard's privileging of metonymy over metaphor and letter over meaning when she theorizes translation as "combinatory rather than substitution" in an earlier essay entitled "Translating (with) the Speculum" (85). Both "with" and "and" are associative terms. They prod us to think about the intersubjective relationship between author and translator (who are both already multiple), or how the movement of sliding signifiers might be translated without causing movement to stop. "With" and "and" are terms that pull us into a middle where translation is a practice built of associations. In the second section I extend Godard's work on translation, employing the terms accumulated in the first section to consider what it might look like to do intellectual history—also a type of translation—by the letter. Just as Godard makes Deleuze ramify by considering him in conjunction with translation, I want to make Godard's "Deleuze and Translation" ramify by considering it in conjunction with intellectual history. What might Deleuze become if we follow him by his associations? As a manner of collaborating with Godard, I renew Deleuze in translation by locating and animating unexpected arrivals and trajectories for his work, illustrating what it means to take Deleuze in the middle.

Translation by Association: Deleuze *and* Parnet *and* Guattari (with) Brossard *and* Irigaray *and* Cixous

"And" is not a simple conjunction. As Godard reminds us, the "and" for Deleuze is a marker of the "disjunctive synthesis," which is "neither conjunction nor disjunction, but both" ("Deleuze and Translation" 60). In order to explain how this can be, Godard draws on Deleuze's work on the fold, which argues that the "and" is a relation of reciprocal implication (the inside folds out and the outside in): "and" does not mark a simple relationship of correspondence between two terms. Godard muses that the major problem shared by philosophy and translation is the gulf between meaning and words. When we rethink translation in terms of the fold—which means accepting and perhaps even accentuating the play between source and translated text—the dominant "abyss-in-need-of-a-bridge" model for translation is replaced with a model of reciprocal implication (60). One is not subject to or subsumed by the other: the one and the other are carried away in the middle. The middle is a site of intermingling and exchange that institutes an aparallel evolution.

The fold is important because it introduces a theory of complex intersubjectivity. Consider Deleuze's collaboration with Claire Parnet. *Dialogues*, Deleuze points out, came out between *Anti-Oedipe* and *Mille plateaux*, and it was written therefore "between Félix Guattari and me" (ix). The collaboration with Parnet was "a new point which made possible a new line-between" (ix), one that moved with its own force and carried with it multiple elements from either side. As Deleuze and Guattari famously argue at the beginning of *A Thousand Plateaus*, names are temporary points of subjectification; each one of the writers involved in a collaboration is already multiple (3). Deleuze thus reflects on the writing of *Dialogues* as follows: "As we became less sure what came from one, what came from the other, or even from someone else, we would become clearer about 'What is it to write?' ... This really was a book without subject, without beginning or end, but not without middle" (x). The book is without subject because it is not rooted in one. The "middle" ground of collaboration is the fold. The inside folds out and the outside folds in. There is a becoming-Deleuze of Parnet and a becoming-Parnet of Deleuze. Not only is this a relation of reciprocal implication, but each of the subjects entering into intersubjectivity is already constituted by many folds, which in turn relate with one another. The folding of reciprocal implication is endless. The question "What is it to write?" can be extended to the question of translation, which is also a collaboration between two or more authors. In the intersubjective relationship between author and translator, there are always more than two authors.

There were certainly more than two authors involved when Godard was translating Brossard. In the middle is where Godard found Deleuze in the early 1980s, amidst a collision between a talk she attended and a book she was translating. Godard's official introduction to Deleuze was a talk being given at the university by Constantin Boundas on the French philosopher, who was then virtually unknown in the Anglo-American academic world, and the book that Godard was translating was Nicole Brossard's *L'Amèr*. As Godard listened to Boundas's lecture, she "heard Brossard's thought expounded under the name of Deleuze" ("Deleuze and Translation" 58). The experience was particularly jarring because Godard had just been advised by a colleague to reconsider her word choice in several instances, and the words that Boundas was using to speak about the work of Deleuze—words like "ramify" and "multiplicities"—were the same ones at issue in her translation because they were not yet common in Anglo-American academic or literary usage. As it turned out, both Boundas and Brossard had Deleuze open on their desks in the early 1980s, a decade prior to his accelerated translation and rise to prominence in the Anglo-American academy during the 1990s and 2000s. While Godard was translating Brossard, she found Deleuze in the fold.

As Godard says of Deleuze's folds, foldings are not simply produced of two entities in reciprocal contact; folding begets folds, relations multiply, and deeper and deeper folds are produced on top of one another. Without going too deep, I want to bring another middle into the fold in order to accumulate another set of terms that are useful for thinking translation associatively. Between her translation of *L'Amer* and her article on "Deleuze and Translation," Godard wrote an article entitled "Translating (with) the Speculum," which draws Hélène Cixous and Luce Irigaray, another theorist of the middle, into the fold in order to elaborate "a theory of translation as combinatory rather than substitution" (85). Much of "Translating (with) the Speculum" is devoted to explaining how the French feminist discourse of Cixous and Irigaray is built on the privileging of metonymy over metaphor. This means that their texts operate by the slippage of meaning as signifiers connect with one another along the horizontal axis of combination rather than the vertical axis of substitution whereby one term pins down and stands in for another. Irigaray in particular subverted the Freudian system, which metaphorized psychoanalysis on the basis of the masculine phallus and feminine lack (transferred by Lacan to language from biology) by focusing on contiguity. As opposed to understanding the vagina as a space of lack, Irigaray, in *This Sex Which Is Not One*, explains that women's "genitals are formed of two lips in continuous contact" (24), and that woman in the "sexual imaginary" devised by Freud is "more or less the obliging prop for the enactment of man's fantasies" (25). Transferred from biology to the economy of writing, the figure of two lips touching, which is itself pleasurable without requiring external stimulus, is a figure for feminine writing as *contiguity*. No phallus is required to fill a void of meaning in the other.

Godard explains that metonymically driven texts pose problems for translation and compares the translation and reception of Irigaray's *Speculum de l'autre femme* and Cixous's *Vivre l'orange* in order to explain that metonymy introduces polysemy, which is often lost in translation. Godard charges that Gillian Gill translated Irigaray's text metaphorically in that she singularized puns, stopping the slippage of signifiers crucial to Irigaray's text by restricting the operation of terms to certain networks (biological in particular) when they were meant to register in, and flow through, several.

Cixous's text, on the other hand, which was a reading *with* Clarice Lispector, was deliberately written with the English and French versions of the text on facing pages so that the slippage or textual contamination that occurred in translation registered alongside the slippage that occurred in the text. The text slides through places and states, beginning with orange and moving through Oran-je, Oran, I/ran, foreinge, and so on. "Foreinge" is a particularly interesting term because it is a neologism only made possible through encounter with the English language. As Godard puts it, by following the course of the orange, "a theory of translation as combination is elaborated in this text in the contamination of French, Portuguese [Lispector's original tongue, also omnipresent in the text], and English" (116). While Cixous's text of contagion moved between languages in translation, Irigaray's metaphorically translated *Speculum* substituted one language for another.

The difference between representational and combinatory approaches is further elaborated in "Deleuze and Translation" with *transcreation*. Beyond introducing intersubjective foldings, the "and" operationalizes a process of becoming. As Godard points out "'ET' (and) exceeds and inheres in 'EST' (being)—E(S)T," and philosophy's fixation on the problem of being has led to the neglect of other relations that exceed being conceived as totality ("Deleuze and Translation" 63). "ET" is not just any relative conjunction, it is a construction that deliberately does away with philosophy's fixation on the question of being and the centrality of the subject in the process. The "and" that is central to intersubjective relationships is also figured by Deleuze as the creative motor that unpins philosophy from its teleological course. For Deleuze (and Guattari and Parnet), philosophy is not a teleological pursuit of being; it is a transcreative process of becoming that is all about the creation of concepts. The movement of reciprocal implication figured by the fold is continuous and, as such, transcreation takes the place of representationalism in philosophy. Via the and (ET)—a perpetual process of becoming—being (EST) is whisked away. To return to the example of Deleuze's collaboration with Parnet, the middle-book without subject is also without beginning or end because it is a *becoming*. Such is also the life of the orange.

The final term that I want to pull from Godard in her ramification of translation as associative is the *event*. Each translation is also an event. The geography of relations that characterize the event—its associations—are precisely what History always fails to capture when it fits events into a narrative trajectory (Deleuze and Guattari, *What Is Philosophy?* 110). In the spirit of the disjunctive synthesis (AND), which is neither conjunction nor disjunction but both, the event is part of a continuity (perpetual movement, becoming), but it is at the same time built of discontinuity; it is the appearance of something new that is irreducible to its appearance. Events are effected by a synthesis of forces. Events, therefore, collect a complex of folds. What the event simultaneously projects is the internal dynamic of the interaction of its constituent forces—a moment of productive intensity, a plateau—whose transcreative becoming moves through the event. The creation of a concept is a philosophical event. The same is true of each new translation. As Godard points out, Deleuze's privileging of parole over langue marked a privileging of pragmatics over semantics and syntactics, which constitutes a turning away from linguistic abstraction toward the performative dimension of language ("Deleuze and Translation" 63). When a concept is created, or a translation is published, a new assemblage is (per)formed.

Always cognizant of the institutions governing reading, Godard points out that the problems of translating Irigaray metaphorically were compounded by the event of *Speculum*'s publication by a university press. Whereas Cixous's *Vivre l'orange* was pitched to an anglophone audience by a French literary press—which meant that it was received and positioned within the "French feminist discursive system" ("Translating (with) the Speculum" 114)—the smoothed out publication of *Speculum* by an American university press meant that it was ultimately read by American feminist readers as though it was written in English. As a result, Irigaray was initially received as an essentialist by American feminists who read the biological signifiers running through her text literally rather than "as a discursive construction deliberately assumed in order to expose the metonymic contingencies of gender operative in the texts of theory" ("Translating (with) the Speculum" 114). Translated metaphorically and released as such into a foreign field, *Speculum* lost most of its associations when it crossed the Atlantic.

Although translation by the letter might, at first blush, seem to be more restrictive than an approach that privileges the communication of meaning because its focus is on the signifier over and above the signified, an approach that privileges the letter is more readily equipped to recognize slippages in the signifier than approaches that privilege the communication of a signified. Slippages in the signifier introduce polysemy, troubling the driving assumption that meaning (the signified) is attainable by, or even the proper object of, the letter (the signifier) in the first place. Associative philosophers both, Irigaray and Deleuze (and/with Guattari, and/with

Parnet) recognize that being is a sticking point, which relations of becoming perpetually exceed. Events, including the publication and translation of texts, are assemblages of complexly enfolded intersubjective relations that continue to become as they are read and written into other associations in a transcreative process of becoming. Operationalizing the "with" and the "and," Godard articulates an ethics of translation that involves the delicate operation of capturing this process without fixing or stopping it.

Expanding Deleuze and Translation: Doing Intellectual History by the Letter

To understand Deleuze and Guattari as post-structuralist thinkers or French theorists independent of the associations that comprise their thought is to interpret their work metaphorically (by substitution) rather than metonymically (contiguously), or to translate their thought by pinning it to meaning rather than by the letter, which slides. In the translator's preface to *These Our Mothers* (and further in "Deleuze and Translation"), Godard reveals the trail she travelled as reader/writer of Brossard and encourages others to blaze their own: "May the intensity of your involvement as reader be as great as mine and you extend its creation in new directions to make this the text of bliss it works to be" (7). Below I extend Godard's work on associative translation in order to think intellectual history by the letter.

What might it mean to do intellectual history by the letter rather than by meaning, as Godard suggested was appropriate when translating with the polysemic work of Cixous and Irigaray? I propose that, by extension, it would mean being sensitive to the sliding of the signifier over the signified, or recognizing that "Deleuze and Guattari," who will be my key example below, cannot be pinned down for making this or that contribution to the history of philosophy because their work does not only cross disciplinary boundaries but is connected to other domains besides institutionally sanctioned and practised philosophy. While Deleuze and Guattari's concepts can be compiled, and their production together can be assembled into a system understood in relation to others articulated in the history of philosophy (it is, after all, a collaborative relationship that culminates in *What Is Philosophy?*), their writings are wrought of relations extending in a number of directions that are opposed to and/or have little to do with the trajectory of Philosophy. This renders metaphoric readings, interpretations, and translations of Deleuze and Guattari—readings that singularize and substitute, that overlook and/or obscure associations—problematic.

The translation of Deleuze (and Guattari) does not follow the trajectory that Godard includes as an appendix to "Deleuze and Translation" (76–78). Brossard was herself a reader/translator of Deleuze whom Godard translated into English in turn. As such, although *Différence et repetition* (1968) and *Logique du sens* (1969) were only translated in the early 1990s, Godard's translation of Brossard's *L'Amer, These Our Mothers* made these books available in translation in 1983. Words like "multiplicities" and "ramify" were being deployed in *These Our Mothers* a decade before they were released as Deleuzian terms. This is translation by association, or the type of relations that I would like to suggest are worth pursuing as intellectual history by the letter. Attention to the letter involves thinking metonymically, not metaphorically: *L'Amer* does not stand in for *Différence et repetition* but extends it by association. And Godard's translation is an extension of *L'Amer*. Brossard *and* Godard *and* Deleuze. In this associative configuration—with Godard taking Brossard and Deleuze in the middle—we witness the "and" as both transcreative extension and fold in the event of translation: Brossard and Deleuze are enfolded, unfolded, and refolded in Godard's *These Our Mothers*. *L'Amer* enacts a becoming-Deleuze of Brossard and a becoming-Brossard of Deleuze, a relationship that Godard unfolds while reading *L'Amer* and refolds into her translation.

Translating Deleuze by Association

Working *with* Barbara Godard, I became interested in doing intellectual history by the letter. Pursuing my doctorate under Barbara's supervision, I set out to rethink the arrival of French theory in America contiguously (via the associations of its thinkers) rather than by substitution (understanding a set of French thinkers as "post-structuralism" or "French theory" *avant-la-lettre*). What I found in my inquiry into the arrival of French theory was that "post-structuralism" was an Anglo-American designation invented in edited collections and special issues of journals at the turn of the 1980s to describe French thought that was produced with no such umbrella term a decade prior. Post-structuralism was born of the need for a new paradigm in the Anglo-American field of literary studies, a field in search of a replacement paradigm for the New Criticism.

I began my inquiry by focusing on two *events*. There was a stark contrast between the conference on "The Languages of Criticism and the Sciences of Man," which took place at Johns Hopkins in 1966, and the 1975 Schizo-Culture conference, organized by Sylvère Lotringer in New York.

The former brought Roland Barthes, Jacques Derrida, and Jacques Lacan, among other French thinkers, to Baltimore in order to introduce structuralism to an audience of 150 academics. The conference is often mentioned in narrative histories of French thought as the moment that inaugurated post-structualism with Derrida's performance of "Structure, Sign, and Play in the Discourse of the Human Sciences," which deconstructed structure by talking about its entry into philosophical discourse as an event (247), and by playing chicken and egg with Claude Lévi-Strauss's distinction between the engineer and bricoleur (252–65). The Schizo-Culture conference, on the other hand, marked the arrival of Deleuze, Guattari, and Michel Foucault, who spoke alongside William S. Burroughs, John Cage, Richard Foreman, and representatives from the anti-psychiatry, prison, gay, and women's liberation movements. While the former conference became *representative* of post-structuralism by the turn of the 1980s, the latter was *associative*, sparking a run of *Semiotext(e)* journals that juxtaposed French thinkers and American artists, writers, and activists without a running meta-commentary. While the proceedings for the Schizo-Culture conference were never printed, the Johns Hopkins proceedings were printed in the early 1970s as *The Structuralist Controversy*, eliding the effects of the late 1960s on the becoming of French thought in the process.

When we return to turn of 1970s France, what we find is, of course, another event. The context for much of the thought that constituted post-structuralist philosophy was May '68. In the late 1960s students introduced social movements into the classroom and demanded that what was discussed in the university classroom be relevant to the outside world. The inside of the university was folded out, and the outside was folded in, a relationship of *reciprocal implication*. One of the manifestations of such folding was that May '68 was a student–worker event.

And May '68 was also a French-American event. What I learned as I pursued May '68 was, first, that May '68 was *much* longer than a month and, second, that it was part of a movement that far exceeded national bounds. It was only days before a research trip to consult Allen Ginsberg and William Burroughs holdings at Columbia and to talk with Lotringer, John Rajchman, and Denis Hollier about Semiotext(e), that I ran into the fact that Columbia had its own '68. I picked up some books and read Joanne Grant's *Confrontation on Campus* on daily subway trips between Brooklyn and Morningside Heights. In Grant's book I read about how students at Columbia threw cobblestones in the spring of 1968, quoting students in Paris (122). Grant's 1969 book began with parallel quotes by Mark Rudd (leader of the Columbia revolt in New York) and Daniel Cohn-Bendit (leader of the March 22 movement, which was a crucial motor for the events in Paris) (xiii–xiv). When I picked up Cohn-Bendit and Cohn-Bendit's *Obsolete Communism*, I found prominent references to Columbia and the mid-1960s Berkeley Free Speech Movement (23–25, 32–33). There was a relationship of reciprocal implication between the movements taking place in Paris *and* New York (*and* Berlin *and* Berkeley *and* Strasbourg, and so on). "May '68" is constituted of a complex set of associations that exceed the temporal and spatial bounds that the term implies; it is a metaphor that does not capture the enfolding, unfolding, and refolding of the events that it is employed to represent. The events of 1968 exceed metaphorical treatment.

So Paris and New York are folded into one another, but what about French theory? Shortly after I arrived in New York, I went to St. Mark's bookstore and found Jean-François Bizot's *Free Press* on a display table. Bizot's coffee table–style book of newspaper covers pointed me to the Underground Press Syndicate (UPS), an internationally networked group of newspapers in which the culture and politics of what was collectively called "the movement" was produced and distributed. Alongside shared advertising revenue, library subscriptions to a microfiche collection of the papers were one of the major ways in which the syndicate was able to keep a growing roster of member papers afloat. Columbia had the collection. With Columbia '68 fresh on my mind, I was drawn to *RAT Subterranean News*, a paper that was produced in New York's Lower East Side and played a significant role in the Columbia revolt. The Columbia–Lower East Side connection was one that I was already pursuing via Lotringer's Semiotext(e) project, which drew uptown and downtown together with the Schizo-Culture conference, and in the run of *Semiotext(e)* journals that followed. Although I did not find Deleuze and Guattari in *RAT*, I did find Jean-Jacques Lebel.

I had run into Lebel's name a few months prior in France. François Cusset's book *French Theory* had just been published, and in it Cusset mentions an eye-catching road trip that Deleuze and Guattari took with Lebel, from New York to San Francisco, after the Schizo-Culture conference in 1975. The trip included encounters with Bob Dylan, Allen Ginsberg, Lawrence Ferlinghetti, and Patti Smith (Cusset 78). Alongside Burroughs and John Cage, whom Deleuze and Guattari encountered at the conference, the names of the American personalities they encountered are peppered through "Rhizome," originally published independently of *Mille plateaux* in 1976, and Deleuze and Parnet's *Pourparler*, which was published in 1977. Deleuze is particularly gushy about Dylan, invoking a lyric from *Writings and Drawings* (which Deleuze likely picked up on the road trip) at length, stating that "[a]s a teacher I should like to be able to give a course as Dylan organizes a song, as astonishing producer rather than author" (Deleuze and Parnet 8). As I researched Lebel's associations further, I found out that he spent time with Burroughs, Brion Gysin, and Gregory Corso in the Beat Hotel in the 1960s and translated their work into French. He met Deleuze in the mid-1950s and attended his seminars at Vincennes and St. Denis, and when Paris started to boil over in May '68, he called Guattari, whom he had met two years prior, to inform him that what he was theorizing and practising at the experimental schizoanalytic clinic La Borde just south of the city was taking place on Parisian streets. What I found was that this "with" Jean-Jacques Lebel produced a lot of "ands," a complex of enfolded relationships marked by reciprocal implication.

Lebel was not simply a go-between who brought Deleuze and Guattari to the American counterculture and vice-versa; Lebel was himself marked by complex foldings and unfolding of the French and American contingencies that he encountered through the 1950s, 1960s, and 1970s and, just as Deleuze (and Irigaray) are folded into *L'Amer*, these complex relationships are themselves folded into, and retrievable in, New York's underground newspaper *RAT Subterranean News*. This is one of the ways in which Deleuze and Guattari were translated for Anglo-American consumption—enfolded, unfolded, refolded, and so on—and "the movement" that Lebel was writing for and about in *RAT* was the very phenomenon that Deleuze and Guattari were attempting to translate in their *Capitalism and Schizophrenia* books. As Kristine Stiles puts it in her introduction to a 2003 exhibit of Lebel's art at the Mayor Gallery in London, Lebel acted as a "radar scout" for Deleuze and Guattari "in terms of his associations, activities, and very life style, which covered territories unknown to them" (5). With not only Deleuze, Guattari, and Beat writers, but also Marcel Duchamp, Guy Debord, Abbie Hoffman, New York anarchist group Up Against the Wall Motherfucker (UAW/MF), Julian Beck and Judith Malina of the Living Theater, Carolee Schneemann—and the list goes on—among Lebel's relations, Lebel's writing, art, and activism took several contingents from either side of the French-American divide down an intensive, middle line.

Even though he played the role of radar scout, Lebel is not, of course, the key to unlocking Deleuze and Guattari. When a line of associations led me to find Lebel, by chance, in *RAT*, I was mesmerized by the encounter. In his *RAT* article, entitled "A French Diary," Lebel relates his experiences at the barricades (where he was *with* Guattari) in a manner that thoroughly resembles the lines of flight that Deleuze and Guattari would write about four years later in *Anti-Oedipe*. When I later found out that Lebel introduced Burroughs, among others, to Artaud's "To be done with the judgement of god" at the Beat Hotel (Lebel, "Burroughs: The Beat Hotel Years" 85), I recalled Deleuze and Guattari's inclusion of Burroughs in their chapter on the Body without Organs in *A Thousand Plateaus*, which led me to consider the chain of translations and associations that landed Burroughs there in the first place. *A Thousand Plateaus* was a book built of associations. As interesting and enlightening as it was to learn about the associations out of which *A Thousand Plateaus* was made, why cut the book from the cloth? If *A Thousand Plateaus* is a rhizome and not a root book, where do its associations lead?

When I opened up a *RAT* paper and found Lebel inside, I was taken in the middle. Barbara suggested I turn to Bruno Latour for help, and when I opened up his *Reassembling the Social* for help, this is what he had to say: "Where should we start? As always, it is best to begin in the middle of things, *in media res*. Will the reading of a newspaper do? Sure, it offers a starting point as good as any. As soon as you open it, it's like a rain, a flood, an epidemic, an infestation" (27). Most supervisors discourage their students from following tangents, but Barbara encouraged me, throwing in Latour—a philosopher of associations—as a lifesaver when the flood came. Enfolded and unfolded in *RAT*, Lebel was laid out in contiguous relation with the movement that was being articulated in the newspaper. Lebel was part of an ongoing conversation. The Lebel that I found in the UPS paper was *RAT*-infested. It was an epidemic. I followed the flood. The crossing of Paris and Columbia became, by late August, the infamous protest at the Democratic National Convention in Chicago and continued to become a complex set of enfolding and unfolding liberation struggles: among others, the black, gay, Palestinian, prison, Puerto Rican, and women's liberation movements.

In *A Thousand Plateaus* Deleuze and Guattari write that "America is a special case.... Everything important that has happened or is happening takes the route of the American rhizome: the beatniks, the underground, bands and gangs, successive lateral offshoots in immediate connection with an outside" (*A Thousand Plateaus* 19). Lebel may have been the "radar scout" who made Deleuze and Guattari aware of the America of the beatniks and underground, but the movement at large was built of events, folds, and transcreative becomings that exceed subjective representation. "The movement" itself operated metonymically and not metaphorically: it was comprised of many contiguous parts standing in for an indefinable whole, and it could only exist as such—as "movement"—if it continued to move. Being was out of the question because without becoming, movement would cease to be.

Conclusion

Translation is never a smooth process whereby a signifier in one language finds its equivalent in another. Even in the most ideal cases, where the equivalency of a term appears indisputable, the position the signifiers of origin and destination occupy differs within their respective languages. Recognizing the associative processes at play in the texts of French and Québécois feminist theorists and writers at a time when equivalency and fluency models of translation were the norm, Godard produced an ethics of translation that was sensitive to writing that was intersubjective and expansive. Godard's translations and translation theory re-inscribe the work of the translator as co-producer and creative interventionist, an associative theory of translation that is true to the spirit of the work being translated.

Just as translation by the letter is an approach that is sensitive to intersubjectivity and becoming, so too can the practice of intellectual history be sensitive to—and even taken away by—the movement that animates it. In the second half of the piece, I employed Godard's associative theory of translation in order to read and rewrite the arrival of French theory in America as a transcreative act. What does theory become when we think it according to its associations? It proliferates; it is taken away by a sea of movement(s). In such a space, tangents are not distractions or asides; they are the lines that take us in the middle, a productive and multifarious space. *And* is how translation works. *And* in the middle is where Godard's theory of translation awaits further elaboration.

Works Cited

Bizot, Jean-François, ed. *Free Press: Underground & Alternative Publications, 1965–1975.* New York: Universe, 2006. Print.

Cixous, Hélène. *Vivre l'orange/To Live the Orange.* Trans. Anne Liddle and Sarah Cornell. Paris: Des Femmes, 1979. Print.

Cohn-Bendit, Daniel, and Gabriel Cohn-Bendit. *Obsolete Communism: The Left-Wing Alternative.* Trans. Arnold Pomerans. New York: McGraw-Hill, 1968. Print.

Cusset, François. *French Theory: Foucault, Derrida, Deleuze & cie et les mutations de la vie intellectuelle aux États-Unis.* Paris: La Découverte, 2005. Print.

Deleuze, Gilles. *Negotiations*. Trans. Martin Joughin. New York: Columbia UP, 1995. Print.

Deleuze, Gilles, and Félix Guattari. Trans of *Mille Plateaux*, 1980. *A Thousand Plateaus*. Trans. Brian Massumi. Minneapolis: U of Minnesota P, 1987. Print.

——. *What Is Philosophy?* Trans. Hugh Tomlinson and Graham Burchell. New York: Columbia UP, 1994. Print.

Deleuze, Gilles, and Claire Parnet. *Dialogues II*. Trans. Hugh Tomlinson and Barbara Habberjam. New York: Columbia UP, 2002. Print.

Derrida, Jacques. "Structure, Sign, and Play in the Discourse of the Human Sciences." *The Structuralist Controversy: The Languages of Criticism & the Sciences of Man*. Ed. Richard Macksey and Eugenio Donato. Baltimore: Johns Hopkins UP, 1972. 247–72. Print.

Godard, Barbara. "Deleuze and Translation." *Parallax* 14 (January 2000): 56–81. Print.

——. "Preface." *These Our Mothers* by Nicole Brossard. Toronto: Coach House, 1983. 7. Print.

——. "Signs and Events: Deleuze in Translation." *Semiotic Review of Books* 15.3 (2005): 3–10. Print.

——. "Translating (with) the Speculum." *TTR: Traduction, terminologie, redaction* 4.2 (1991): 85–121. Print.

Grant, Joanne. *Confrontation on Campus: The Columbia Pattern for the New Protest*. New York: Signet, 1969. Print.

Irigaray, Luce. *This Sex Which Is Not One*. Trans. Catherine Porter. Ithaca: Cornell UP, 1985. Print.

Latour, Bruno. *Reassembling the Social: An Introduction to Actor-Network Theory*. Oxford: Oxford UP, 2005. Print.

Lebel, Jean-Jacques. "Burroughs: The Beat Hotel Years." *Naked Lunch @ 50: Anniversary Essays*. Ed. Oliver Harris and Ian MacFayden. Carbondale: Southern Illinois UP, 2009. 84–90. Print.

——. "A French Diary: At the Barricade." *RAT Subterranean News* 1.14 (June 1968): 3, 11. Print.

Stiles, Kristine. "Jean-Jacques Lebel's Phoenix and Ash." Introduction. *Jean Jacques Lebel: Works from 1960–1965*. London: Mayor Gallery, 2003. 3–15. Print.

Chapter 11
Gail Scott and Barbara Godard on "The Main": Borders, Sutures, Micro-cosmopolitan Interconnectivity, and Translation Studies

GILLIAN LANE-MERCIER

This essay examines productive resonances between Gail Scott's novels and essays,[1] Barbara Godard's 2002 article entitled "Writing from the Border: Gail Scott on 'The Main,'"[2] and the concept of micro-cosmopolitanism recently defined in the area of translation studies by Michael Cronin in *Translation and Identity*, published in 2006. I shall argue that while, on the one hand, Scott's writing and Godard's analysis could be seen to uphold the translational paradigms inspired by Antoine Berman and Lawrence Venuti, both of whom seek to avoid assimilating the cultural other through "non-fluent" translation strategies based, respectively, on the source text's material "strangeness" and on foreignizing or minoritizing practices, on the other hand, they point to ways of going beyond the binaries in which these paradigms remain grounded.

More specifically, Scott's experimental aesthetics and Godard's critical reading combine to suggest new routes of reflection on the theory and practice of translation in the age of globalization. These routes echo Cronin's exploration of the way in which translation at once upholds and enhances cultural diversity in an ongoing effort to counter more conservative tendencies toward monoculturalism and monolingualism. If, as Cronin states, a micro-cosmopolitan vision of translation implies a conception of cultural experience predicated on post-Newtonian ideas of non-linearity, mobility, random bifurcation, non-equilibrium, intrinsic uncertainty, complex allegiances, and poly-identity, then it is possible to see in Scott's writing and Godard's analysis the conceptual and material contours of a new paradigm for translation studies akin to the one he proposes.

This new paradigm enables the foregrounding of alternative forms of connectivity that, by dismantling the dichotomies still implicit in much contemporary thinking on literary translation in particular and cultural difference in general, entail an open-ended interdependency in which "where-questions" remain crucial to a proper understanding of the trans-local. Moreover, hitherto ungrammatical formulations such as "Who am ... WE?" (Scott, "Mrs. Beckett's" 91) acquire unexpected ethical, cultural, and political relevance insofar as they articulate less abstract processes of globalization. For translation not only ensures the movement of goods, information, and texts across territorial, linguistic, and cultural boundaries, it also plays a role in the migratory movements of people themselves. Accordingly, translation is not merely concerned with theoretical reflections on linguistic equivalence or cultural transfer, but is also and perhaps more urgently a very real question of everyday survival for an ever-increasing portion of the world's population.

In what follows, I propose to draw out the connections between Cronin's account of the stakes of translation in a global context, Godard's analysis of Scott's novel *Main Brides*, and my own attempt to extend and complicate her analysis through a reading of Scott's latest novel, *The Obituary*. As I hope to demonstrate, the politics of survival informing Cronin's concept of micro-cosmopolitanism also informs the aesthetic notion of suture and the critical category of metonymic accretion as defined, respectively, by Scott in her essays and Godard in her analysis. My general hypothesis is that a politics of survival forms the basis of the new paradigm for translation studies, which these concepts and categories implicitly or explicitly help to shape.

First, however, a brief definition of micro-cosmopolitanism is necessary. While Cronin's overall goal is to provide an alternative to the binary opposites, universalisms, and absolutes that continue to inform current debates on translation and identity in relation to questions of cultural diversity, migration, citizenship, and globalization, he nonetheless posits an initial series of distinctions operating within modern visions of what he calls macro-cosmopolitanism. The most obvious distinction, of course, is between the delocalizing processes typical of macro-cosmopolitism versus the localizing processes it opposes, as expressed by any number of binaries such as the general versus the particular, the plural versus the singular, the universal versus the specific, the post-national versus the national, cultural non-determinism (sameness) versus cultural determinism (difference). This leads him to reiterate the duality of the translator's task insofar as it transcends the binaries just enumerated: as "cultural cosmopolitans" (Cronin 11), translators must go beyond the singular location and yet they must recognize the importance of that location's idiom "without which translation as a meaningful activity would cease to exist" (12).

Rather than seeing these binaries as mutually exclusive or attempting to deconstruct them, Cronin defines the concept of micro-cosmopolitanism as a way of asserting their interconnectivity. Not only do macro- and micro-cosmopolitism share certain ideals, most notably "a concern for freedom, an openness to and tolerance of others, a respect for difference" (14), but micro-cosmopolitism contains the global on a local scale:

> The micro-cosmopolitan movement, by situating diversity, difference, exchange at the micro-levels of society, challenges the monopoly (real or imaginary) of a deracinated elite on cosmopolitan ideals by attempting to show that elsewhere is next door, in one's immediate environment, no matter how infinitely small or infinitely large the scale of investigation. (16–17)

Put differently, micro-cosmopolitanism allows for the diversification and layering of the local that foregrounds difference and foreignness as occurring at once within and beyond a given boundary, be it geopolitical, cultural, linguistic, or identitarian. Specificity is "defined through and not against multiplicity" (18), context-bound cultural formations or practices can be seen as having global origins or resulting from multiple influences, and globalizing processes are no longer the unique preserve of borderless forms of interconnectivity. By revealing connections between the local and the global, micro-cosmopolitism contests "disabling" and discriminatory "either/or" modes of thinking in favour of what Cronin terms an "enabling," progressive bottom-up approach that "admits the importance and complexity of the local as a basis for the formation of solidary relationships but allows for the trans-local spread of those relationships, i.e., for the establishment of solidarities that are not *either* local *or* global but both *local* and *global*" (19).

In this perspective, global issues of rights and freedoms so central to rationalist liberal individualism and macro-cosmopolitanism are inextricably intertwined with multiple local (political, cultural, etc.) allegiances that comprise most people's sense of identity and rootedness. At the same time, the macro-cosmopolitan, anti-essentialist notion of an uprooted, borderless poly-identity is no longer at odds with context-bound aspirations to difference and a sense of belonging. These proliferating, non-linear, unforeseeable interconnections between the local and the global are what

Cronin terms the inward/outward networking of the micro-cosmopolitan moment, "when context-bound cultures encounter each other and undergo transformation as a result. Only in this way can the twin pitfalls of the false universalism of liberalism's universalistic morality and the communitarian retreat into the particular be avoided" (Delanty qtd. in Cronin 23).

At least three aspects of Cronin's conception can be singled out here. First, the notion of place, no matter what the scale, is metonymically construed as multi-faceted, layered, culturally diverse, informed as much by (traces of) difference as by fluid, non-linear inward/outward connections, and an ensuing sense of interdependency that eschews absolutes in favour of transformative linkages.

Second, instead of being considered a purely extrinsic, outward-bound phenomenon that mediates languages, cultures, and traditions across national borders, as current theories of translation tend to support, be they source- or target-oriented, translation is increasingly becoming an intrinsic, inward-bound phenomenon called upon to mediate language or community rights, ethnic solidarities, cultural difference, cultural memory and loss within a given local setting. While intrinsic translation is a direct result not only of the "remembering" inherent to various forms of identity politics but also of the impact of globalization and (im)migration on contemporary societies, this micro-cosmopolitan turning away from the assimilative diktats of translational equivalence, transparency, and bridge-building and from the non-ethnocentric practices of foreignizing (Venuti) and neo-literalism (Berman), both of which are based on the idea of discrete languages/cultures/identities/nations and "top-down" localization, points to translation's transformative, overlapping (metonymic) potential as it is called upon to connect constantly shifting differences and similarities at the local and global levels. As Cronin remarks:

> If in one of the senses of cosmopolitanism (…)[3] being a citizen involves an awareness of connectedness beyond the local and the immediate, then it is important to identify mobilizing paradigms that can usefully link the local to what lies beyond the local. One of the ways in which we connect with others from different languages and cultures is through translation, so commitment to appropriate, culturally sensitive models of translation would appear to be central to any concept of global citizenship in the twenty-first century. (30)

Finally, by drawing attention to questions of interconnectedness, micro-cosmopolitanism requires new avenues of thinking about borders, be they external or internal, which adhere to an "and/both" logic as opposed to an "either/or" logic. If the fluid, mobile, open-ended, transformative properties that constitute the micro-cosmopolitan moment stop short of synthesis, on the one hand, and, on the other, of free-flowing porosity, this is because the micro-cosmopolitan moment foregrounds not so much the entities it connects as the point at which they connect, namely, the border or fault line itself. Indeed, it is precisely this "form of triangulation or (…) 'broken middle'" (118) at the basis of micro-cosmopolitanism, along with the type of translation processes it fosters, that resonate with Godard's critical reading of the "strained encounters" (123), "movements of accidental assemblage" (122), and metonymic accretion she sees as constituting the aesthetic project of Scott's second novel, *Main Brides* (1993), and with Scott's notion of the sutured subject, the most striking illustration of which can be found in *The Obituary* (2010).

The unifying thread that links the notions of suture and metonymic accretion to Cronin's concept of micro-cosmopolitanism resides in the paratactic relations all three terms imply. Whereas parataxis as a stylistic device is most frequently construed as operating along a horizontal axis through juxtaposition, sequencing, combination, insertion (incision), addition, repetition, disassociation, or digression, it can also operate on a vertical axis through superposition, overlapping, (over)layering, ventriloquism, footnotes, palimpsest (trace), suppression, or *rature* (censure). Despite their apparent diversity, paratactic strategies eschew both resolution and synthesis, relying on reversible, incomplete, hence open-ended disjunctive/conjunctive processes similar to those underlying the rhetorical figures of metonymy and synecdoche in which intervals (gaps) and layerings (patches) allow multiple articulations between two or more elements—textual spaces, voices, languages, cultures, identities, communities—to emerge and proliferate along the "fault lines of the fissured, and often campily re-sutured subject-in-becoming" (Scott, "The Sutured Subject" 69).

As will become clearer below, in the same way that sutured narrative surfaces and subjects "hol(d) out the promise of the manageability of unspeakable loss (…), with the displacement of the referent and the multiplication of signifiers at the site of the lost referent" (Godard, "Writing from the Border" 138), translation conceived as "the subtle metamorphosis of the metonymic rather than the absolutist expropriation of the metaphorical (…) will give rise to a different idiom with its multiple translation traces where the overlapping and the partially corresponding will tilt the language in new directions" (Cronin 55). Anchored in a logic of contiguity, connection, transformation, diversity, and multiple futures, such a conception contests the "either/or" logic of substitution and equivalence in which the ability to translate or be translated "can imply a painful stretching, bending, conceding when it is an everyday necessity, a tool of survival" (Scott qtd. in Godard, *Collaboration* 18) that fosters, at best, a forced duality within speech, at worst, the suppression of difference, loss, and death.

The "and and" or, if one prefers, the "both/and" logic inherent to the notions of sutured subjects, metonymical accretion, and micro-cosmopolitanism defines these notions as a semiotic process deployed along borders between two entities according to a dynamics of disjunction and (re)connection that leads to the transformation of both entities without completely dissolving either. This dynamics is designed to defuse all attempts to separate or to synthesize associated with ideologies of difference seeking to reinforce boundaries by strengthening the "either/or" binary or, conversely, to dispense with them altogether through radical deterritorialization, examples of which can be found, respectively, in the official definition of Canadian multiculturalism and in conventional forms of macro-cosmopolitan thinking, notably the translation concept of creolization, as recently defined by Edouard Glissant.[4]

More importantly, however, "both/and" logic further serves as a political and ethical response to "History's 'homocidal' propensities where sameness has a killing effect" (Godard, "Writing from the Border" 138), where the "closing of the gap (…) leads almost invariably either to the Hegemony of the One (…) or the Tyranny of the Two (there is My Language and Your Language and anything else between disappears)" (Cronin 135), and where, given "(t)hey also hated Indians. (…) By the end of our tale, we may likewise be dead" (*The Obituary* 13), including "our Native narrator" (14), as a result, among other expropriating factors, of "(n)o one teaching anything Algonquian" (153) even though "(e)veryone knew the words of the new concept anthem: *The Maple Leaf Forever*" (121). Scott cites as a quintessentially Canadian case of "homicidal propensities" the (in)famous notwithstanding clause, which authorizes the federal government or a provincial legislature—namely those of Alberta, Saskatchewan, and Québec—to enact legislation in order to override one or more sections of Canada's Charter of Rights and Freedoms, including freedom of expression and freedom from unreasonable search and seizure.[5]

I should like to suggest that the explicit and implicit references to the overriding properties encoded in the notwithstanding clause are fundamental to the very intense sense of place all Scott's novels seek to denote, as well as to her critique of the hypocrisy of Canadian multiculturalism and the corresponding suppressed genocide of the indigenous peoples, which is expressed by—or, more properly, heard through—the gaps and layers that constitute the ~~Native~~ narrator's "inchoate origin" (12), together with her dissociated (metonymic) subjectivity. Recalling that "inchoate" signifies (1) only partly in existence (gap); (2) a criminal offence liable to lead to another (accretion), the term points simultaneously to the novel's epigraph: "What haunts are not the dead but the gaps left within us by the secrets of others – Abraham + Torok" (5) and to the central issue Scott wishes to address: "The question being, in the case of the dissociate, or of any child having parents whose talk not complementing the interior who-am-we: What part of her (…) crossing the great divide? What part [if any] left to speak?" (46).

In other words, the overriding properties of the notwithstanding clause and its derivative, the adverb itself, serve as highly politicized tropes for Scott's writing project from both a thematic and a formal point of view. On one level, these properties uphold "either/or" conceptions of translation as expropriation, containment, and silencing; on another level, they inadvertently reveal the intervals and layers such conceptions refuse to acknowledge. The notwithstanding trope thus paradoxically also upholds, via the related tropes of suture and metonymic accretion, "both/and" visions of translation as micro-cosmopolitan inward-outward interconnectedness, perceived by Cronin as offering a cultural, ethical, and political framework from which to account for issues pertaining to identity and cultural diversity in the contemporary global moment. I shall now attempt to describe the nature of this conceptual link, bearing in mind the importance attributed by Cronin not only to the role literature and literary translation can play in fostering cultural diversity and cultural policies, but also to the ways in which multilingual nation-states such as Canada or Ireland and supranational formations such as the European Union can give political effect to the version of the cosmopolitan he articulates.

Godard's insightful reading of Scott's second novel focuses on the multiple border positions the narrator, Lydia, occupies and on the "small solidarities" (*Main Brides* 16) these positions enable her to forge. Drinking wine in a café on Montreal's boulevard St-Laurent—also called The Main—Lydia wavers between verbal categories, subject positions, languages, cultures, centuries, identities, and several states of consciousness as she successively juxtaposes images of the seven women ("brides") she observes onto pediments of the buildings across the street, thereby connecting "art and life to make a new history based not on violence but on aesthetic detail" (Godard, "Writing from the Border" 118). Referring to the influence of Deleuze and Guattari's concept of minoritizing on Scott's narrative prose, which manifests itself through the intensive, non-referential use of language based on various disruptive paratactic strategies designed to exceed rational boundaries of self, language, time, and place, Godard accentuates the transformative potential of these strategies, underscoring the disjunctive, "disidentifying" effect they have on the form, indeed the very texture of Scott's writing practice:

> Writing between languages has obliged (Scott) to (…) engage in "language-centred" work on signs as affective and effective relays rather than cognitive representations and so to make English vibrate differently with (Latin) rhythms from Quebec. Such bilingual confluency introduces a contradictory dynamic (…), where signifying surfaces bounce off each other in a movement of proliferation and dispersion, rather than one of centring and integration. Fictional events occur at the level of discourse in such movements of accidental assemblage. (122)

Godard singles out parentheses as one of the principal formal devices used by Scott in *Main Brides* to denote the excesses of intensive, a-signifying language practices. By "ruffling smoother syntactic links" and performing "the zigzag movement of narrative semiosis" (122), parentheses introduce incisions into normative grammatical relations—especially those between subject and verb or subject and object—that cause identities to vacillate, splinter, and reconnect anew, "campily re-sutured" *through*, *within*, and *over* the space of the parenthesis. Such displacements along the syntagmatic (metonymic) axis transform identity into "a moving site of signifying effects" (124), which, due to their implicit or explicit bilingual confluency, also function as translation effects.[6] Moreover, given that parentheses further interfere with normative spatial and temporal relations, Scott's translating subject-in-becoming, seated in a café on The Main—itself a complex, multi-ethnic, multilingual, hence fluidly zigzagging, disruptive border between francophone and anglophone Montreal—finds herself disconnected from (patriarchal) History and projected outward onto architectural details as fantasized, desiring images of women with rebellious pasts and multiple futures.

Parentheses operate, then, as internal borders, construed simultaneously as non-linear bifurcations, proliferating contiguities, gaps (holes), patches (fillings, accretions), and haphazard triangulations (asides), designed to wreak havoc with fixed categories and their conventional correlations, in accordance with a "both/and" dynamics that attempts "to articulate strategies of the real" (137). In this perspective, borders are themselves complex, paradoxical, moving sites of excess designed not so much to be inhabited as to link, through a politics of address (128), the writing subject's oscillating "I" with a bilingual "You" and the ever-dissolving/recomposing "We" of the community of "brides" via the ungrammatical "are" and a series of hesitating, affect-laden dots, which combine to prefigure the fractured, dissociated solidarities typical of Scott's current questioning: "Who am ... WE?"

Perceived as both an inward-oriented incision and an outward-oriented interstice that offers the subject-in-becoming "a space of differentiation" (128) and interconnectivity denoted by the The Main, the parenthesis figures a "thin or permeable border (which) does not reunite but stutters, as trace of a frayed line that breaks off in connecting" (128). Godard correctly describes the resulting transformative process as akin to the metonymic (metamorphosis, difference, excess) as opposed to the metaphoric (synthesis, resemblance, loss),[7] noting that "the café on The Main is not so much a site for marking distinctions as for facilitating overlaps, contradictions, paradoxes," "a site of charged encounters and superpositions" (131), of the "overflowing" and "blurring" (132) of borders and the entities they "accidentally" connect/disconnect, which nonetheless avoid erasure and indistinction.

Godard's critical notion of metonymic accretion is invaluable for apprehending the ways in which Scott's narrative holes and patches allow for the proliferation of "impossible or illegitimate combinations" (134) and "irrelevant or multiple groupings" (139) destined, through segmentation, dislocation, and the releasing of affect (desire, pathos, nostalgia, fear, pain), to "send things spiralling in every direction, rather than forward in a single logical causal construction" (134). In this sense, her notion is well suited to capture the experimental dimension of Scott's prose, which constantly calls attention to "sentencing" (Scott, *Spare Parts* 87)—that is, to the spaces between words, sentences, and paragraphs that redistribute the subject "across hazardous abutments, torqued by inner syntax in dissonance with outer or the reverse" (13). In this way, it is equally well suited to capture the "small solidarities" that "generat(e) new localisms through gossip, through performing for each other" (Scott qtd. in Moyes 213), through the porosity of a text that knows how to listen by allowing the subject to "bleed" into inner-outer context without entirely disappearing so as to avoid assimilation, thereby "projecting a contiguity (...) which is not a relationship of trying to mirror reality" (Scott qtd. in Eichhorn 55).[8]

I would argue, however, that the notion of metonymic accretion is unable to articulate the inevitable suppressions, censuring, losses, and deaths (genocides) for which not only the homogenizing, metaphoric processes of the exclusive "either/or" logic must be held accountable, but the layering, transformative metonymic processes of the supposedly inclusive "and/both" logic as well. The image of accretion (proliferation, spiralling, combination, excess) as it is used by Godard "hides" the darker sides of metonymy, namely, the suffocating potential of proliferating phenomena, together with metonymy's reductive rhetorical properties whereby the part selected to signify (stand for) the whole transforms the latter by also rendering it partially invisible and/or inaudible. More significantly, such an image cannot fully account for the risks associated with a porous, vacillating, "both/and" subject position (or writing subject) that, while it may enable the "line of flight" or "breaking out" (Godard 128) of fear toward a new future and a new way of thinking about history, remains connected to the realities that have inspired this fear. Poverty, homelessness, immigration, prostitution, drug addiction, rape, and murder are thematized in *Main Brides* not as tropes, but as "real" life contexts of the "brides" Lydia wishes to superimpose on the neighbouring rooftops and, by metonymic proximity, of Lydia herself.

The Main as border or, more accurately, as "broken middle" of a triangulation designed to ward off the violence of resolution, is thus caught up, along with the parentheses that forge Scott's inchoate subject-in-becoming, in a wavering intensive-extensive use of language that, contrary to what Godard suggests, does not completely "lose" the referent (context) in the process of proliferating semiosis, but, rather, loses sight of the damage this proliferation can cause, such as the inchoate, recurring criminal offences it covers up. Whereas Godard's critical analysis resonates with Scott's formal project and, by anticipation, with certain facets of Cronin's concept of micro-cosmopolitanism, thereby pointing to their respective impact on binaries in general and on translational binaries in particular,[9] the emphasis placed on metonymic addition (excess) to the detriment of metonymic subtraction (reduction) obscures more negative forms of interconnectedness raised by Scott's experimental prose and implied by Cronin's concept. This is partially due to the evolution of Scott's thinking on subjectivity as it moved away from the formal effort to grasp the "feminist," "queer," "Anglo-Québec" moment inspired by the notion of the porous text/subject, so predominant in *Heroine* and, especially, *Main Brides*, toward "the formal attempt to grasp the total moment of time in which one happens to be writing a particular piece of prose" (Scott, "The Sutured Subject" 90), henceforth informed, on the one hand, by the notion of the sutured text/subject and, on the other, by the theme of the notwithstanding clause, to which I shall return after one more detour through Cronin's book.

Cronin is careful to point to the life and death consequences for translators, in particular oral interpreters, in situations of conflict—resistance, imperialistic expansion, colonialism, imprisonment, trial, exile, war—where "fidelity is a relative rather than an absolute notion" (86) and "metamorphosis (…) is not simply a benign shift in state, (…) but can involve a violent alteration of state, a brutal transformation of one's condition" (108). Despite their apparent support of peaceful cohabitation, metonymical processes based on permeability and transformative interconnectivity that leave (traces, fragments of) the border intact are just as susceptible to power imbalances, manipulation, control, betrayal, persecution, loss as other, more overtly aggressive forms of border reinforcement (e.g., nationalism), crossing (e.g., invasion), or dissolution (e.g., macro-cosmopolitanism).

Conversely, while translation's perceived marginal status has often been attributed to the translator's "monstrous doubleness" (114), together with his or her well-documented invisibility, it is this very marginalization, according to Cronin, that ensures innovation and connectivity in a global situation, given that "weak" ties are less binding than "strong" ones, enabling greater freedom from the local accompanied by greater randomness and farther-reaching links. If one also subscribes to the micro-cosmopolitan premise that difference binds rather than divides, then it is possible to recognize the "vital necessity of factoring in translation to any proper understanding of debates around contemporary identity" (142).

In this light, Scott's more recent essays and experimental prose present overt affinities with micro-cosmopolitan thinking as a dynamics of proliferating resurfacings—in the dual sense of emerging and patching—that bespeak simultaneously of loss and of gain. As she noted in a 1999 interview: "Something is breaking down. Identity is becoming a parody of itself as people drift and merge in new cultures" (Scott qtd. in Frost, n.p.), opening up the local to global influences, which allow for new links not only to the future but to the past as well. *The Obituary*'s awkward sentences, the moving inward-outward possibilities they create, and their palimpsestic (over)layering thus suggest new ways of apprehending the notion of interconnectedness. By calling into question the relationship between citizenship and the writing subject, as well as the spaces they occupy—in this case Montreal's multi-ethnic, "noisy" Mile-End, which includes a section of The Main—her prose reveals through what she calls a performance of the cicatrice censured, acculturated, lost interconnections that can still be heard if one listens to the sounds emanating from the suture's metonymic seam/scar in the form of haunting translation effects.

More specifically, if storytelling can be characterized as "the questioning of the storyteller and her work in the aesthetic (re)production of social relationships" (Scott et al., 10) and as a practice "pressed on by [...] the rhythms and complexities of multiple-language and cultural contexts" (24) that form our contemporary societies, then story-telling also becomes a site for the abrupt resurfacing of silenced languages and cultures such as ~~Algonquian~~ through the stereoscopic links created by "sentencing," footnoting (♥), and multilingual confluency:

> R ~~faux~~-confidential laugh + slippy-slidey sentences, switching♥ this way + that.
> ♥Reader, the past carries a secret index. Little by little revealing why one meandering in speaking, (…) disparate in our associations (…). (*The Obituary* 39)

In other words, by releasing along a series of fault lines the painful noises ("timeless secrets + ressentiments" [38]) of the supplement (excess) and of repression (reduction), the suture produces a chain of slippages (possible stories declined in the future anterior tense) that provoke the dissociation of the narrating/social/historical/female subject, "halfway between melancholia + paranoia" (134), into ever shifting metonymic parts: I, Rosine, Rose, I/little Rosie, I/Rosine, I/R, R surrogate, I/th' fly, *Face*, the Bottom Historian (author of the footnotes): "Dear Grandpa, I/your granddaughter ~~am a liar~~ wanted to be authentic. After, I mean just before the future. [And the future tale within, which is the realm of the ancestors. (…).]" (152). These disjunctive speaking subjects combine to form an unstable, sutured text/"WE" comprised of additions (footnotes, parentheses, and plus [+] signs), subtractions (*ratures* and minus [–] signs), fissures (obliques [/]), and equal signs (=) that denote (im)possible past, present, future dénouements:

> Never say you're an Indian. If. You're. Not. (22)
> ~~th' freedom I looking for all–"~~ (146)
> (…) when understood, fully. Will restore to rightful status the discerning Indigenous peoples. Who knowing nothing happening in any one planetary domain or moment. Ever definitively lost to any other. (118)
> For we th' livin' obliged to keep movin'. Toward that monstrosity: th' future [+ th' anterior within it]. (144–45)

Which brings us back to the notwithstanding clause and the very real "cicatrices" it can legally perform through its overriding powers.

Qualified at the beginning of the novel, in a parenthetical remark inserted into one of the numerous footnotes written by the "Bottom Historian, ever in denial about her secret desire for omniscience" (165), as having been "[summoned for defence of French-language and other collective rights]" (16), the notwithstanding clause, together with the ethical issues it raises, informs not only the formal and narrative devices just referred to, but many of *The Obituary*'s thematic layers as well. On one level, the provision's overriding prerogatives operate grammatically in a rather large array of supposedly innocuous adverbial "sentencings": "Multicoloured tree lights [notwithstanding season]" (97); "And at night, notwithstanding those nailed planks blocking bedroom doors: cries of rats. Trying to get in" (38); "Though (the *Book of Genocides*) containing no mention of people camping there ere establishment of (…) Crystal Palace's (…) central nef—notwithstanding Palace's exposition vocation—reserved for skating" (24). Offering semantic reinforcement for Godard's more semiotic vision of the "both/and" properties of metonymic accretion, the recurrence of the term "notwithstanding" throughout the novel overrides established categories (e.g., seasons), protective boundaries (e.g., restraining planks), and predetermined functions (e.g., exhibits) in favour of other possibilities and sensations based on an idea of the exception as excess or surplus and borders as porous.

On another level, however, these same overriding prerogatives take on different hues, serving on occasion "to cover hesitation, dubiety, rooted in (Canadians') fear of offending" (16) or, as stated above, to enact legislation that operates in spite of some Charter rights the latter appears to violate. Based on the idea of the exception as, at best, a form of hypocrisy (or political correctness), at worst, a legally sanctioned act of restriction and exclusion that supports the interests/rights of some to the detriment of others, the term "notwithstanding" used in these ways reactivates the "homicidal propensities" of "either/or" logic, in which to override is to simultaneously silence through temporary exclusion (a notwithstanding clause expires after five years) and indefinitely perpetuate the same silencing (a notwithstanding clause can be re-enacted).

Even though the Bottom Historian (and Scott's readers) "must guard against overinterpretation" (16), it is difficult not to read into these allusions and references to the notwithstanding clause a critique of theories of diversity that work to the advantage of the privileged by teaching, for example, English, French, and Latin, but not ~~Algonquian~~ or by embracing certain official definitions of multiculturalism. Thus in a footnote:

> But what leads generation after generation of new arrivals in the Americas to declare: *In this country everyone an immigrant*? (...) soldiers shooting, "when required"; otherwise, deviously kidnapping Aboriginal children into conditions killing thousands [strangely, the word *genocide* refused.] Notwithstanding contemporary acknowledgement of guilt, voices on state radio still regularly iterating *In this country everyone an immigrant*. (85–86)

Scott's sutured narrating subject is thus in every way an inchoate subject, only partly in existence as a result of recurring, unacknowledged criminal offences that figure as gaps in the *Book of Genocides* from which she tears out leaves, torquing her Grandfather's unspoken/unspeakable tale into a tale she will have told, "(t)here being no redemption in ~~origins~~ extinct matter" (117) and no closure to the future anterior of remembering. Resonating with Godard's critical notion of proliferating, a-signifying, metonymic accretions that override the silencing of diversity and the fixity of identity politics, the notion of the sutured subject, through which ghostly ventriloquist-translators of lost indigenous languages and lineages become audible, also resonates with Cronin's micro-cosmopolitan conception of translation as a form of ethics predicated on the complexity, distance/closeness, and desire of triangulation (135). As Cronin argues, "it is high time that translators were not merely seen but heard" (74), for a translator who is merely visible is not translating at all.

As we saw, micro-cosmopolitanism is not only an outward-oriented movement from the particular toward the global, but also an inward-oriented movement toward "the omnipresence of traces of foreignness, of other languages and cultures" (16) within the local, even when the "omnipresence" of diversity has been reduced to "its shadow, memory" (*The Obituary* 118). Refusing the false rhetoric of the overriding "either/or," the (writing) subject is a translating subject who "speaks à côté. She is constantly recomposing. And that makes her utterly contemporary" (Scott qtd. in Eichhorn 60), indeed, utterly micro-cosmopolitan. Scott's inchoate narrative of suppressed genocide gestures, within a composite local-global moment of time, toward the future anterior of (the past (his)story of) the translating subject, whose suture can be read as the metonymical scar of forced assimilation (junction) and the impossibility of total silencing (disjunction). By so doing, it also gestures toward the inward-bound diversity of space and of self—"Do not skyscrapers bear, deep within, straw huts? The person, her ancestors?" (*The Obituary* 117)—that at once mirrors and fosters proliferating outward-bound, trans-local interconnectivities.

Translation theorists who continue to subscribe to tight definitions of the local, the trans-local, and the multicultural are unable to sufficiently account for these translational movements of intrinsic/extrinsic metonymic accretion based simultaneously on the "manageability of unspeakable loss" (Godard), ever shifting gains, triangular relationships, and a politics of survival. In this respect, the multilingual experimental works of Anglo-Québec (the term itself displays a suture) writers like Scott, together with the critical concepts their works have inspired, offer an extremely rich terrain for theorists who, following Cronin, seek to develop enabling paradigms in response to the new questions posed by globalization, "some of them, grant it, quite scary, such as the question that brooks no answer, for it allows no singularity [...]: Who am ... WE?" (Scott, "Mrs. Beckett's" 90–91).

Notes

1. Scott has published four novels: *Heroine* (1987), *Main Brides* (1993), *My Paris* (1999), and *The Obituary* (2010), a collection of short stories, *Spare Parts Plus Two* (2002), a collection of essays, *Spaces Like Stairs* (1989), and two co-edited books, *La théorie, un dimanche* (1988) and *Biting the Error* (2004).
2. An earlier, slightly different version of this article was published in *Trois* in 1996. To the best of my knowledge, this is Godard's only in-depth analysis of one of Scott's novels, despite many references to her work in other articles and their collaboration on *Tessera* (see Godard, *Collaboration*).
3. In order to distinguish between Scott's use of square brackets in *The Obituary*, I have used rounded brackets throughout the essay to indicate omissions from the passages I quote.
4. I am referring here to Glissant's more recent claim that "(...) la créolisation qui se fait dans la Néo-Amérique, et la créolisation qui est en train de gagner les autres Amériques, est la même qui opère dans le monde entier. La thèse que je défendrai (...) est que le monde se créolise (...). Et c'est cette mutation douloureuse de la pensée humaine que je voudrais dépister (...)" (14).
5. The clause, which can be found in section 33 of the Canadian Charter of Rights and Freedoms, reads as follows: "Parliament or the legislature of a province may expressly declare in an Act of Parliament or of the legislature, as the case may be, that the Act or a provision thereof shall operate **notwithstanding** a provision included in section 2 or sections 7 to 15 of this Charter." For an excellent overview and explanation of the Notwithstanding Clause, see Makarenko.
6. For an analysis of translation effects in Scott's novels, see Lane-Mercier ("Écrire-traduire") and Simon.
7. For an analysis of the processes and images of metonymy in *Main Brides* from a translations studies perspective, see Lane-Mercier ("La traduction").

8   See especially Scott ("The Porous Text," "Le texte poreux"); Frost. See also *My Paris*.
9   It is worth stressing Godard's sensitivity to the translational dimension of Scott's writing, already apparent in her first novel, *Heroine* (1987), in the form of words, expressions, and phrases in French, and subsequently radicalized in *My Paris* and *The Obituary*. Godard was well aware of the importance of The Main as a (symbolic) porous linguistic border, as well as of Scott's position, as an Anglo-Québec writer, between languages and literary institutions. Although she does not elaborate on Scott's "bilingual confluency" (122), Godard's remarks provide a further link with Cronin's work and a springboard to Scott's more recent notion of the sutured subject, with which Godard could not have been familiar when the 2002 reprint of her initial text appeared. It should also be stressed that Godard was well versed in feminist translation theory and herself a literary translator. Her numerous articles on translation represent a significant contribution to translation studies in Canada (see especially Godard, "Theorizing Feminist Discourse/Translation," "Writing Between Cultures," "Culture as Translation," "Une littérature," "La traduction").

Works Cited

Cronin, Michael. *Translation and Identity*. London: Routledge, 2006. Print.
Eichhorn, Kate. "Interview with Gail Scott." *The Belladonna Elders Series* 6 (2009): 53–64. Print.
Frost, Corey. "'Some Other Kind of Subject, Less Bounded': Gail Scott in Conversation with Corey Frost." Web. June 26, 2005. <http://www.scc.rutgers.edu/however/vl_4_2000/current/workbook/ index.html>.
Glissant, Edouard. *Introduction à une poétique du divers*. Montreal: Presses de l'Université de Montréal, 1995. Print.
Godard, Barbara, ed. *Collaboration in the Feminine: Writings on Women and Culture from Tessera*. Toronto: Second Story, 1994. Print.
———. "Culture as Translation." In *Translation and Multilingualism: Post-colonial Contexts*. Ed. Shantha Ramakrishna. New Delhi: Pencraft International, 1997. 157–82. Print.
———. "Theorizing Feminist Discourse/Translation." *Translation, History, and Culture*. Ed. Susan Bassnett and André Lefevere. London: Pinter, 1990. 87–96. Print.
———. "La traduction comme réception: Les écrivaines québécoises au Canada anglais." *TTR* 15.1 (2002): 65–101. Print.
———. "Une littérature en devenir: La réécriture textuelle et le dynamisme du champ littéraire. Les écrivaines québécoises au Canada anglais." *Voix et Images* 24.3 (1999): 495–527. Print.
———. "Writing Between Cultures." *TTR* 10.1 (1997): 53–99. Print.

———. "Writing from the Border." *Trois* 11.1–2 (1996): 169–80. Rpt. in *Gail Scott: Essays on Her Works*. Ed. Lianne Moyes. Toronto: Guernica, 2002. 117–41. Print.
Lane-Mercier, Gillian. "Écrire-traduire entre les langues. Les effets de traduction et de bilinguisme dans les romans de Gail Scott." *Voix et Images* 90 (2005): 97–112. Print.
———. "La traduction comme 'performance de la cicatrice.' Vers de nouveaux paradigmes traductologiques?" *Québec Studies* 50 (2010/2011): 127–48. Print.
Makarenko, Jay. "The Notwithstanding Clause: Section 33 of the Charter." June 1, 2006. Web. February 27, 2012. <http://www.mapleleafweb.com/features/notwithstanding-clause-section-33-charter>.
Moyes, Lianne, ed. *Gail Scott: Essays on Her Works*. Toronto: Guernica, 2002. Print.
Scott, Gail. "Finding Her Voice." *Canadian Forum* 65 (1985): 39–44. Print.
———. *Heroine*. Toronto: Coach House, 1987. Print.
———. *Main Brides Against Ochre Pediment and Aztec Sky*. Toronto: Coach House, 1993. Print.
———. "Mrs. Beckett's Old Steamer Trunk." *Québec Studies* 44 (2007/2008a): 89–94. Print.
———. *My Paris*. Toronto: Mercury, 1999. Print.
———. *The Obituary*. Toronto: Coach House, 2010. Print.
———. "The Porous Text, or the Ecology of the Small Subject, Take 2." *Chain* 5 (1998): 202–8. Print.
———. *Spaces Like Stairs*. Toronto: Women's, 1989. Print.
———. *Spare Parts Plus Two*. Toronto: Coach House, 2002. Print.
———. "The Sutured Subject." *Review of Contemporary Fiction* 28.3 (2008): 62–72. Print.
———. "Le texte poreux, ou l'écologie d'un modeste sujet." *Écrits* 95 (1999): 203–7. Print.
Scott, Gail, et al., ed. *Biting the Error*. Toronto: Coach House, 2004. Print.
Simon, Sherry. "The Paris Arcades, the Ponte Vecchio, and the Comma of Translation." Ed. Lianne Moyes. *Gail Scott: Essays on Her Works*. Toronto: Guernica, 2002. 142–52. Print.

PART FOUR

Public Memory and the Archive

Chapter 12

Linked Histories and Radio-Activity in Marie Clements's *Burning Vision*

SOPHIE MCCALL

The play *Burning Vision*, by Métis writer and filmmaker Marie Clements, is an extraordinary exploration of historical relationality in the transmission of trauma, disease, and environmental poisoning. A play in four movements, it traces the journey of uranium from its origins deep underground in Sahtu Dene territory, in the air as malignant dust, across the water in ships to Los Alamos, New Mexico, and finally into fire as the bomb that dropped on Hiroshima in 1945. Through a series of repeated images that move in a circular pattern around the stage, as well as through a recurring soundscape made up of clicks, coughs, footsteps, heartbeats, radio static, radar frequencies, drums, and explosions, the play confronts its audience with a "burning vision" of intergenerational correspondence that demands both a response and an acceptance of historical responsibility. Some of the correlations that the play draws are direct, such as escalating rates of cancer in regions surrounding Port Radium in Northwest Territories, in Los Alamos in New Mexico, and at other uranium mining sites in the southwestern United States (affecting Navajo, Pueblo Indian, and Zuni peoples there),[1] and in Hiroshima and Nagasaki in Japan. Other overlapping histories are more ironic, such as the connection between Japanese Canadian citizens, labelled as "enemy aliens" during World War II and forced to carry identification papers, and Native peoples, who also had to carry ID at that time, who encountered Japanese Canadians in "ghost towns" in British Columbia in the 1940s, and who at once were excluded from and incorporated within Canadian citizenship structures.[2]

Given Clements's exploration of the interconnectivity of traumas, in which victims of one catastrophe potentially are implicated in another, questions of apology, reconciliation, and reparation become particularly fraught. Writing in 2002, and evoking several high-profile public apologies, such as the spate of Church apologies to survivors of Indian residential schools in the 1990s in Canada, as well as Iva Toguri's unsuccessful bid for an apology from the American government, Clements indirectly comments on the global turn to apology and state-sponsored processes of reconciliation.[3] This shift to reconciliation demands careful attention: reconciliation for whom and to what? Can reconciliation mean more than an absolution of guilt for those who have benefited from social inequalities and an enforced relinquishing of a project of social justice for those who have paid a high cost for those privileges? In the play, the character of Round Rose comments sardonically on the current era of the public apology: "The politicians are sorry, the cops are sorry, the priests are sorry, the logging companies are sorry ... everybody's sorry they got caught" (Clements, *Burning* 100–1). Getting caught breaks the silence surrounding historical wrongdoing, yet the legacy of secrecy may continue to haunt formal processes of truth-telling and reconciliation. Thematically, the play is concerned with the questionable effectiveness of an apology in contending with living legacies such as colonialism, racism, and environmental devastation. For example, the character Fat Man, the nuclear bomb test dummy who shares the same code name as the bomb that was dropped on Nagasaki, states: "I'm sorry. What did I do wrong?" (99), highlighting the empty formality of official apologies, which often lack a wider historical consciousness.[4] Clements is underlining the gap between the concept of "doing wrong" (a discreet, completed action) and living legacies of historical injustice: while reconciliation and apology enact a retrospective orientation to the problem of injustice, "getting caught" implies the idea of present, ongoing injustice.

Though Clements's play is, for the most part, cynical about corporate and state-imposed models of reconciliation, it does reference favourably the 1998 delegation of Dene people who travelled to Hiroshima to meet with survivors and express their shared grief. The play suggests that this grassroots-led project may provide an alternative model for reconciliation, one connected to a process of sharing testimony across the boundaries of language, history, and geography, and one flowing from a Dene-centred understanding of historical accountability. George Blondin, a Dene elder and storyteller who worked as an ore carrier in Port Radium, and who lost his wife and four of his seven children to cancer, was a member of this delegation. He also played the part of the Dene See-er in the 2002 production of *Burning Vision* in Vancouver. His many stories collected in *When the World Was New* (1990), *Yamoria the Lawmaker* (1997), and *Trail of the Spirit* (2006) suggest that an understanding of the world based on the precept of relationality is foundational to Dene cultural contexts. More specifically, Dene people have their own traditions of acknowledging wrongdoing, making amends, and paying reparations, traditions that emerge from a deep sense of responsibility for, and to, the land. This responsibility extends to an ongoing duty of guardianship for resources taken out of the land. In Peter Blow's documentary film, *A Village of Widows* (1999), Blondin articulates a Dene-centred principle of historical responsibility to a group of Korean Japanese labourers suffering from illnesses related to radiation poisoning and explains his reasons for travelling to Hiroshima: "We, as an Indian, we share your sorrow, our sorrow, and we share that together. I am part of you, Indian law goes like that, there is no stranger in the world, everybody is your brother and sister. And as an Indian, we love each other, so therefore I love you people. I see you that you are my brother and sister. That is my general thinking as an elder." Sharing, as a "foundation of Dene law," as he states later on, undermines the strict demarcations of subject location between perpetrators and victims that sometimes animate discourses of reconciliation and that risks installing a politics of blame that may not adequately represent the complexity of both loss and accountability.

Following Blondin's cue, I want to advance the hypothesis that relationality may be one of the keys to understanding reconciliation. *Response, Responsibility, and Renewal* is the title of one of the volumes published by the Aboriginal Healing Foundation, an organization that was founded as part of the 2007 Indian Residential Schools Settlement Agreement. As the editors Gregory Younging, Jonathan Dewar, and Mike DeGagné explain, the book's title emphasizes the necessity of foregrounding relationships as sites of dynamic exchange and as a means of bringing about healing and change (1–6). In order for reconciliation to function differently from amnesia, it must begin with a recognition of interrelationships, as well as with an acknowledgement of how benefits and privileges are accrued for one group at the expense of another. Reconciliation is not a *goal* so much as a *process* of re-establishing those relationships and redistributing land and resources as a way to address and lessen the economic and political gaps that have developed between Indigenous and other communities in Canada. While the play explores unexpected historical contiguities between migrant and Indigenous groups, it also foregrounds how Aboriginal populations and the history of the land are defined not only by colonizing definitions, but also by a longer, pre-Contact historical consciousness. *Burning Vision* explores an ethics of land rights as practised across the boundaries of time and space, drawing attention to the unique relationship to land that Indigenous peoples continue to maintain whether they live on their ancestral territories or not.

What is especially distinctive about Clements's play is how, in creating a nexus of interpenetrating histories, the text moves fluidly within and across Indigenous and diasporic narratives without losing sight of or effacing the differences between Indigenous and minority groups. In Canadian literary studies, connecting the dots between Indigenous and diasporic histories usually means approaching Indigenous identity in relation to a Euro-Canadian, white, settler identity.[5] Barbara Godard's work comments extensively upon the politics of difference, including difference *in relation* to a dominant identity formation, and the asymmetries that necessarily inform a process of building affiliations. Studying her writing in a range of fields has helped me develop an approach to history, people, things, power, and ideas in terms of how they make or break social relationships, transforming objects of discourse into speaking subjects, into dynamic sites of exchange and potential change. Her consistent attentiveness to the ways in which language creates relationships and produces differences among cultures, social groups, and individuals has become at once foundational to, and prophetic of, emergent concerns in literary and cultural studies in Canada. *Burning Vision* uses techniques of code-switching between the languages of English, Japanese, and Slavey to convey a disequilibrious range of differences between groups and individuals who encounter one another as a result of chance historical convergences. The play's soundscape of clicks, ticks, and static suggests that language differences are generated by underlying structures of mediation; in the traffic of languages, systems of hierarchically arranged differences speak at cross-purposes, undermining the apparent fixity of difference in relation to the dominant language.[6]

In *Burning Vision*, Clements excavates historical correlations between groups that skirt around the dominance of a Native–white axis, with the aim of crafting a new politics of shared historical responsibility among migrant and Indigenous groups in Canada, one that acknowledges the primacy of Indigenous rights to land, while at the same time crafting new "site[s] of movement and change" (Godard, "The Politics" 197). One of the principal characters is Rose, a mixed-race Métis woman whose Dene mother "saved [her] father, the Irishman, softening him from a journey of Irish potatoes,

Indian curries and Chinese noodles" when he arrived as "a stowaway at fourteen on a clipper that traveled the orient and by accident discovered [her] Indian mother" (Clements, *Burning* 58). Much of Rose's preoccupation centres on finding a place for herself, trying to figure out how, as a Métis woman, she connects to her Dene relatives. She recalls her feelings of displacement in the company of her mother's family: "Their red feet never touch[ed] the floorboards of our cabin. Never touching us, the half-breeds, breeded to be more European than someone from Europe. Bred to be white in the Indian-est of land" (38). This neither-nor conceptualization of cultural difference is a constant irritant for Rose, alleviated only when she falls in love with Koji, a Japanese fisherman, described as "Indian enough from the other side" (105), suggesting his possible connection to the Ainu people, an Indigenous group in Japan.[7]

Like Indigenous peoples in Canada, the Ainu were both excluded from and obliged to assimilate into Japanese culture and citizenship.[8] Clements's evocation of the Ainu people occurs principally through Koji, whose world view is strongly informed by his connection to the natural world and his animistic philosophy. Through Koji's voice, Clements retells a legend concerning the proper handling of trout:

> You fish, you and me meeting here at the end of a line. Here, let me take you off the hook. The legend about you says, there should be one hand on you at all times.... I will put one hand on you, gentle right in the middle, so that the world will not quake when your tail shakes the world's air.... You will no longer breathe water and send out the sea through your mouth. You will no longer lie beneath the world. (27)

Though he says "there should be one hand on you at all times," Koji later drops the trout (33), suggesting a certain failure in his efforts to follow customary law and cultural traditions. Koji's retelling of the legend, as well as his mistake in dropping it, resonates with George Blondin's stories, which explore both the persistence of Dene traditions and the cultural dissonance produced by his people's encounters with modernity. Over the course of at least fifteen years, Blondin collected and wrote stories told by elders living in Denendeh (the Dene people's territory, which stretches across parts of Northwest Territories, Nunavut, and northern British Columbia). Blondin's retellings often expose the pressures of colonial and capital incursions on Dene territory as a force of cultural transformation. This is especially palpable in his retelling of a vision by a medicine man from the 1880s. This medicine man foresaw the extraction of a rock from a site on the east side of Sahtu or Great Bear Lake, where Port Radium is today, as well as the terrible consequences of transforming that rock into fire (Blondin, *When* 79).⁹ At a reading at Simon Fraser University in 2009, Clements acknowledged the influence of Blondin's work while she was writing *Burning Vision*: "By chance I picked up George Blondin's book *When the World Was New* ... in that book was the story of the see-er who had foreseen the discovery of uranium up north over four nights.... I carried this book with me for ten years" (Clements, Reading). The tension in Blondin's work between the loss and renewal of traditions is also palpable in Clements's play, particularly in characters such as Rose and Koji, who must negotiate numerous cultural contact zones.

Koji, the Japanese/Ainu fisherman, is simultaneously Koji, the victim of the bombing at Hiroshima, as well as the survivor who meets Rose, the Métis bread-maker. Koji is strongly associated with the idea of transformation, and his journey from Japan to Sahtu Dene territory takes place through a hole in the sky (Clements, *Burning* 89), evoking other stories collected by Blondin.¹⁰ The birth of Rose and Koji's son, also named Koji, enables a recognition of accumulated histories—Dene, Ainu, Japanese, Métis, and Japanese Canadian. This baby symbolizes for Rose a certain hope in the redemptive potential of cross-cultural intermingling: "My baby's going to be mixed again, but I am happy about that 'cause I think he can give the world my hope" (114). "Mixed again" suggests that, like Rose, Koji will grow up navigating communal divides, thereby supplementing genetic notions of ethnic mixing with a social understanding of negotiating collectivities. Yet moments after Rose expresses this hope, the sound of an explosion and a blinding white light signal the detonation of the 1945 atomic bomb. The play stages the nuclear blast no less than five times, demonstrating how, as Meagan Dallimore comments, "the impact of the event is by no means *past*—although it may be *passed on* to future generations" (Dallimore 2).

As bread-maker, Rose is fascinated by the transformative effects of mixing the liquid with the dry ingredients: "Two substances meeting like magic," she says, just before another H-bomb explosion is triggered (Clements, *Burning* 39). In many ways, the play embodies an argument "for" cultural hybridity, as characters such as Koji and Rose, with little in common in the way of history or ethnic ancestry (beyond accidental connections), come together and create intimate connections. This hybridity functions to counteract a rigid cultural Manicheism and ethnic absolutism (a problem particularly apparent in world history in the 1940s). Yet Clements's play, as much as it holds out hope for a new world order of cultural mixing, simultaneously draws attention to the more sinister forces that are driving these connections—forces such as war and large-scale capital development that strip the land of its wealth for communities living on it. Cultural hybridity can serve the interests of a voracious, exploitative capital searching for new territories and new bodies to conscript for its projects of development. For example, the Widow, who is mourning the loss of her husband, the Dene Carrier, to cancer following his work hauling uranium, notes that the uranium ore carriers were called "coolies." She comments that "coolies" are "Some word for people that do the dirty work, I guess. The people that get their hands dirty.... Hauling those sacks, in long lines, from one man to the next, one coolie to one coolie, one Indian to another" (Clements, *Burning* 80). "One Indian to another" invokes Canada's reliance on Indigenous and Asian migrant labourers who were uprooted and moved to follow capital, as well as culturally dispossessed and homogenized as "coolie." The phrase, which effaces the differences between diasporic and Indigenous peoples' experiences of the force of capital expansion through displacement and dispossession, also draws attention to the limits of discourses of interconnectivity.

When Rose says "my baby is going to be mixed" just before the play's final dramatization of the bomb's explosion, the audience is meant to hear the more ominous implications of "mixing"—that is, getting *mixed up with* radioactive material. "Fusion" (along with "fission") are hardly innocent concepts in this play, and the insidious consequences of radioactive contamination are everywhere apparent. Referring to the black dust that fills the air as a result of uranium mining, Rose says: "The wind's blowing it everywhere. The kids are playin' in the sandboxes of it, the caribou are eating it off the plants, and we're drinkin' the water where they bury it" (103). Yet Rose does not recognize the potential danger of these amalgamations: "I guess there's no harm if a bit gets in my dough. It's as fine as flour anyways" (103).[11] Jim Harding, a scholar of environmental studies, argues that in assessing the damage caused by mining uranium and other radioactive elements, it is necessary to address the cumulative effects of radioactive waste and its high levels of interactivity. Like other scholars in this field, he argues for the need to "trace the yellowcake" (Harding 21)—that is, to map how the material warps and changes as it comes into contact with other elements. In Clements's words: "Everything is innocent on the table but when you put it together, it can cause a lethal reaction." She adds, "when you look at uranium, you look at world events. Uranium had always been in the centre of the Dene world ... when it was exposed, it created a domino effect" (Clements, Reading).

Clements's own family history is deeply embedded within the history of uranium as a number of family members worked on the transport boats as well as in the mines (Reading). According to the Northwest Territory Cancer Registry, by 1998, fourteen of the thirty Dene workers who hauled and ferried uranium from 1942 to 1960 had died of died of lung, colon, and kidney cancers (Nikiforuk A1). In the film *A Village of Widows*, Deline residents speak of the many losses in their community to cancer, including women and children who were in close contact with the workers, and throughout the film interviewees contribute to an ongoing verbal memorial of those who have passed on. The words of Shirley Baton, daughter of the late John Baton who hauled uranium, opens the film: "My dad died of cancer, my aunt died of cancer, my grandmother died of cancer, my mum is suffering because of her sickness, and what about my children? Because I believe once there's something in a person's genes, it carries on."[12] The idea that a family's genes are imprinted by a history of radiation ironically underlines an orientation toward interconnectivity and relationality that Blondin claims is at the heart of Dene cultural and philosophical traditions. This doubled sense of correlation—as the fear of deadly contamination and as the hope for a renewed sense of collectivity based on the community's understanding of their cultural and philosophical inheritance—remains an insoluble tension in both the film and the play. Deline is not an isolated case: communities located downriver from other uranium mines and refining plants across North America—such as the Chipewyan and Métis people near Uranium City in northern Saskatchewan, the Snake River First Nation near Eliot Lake in Ontario, and the Navajo communities in the southwestern United States—have witnessed rates of cancer two to four times higher than those found in the national populations.[13] Thus, "tracing the yellowcake" in Clements's play takes the form of connecting up the poison and the cure: in other words, revealing the unwitting correspondences between the source of the harm (the uranium) and its treatment (revitalizing Dene philosophical and storytelling traditions with the aim of crafting a new ethics of living on the land). Clements may also be implying the need to connect those responsible for knowingly exposing communities to dangerous conditions and those who have suffered the consequences (as might occur in a restorative justice paradigm). Her aim is not to relativize these oppositions, but rather to reveal the dynamism of relationality in which chains of reaction with unpredictable results are set off.

In Clements's play, many of the characters have doubles, and as the actors move from one role to another, the audience is confronted with a series of uncanny connections between traumatic histories of loss and displacement—from the Pacific War, to Japanese Canadian internment camps, to Indian residential schools, to environmental deterioration. The son of Koji and Rose, also named Koji, is raised by Rose's grandmother, the Dene Widow, who is a double cast with the character of the Japanese Grandmother. The part of Koji the child is played by the same actor as Little Boy. Little Boy, more symbol than character, is described as "[t]he personification of the darkest uranium found at the centre of the earth" (Clements, *Burning*, "Characters" n.p.). He is also the medicine man's prophesy and an adopted Native child, displaced from his family and ancestral territory. Along with the uranium ore, Little Boy was shipped from Sahtu Dene territory to the nuclear test site in New Mexico. "Little Boy" is also the code name of the atomic bomb dropped on Hiroshima. In closely linking Koji, the Ainu-Japanese-Canadian-Dene-Métis child, with Little Boy, the embodiment of Dene territory and its associated prophetic traditions, as well as with the exploitation of land in mining and developing uranium as war arsenal, Clements is putting within earshot multiple histories whose connections have not been adequately acknowledged in dominant narratives of nation. Clements's technique of creating recurring patterns of ironic historical echoings—echoings that repeat with a difference, to evoke again the work of Godard[14]—suggests that writing history involves a process of tuning into conversations taking place in a variety of places and time frames but irrevocably tied to the here and now. In Clements's play, history becomes a series of imperfectly overheard conversations mediated through multiple channels whose crossed signals have created a background of distortions and static.

This background of "white noise" (as both multiple, crossed channels and as the homogenizing force of dominant, nation-based media channels) has obscured the fact that Indigenous groups are not just another minority group; they are the First Peoples of this land. Clements's play underlines the unique relationship between Indigenous peoples and the land by developing an ethics of relationality: not "claiming" land as a prospector would, but rather living with/in the land. The opening scene of the play creates a dramatic contrast between the Brothers Labine, who view the land as something from which to extract resources to become rich, and Little Boy, who embodies the centre of the Dene world and of the Earth. The Brothers Labine represent the historical figures of Gilbert and Charlie LaBine who are attributed with discovering high-grade pitchblende stake at Eldorado claim near Cameron Bay on Great Bear Lake, Northwest Territories. Little

Boy critiques their prospecting ethos, which equates discovery with possession: "It is only a matter of time [...] before someone discovers you and claims you for themselves. Claims you are you because they found you" (20). Little Boy ultimately overturns this act of subjectification by successfully leaving Fat Man's house in New Mexico and returning home to Sahtu Dene territory via the TV screen (99). As he emerges "from the back of the TV," Little Boy becomes an embodiment of the Dene See-er and of the prophesy itself, thereby making explicit the links between voice, land, and belonging in a Dene-centred expression of home (102). His mediation through an electronic form of communication provides an "explanation" for his ability to travel instantly between worlds in the way that Blondin describes the powers of certain medicine men of the past.

Recognition of the primacy of Indigenous land rights provides the backbone for understanding the play's engagement with discourses of reconciliation and of apology for historical wrongdoings.[15] In the play Rose, who is working at a Hudson's Bay Company store managed by her father, is searching for her family on her maternal side, with whom she apparently had lost touch following her mother's death. She encounters the Widow mourning the loss of her husband, the Dene Carrier. The Widow jokingly refers to the HBC store as the "Half Breed Curse Store" or the "Here Before Christ Store," adding "but not before me" (55–56). In asserting her ongoing and historic presence in this land, the Widow sets the terms by which Rose will reconnect to her mother's community. It is strongly implied that the Widow is Rose's grandmother, who announces at one point that "you are like my daughter" (105), though when they first meet, they do not appear to recognize each other. The cool distance between them stems at least in part from the mother's uprooting from her place in the community, like others of her generation who attended residential school. Part of the play's thematic focus is on Rose's efforts to reconcile with her "home" community through her attempts to befriend the Widow. Thus, the scenes between Rose and the Widow consider what reconciliation means, how it is to be achieved, and what its purpose might be, particularly within families whose members have become estranged as a result of colonial policies:

> THE WIDOW: Why you standing way over there? Why don't you come closer so I can get a good look at you. [...]
> ROSE: How did you know I was here?
> THE WIDOW: I can feel your eyes looking in.
> ROSE: I'll just stand here if that's fine. [...]

ROSE: I just wanted to ask you if …
THE WIDOW: If I knew your mother. Just because I'm an old widow doesn't mean I know everybody that's dead.
ROSE: I thought maybe you might know her because she came from these parts.
THE WIDOW: What, you think I know everybody's mother in the world?
ROSE: No. Sorry. I just …
Rose begins to walk away. (53–55)

Throughout the play, Rose and the Widow are engaged in a recurring pattern of reaching out to each other and then walking away. If reconciliation is conceived as a return to harmony, as implied by the term "re-conciliation" and by some of the literature concerning the Truth and Reconciliation Commission (TRC) in Canada and elsewhere,[16] there is little possibility of reconciliation occurring between Rose and the Widow since Rose was never a part of the Dene community, and Rose's mother's relationship to the Dene community was, to a large extent, severed by her experiences at residential school. Thus, the scene between Rose and the Widow becomes a parable of reconciliation and the limits of what it can do given the deep schisms that residential schools have created. Rose partially integrates herself in the community by giving away loaves of bread from her father's store; however, in making the bread, she uses flour contaminated by the uranium ore dust, which covers everything in the vicinity of Port Radium (103). Her symbolic gift of sustenance, the bread, becomes a poisonous gift, not unlike the "gift" of uranium mining and other large-scale industrial developments: new jobs at the cost of environmental and health degradation.

The repeated interplay of coming together and pulling apart, as demonstrated by the dialogue above, evokes the play's fascination with the politics of listening across great distances and the accidents of historical and geographical overlappings. Characters who are located thousands of miles away from one another in various locations in the Northwest Territories, the United States, and Japan, hear one another imperfectly across the permeable distances of time and space. When Rose drops her heavy sack of uranium-contaminated flour (21), when the Widow strikes a match and makes a "sheeek sound" (22), and when Koji's fishing line goes "whizzz" (26), the Brothers Labine ask each time with minor variations: "Did you hear that?" (28). Fat Man, in his house in New Mexico, and the Miner, deep underground at Port Radium, also hear sounds from different parts of the world (28, 57, 96). Indeed, listening becomes an important element of Clements's historiography, which involves understanding histories in relation to one another. For the performance in Vancouver in 2002, the play was staged in the round, the space of the stage divided into four sections representing the four principal "worlds" of the play: the Widow in Sahtu Dene territory, Fat Man in New Mexico, Rose at her bread-making table in her father's HBC store, and Koji in Hiroshima. For each scene, one world would be lit up, leaving the rest in darkness. As the interrelationships between the worlds emerge, and as the conversations become increasingly overlapped, the stage directions describe the worlds as "colliding" (102).

The soundscape, which rips through the boundaries of time and space, and which consists of a tremendous diversity of non-verbal sounds—heartbeats, explosions, wind, drums, coughing, babies crying, fire crackling, hooves pounding, water running, clocks ticking—draws attention to the more menacing implications of interconnectivity. The predominance of clicks and ticks, including the Geiger counters, which measure the degree of radioactivity in a person's body, suggests an ominous countdown to Armaggedon. Indeed, the play's multiple detonations of the 1945 atomic bomb, including at the opening and the conclusion of the play, suggests that the effects of this event are so far-reaching as to be immeasurable. Though the soundscape is made up of noises from bodies, nature, the elements, and other "natural" sources, the audience is not permitted to forget that all is electronically mediated, since the sounds of feedback, static, and tuning intrude throughout. This emphasis on electronic mediation is particularly evident in a class of sounds that might be described as "radio-activity": a combination of war propaganda from the 1940s on CBC radio, static, radio scratching (in which the dial slides over the channels), and community radio in northern Canada.

The soundscape suggests that the play is itself radioactive, simultaneously an agent of contamination that implicates the audience in linked histories of dispossession, and an intermediary of social justice demanding official recognition of the interpenetration of communities and their stories. One of the recurring sounds in the play is that of a radio dial gliding over stations. It becomes a manifestation of the dominant media's power as it determines the "cultural tones" of the "stories sitting on radio waves" (19). At times we hear Round Rose, in her persona as Tokyo Rose, mocking American soldiers while simultaneously sending them covert messages to evade the Japanese army. At other times we hear Lorne Greene, described as "the voice of doom" on CBC Radio, making wartime announcements in the 1940s. Static is another important component of the soundscape, at once emphasizing how white noise contaminates all of the communications, particularly those that inform the official narratives of the nation, while at the same time defamiliarizing these narratives of nation by running interference through them. Radio becomes the voice of official nationalist discourse, saturated by, as the stage directions state, "the static of propaganda, the sound score of western civilization building a country" (75). This nationalist soundscape is simultaneously transnational, suggesting a confluence of agendas between federal and global corporate powers, especially as facilitated by the reach of dominant media outlets; in the third movement, "world broadcasts rise over in a frequency that goes through the walls of the world. The broadcasts are a collage and build under the tensions of the scenes accelerating" (94).

The radio, however, like everything else in this play, is not simply a negative force that facilitates national jingoism, transnational capital exploitation, and cultural assimilation. Radio-activity signifies as much the vital role of radio as a means of communication in the North as it does deadly toxicity. Radio broadcasts in the language of Slavey, made up of a series of community concerns, call-home or come-home requests, echo like a refrain throughout the play. In one instance, the Slavey announcer, in a voice-over, says, "Hey, naga, tack-ohtay. We have brought the dogs in for the feast. Your grandchildren are getting real good looking.... I am so proud of them. You would be too. Love, your friend Ethel" (87).[17] These personal messages on CBC's northern radio frequencies underline the potentially transformative power of the interconnections of love, hope, and community. Radio-activity also stands for the unpredictable transformation that is involved in mixing previously discrete elements, materials, cultures, people, stories, and traditions. The repeated parallel drawn between Rose's sack of flour and the Labine Brothers' sack of ore (25, 28, 39, 79) perhaps best captures the play's principled rejection of easy oppositions of sustenance and danger, of wealth and impoverishment. TV also functions ambiguously as an agent of radiation, a tool of social control, and a conduit of connectivity that (re)establishes community ties. It is through the static of Fat Man's TV, tuned to the after-hours' "high-pitched sound of broadcast bars" and accompanied by "[t]he image of a multi-coloured Indian Chief on the screen" (34), that we hear the voice of the Dene See-er and his prophesy of radical transformation for all living beings. Played by Blondin in the Vancouver production in 2002, the Dene See-er confronts the audience with both the high cost and political potential of acknowledging one's implication in an interconnected world: "The people they dropped this burning on, [they] looked like us, the Dene" (119).

The phrase "they looked like us" reiterates the play's implicit argument for an ethics of interconnectivity, and underlines the play's motif of the uncanny, in which seemingly unrelated objects, people, or histories inexplicably become drawn to and familiar with one another. Though these weird doublings might suggest the recuperation of a lost, original unity, Clements's play places the stress on accidental minglings. In other words, although they "they looked like us" (and could be us), what creates this sense of resemblance is not so much *identity* as *contiguity*—a nearness produced as much by the compulsion of capital development and the transport of uranium within and across territories as it is created by an otherworldly sense of recognition. Contiguity also produces the conditions that enable the building of political and cultural affiliations across national borders. Blondin's presence on stage recalls the Dene-led initiative of retracing the journey of the uranium from Sahtu Dene lands to Hiroshima. There the Dene representatives initiated a politics of reconciliation that involved not only paying respects to survivors, but also asserting the Dene people's connection to the place where part of Sahtu Dene territory burned in fire. Through conversation and symbolic action, the visitors acknowledge the insoluble links that now exist between Denendeh and Japan. In the play's final movement, entitled "Radar Echoes," following Koji's arrival in Canada from Japan, the action shifts to the 1880s, when the medicine man uttered the prophesy. It then shifts to 1945, when the character of the Japanese Grandmother loses her grandson, and, removing her kimono, becomes the Dene Widow. The transformation of the Japanese Grandmother into the Dene Widow, as well as the switch of Koji the grandson into the Widow's husband, the Dene Ore Carrier, create a sense of shared responsibility for unwitting historical correspondences. Neither the film, *A Village of Widows*, nor Clements's play, *Burning Vision*, suggests that apology plays a significant role in this process of establishing and accepting ongoing relationships. Round Rose, remarking cynically upon the current ubiquity of the public apology, states: "half the time we don't even know what we are sorry about, it [the apology] just squeaks out of our sorry gaps before we've even clued into the conversation.... You can't really be sorry for something you don't want to remember can you. Selective memory isn't it? ... Indian residential schools, Japanese internment camps, hell, and this is just in your neighbourhood" (100). Yet, as much as the play is skeptical about public apologies, it nevertheless insists that a politics of reconciliation is possible if we are willing and able to "clue into the conversation," overcome a case of "selective memory," and understand the world as "your neighbourhood" (100). Initiating a politics of reconciliation must begin with a recognition of the personal and political stakes of an affiliative politics. A diversity of forms of affiliation is possible and indeed necessary to recognize the struggle of writing and of telling a more just story of the intersections of Indigenous and diasporic histories in Canada.

Burning Vision ultimately affirms the transformative potential of relationality in discourses of reconciliation; as Sherill Grace remarks, the play ends "on a note—or a combination of notes—of hope" (Grace 15). The voice-over of radio announcers in Slavey and Japanese is followed by the Canadian announcer whose English reveals what we have heard: "Hello, Granddad, brother, sister, son, husband, father, cousin, nephew, friend, my teacher, my love ... We love you and miss you" (Clements, *Burning* 122). Koji—Japanese survivor, Japanese Canadian diasporic subject, Ainu dissident, father of Dene-Métis child—answers this radio call: "They hear us, and they are talking back in hope over time" (122). Koji's words are themselves an echo of the words of the Dene See-er: "Can you hear through the walls of the world? Maybe we are all talking at the same time because we are answering each other over time and space" (75). The play's nuanced exploration of radio-activity highlights both the dangers and the possibilities of this interconnectivity of "time and space." In Rita Wong's words, "the complex relationships presented in Clements's visionary play interrogate the possibilities and limits of interracial affiliations" (Wong 170). The "relational logics" of the play emphasize reconciliation as a process of building relationships across borders, but with an acknowledgement of the need to address the psychic and material gaps between Indigenous and migrant communities in Canada, and to work toward a politics of reparation and redistribution. As much as *Burning Vision* creates shared ground between Indigenous and ethnic minority communities, it foregrounds the rights of the First Peoples of the continent and explores an ethics of land rights that underlines Indigenous peoples' historic and ongoing relationship with the land.

Notes

1 Indigenous rights and environmental activist Winona LaDuke has written extensively on the deaths and severe health problems that more than three thousand Navajo workers and their families have suffered as a result of working at or in the vicinity of the one thousand uranium mines operating on Navajo territories from the 1950s to the 1980s. See LaDuke, "Uranium Mining" and *All Our Relations*.

2   That is to say, both Japanese Canadians and Indigenous peoples in Canada in the 1940s became implicated in what Katja Sarkowsky has called the "continuous struggle for the meaning of citizenship and its application based on processes of constructing necessary 'others' against which to define 'the citizen'" (30). Sarkowsky makes clear that procedures of exclusion necessitate concurrent procedures of incorporation. Clements further draws out this connection between exclusion and incorporation in the character of Fat Man, a nuclear test dummy who waits for the atomic blast in a plywood house in the desert in New Mexico. Before his annihilation, he kicks out his two companions whom he considers "enemy aliens": his adopted son, a Native boy, and his wife, Round Rose, based on Iva Toguri, a Japanese American university student coerced by the Japanese government to play the role of the radio personality, Tokyo Rose, and later tried for treason by the American government. Disavowing Indigenous peoples' rights as the First Peoples of this continent, while mobilizing racist language to falsely "indigenize" white settler subjectivity, Fat Man says to Little Boy and to Round Rose: "I want you two aliens to get the hell out of my living room.... [G]o back to where you came from" (Clements, *Burning* 98, 99).

3   Clements was writing immediately following the federal government's Statement of Reconciliation in *Gathering Strength—Canada's Aboriginal Action Plan* (1998) and the release of apologies made by churches in the late 1990s. See Younging et al. for a useful timeline of these Church apologies (176–77). In the notes on the play's characters, Marie Clements writes that Iva Toguri (the inspiration for the character Round Rose) is "still waiting for an apology by the U.S. government for her prosecution as 'Tokyo Rose'" (Clements, *Burning*, "Characters" n.p.).

4   A number of commentators have noted that Stephen Harper's denial that colonialism has occurred (and is occurring) in Canada, articulated in October 2009, sixteen months after his formal apology in the House of Commons on June 8, 2008, is an example of how apology can become a tool of forgetting. See Henderson and Wakeham (1–2).

5   Rita Wong and Lee Maracle are just two critics who have attempted to realign the comparative field in Canadian literary studies by emphasizing, in the words of Wong, "moments of reciprocity and solidarity between racialized bodies" such as "'Asian' and 'First Nations' characters" (168). Wong's article "Decolonizasian" reads *Burning Vision* in relation to, among other texts, SKY Lee's novel *Disappearing Moon Café* and Maracle's short story "Yin Chin." The latter, one of the first short stories in the Canadian literary context to address the problem of perpetually understanding racial differences in relation to whiteness, reconstructs Maracle's memory of Asian and Native writers speaking at length with one another "and not once did the white man ever enter the room" (Maracle, "Yin Chin" 291). See also Maracle's "Oratory on Oratory."

6   In "The Politics of Representation," Godard draws attention to the asymmetries between languages, as well as to the potentiality for change at the site of the

"in-between," by developing a reading of M.M. Bahktin's work on heteroglossia: "Bakhtin's elaboration of the dialogue, a double-voiced discourse ... is oriented towards someone else's discourse.... Points of antagonism overlap, collide, and explode. They interrogate boundaries, challenge the hierarchy of sites of discourse, force the threshold, and move into the liminal, working the in-between, site of movement and change" (Godard, "The Politics" 127–28). In the 1990s Bakhtin's social semiotics became a popular approach by which critics approached Native writing. In more recent years, Indigenous critics have questioned the uncritical application of Bahktinian dialogue as if it were, in Louis Owens's words, a "topical ointment applicable to virtually any critical abrasion" (256). Ironically, Owens himself has been criticized for an overreliance on Bahktin (Womack 47). It should be noted that Godard's article, which provides a detailed discussion of the structural inequalities in Canadian publishing as a result of systemic racism, as well as a precise picture of the politics of representation in the early 1990s, avoids some of the pitfalls of those Bahktinian readings that risk divorcing discussions of the "in-between" from an analysis of unequal access to institutions, publishing, and other channels of "voice."

7   My thanks to Meagan Dallimore for suggesting Clements's possible reference to the Ainu people in this line.

8   Beverley Curran describes the Ainu as the Indigenous people of Japan who inhabit the northern part of what are now Honshû, Hokkaidô, Sakhalin, and the Kurile Islands. Since the mid-fifteenth century, for trade reasons, Japanese people sharply distinguished themselves from the Ainu people, forbidding the Ainu to speak in Japanese or wear Japanese clothing; however, by the mid-nineteenth century, colonial policies of assimilation were aggressively pursued and Ainu lands, put under state control, were confiscated if they were not developed agriculturally (451–52). This tension in Japanese state policy between segregation and assimilation also lies at the heart of Canadian policy on Aboriginal peoples and highlights another point of connectivity between Koji and Rose. For more on the Ainu people and other minority communities in Japan, see Morris-Suzuki, Fitzhugh, and Lie.

9   To read the prophesy as recounted by Blondin, see "An Oldtimer's Prophesy" in *When The World Was New* (78–79). Clements borrows some of its language in her play. Blondin retells the prophesy with some variations in Magnus Isacsson's film, *Uranium* (1990).

10 In *Yamoria the Lawmaker*, Blondin retells a number of stories concerning Yamoria's extraordinary medicine powers, including his ability to travel instantly from one place to another. Another medicine man, Tacheam, receives his powers by travelling between Earth and space: "I travelled in spirit form on earth and in space and that is when I received my powers. At one time I became a giant. I was standing on earth with my head in the heavens. My head went through the three protective layers around the earth" (159). The fluidity of time and space in Blondin's retellings of his people's oral traditions is

also apparent in Clements's play, particularly in its innovative staging, in which four worlds collide and separate as the characters move between them. At a reading at Simon Fraser University, Clements explained that the play, staged in the round, "looked like a clock." Each quadrant of the clock represented a world; as the action shifted, one world would light up, the rest remaining dark. The stage became "one big circle when the worlds were colliding" (Clements, Reading).

11 Rose's lines echo those of Derek Likert, who was interviewed for the film *A Village of Widows*, and whose father, the school superintendent in Port Radium in the early 1940s, filled the sandbox with uranium tailings since there is no naturally occurring sand in the area. Likert describes the ubiquity of the fine uranium dust while he was growing up: "It's just like flour. It pulverized to nothing. Just blows around just like flour—it was in your cupboards, in your bed, it was everywhere." The strong echoes between Likert's and Rose's words suggest that Clements viewed this film before or while she wrote the play.

12 Another contribution to this verbal memorial in *A Village of Widows* is provided by Blondin: "Out of my seven children, four died of cancer plus my wife—all died of cancer. I have spent fifteen years right outside of Echo Bay mine. My dad lost three children. Almost all the families from Great Bear Lake that lived close to Echo Bay mine lost half of their children. You don't have to be very educated to know that ... [the] uranium that they threw in the water affect[s] our life."

13 For testimonials and analyses on the impact of the mining on local communities, see Isacsson's film, *Uranium*. This film points out that it has become a challenging political and medical task to draw direct causal links between cancer and radiation exposure since the affected communities are often too small in number to generate what are considered reliable data sets. The communities themselves, however, have few doubts about their experience with escalating rates of cancer. See also LaDuke and Eichstaedt.

14 Many of the turns of phrases that Godard has mobilized or coined over the course of her career could be placed under the umbrella term "repetition with a difference." These *répétitions* or rehearsals, which are borrowed, invented, translated, or written anew, include: parallels and parallax; difference from and self-differentiation; *l'interdit*, the forbidden and the in-between; versions and subversions; binds and double-binds; and, most potently for me, the relations of exchange, change, and interchange (Godard, "Relational Logics" 318–19). It is only through an exchange that change can occur, and only through changing our positions that exchange can occur. An interchange can also occur, and risks becoming an endless substitution of the same, but by intervening with the sharpness of juxtaposition, Godard derails this repetition of sameness, moving to new sites of (ex)change (320). Exchange, or talk, saturates my memories of Barbara—in her living room, garden, or over email. Exchanging ideas in the name of change.

15 The idea that the recognition of Aboriginal land rights must precede a process of reconciliation is echoed in many of the contributions to the Aboriginal Healing Fund's three volumes of writings on the concept of reconciliation. For example, Fred Kelly, residential school survivor and Anishinabe elder, argues that "[i]f reconciliation is to be real and meaningful in Canada," it must take place within a context of just self-government agreements, the honouring of treaties, and the timely processing of land claims (22–23).

16 For example, John Amagoalik, former vice-president of Inuit Tapirisat of Canada and chief commissioner of the Nunuvut Implementation Commission, argues that the word "reconciliation" suggests that there was once a time of "conciliation," thereby giving a false impression of the challenges facing the TRC in Canada: "Since Europeans arrived on our shores more than five hundred years ago, there has never really been a harmonious relationship between the new arrivals and the original inhabitants on North America.... Because there has been no harmonious relationship, we have to start with conciliation" (Amagoalik 93). It should be noted that Amagoalik is referencing Inuit–settler relationships, while Clements is exploring the challenges of reconciliation between family members. Presumably within families there is a greater possibility of uncovering a history of conciliation. This is an important distinction to make; yet Rose's mother's residential schooling virtually precludes Rose's retrieval of this history of conciliation. Another part of the difficulty for Rose is that her Irish father, manager of an HBC or "Half-Breed Curse Store," implicates her in a larger history of Indigenous–settler conflict and misunderstanding.

17 "Ethel" may be a reference to Ethel Blondin, who was the member of Parliament for the district of Western Arctic in the Northwest Territories and the first Aboriginal (Dene) woman to be elected to the Parliament of Canada in 1988.

Works Cited

Amagoalik, John. "Reconciliation or Conciliation? An Inuit Perspective." *From Truth to Reconciliation: Transforming the Legacy of Residential Schools*. Ed. Marlene Brant Castellano, Linda Archibald, and Mike DeGagné. Ottawa: Aboriginal Healing Foundation, 2008. 91–100. Print.

Blondin, George. *Trail of the Spirit: The Mysteries of Medicine Power Revealed*. Edmonton: NeWest, 2006. Print.

———. *When The World Was New: Stories of the Sahtu Dene*. Yellowknife: Outcrop, 1990. Print.

———. *Yamoria the Lawmaker: Stories of the Dene*. Edmonton: NeWest, 1997. Print.

Blow, Peter, dir. *Village of Widows*. Peterborough, ON: Lindum Films, 1999. Film.

Clements, Marie. *Burning Vision*. Vancouver: Talon, 2002. Print.

———. Reading and talk. Simon Fraser University, Burnaby. November 26, 2009. Talk.

Curran, Beverley. "Invisible Indigeneity: First Nations and Aboriginal Theatre in Japanese Translation and Performance." *Theatre Journal* 59 (2007): 449–65. Print.

Dallimore, Meagan. "'Ikoyo!'/Let's Go/[Let Us] Go: Connective Tissues in Marie Clements's *Burning Vision*." 2010. TS. Simon Fraser University, Burnaby. Print.

Godard, Barbara. *Canadian Literature at the Crossroads of Language and Culture*. Ed. Smaro Kamboureli. Edmonton: NeWest, 2008. Print.

———. "The Politics of Representation: Some Native Canadian Women Writers." Godard, *Canadian Literature at the Crossroads of Language and Culture*, 109–59.

———. "Relational Logics: Of Linguistic and Other Transactions in the Americas." Godard, *Canadian Literature at the Crossroads of Language and Culture*, 315–57.

Grace, Sherill. "The True North Strong and Free: War, the Arts, and the Canadian North." UBC Killam Lecture, Vancouver, 2008. Web. October 21, 2010. <http://www.english.ubc.ca/faculty/grace/news.htm>.

Eichstaedt, Peter H. *If You Poison Us: Uranium and Native Americans*. Sante Fe: Red Crane Books, 1994. Print.

Fitzhugh, William. "Ainu Ethnicity: A History." *Ainu: Spirit of a Northern People*. Ed. William Fitzhugh and Chisato O. Dubreuil. Los Angeles: Perpetua, 1999. 9–27. Print.

Harding, Jim. *Canada's Deadly Secret: Saskatchewan Uranium and the Global Nuclear System*. Winnipeg: Fernwood, 2007. Print.

Henderson, Jennifer, and Pauline Wakeham. "Colonial Reckoning, National Reconciliation? Aboriginal Peoples and the Culture of Redress in Canada." *English Studies in Canada* 35.1 (2009): 1–26. Print.

Isacsson, Magnus, dir. *Uranium*. Montreal: National Film Board of Canada, 1990. Film.

Kelly, Fred. "Confession of a Born Again Pagan." *From Truth to Reconciliation: Transforming the Legacy of Residential Schools*. Ed. Marlene Castellano, Linda Archibald, and Mike DeGagné. Ottawa: Aboriginal Healing Foundation, 2008. 11–40. Print.

LaDuke, Winona. *All Our Relations: Native Struggles for Land and Life*. Cambridge, MA: South End, 1999. Web. October 28, 2010. Print.

———. "Uranium Mining, Native Resistance, and the Greener Path: The Impact of Uranium Mining on Indigenous Communities." *Orion* (January/February 2009). Web. October 28, 2010. < http://www.orionmagazine.org/index.php/articles/article/4248>.

Lie, John. *Multiethnic Japan*. Cambridge, MA: Harvard UP, 2001. Print.

Maracle, Lee. "Oratory on Oratory." *Trans.Can.Lit: Resituating the Study of Canadian Literature*. Ed. Smaro Kamboureli and Roy Miki. Waterloo, ON: Wilfrid Laurier UP, 2007. 55–70. Print.

———. "Yin Chin." *Sojourner's Truth and Other Stories*. Toronto: Press Gang, 1990. 65–72. Print.

Morris-Suzuki, Tessa. *Re-inventing Japan: Time, Space, Nation*. Armonk, NY: M.E. Sharpe, 1998. Print.

Nikiforuk, Andrew. "Echoes of the Atomic Age: Cancer Kills Fourteen Aboriginal Workers." *Calgary Herald* March 14, 1998: A1, A4. Web. October 20, 2010. <http://www.ccnr.org/deline_deaths.html>.

Owens, Louis. *Other Destinies: Understanding the American Indian Novel*. Norman, OK: U of Oklahoma P, 1992. Print.

Sarkowsky, Katja. "Nesei Negotiations: Citizenship and the Nation in Japanese Canadian Writing." *Citizenship and Cultural Belonging: Special Issue of West Coast Line*. Ed. David Chariandy and Sophie McCall. *West Coast Line* 59 (2008): 28–41. Print.

Womack, Craig. "A Single Decade: Book-Length Native Literary Criticism Between 1986 and 1997." *Reasoning Together: The Native Critics' Collective*. Ed. Janice Acoose et al. Norman: U of Oklahoma P, 2008. 3–104. Print.

Wong, Rita. "Decolonizasian: Reading Asian and First Nations Relations in Literature." *Canadian Literature* 199 (2008): 158–80. Print.

Younging, Gregory, Jonathan Dewar, and Mike DeGagné, ed. *Response, Responsibility, and Renewal: Canada's Truth and Reconciliation Journey*. Ottawa: Aboriginal Healing Foundation, 2009. Print.

Chapter 13

Memory as Fracture: French Mnemotechniques in the Erasure of the Holocaust

MICHAEL DORLAND

While Barbara Godard was best known for her work in semiotics, translation theory, and narratology, it was not until her later years, in a number of fugitive pieces,[1] that she found herself attracted to questions of public memory, and the struggles over them in space and time that she came to term broadly "mnemotechniques."

For Barbara Godard, mnemotechniques, "the practices through which contests over time and space have been carried out" ("Contested" 59), played themselves out in particular in the practice and theory of the archive, the monument, the performance, and, above all, in the various forms in which memory is written and who is writing. She recognized that the problems of public memory were fraught ones for the modern state, and that numerous sites of contest over memory informed the social imaginary. She also was clear that many of the modern debates over memory had originated in Third Republic France, notably with Renan. It was in France, too, that the study of memory had been formed into a new branch of sociology in the work, as of the 1920s, by Maurice Halbwachs. Furthermore, she had learned from Freud that questions of memory, especially at the individual level, were deeply tied up with repression. The archive was not, as Freud wrote, open to anyone, but was instead a site of restriction and taboo. But Godard, other than a few key references, did not specifically look at the case of France itself as a site of recent, major memory wars, which is what I am proposing to do here for a number of reasons.

Godard was, after all, principally preoccupied with the puzzles of the Canadian case. "Why memory? Why Canada?" she asked, "A country so young would seem to have little to recall" (59). "Youth," however, may not be the central issue when it comes to the writing of history. Barbara Godard did recognize that "the contemporary obsession" with memorialization was tied to an economy of publicity that had severed the sensorial and affective aspects of remembering from "the networks for conceptual generalization and transmission" (62). Accordingly, numerous countries have problems with the writing (and rewriting) of their own history, and these problems seem to especially afflict the writing of twentieth-century history. In a famous quip, the former Chinese premier Chou En-lai once remarked that it was still too early to pass judgment on the French Revolution.

The French themselves, however, have fought over the meaning of the French Revolution for over two hundred years. One of the burdens of the "universal" principles of the French Revolution was their applicability to local populations within France (e.g., the Basques), to "particularistic" religious ethnicities (e.g., Jews), but then also later to immigrant populations, whether from eastern Europe around the turn of the last century or to former colonial populations from Africa or the Magreb. For all the vigorous debates over the nature of history, the French historical archive is surprisingly very full of silences, ghosts, and prohibitions. The list is long, but no doubt the two principal ones of the latter half of the twentieth century concern the sixty-year-long erasure of France's participation in the Judeocide of World War II, followed by the continuing silence over the Algerian War (1954–62). It is the first of these that will concern me here, for we are far from finished with understanding the Holocaust.

Just recently, in a major work of historical revisionism, historian Timothy Snyder almost singlehandedly tilted the fulcrum of the geographic locus of the Holocaust from the largely accepted centrality of the killing sites of eastern Poland to the even more bloody slaughters that took place further east, in the Baltic states and farther south.[2] At the other end of the spectrum, while there is some familiarity with the memory wars over the Holocaust regarding Poland or Germany, France continues to provide an instance of a long-running case of a site of effaced World War II memory. As Elizabeth Bellamy puts it importantly, France's "own scarcely confronted 'Jewish Question' [is] even *more complex* than Germany's" (12–18; emphasis added).

The outbreak of World War II, and Nazi Germany's rapid defeat and occupation of France as of 1940 entailed a new twist to the scarcely confronted French Jewish Question, but which was now blatantly manifested in the form of the persecution, deportation, and almost total extermination of over 75,000 French Jews and non-French Jews living as refugees in France. The result of this accumulation of trauma, post-1945, was the repression of the French Judeocide from public memory, which lasted, except for occasional symptomatic outbreaks (in which films played a key role), until the mid-1990s, when Jacques Chirac, in his first term as president, formally recognized that the Republic had committed against its Jewish citizens crimes "without statute of limitations" (Wiedmer 53).

In the French context (and in the theory of post-Holocaust affect more broadly), the struggle over public memory is thus framed and infiltrated by: (1) oscillations from collective to individual trauma, (2) failed attempts at re-membering (trying to put back together what was sundered), which (3) eventually take the form of symbolic acts of commemoration (for some) and the injunction to bear witness (for others). All these tactics of mnemotechniques are ultimately articulated through various practices of writing (novels, memoirs, historiography, as well as films) that are always, at the same time, acts of rewriting and transformation. As the Holocaust remains the primary template for all the other struggles over memory, I will focus below mainly on the contradictions between historiography, remembering, and commemoration, while foregrounding important aspects of Jewish memory, so central both to the Holocaust itself and to its French context in particular.

I

Ruth Leys observes, usefully for the discussion to follow, that "Post-traumatic disorder is fundamentally a disorder of memory" (2). One of the central themes running through the entire discussion on trauma accordingly concerns its relationship to memory, and recent French thought would prove to be particularly enlightening in this respect.

A related corollary here is that the difficulties of remembering recollections often take the form of unconscious *strategies of forgetting*, such as amnesia or falling into silence. As Alain Finkelkraut remarked on the problem of thinking about the twentieth century—"a historical monster" completely refractory to any ordering of human time—one of the main dimensions of such temporal monstrosity had to do with the *inability* to remember (15). As a result, a large literature developed dealing with the problems of memory from every conceivable perspective: biological and neurological, cultural, historical, and sociological, with one portion devoted, not surprisingly, to the Holocaust. Here, however, much of the emphasis seemed to be on reclaiming memory,[3] and Holocaust memory in particular, thus the resulting examination of artworks, public monuments, and Holocaust museums, which were, at the same time, a *displacement* of memory onto either particular objects or collective rituals of commemoration. It is as if, given our individual problems with our own personal memories,[4] remembering and commemoration had become socialized in ways not previously understood.

French philosopher Paul Ricoeur's *La Mémoire, l'histoire, l'oubli* (2000)[5] explores the complex imbrications of contemporary memory, history, and forgetfulness. His motives in writing this book stemmed from a lengthy professional preoccupation with historical writing, but also from a "civic" sense of being troubled by the public implications of "the worrying spectacle" of too much memory here, too much forgetfulness there, compounded by "the influence of commemorations and the abuses of memory" (1).

Ricoeur turned to the work of the founder of the twentieth-century sociology of memory, Maurice Halbwachs (1877–1945). Halbwachs died at Buchenwald; his last days have been written about by Jorge Semprun in his 2002 *Le mort qu'il faut*, and movingly sketched by fellow detainee, artist Boris Tsilitsky.[6] In 1925, Halbwachs had published *Les cadres sociaux de la mémoire*, which defined the field of social memory; he returned to it in his posthumous 1949 *Mémoire collective*.

Ricoeur, however, insisted in *MHO* on the previously unnoticed radicality of Halbwach's distinction between collective memory and historical memory (512). In Halbwach's earlier work, the fundamental distinction had been between *individual* and *collective* memory, two very different ways of organizing memory, but nonetheless still interconnected. Not so with the idea of *historical* memory, which, Halbwachs argued, went back to school days in which the student was first exposed to history primarily as dates that had to be memorized (facts, major events, and people)—that is, as material completely *exterior* not only to a young life but to that life's experience. While the historically obsessed Third Republic made some headway in bringing the teaching of history closer to lived memory, Halbwachs noted that this had mainly occurred after the fact, and largely by way of national commemorations, including national narratives, myths, and so on.[7] For Halbwachs, the teaching or construction of history was a form of violence from the outside exerted upon memory that resulted, in Ricoeur's words, in "the uncanniness of the historical past" (513).

The ensuing problem concerned that of the trans-generational transmission of this uncanny form of history that operated first through the construction of the idea of a generation as a "we-group" of a common age and culture, but that was also anchored biologically in sexual reproduction and in the succession of generations: the old die out and are replaced by the new generation. Social links were thus firmly codified in the parental system of our societies where the biological and the social are brought together by affective familial ties as well as by juridical mechanisms like adoption. However, given the long chain of the succession of generations in an immense genealogical tree whose roots are lost in the soil of history, the ancestral stories, so familiar to so-called traditional societies, were eventually forgotten, and what remained was only the abstract and anonymous idea of generational succession.

In this way, living memory fell into the clutches of history. While traces of the past remained in the form of books, the archaeological discovery of monuments, and public efforts by city authorities not to entirely obliterate the historical urban architecture, there still lingered on the horizon a historical will-to-power that sought to integrate into "an integral memory" the separate forms of individual, collective, and historical memory so that it became possible, in Halbwachs's words, "To never forget anything" ("*On n'oublie rien,*" cited in *MHO*, 515).

Except that the complete absorption of lived memory by history did not fully happen. For one, Halbwachs noted a "malaise" regarding the methodological delimitation of the discipline of history and the ensuing endless turf wars over control of and subdivisions within the historical field (as also in most other fields of knowledge). Secondly, the major frame of reference for historical memory remained predominantly that of the nation, although between the nation and the individual there are already countless intervening variables and groups. Thirdly, the role of historical writing and historiography assumed ever-greater distance from collective memory in the name of the pursuit of scientific objectivity.[8] (On a personal level, for Halbwachs, the opposition between the procedures of scholarly history and the exercise of collective memory also took the form, as Ricoeur put it, of "a challenge addressed to his close colleagues [the historians of the so-called *longue durée*]" (*MHO* 516). For Halbwachs, the very notion of "historical memory" became ever more problematic—as a result of which "memory" and "history" remained suspended in an uneasy, forced cohabitation.

The late Yosef Hayim Yerushalmi's *Zakhor: Jewish History and Jewish Memory* (1982) took the next step opened up by Halbwachs of further separating "scientific" historiography from the sense of history that, Yerushalmi argued (24), had been invented by ancient Israel. If by historiography is to be understood a self-reflexive discipline that analyzes over time the methods and interpretations used by historians, such a self-understanding openly revealed the crisis that it had generated in the very heart of memory, both personal and collective, that otherwise maintained itself alive through narrative transmission from one generation to another. In Halbwachs's words, "History begins where tradition ends" (cited in *MHO*, 518). Modern historiography, however, attacked lived memory by "correcting it, displacing it, contesting it, interrupting it, and destroying it" (Ricoeur 518).

Yerushalmi's account of Jewish memory revealed itself to be both singular and exemplary. It was not to be confused with the oral tradition, especially not among a people as highly literate and devoted to reading and commentary as the Jews. Jewish memory, then, was highly charged with a sense of history, but *not* of historiography. The title of Yerushalmi's lectures, *Zakhor*, is the injunction of the Torah to remember, not through the verbal, discursive, or literary ways by which, according to Ricoeur, the operations of historical distanciation worked (519). Rather, the Jewish sense of history was sustained through the injunction to transmit the stories and laws of the Jewish experience, beginning with those stories closest to us familially, and moving to the entire collectivity interpellated by the words, "Hear, oh Israel" ("Shema Yisroel," the holiest of Jewish prayers),[9] words that abolish the distance between those close and those farther away. Not only did the Jewish sense of history ignore historiography, but, as Yerushalmi puts it, "there is no equivalence between meaning in history, the memory of the past, and the writing of history" (cited in *MHO*, 520).

Such a view of ancient Israel's sense of history, however, ran into problems, with the secularizing impulses of the Jewish Enlightenment and the early nineteenth-century rise of the professional Jewish historian in the project of "a science of Jewishness" (*Wissenschaft des Judentums*). But this science was, Yerushalmi argued, less the adoption of the methods of scientific history than the radical critique of the theological sense of Jewish memory. Historiography thus equated to secularization; as Yerushalmi put it, "assimilation from without [and] collapse from within," so that secular Jewish history—and particularly that of post-1948 Israel—succumbed in many ways to the problems of any other national history. As Ricoeur remarked, for Yerushalmi, historiography had nothing to do with restoring memory; on the contrary, it represented an entirely *new* kind of memory, that of the rational project of wanting to save the past in its entirety. This "delirium of exhaustivity" (Ricoeur 522) became self-perpetuating and Faustian; and also, as Nietzsche had remarked, there was something in the "'historical sense' that injures and finally destroys the living thing, be it a man or a people or a system of culture" (cited in *Zakhor* 145 and not 147 as Ricoeur has it, 522).

The third prong of Ricoeur's (and Yerushalmi's) powerful assault against historiography dealt with the differences in the treatment of history between the first (1984) and third volumes (1992) of Pierre Nora's monumental compilation, entitled *Les Lieux de mémoire*. As we saw, memory progressively displaced itself from lived forms and became re-deposited in various "sites" (*lieux*).[10] For Nora, the *lieux* or sites of memory became more important because there no longer existed *milieux d'histoire* or lived environments of history. The consciousness of a break with the past was bound up with the sense that memory had been torn apart. History had led to "the eradication of memory" (Nora, "Between" 632). Accordingly, "Memory and history, far from being synonymous, appear now to be in fundamental opposition" (Nora, "Between" 633; Ricoeur, 523-28). Memory was "life," while history was the "always problematic and incomplete" reconstruction of what is no longer. History is a critical discourse, antithetical to memory, perpetually suspicious of it, "and its true mission is to suppress and destroy it" (Nora, "Between" 633). "The equation of history and memory" (Nora, "Between" 633)—*histoire-mémoire*—the devouring of memory by history, in turn gave rise to, as Ricoeur put it, "*a new figure*" that Nora termed "memory seized by history" (*MHO* 525; emphasis added). This new figuration of history had three characteristics or "symptoms," as Ricoeur noted. One, it was an "archival" (Roudebush's translation of Nora, 636) form of memory—Nora used the word "archivistic" (*archivistique*), which better captures the precariousness contained by what Liebniz, as long ago as the eighteenth century, had called "paper memory." Ricoeur commented that the essays Nora gathered in volume one of *Les Lieux de mémoire* attested to the resulting corrosive and constraining character—again, of the violent imposition—of history from the outside. And this especially in the form of a materialization of history that, as of 1980—in France, the year of the Cultural Heritage (*patrimoine*)—inflated the inverse correspondence of the former sites of memory to topographical sites given over to commemoration (Ricoeur, 525-26).

This process entailed the reduction of memory to that of *individual psychology*, as a product of cultural compensation for the historicization of memory. Memory thus became a form of cultural duty or obligation. To paraphrase Nora, if memory was no longer everywhere, it was nowhere. Or, put differently, it had been taken in charge by the culture industry and so placed before an individual consciousness' dutiful appreciation, in the appropriate official locations (museums and so on). Ricoeur observed in a footnote (526n94) that Nora's point about the individualization of memory as duty made an explicit parallel with the recent turn of many non-religious French Jews to a reactivation of Jewish memory. As Nora put it,

> In this tradition which has no other history than that of its own memory, to be Jewish is to recall Being, but this non-refusable ("*irrécusable*") obligation to remember, once interiorized, places you, one after the other, in an entirely new situation. Memory of what? Memory of memory. The psychologization of memory leaves everyone with the sentiment that one's salvation, finally, depends upon acquitting this impossible debt.[11]

The third symptom, the first two being memory-as-archive to memory-as-duty, was memory-as-fracture (*MHO* 526; Nora xxxi). In volume one, Nora had remarked that "museums, archives, cemeteries, festivals, anniversaries, treaties, depositions, monuments, sanctuaries, fraternal orders" (Revel and Hunt 636) were "the beleaguered and cold" markers of a society without ritual, "a society deeply absorbed in its own transformation and renewal, one that inherently favors the new over the ancient, the young over the old, the future over the past." This gave Ricoeur several further openings for his reflections later in *MHO* that the sites of memory are forms of transcription—that is, of *writing*. Second, it allowed Ricoeur to elaborate via the essay on "Generations" (in Nora, vol. 1) on some of the problems he had mentioned in discussing Halbwachs: namely, that the idea of "talking about my g-g-g-generation" (as the song by The Who put it, not Ricoeur) had inaugurated a symbolic rupture that resulted in a purely horizontal vision of the social bond in which one generation simply replaced another in a process of perpetual substitution (530). For one example in France, take the immense resonances of "the May 68 generation." The implications for Ricoeur as for Nora (who in volume two is especially attached to the vertical idea of the memory-nation) were considerable. Memory, as predominantly generational, turned increasingly to commemoration. In Ricoeur's words, "We are thus in the realm of pure memory, that which makes a mockery of history, and abolishes duration to turn it into a present without a past" (531). The past, *if there at all*, exists only to "memorialize" the present. As such, Nora wrote, "Commemoration has emancipated itself from its traditionally designated space, and it is the entire epoch that has become commemorative" (3: 998). The "era of commemoration" had become "infinite" (1005).

The above discussion sheds light on several problems relevant to the study of recent French historical writing at the narrow end and then to the broader question of memory in the Western invention of tradition. At the narrow end, it helps explain the persistent problems around the French writing of the history of the Resistance until the 1980s in its inability to recognize the important role played by Jewish Resistance groups.[12] In effect, that until further problematization of the nature of historical writing itself, the "history" of the Resistance could only be at best a generational one, that of the memoirs of the official Resistance generation, and only that. This, then, also explains the separate and parallel characteristics of early postwar studies by French Jewish historians as being framed by a different historical sense of the idea of history. Their studies were framed in relation to a millennial background of specifically Jewish history with its catastrophic antecedents going back to the Roman destruction of the Second Temple. Accordingly, for the *goyim*, to put it this way, writing the history of the Holocaust—and, for that matter, of the persistent uncanniness that Jewish survivors aroused among non-Jews—posed an even greater problem. In other words, and to be charitable about it, that part of such a history was itself enfolded within the long history of Christian anti-Semitism, and so called for a form of reflexivity regarding Western culture as a whole that was challenging, to put it mildly. It was easier, as it were, to ignore, repress, or *pathologize* the matter, as a further part of this larger challenge also had its specific ramifications for a potential rewriting of the various national histories of Europe, thus demanding a *double* self-reflexivity (the critique not only of Western culture but within it, that of the nation). The difference between these strategies was that to ignore or repress were still only largely unconscious acts, whereas to pathologize drew upon the formidable knowledge/power resources that, after Freud's opening up of that continent, Michel Foucault's work was among the first to unveil to the present generation.

These differences, in turn, suggest another point, namely, the extent to which historiography itself, because of its problematic and uneasy relationship to lived memory as well as to trauma, or the traumatic nature of historical events, is profoundly entangled with related psychological phenomena—as a form of the will-to-power, for example, or even more clearly as a neurosis. Not for nothing did Henry Rousso frame his study of the problem of Vichy memory (*Le Syndrome de Vichy*) as a manifestation of neurosis. Finally, if the argument made by Nora about the dissolution of the past by an infinite era of commemoration holds, this also connects the interrelationship of acts of commemoration with the collective burden imposed upon survivors of being living witnesses to the bad events of recent history.

II

In France, the 1980s saw the biggest commemoration of all, the 1989 Bicentennial of the Great Revolution of 1789. One of the many books on the "The Commemoration" is a 1999 reprint of a collection of articles by various leading historians, sociologists, and so on, published in the journal *Le Débat* from 1983 on. Its cover, a photograph taken from the official, televised ceremonies, shows black American opera star Jessye Norman, who rendered "La Marseillaise" at the Commemoration opening night, draped in a long dress made from the tricolours of the national flag. The photograph powerfully recalls Roland Barthes's famous essay in *Mythologies* (1957) about the black soldier saluting the French flag. There, he analyzed the signifier of this sign system as being, on one level, about France's "imperiality," although he went on to show that, in fact, it signified nothing at all. It was not, he wrote, about French imperiality "tied to the totality of ... the general History of France," but rather a mythical concept "made of yielding, shapeless associations" and one "must firmly stress [that] ... it is a formless, unstable, nebulous condensation," something whose fundamental character "is to be *appropriated*" ("Myth Today," esp. 105).[13] But if commemoration is fundamentally about "appropriation," it should not be forgotten that the late 1980s through mid-1990s was also when France at last began to appropriate into what Nora had called the "mémoire-nation," the French Jewish Question. Or at least, the beginnings of what sociologist Pierre Birnbaum, in volume two of *Les Lieux de mémoire*, saw at the time as a possible "new deal" for Franco-Judaism (2: 2679).[14]

On July 16–17, 1942, some 4,500 Paris police, aided by the bus drivers of the CTRP (as the RATP was called then), rounded up between 12,500 and 13,200 Jews—men, women, and children—interning just over 8,000 at the Vélodrôme d'Hiver (or Vel d'Hiv, for short),[15] not far from the Eiffel Tower at the time, but demolished soon after the war. The rest were sent directly to Drancy, and then all were deported to Auschwitz, where they were murdered. This was the largest deportation of Jews from Paris by the Vichy government.

In 1949, de Gaulle had a square, bounded by the quais de Grenelle and Branly, the boulevard Grenelle, and the Bir-Hakeim bridge, dedicated to the memory of the "thirty thousand Jewish ... victims of racial persecution ... confined in this space by order of the Nazi occupier" (Wiedmer 44). In the early 1960s, an architecturally stark Memorial to the Deportation was built at the tip of the Ile de la Cité, just behind Notre Dame, although French Jews are not mentioned explicitly there.

De Gaulle's plaque was removed in 1986 to make way for a new one dedicated by then-mayor of Paris, Jacques Chirac, on July 18, 1986. The Chirac plaque gave more details, corrected the numbers arrested, broke them down by gender and age (4,115 children, for instance), and restated that the deportation had been done by the police of Vichy on order of the Nazi occupier. As Wiedmer notes, while giving more information, the new plaque still did not tell the whole story: for instance, that the members of the police involved stayed in their jobs after the Occupation (45–46). The annual commemoration of the Vel d'Hiv remained privately observed by various Jewish organizations until 1993, when President Mitterand made it a National Day of Commemoration of the racist and anti-Semitic persecutions committed "under the de facto authority" of Vichy or, by its official name, the Government of the French State. There was further fiddling about with plaques and a kitschy monument was put up by Mitterand.

But it was not until the July 1995 commemorative ceremony that Chirac, beginning his first mandate as president of the Republic, admitted that "France," *patrie* of the Enlightenment and the rights of man, had, on July 16, 1942, "accomplished the irreparable," broken its promises, and delivered its wards to their executioners: "We owe [the Jews deported from France] a debt without statute of limitations" (cited in Wiedmer 53). Even so, it was not until 1997, emblematized in part by the trial of Maurice Papon—a Vichy *préfet* in charge of deportations in the Gironde, who later rose under de Gaulle to head the Paris police and oversaw the 1961 police riot and murder of several Algerians protesting the war in Algeria[16]—but also because then–Prime Minister Lionel Jospin had committed his new government to assist the commission recently formed to (finally) investigate the wartime appropriation of Jewish property, to open up the official archives of the Vichy period, and to fund the creation of what became the Mémorial de la Shoah, that the French Holocaust became part of the national memory. The 1997 commemoration of the Vel d'Hiv also marked its full entry into the commemorative pantheon and, today, where only a few thousand commemorants once stood in memory, it has become a major media event. It's the same story for the site of the Drancy camp: speeches by the president of the Republic, solemn media coverage, and so on. As Wiedmer also notes (49), since April 25, 1954, every last Sunday in April is the National Day of Memory of the Deportation to remember the liberation of the camps and, as she puts it bizarrely given her book's topic, "the end of suffering" (49).

Of the subsequent French debates over Holocaust memory and representation, I'll briefly mention two. One began in March 1966 when a young French journalist, Jean-François Steiner, published his *Treblinka: The Revolt of an Extermination Camp*, a mix of history and fictional "reconstructions"[17] that went on to become an international bestseller and was quickly translated into English, German, Spanish, Italian, Portuguese, and Japanese. In Paris, the book became the centre of an intellectual scandal that raged for the next six months, involving leading figures like Simone de Beauvoir, who had written a glowing preface, the critic George Steiner, and other literary luminaries (Elie Wiesel, Sartre, etc.). In an interview, Jean-François Steiner himself started the controversy by raising the question of the extent to which the Jewish deportees, here members of the *Sonderkommando*, were "complicitous" in the Nazi extermination machine. The same claim made in the United States about the *Judenrate* (Jewish Councils) by Hannah Arendt in 1963 and earlier by historian Raul Hilberg in 1961 had unleashed furious controversy, though far more so for Arendt at the time than over Hilberg's extremely meticulous study. The "Steiner Affair" raised similar hackles in France, but, as Samuel Moyn noted in his 2005 study, for different reasons. The predominant French view of the Holocaust had paid much more attention to the concentration camps, where most of the (non-Jewish) French Resistance fighters were held, than to the *extermination* camps. In discussing the extermination camps, there was no avoiding the fact that the vast majority of the exterminated were Jews. In this sense, as Moyn remarked (5), Steiner's *Treblinka* was a watershed in France in the public uses and discussion of Holocaust memory that opened it up from its previous restriction to a small and unknown coterie of scholars, marginal to the established disciplines. If *Treblinka* was able to produce such forceful affects, it was also because Steiner consciously wrote his book "as a popular 'Western,'" as Moyn put it (7), freely admitting that he had "imagined" parts of it, to make the facts speak more truly, so to speak. His French publisher, Fayard, had forced him to remove some unflattering remarks about professional historians, people who do not take journalistic arrogance lightly.

In 2003 a further controversy broke out with the publication of art historian Georges Didi-Huberman's *Images malgré tout*. Claude Lanzmann, explaining why his 1984 film *Shoah* had not used conventional documentary footage, had famously remarked that it was because such images from within the death camps did not exist, adding that if he had found such in the many years of research on the film, he would have destroyed them. Didi-Huberman's book was a response to Lanzmann as well as other critics that such images did in fact exist—and in particular four photographs ostensibly taken from within Auschwitz gas chamber V by an anonymous member of a *Sonderkommando* in August 1944, photographs that showed gassed bodies being cremated in outdoor incineration pits.[18] Much of the resulting argument had to do with technical discussion of what images do and do not show, and how the person taking the shots could have gotten hold of a camera. Didi-Huberman's main point, however, was to stress the idea of "in spite of it all" (*malgré tout*)—that is, that the debate over "how to read" the Holocaust was not settled at all.

III

This brings us appropriately to the problems of bearing witness or testimony. Historian Annette Wieviorka, in 1998, published a small book entitled *L'Ere du témoin*, the era of the witness.[19] It was dedicated to psychoanalyst Anne-Lise Stern whose long-running seminar at the Maison des Sciences de l'Homme as of the 1970s had centred on uncovering the often unconscious but continuing presence of echoes of the Holocaust in contemporary European culture.

Wieviorka opened with the words spoken by Jewish historian Simon Dubnov to his comrades in Riga in December 1941, just before being murdered as part of the liquidation of the ghetto: "Good people, do not forget; good people, tell the story; good people, write!" (9). Not only were numerous written accounts, diaries, and so on found buried in the ruins of the ghettos and death camps of eastern Europe[20] and later rediscovered, but between 1944 and 1948, the work of the Central Commission of Jewish History in Poland had gathered over seven thousand testimonial accounts from survivors. Raul Hilberg recalled the Yiddish Scientific Institute's (YIVO) research director Philip Friedman, who died in 1960, telling him that there were, by the 1950s, some eighteen thousand writings by survivors, and that those numbers were already out of date (Wieviorka 9–12). Since then, to manuscripts have been added countless numbers of audio cassettes and tapes, videotapes, CD-ROMs, DVDs, gathered and stocked in numerous archives and libraries in sites throughout the West. Wieviorka remarked that historians had seldom looked at this recorded material, leaving the "gigantic corpus" either to literary scholars, or to diverse psychiatrists (15).

Most importantly, all this material provided a "model of the construction of memory"—in other words, "a figure of testimony" (16). She proposed to investigate the archival materials in three expanding dimensions: (1) those left by the ones who were killed; (2) how the Eichmann trial made the emergence of the figure of the witness possible; and (3) how the figure of the witness had become sociological in the sense that one could speak meaningfully of an era of testimony. Still, it is important to note that there is no unanimity on the obligation to bear witness.[21]

In French, a *témoin*, in its most banal sense, is someone who tells what he or she saw, usually to a police officer or in a courtroom, about an accident or a crime, or gives visual identification of those involved. There are degrees of witnessing and testimony, accompanied by increasing levels of formality: depositions, attestations, etc., in which what is being recounted is written down, transcribed, and signed, all of which guarantee the veracity of the account. The formalization aspects also increase the stakes, and no doubt reach their pinnacle in the eternal Covenant of G-d with the Jewish people. The Covenant is a legally binding contract, sealed by the Law, the Ark of the Covenant, and the mark of circumcision.

Moving from theology to historiography reveals different problems. Holocaust historian Raul Hilberg, in his 2001 *Sources of Holocaust Research*, classified "testimony" into four categories, noting that the word itself referred to sources that were "highly varied and widely scattered," and depended on whether the testimony is from a perpetuator, a bystander, or a survivor (44). His four categories were legal testimony, interviews of specific people, oral history, and "memoir literature." He raised a number of problems with the testimony of survivors: Were they representative of the Jewish community that was destroyed? Were they a random sample of survivors as a whole? Did their testimony reflect a random sample of their experiences? In fact, unless a number of surviving witnesses could testify about a common experience in a specific case—as he noted, such as historian Christopher Browning found in the 134 accounts of shared memory of survivors of the Starachowice labour camp—Hilberg himself had little use for survivor testimony as a historian. There was simply too much individual variation to guarantee reliability.

But we can leave the historians to the dilemmas of their professional activities as there are other ways to look at the matter. Besides, we have already sufficiently seen the kinds of crises of veracity that affect the historical profession and, as psychiatrist Dori Laub remarks, it was that very crisis of the profession that led to the move to "history as trauma" (255), and so the shift, for Laub, to psychoanalytic approaches to survivor accounts—that is, as forms of narration, with distinctive styles, and rhetorical figures.

As a system of law, Judaism is characterized by a *style* of legal reasoning and modes of argumentation. As such, these are rhetorical acts that generate figures of discourse. One of these figures is the witness testifying to God's injustice. As Anson Laytner proposed in his fascinating *Arguing with God: A Jewish Tradition*:

> As God has not acted toward His people as a God should act ... His people have known it. The Jewish literary heritage is replete with laments and dirges, complaints and arguments, all protesting God's mistreatment of His people.... This history [of Jewish suffering since Roman times, if not long before] has given rise to a unique literature of argument prayers ... that, though rooted in deep faith, nevertheless calls God to task for His Lapses of duty.... [Th]is is the Jewish mode of appealing to God the Chief Justice of the Supreme Court against God the Partner. (xv)

In historical terms, the predominant mode of address here has tended to take the form of prayer/appeal, but this was not always the case, and particularly not in the Holocaust and post-Holocaust period. Laytner specifically discusses "the prose arguments" of Elie Wiesel (214–27).[22] For Wiesel, and in turn reflecting many of the dilemmas of post-Holocaust theology, God was both alive and dead, or was alive but absconded during the Holocaust. Much of the argument relies heavily on the figure of paradox, but certainly one thrust concerns a rejection of the ancient doctrine of *u'mipnei hata'einu*—for our sins we are punished. That the Holocaust was a form of divine retribution is an utter obscenity for Wiesel. In the absence of God, one's obligation as a Jew is to one's fellow human beings, to one's fellow survivors, as well as to the millions of others who died, to whose memory one must remain a living witness. Wiesel's stance, Laytner noted accurately, was one of "defiance" (226): he continued to argue with and question God, even if he was no longer sure that he was there, while still adhering to the Covenant *in spite of God*. As with Didi-Huberman, his was a philosophical version of the *Malgré tout*.

For sociologist Renaud Dulong, the phenomenon of the witness "is that a narrative is factualized by ... the presence of its narrator in regard to the reported event" (*Le Témoin* 10–11).[23] And, to be sure, the problems of witnessing change along with the nature of the events as well. One is dealing with greater matters than, say, just the communication of information.

Thus, a 2005 collection of essays, edited by Dulong and Carole Dorniers, deals frontally with war-related trauma and memory, but now also as a problem of the *aesthetics* of witnessing. Any account, in its dual ambition of "telling the truth" and of adequately transmitting experience to others, necessarily entails aesthetic (stylistic and formal) issues that range across the variety of media of expression from the "high" style of literary writing (including poetry), to theatrical representation (of the Rwanda genocide in this collection), to film. For example, Emmanuel Finkiel's 1999 feature film *Voyages* focuses upon four Jewish women survivors' experience decades later, opening with the return of sixty-five-year-old Riwka to what remains of Auschwitz.[24] As in Alain Resnais's *Hiroshima mon amour* whose leitmotif is "Tu n'as rien vu à Hiroshima," Riwka too "ne verra rien d'Auschwitz."[25]

In the same collection, historian Frédéric Rousseau returns to Jean Norton Cru's 1929 book, *Witnesses: An Essay of Analysis and Critique of the Memoirs of Combatants Published in French, 1915–1928*.[26] The book caused a scandal at the time because the story it told so completely flew in the face of the commemorative memory established since World War I—the heroic sacrifice of the Unknown Soldier, the glory of dying *pro patria*, but as well of such supposedly realist, anti-war novels as Henri Barbusse's *Le feu* (1916). The still unanswered question Norton Cru raised was "How does one write about war?" Rousseau demonstrates the various stylistic artifices—exaggeration and sensationalism, the abuse of local colour such as regional accents, as well as a stylistic verve that said more about the author than those whose experience he was trying to get at—that Norton Cru had denounced in others while using them himself. The Rousseau contribution to this 2005 collection thus shows that the debate around such questions has gone on for seventy years and specifically raises that of the "fictionalization" of the concentrationary universe violently denounced by some survivors as having made of "the deportation a best-seller" (13–14). He combines Cru's question from the 1920s as to how to write about war with a second question raised by the British historian Eric Hobsbawm in *The Age of Extremes* (1994), namely, "How does one write about the concentration camps?" For Rousseau, the two questions had "become one and the same" (14).

As a result, writing about war and the concentration camps entails the social emergence of what Dulong called "new figures of testimony" (*Le Témoin* 17), in the form of the "new type of witness" exemplified by the former soldier or concentration camp returnee, whose testimony is all the more precious as the generations contemporary of the great catastrophes of the twentieth century die out (16). Their testimony is an essential element of what he terms "a dispositive of vigilance" that permanently reminds us of the murderous outcomes of totalitarian and racist logics. But also they are living reminders of the obscenity of some political positions and slogans; living proof of the lies of Holocaust deniers; brakes upon our own forgetfulness; as well as enabling us to continue to reflect upon the past, and pursue the debate about our civilization and its future (16).

Notes

1. Notably "Contested Memories" and a doctoral seminar she taught in 2007 on "Theorizing the Archive in the Canadian Context."
2. See Snyder.
3. For example, but not exhaustively, Ahokas and Chard-Hutchison. See also Wiedmer. But, on another level altogether emphasizing the ambiguity of memory and the rhetoric of ruins, see especially Young.
4. The ability to recall a personal memory is, as Ricoeur remarked near the end of a long life (1913–2005), "a small miracle."
5. Hereafter referred to as *MHO*.
6. Tsilitsky's sketches of deportation, in particular the so-called "small" Jewish camp within Buchenwald, and later paintings were displayed at an exhibition by the Museum of Jewish History and Culture in Paris in 2006.
7. See, for example, Citron.
8. On this, in the American context, see Novick.
9. A parody of which, refracted through his Auschwitz experience, opens Primo Levi's *If This Is a Man* (*Si questo un uomo*, 1958), first translated into English under the title *Survival in Auschwitz* (1960).
10. For Nora (1984) in English and related debates from the late 1940s through to Henry Rousso's 1987 book on the Vichy syndrome, see Revel and Hunt. Nora's text, "Between Memory and History," is on 631–43.
11. This passage from Nora (1984, xxx–xxxi) does not appear in the Roudebush translation in Revel and Hunt.
12. See especially Douzou.
13. See Barthes, especially 105.
14. Copernic refers to the Paris street in which a synagogue was firebombed in 1980. The Abbé Grégoire, at the time of the Revolution, fought for the recognition of French Jews as citizens, but not as Jews. Drancy was the terminal outside Paris from which convoys were assembled for Auschwitz or equivalent one-way destinations. Drancy is also a central reference point in a 2007 feature film, *Emotional Arithmetic*, drawn from the novel by Canadian writer Matt Cohen and directed by Paolo Barzman.
15. As Sarah Schladow writes:

    In France, the earlier discovery of damning government files and the opening of government archives had brought France's war history, and the gap between national and Jewish perceptions of French complicity, again into question. While Vichy was now a subject for popular representations, the French government still avoided addressing the relation of various war criminals to genocide.... The passage in 1990 of a parliamentary bill against public denial of Nazi crimes sat in tension with hitherto tolerated liberal publication and legitimisation of revisionist views.

16 Papon died in 2007 and was quietly buried, wearing his Legion of Honour.
17 Unsourced paraphrases, putting words into the mouths of historical people that they did not say, and so on.
18 Photo negatives no. 277–278, 282–283, State Museum of Auschwitz-Birkenau, published in Didi-Huberman (24–27).
19 The originator of the idea of an era of testimony was Felman ("In an Era of Testimony"). Felman also suggests *Shoah* was less a "historical document on the genocide" and more a "film about witnessing": its "disorienting vision of the present" (40) rewrites the past "event-without-a-witness into witnessing, and into history" (53).
20 Among many, see, for example, "Des voix sous la cendre: Manuscrits des Sonderkommandos d'Auschwitz-Birkenau."
21 See, for example, Kluger's *Refus de témoigner*, translated from "the American," as the French say; also Anne-Lise Stern's "Sois deportée ... et témoigne!" (105–13).
22 For a brilliant discussion of Yiddish poetry of the "annihilation," see Rachel Ertel's *Dans la langue de personne*, a title one can translate with two meanings: (1) as a language that itself disappeared in the flames of the Holocaust, but also (2) as the traces left by the annihilated *people* turned by the Nazis into nothing and nobody: *personne* means both someone and no one.
23 Schladow remarks that:

> Witnessing is a process of positioning, both specular and active, whereby the subject is constructed in terms of what s/he has seen or experienced. In relaying that experience, not only is the subject positioned in relation to others, the recipient is also positioned to accept/believe or refuse/disbelieve the testimony. The process of witnessing, officially or unofficially, is therefore ineluctable: what has been witnessed cannot be changed for the subject; nor can it be changed for the recipient of the testimony, who essentially can no longer remain neutral. In the Eichmann trial, for instance, both the witnesses and the recipient audience were positioned by the act of relaying testimony—the former, as subjects of the experience; the latter, as judging subjects of Jewish testimony and experience and of Eichmann and the trial itself. Jewish experience could no longer be ignored or discounted, only accepted or refused, creating the conditions for subsequent discourse about Jewish victimhood and the Holocaust. (n.p.)

24 On this more generally, see interview with Auschwitz historian Jan Van Pelt.
25 The script is appended to Dulong and Dornier, along with an interview with Finkiel (251ff.).
26 Obviously I am translating the French title, first published by Editions Les Etincelles in 1929, and republished in 1993.

Works Cited

Ahokas, Pirjo, and Martine Chard-Hutchison, eds. *Reclaiming Memory: American Representations of the Holocaust*. Turku: U of Turku, Finland, 1997. Print.

Barthes, Roland. "Myth Today." *Mythologies*. Paris: Seuil. 1957. Introductory essay rpt. in *A Barthes Reader*. Ed. and intro. Susan Sontag. New York: Hill and Wang, 1982. 93–149. Print.

Bellamy, Elizabeth. *Affective Genealogies: Psychoanalysis, Postmodernism, and the "Jewish Question" after Auschwitz*. Lincoln: U of Nebraska P, 1997. Print.

Birnbaum, Pierre. "Grégoire, Dreyfus, Drancy, et Copernic." Rpt. in Nora, *Les Lieux de mémoire*, 2679–717. Print.

Citron, Suzanne. *Le Mythe national*. 2nd ed. Paris: Editions ouvrières, 2008. Print.

Cru, Jean Norton. *Témoins: Essai d'analyse critique des souvenirs de combattants édités en français de 1915 à 1928*. 1929. Paris: Reprinted Editions de Les Etincelles, 1993. Print.

"Des voix sous la cendre: Manuscrits des Sonderkommandos d'Auschwitz-Birkenau." *Revue d'histoire de la Shoah* 171 (January–April 2001): 388 pp. Print.

Didi-Huberman, Georges. *Les Images malgré tout*. Paris: Editions de Minuit, 2003. Print.

Douzou, Laurent. *La Résistance française: Une histoire périlleuse*. Paris: Seuil, 2005. Print.

Dulong, Renaud. *Le témoin oculaire*. Paris: Editions de l'EHESS, 1998. Print.

Dulong, Renaud, and Carole Dorniers, eds. *Esthétique du témoignage*. Paris: Editinos de la Maison des Sciences de l'Homme, 2005. Print.

Ertel, Rachel. *Dans la langue de personne*. Paris: Seuil, La Librairie du XXe Siècle, 1993.

Felman, Shoshana. "In an Era of Testimony." *Yale French Studies* 79 (1991): 39–81. Print.

Finkelkraut, Alain. *Penser le XXe siècle*. Paris: Editions le l'Ecole polytechnique, 2000. Print.

Godard, Barbara. "Contested Memories: Canadian Women Writers in and out of the Archive." *Annual Review of Canadian Studies* 27 (2007): 59–88. Print.

———. "Theorizing the Archive in the Canadian Context." Doctoral course syllabus, Fall 2007. Print.

Halbwachs, Maurice. *Les cadres sociaux de la mémoire*. 1925. Paris: Mouton, 1976. Print.

———. *La mémoire collective*. Paris: Presses universitaires de France, 1968. Print.

Hertel, Ruth. *Dans la langue de personne: Poésie Yiddish de l'annihilation*. Paris: Seuil, 1993. Print.

Hilberg, Raul. *Sources of Holocaust Research*. Chicago: Ivan R. Dee, 2001. Print.

Hobsbawm, Eric. *The Age of Extremes*. New York: Pantheon Books, 1994. Print.

Kluger, Ruth. *Refus de témoigner*. Paris: Vivian Henry, 1997. Print.

Laub, Dori. "From Speechlessness to Narrative: The Case of Holocaust Historians and of Psychiatrically Hospitalized Survivors." *Literature & Medicine* 24.2 (Fall 2005): 253–65. Print.

Laytner, Anson. *Arguing with God: A Jewish Tradition*. Northvale, NJ: Joseph Aronson, 1990. Print.

Levi, Primo. *Survival in Auschwitz*. New York: Collier, 1960. Print.

Leys, Ruth. *Trauma: A Geneaology*. Chicago: U of Chicago P, 2000. Print.

Moyn, Samuel. *A Holocaust Controversy: The "Treblinka" Affair in Postwar France*. Waltham, MA: Brandeis UP, 2005. Print.

Nora, Pierre. "Between Memory and History: Les Lieux de Mémoire." Trans. Marc Roudebush. Revel and Hunt, *Histories*, 631–43. Print.

———. *Les Lieux de mémoire*. 1984. New ed. Paris: Gallimard, 1997. Print.

Novick, Peter. *That Noble Dream: The "Objectivity Question" and the American Historical Profession*. Cambridge: Cambridge UP, 1988. Print.

Revel, Jacques, and Lynn Hunt, eds. *Histories: French Constructions of the Past*. Trans. Arthur Goldhammer. New York: New Press, 1995. Print.

Ricoeur, Paul. *La Mémoire, l'histoire, l'oubli*. Paris: Seuil, 2000. Print.

Rousso, Henry. *Le Syndrome de Vichy de 1944 à nos jours*. Paris: Seuil, 1987. Print.

Schladow, Sarah. "Regenerations of the Holocaust: From the Politics of Identification Towards a Political Identity." Diss. Curtin University, 2007. Print.

Semprun, Jorge. *Le mort qu'il faut*. Paris: Seuil, 2002. Print.

Snyder, Timothy. *Badlands: Europe Between Hitler and Stalin*. New York: Basic Books, 2010. Print.

Steiner, Jean-François. *Treblinka: The Revolt of an Extermination Camp*. Pref. Simone de Beauvoir. Trans. Helen Weaver. New York: New American Library, 1979. Print.

Stern, Anne-Lise. *Le Savoir déporté: Camps, histoire, psychanalyse*. Ed. Nadine Fresco and Martine Leibovici. Paris: Libraire du XXe siècle, 2004. Print.

Van Pelt, Jan. "Auschwitz in the Age of Mass Tourism." *Fuse* 23.4 (2000): 34–38.

Wiedmer, Caroline. *The Claims of Memory: Representations of the Holocaust in Contemporary Germany and France*. Ithaca/London: Cornell UP, 1997. Print.

Wieviorka, Annette. *L'Ere du témoin*. Paris: Hachette Pluriel, 1998. Print.

Yerushalmi, Yosef Hayim. *Zakhor: Jewish History and Jewish Memory*. Seattle: U of Washington P, 1982. Print.

Young, James E. *The Texture of Memory: Holocaust Memorials and Meaning*. New Haven/London: Yale UP, 1993. Print.

Chapter 14
Gender in the Shaping of Public Memory: *Arms (Monumental) for Montreal*

SUE LLOYD

On April 8, 2003, at York University, Barbara Godard held a seminar entitled "Gender in the Shaping of Public Memory: Issues in the Canadian Context."[1] She invited me to speak about my work, *Arms (Monumental) for Montreal*, a site-specific photographic mural work, memorializing the fourteen women murdered in Montreal on December 6, 1989, at the École Polytechnique, where they were studying engineering. The work was commissioned by York University and installed in the east lounge of the Student Centre in the fall of 1997. Presently, the work is still in its original location. What follows here is the result of my revisiting the talk I gave on the occasion of the seminar, a discussion of specific decisions I made in creating the memorial.

A central problematic in working with the female body in visual work is the very fact of its presence or absence, its visibility or invisibility. A conversation with Barbara Godard focused my attention on her premise that visual art was all about making visible what cannot be seen. And while I haven't yet decided once and for all if this is true or not, at the time it spurred my thinking. To consider the role of gender in shaping public memory, it is important to consider the possibilities for the presence of, and representation of, the female body in the public realm. These issues have been and continue to be prominent in feminist discourse regarding visual culture. In the history of visual culture, two opposing premises exist. On the one hand is the premise that visibility of the female figure is equivalent to the objectification and victimization of females. For the female body, being seen does not necessarily mean empowerment; being seen may mean vulnerability. The basic problem is the equation of visibility with sexual availability, passivity, and being objectified. In this paradigm, the degree of visibility is presumed to be proportionate to the degree of availability. On the other hand, in identity-based politics and work, the premise is that visibility is equal to power; to make visible representation of one's marginalized or oppressed identity group is to refuse the invisibility that is fundamental in oppression. Making one's self or representations of the group identity visible is considered an act of empowerment and a demonstration of agency. In a further twist, there are also traditions in which forms and degrees of invisibility are modes, not of subjugation, but of moving with choice and power: disguises, masks, drag, wearing the veil, assumed identities, costumes, magical powers, shape-shifting, etc.

In my own work, I am preoccupied by the pursuit of making visible, and therefore possible, what seems to be a kind of impossible figure: a female figure that exceeds the limited shape popularly allowed to females. Perhaps this figure is "impossible" because she represents a combination of attributes that are incompatible in the dualistic logic that delineates male and female attributes. This impossible figure is a female figure that defies externally imposed limitations. Her visibility, including her nudity, is equal to power and sensual being, not sexual availability. Her qualities of physicality and sensuality belong to her. I portray gender as detachable from proscribed behavioural roles, and each gender as able to assume roles prescribed by both conservatism and political correctness. I investigate the positions and roles of being passive and of being more active or aggressive, with the intent that each is a role taken on occasion for pleasure, one of many possible facets. This figure is not impossible in real life, but in visual culture there are limited models. We cannot see her, cannot even picture her because the collective public vision of gender does not allow her to exist, at least visually, as a symbolic type. She is just one of a number of impossible figures in visual culture. To pursue this impossible figure is to pursue a similarly impossible vision of gender.

I try to make visible the discourse and dynamics of my problematic, working with visibility, invisibility, and fragmentation in order to examine and to expose the power and the inadequacies in each. The difficulty of visually representing any facet of female sexual existence, for example, the representation of lesbians, is evidence of this problematic, particularly in photographic and lens-based work. Logically, what might make a lesbian most visually identifiable is lesbian sexual practice. When lesbians are not engaged in sex, they might look just like other women. But lesbians are not necessarily any more comfortable than other women in being portrayed nude and/or engaging in explicit sexual acts. The desire to be visible and proud as a lesbian can be entirely and understandably overshadowed by an unwillingness to be so visible and vulnerable in a visual image publicly exhibited. Moreover, if lesbians are identifiable only through sexual acts, how can lesbian point of view (different from lesbian appearance) ever be expressed? The development of visible dyke culture offers one solution. Much like the business suit, a visible culture of hair and clothing styles identifiable as "dyke" has evolved to satisfy a need for visibility, as an alternative to explicit statements and bodily exposure. The problem in becoming visually identifiable is the simultaneous result of visual clichés and stereotypes. Interestingly, and problematically for many lesbians, "dyke" culture and appearance suggest (demand?) a conflation of lesbian sexual practice with a challenge to, or refusal of, self-presentation complicit with gendered roles. Visual representation of a lesbian is a fraught and impossible task. The lesbian is a visual problem and an impossible female figure within visual culture: able to be seen only if she is exposed in sexual acts or presented in identifiable "dyke" costume.

My considerations in making the memorial work, *Arms for Montreal*, relate to the representation of women in general, but also in this case to women who had been violently murdered. The fourteen women, or perhaps more accurately, the event of their murder, has come to be seen as symbolic of violence against women. The way that these women are represented impacts, and is impacted by, public memory as well as public perception of gender. The problem of the impossible female figure is central in public memorials if one wants to create images of females who represent and claim certain attributes, especially those consistent with acts worthy of memorializing other than being victimized (or perhaps even more especially when the women are victims). Can we conceive of a female figure as a representation of courage, bravery, heroism, action, honour, or any of the other qualities that a memorial or commemorative work might require? Will women appear only in memorial or commemorative works that are biographical, and therefore demand a specific female figure? Can we conceive of visible female bodies as representative of forms of power other than those operating through indirection: being passive, charming, persuasive, underhanded, flirting, dealing in the dark arts, or being a temptress? Once we begin to list the kinds of powers that female bodies symbolize, the continuum takes us into areas that are (ambiguously) powerful, and not necessarily heroic.

I wanted to represent the fourteen women as embodied.[2] One of the reasons for this was to focus on the women rather than on the event of the massacre, or our own responses of mourning and grief. The most popularly known visual symbols of the Montreal Massacre (roses and candles) have been associated with mourning and have, it can be argued, functioned to disembody the women. Murder is the ultimate disembodiment and, by all accounts, a primary reason for the women being targeted was their female bodies. It was important to me, then, that they be represented as bodies, and as bodies capable of action. The representation of absence, and absent and missing bodies is often used in memorial work; I felt in this case the presence of the body was more powerful and empowering.

The women in *Arms (Monumental) for Montreal* are represented as embodied but that representation is somewhat ambiguous and perhaps might be seen as somewhat ambivalent. I decided to use a body part, rather than a whole body. I chose the forearm and the hand because of the capability and potentiality of that part of the body for action, in fact, for a great range of actions, powerful actions: working, typing, drawing, striking, caressing, loving, building, lifting, carrying, etc. I decided also not to make the body or body part gendered in any obvious way. It is difficult to present images of women that are physical and embodied but that do not make the women visually available to viewers in a manner that perpetuates the history of images of women. In this case, the relative invisibility of the women's bodies, although they are embodied, is the effect of a dual strategy. The visual work enacts a paradox: it insists that the women be embodied and empowered through the choices made in representing them through their bodies; however, because each body can be only partially viewed, there is equal insistence on the protection of the bodies. To fully respect the women, already violated physically in real life, I did not make them visually available.

My representation of female bodies in *Arms for Montreal* employs ambiguity to empower and to protect the women represented, and to create questions in the minds of my viewers.[3] I have always believed that the sex of bodies can usually be identified through almost any body part if the viewer looks carefully. And when it cannot, the occasion gives rise to productive consideration of the importance of gender in knowing and judging. The absence of an easy method for identifying the bodies as female might also lead the viewer to question where exactly femininity (or masculinity) resides in the body.[4] What might make the actual hand and arm that I photographed more difficult to identify as female is that the qualities the arm possesses might not be read as female. I photographed a friend of mine, who is female and a welder; she has very strong and visibly muscled arms. I liked the idea of using this very simple visual representation of strength and power for the female engineering students. Wherever the strategy was most effective, I used a lack of ambiguity to deliver a political message. For example, I reduced the possibility of ambiguity by the specific use of text: the date, time, place, and context of the event were clearly given. Basic information should not be misread. There were a few things I did not want to explicitly restate: the murderer's name, as well as the actual fact that they were murdered. My rationale here was that I neither wished to memorialize the murderer, nor to reiterate the act of murder.

To me, the memorializing of the fourteen women and their violent death has become popularly established as an occasion for mourning instead of an occasion for more political responses and actions. I did not wish to focus on mourning. Instead I chose to focus on being galvanized into action as a response (or at least as one possible response) to the murders on December 6, 1989. For this reason, I depicted the sequence of the hand and forearm. For this reason also I chose to use the quotation from the Québec licence plate ("je me souviens"), importantly in French. I also understood that it invokes memories of a defeat (the fall of New France at the Plains of Abraham in 1759 to the English) with the purpose of transforming and utilizing that memory to create resolve to remember and to live Québécois identity, culture, and language. In the case of the Montreal Massacre, the predominant strategies in both visual work and memorial rituals have focused on mourning. I prefer to make a connection between memory and motive for action: to incite vigour and energy, not sorrow.

The clenched fist is clearly a symbol of resolve and of action, but it is unclear as to what nature and extent of action. I am not condoning a response of physical violence as an appropriate response to physical violence; however, a work of visual art can certainly generate questions: What kind of response is justified? What degree of physical action is needed? How violent are the emotion and the resolve that one feels in response to atrocities? The forearm and hand progress through a sequence where a limp hand, palm open and upturned, becomes, in the fourth panel, a clenched fist. The clenched fist has a range of associations, but basically all of these associations relate to action and resolve, less or more extreme. Also, the title "arms" suggests an entire range of weapons that might be employed to respond to a massacre. While I do not advocate violence, I request that the full range of emotions be allowed and considered in response to such violence. For me, focusing on mourning appears insufficient, a polite and appropriate gendered response by and for women. That gendered behaviour in response to such atrocities even exists raises other possible avenues of critical questioning.

Representing and identifying the women as engineers was accomplished through the naming of the four areas of engineering (one panel for each), as well as the accompanying diagrams for each area, which appear to be tattooed on the forearms. I wanted to identify my subjects as engineers as well as women as that is the goal and the knowledge that they chose for themselves, and again it was this intersecting combination that made them the targets of violence. I chose to tattoo the diagrams on the women's forearms. In popular and visual culture at the time, tattoos signified the recognition of the importance of embodied experience in forming interiority, as well as the possibility of expressing interiority through external visual devices such as tattoos. Diagrams representing the body of engineering knowledge attribute power. In this way, the women possess and are identified by what they wished for themselves. It is significant that engineering is still a profession dominated by men.

Within visual culture, the role of gender in shaping public memory seems to be a specific sub-question of the larger question of how gender is experienced, communicated, and taught through visual imagery. I therefore return to the premise that one of the roles of visual art is to make visible what cannot be seen. At the outset of considering this problem, I proposed that I have been working to make impossible figures visible, one of them being a female figure that could be a representation of power and self-possession in the many ways that are typically identified as not-female. I still think that this may be true. What I have discovered is that I have also been engaged in articulating and making visible not only the *figure* but the whole *problem* of presenting that figure (and others) visually.

Appendix: "Gender in the Shaping of Public Memory: Issues in the Canadian Context," April 8, 2003, York University (Call for papers by Barbara Godard)

"Looking Forward, Reaching Back." This mandate of the Canadian Women's Movement Archives exemplifies the contradictory logic of memory work, its attempt to stop a temporal flow in a return to the past to launch that instant more powerfully forward in the movement of time. Memory work is paradoxically predicated on this constitutive rupture, inducing a necessary forgetting, which narratives and other representational practices work to make continuous. Despite the apparent "presentness" of contemporary society, these are memory-obsessed times. The function of memory in individual and collective identity has become an object of inquiry in many disciplines.

How is the past made to work in the present to constitute sociality for women? The symbolic activation of time—and space—gives shape to imagined communities. Collective memory through the interconnection of an elaborate network of social mores, values, and ideals generates the shared images forming the social frameworks within which individual memories and identities are created and sustained. Attention to *nachtraglichkeit* or deferred action as it becomes legible through anemnesis in psychoanalysis has accorded considerable importance to the role of memory in personal identity. Collective identities are fostered and often largely defined by a number of symbolic processes that create an emotional bonding with particular histories and geographies. The material rendering of social memory makes use of many mnemonic devices to transform and external phenomenon to be engaged visually into a psychic terrain of internalized symbolic meaning. While accumulation and classification of material traces of the past were the principal concerns in previous eras, today the focus is on their display. Possibly this is a consequence of the advent of digital technologies, which, with their shift in the techniques of conservation and classification, have provoked a sense of imminent crisis in the transmission of traces of the past and given rise to a rhetoric of instantaneity and simultaneity. Digitization renews the utopian impulse of such memory work, however, embodying the hope of mastery of a quasi-infinity of cultural materials.

What are the forms of collective memory work in Canada? How does gender figure in memorializing practices? This is a critical question, since recall is inevitably a selective process. Transmission of knowledge of the past occurs under contested conditions: communities are dissolved as well

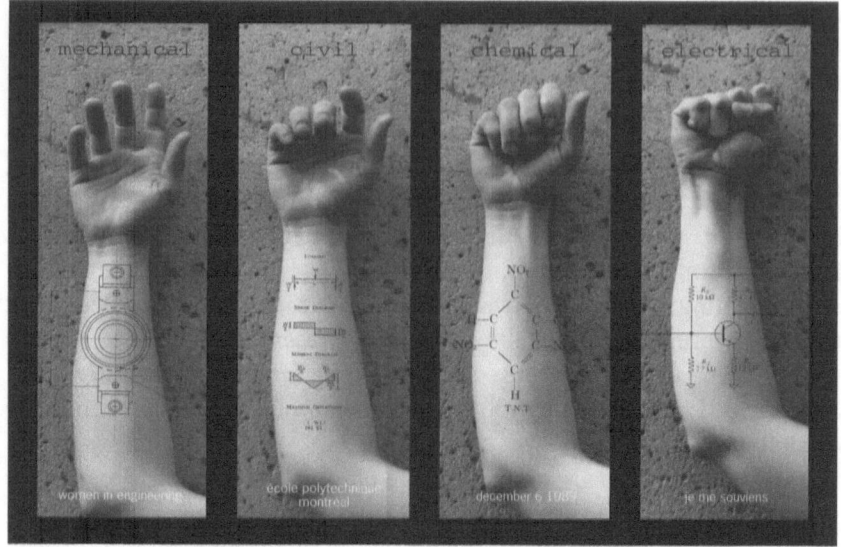

Figure 14.1: *Arms for Montreal (Multiple)*; edition of 150, signed and numbered offset print on paper; 11 inches high by 18 inches wide, 1997; image courtesy of the artist.

as made in the interlocked processes of forgetting and remembering. Memorializing practices exercise the power of exclusion as well as of inclusion. Who writes the narrative? Whose markers of the past are accorded public space?

The question of public memory has been a fraught one for feminism. The absence of public sites of memory for women was regretted by previous generations of feminists. In *A Room of One's Own,* Virginia Woolf commented on the necessity for women to have mothers "to think back through" and decried the absence of any historical information about women in the university libraries. An important accomplishment of second wave feminism has been the (re)writing of history to develop metanarratives inclusive of women's activities in creating social community. And in Canada there has been much significant work done in women's history, including the collaborative projects of the Clio collective and the Canadian Women's History group, while individual literature scholars have located and explicated the works of earlier generations of women writers. As well, there have been initiatives to establish such sites of memory as the Canadian Women's Archives, the Gay and Lesbian Archives, and, recently, the erection of monuments to commemorate exceptional women—such as the

Gender in the Shaping of Public Memory 295

Figure 14.2: *Arms for Montreal (Monumental)*; installation shot; four mural panels: black-and-white resin-coated silver prints, laminated; each panel 12 feet high by 30 inches wide; commissioned site-specific work installed in second-floor Students' Lounge at York University, 1997; image courtesy of the artist.

Person's monument. In addition to such *denkmal*, there have been admonitory *mahnmal* in the form of memorials to women victims of misogyny. Public memory may be an instrument of power and authority, or of resistance and rebellion.

In Canada, the creation of symbols and myths of national identity—the stuff of history, tradition, and cultural heritage—has officially taken the form of the cult of the hero (or shero?), the transformation of the wilderness into home (and commodity), the celebration of the spirit of the land. Divergent representations have been produced by more recent migrant communities who contest the very concept of space as mnemonic and the events specified in these narrations of the past. The forms in which official and vernacular or resistant memories have been preserved and represented are virtually endless. Among the most observed memorializing practices are histories and narratives, high art and literature (memoir, autobiography, biography), oral legends and popular tales, encyclopedias, *Dictionary of Canadian Biography*, archives, landmarks (*lieux de mémoire*), monuments, public art, commemorations, memorial events, performances/

re-enactments, symbolically loaded sites (*genius loci*), parks, buildings, museums, cultural productions (music, literature, film, video, theatre, Internet, folk productions), walking tours, historical tourism, sporting events, national holidays, etc. The communities initiating or funding such practices and so brought together or sustained through the processes of creating or the rituals embodying commemoration are diverse and differentially situated within the field of social relations of power.

These are the issues that inform our seminar this afternoon. We shall approach them through panels on Monumentalizing Memory, Archives and the Commemoration of Women's Acts, and Memory in Transit.

Notes

1 Included as an appendix is the text of Barbara Godard's original call for the seminar.
2 I also decided to represent the women collectively and anonymously, not individually. I cannot argue that one strategy is better than the other, just that they are different. Since I didn't know the women individually, it never occurred to me to relate to them or to represent them in that way. Since making that work, I have a deeper appreciation of why it might be important to work with individual names of the dead even though no other information is known. This is, for example, the tradition used in memorializing soldiers who have died serving their country. It is true that in my work, the women and their bodies remain in the symbolic realm.
3 *Arms (Monumental) for Montreal* is probably the least ambiguous work I have ever made. Except for a few strategic places and ideas, ambiguity appears to be mostly inappropriate in a memorial work. The power of ambiguity is the richness that results from a multiplicity of meanings; each viewer brings his or her knowledge to inform the meaning of the work. My own visual practice has developed in an era of art production in which meaning is less likely to be straightforward and didactic, and my own work participates in the use of visual imagery in an open-ended and sometimes metaphoric way.
4 When such ambiguity is present, viewers frequently make assumptions that are wrong. I previously experienced this occurrence with several viewers' misreadings of *searchworks*, an earlier body of my work where female bodies often are misread as male because they are interpreted as the more powerful of two figures (they are "on top" or carry what are misinterpreted as weapons, plus there are no obvious female identifiers: no long hair, no dresses). I imagine that the drawn-out process of trying to reconcile one's assumptions with the facts (when, if ever, they can be known) is a worthwhile process in making viewers (the public) question and rethink assumptions about gender.

Chapter 15

Contested Memories: Canadian Women Writers in and out of the Archive

BARBARA GODARD

Why memory? Why Canada? A country so young would seem to have little to recall, or so Earle Birney laments in a poem about the absence of tradition in Canadian literature and a consequent lack of national identity: "it's only by our lack of ghosts / we're haunted" (138). As Canada prepared to commemorate 400 years of European settlement in Quebec in 2008, following similar festivities in Acadie in 2004, and after First Nations' land claims were pressed in court and on the ground at Oka, Quebec, in 1990 and Caledonia, Ontario, in 2006, it is clear that Canada not only has a long history of remembering but, like many modern states, it has its own memory wars. The question of public memory is a fraught one for the modern nations such as Canada, which, despite a liberal democratic commitment to equality, is riven with divisions, those of the linguistic and cultural divide between French and English and between these "Founding Nations" and those they have colonized, "First Nations," the Métis and the Inuit, as well as gendered and class conflicts. How such contests over memory inform the social imaginary—that is, the representations that bind a population to the abstract form of the state to produce a subject or citizen through this process—is my concern in this essay. I want to introduce briefly some of the memory wars of a haunted Canada through analysis of a few representational practices or mnemotechniques through which the contests over time and space have been carried out, namely those of the archive, the monument, and the performance.

The role of memory as a constitutive element in collective and personal identity has emerged as a matter for academic research in recent years. Some of the interest in public memory arises from the understanding that the nation is a "cultural artefact," something "imagined" (Anderson) through the "invention of tradition" (Hobsbawm). The forms and practices of making tradition or mnemotechnics interest me, less those triumphs of the victors with their *denkmal* than the *mahnmal* or counter-monuments of those who have gone through the slaughterhouse of history. How is the past made to work in the present to constitute sociality? To what ends is memory work performed? What are the representational practices employed in such monumentalizing gestures? These are questions that resonate in my brief account of some of the strategic uses of memory for political ends to produce new kinds of subjects for the Canadian nation.

Why Remember?

The problemization of cultural memory and its investigation in the last couple of decades has been building on thought of a more than a century earlier. During the Third Republic in France, Ernest Renan wrote in "Qu'est ce qu'une nation?" (1882) that the modern nation is a historical result of remembering: "The essence of a nation is that all individuals have many things in common, and also that they have forgotten many things" (11). Unity is always effected by means of brutality, the violence not only of certain deeds of exclusion but subsequently the violence of a certain kind of forgetting. There is no civility without barbarism, as Walter Benjamin concluded a century later (256). The capacity to remember creates a dialectic in which marginalized groups often attempt to maintain at the centre of a national memory what the dominant group would rather forget. There is not just one public memory but the memories of multiple groups constantly battling for attention in public space. Collective memory is consequently always in flux responding to political forces. As Maurice Halbwachs (1920) later elaborated on these processes, we remember the events, language, actions, attitudes and values that are aspects of our membership in groups. Individual memory is a function of a network of these relationships not an autonomous entity. Memory is one of the ways our consciousness connects events and experiences in the web of language or other symbols. However, such connections are reconstructed in the context of the present and never dissociated from considerations of power. Any national meta-narrative seeking to construct community needs to link events and actors to sites of symbolic of power in such a way as to forge a mythic bond, gathering its many contested stories into the horizontal time of the enduring present of the nation. However, as Marcel Proust demonstrated, what is forgotten is what most endures: within the meta-narrative, absence or silence constitutes a residual reservoir of oppositional or ex-centric narratives.

In the same period as Renan was writing about collective memory with respect to forgetting, Sigmund Freud was theorizing the role of memory in individual identity in relation to repression. He posited that a subject was formed in the act of forgetting, which constituted the unconscious as the repository of what individuals found most troubling and so repressed. As he wrote in his analysis of "The Psychical Mechanisms of Forgetfulness," the "function of memory, which we like to regard as an archive open to anyone who is curious, is in this way subjected to a restriction by a trend of the will." In "hysterical amnesia," people "do not know they do not want to know." "[P]sycho-analytic treatment endeavours to fill up such gaps of memory in the course of the work" (296). However, this anamnesis or memory work reveals the unconscious desires creating a "certain resistance" to recovery of a repressed trauma. What both these theories of collective and personal identity expose is a gap between an event and its remembered representation as they point to the role of violence and desire in the activities of seeking to remember as well as of trying to forget.

Why memory? This question is posed as a response to another question, *Who Killed Canadian History*? (1998), raised in what has become a controversial book by Canadian historian Jack Granatstein. In this book he claims that Canadian history is in crisis because there has been a turning away from political history, a "national" history, or what he sees as public events from his particular perspective as a military historian. With a turn in historiography to the study of social history, to everyday life and especially to history from below, that of ethnic and racial minorities and women, he claims, a nostalgia for memory has taken centre stage. His book expands upon the work of the Dominion Institute, a Toronto think tank that focuses on making Canadians more aware of their national history. In 1997 the Institute had launched itself with a survey, which found that most Canadians could not name the dates of significant events in the formation of Canada as a nation, such as Confederation, or the names of the major actors in these events and called for a renewed emphasis on the teaching of Canadian history—or of a certain Canadian history. What is at stake, in fact, is a change in historiography that has been brought about by a number of feminist historians who have been a leading group in the Canadian context in the disciplinary turn to social history seeking to introduce as actors on the national scene many who were excluded from the "great man" history of an earlier nationalist school of historiography, which had charted the progress from wilderness through colony to nation with World War I a defining moment in the transformation. Despite an apparent crisis in memory that the above texts might suggest, these are memory-obsessed times. The crisis is not that there is no national history but rather that there are many stories all contesting the understanding of the historical and seeking designation as "factual." Consequently, the function of memory in individual and collective identity has become an object of inquiry in many academic disciplines other than history, in particular geography, the fine arts, and literature.

Why remember? The question has been asked with increasing insistence in the last few decades because it is symptomatic of what Andreas Huyssen (1995) has called our "museal culture." The contemporary speeding up of media images elides space and erases temporal distance. Rather than amnesia, though, this condition has induced an "expansive historicism" for which, Huyssen proposes, the museum functions as a key paradigm. In what is predominantly a visual culture, the contemporary mode of engagement with the past has increasingly become one of display. Objects that would otherwise be lost in the flux of time are made concrete to us, preserved against dispersion and fragmentation, within the simultaneity of an elastic present. The dynamic role of memory in cultural transmission works now to exteriorize tradition. In this, it differs from the mediaeval period, which was concerned with collecting memory, accumulating and storing it, and the modern era, which was concerned with developing methods for classifying the traces so saved from the past.

Taken to an extreme as spectacle, the contemporary obsession with memorialization participates in an economy of publicity from which has been evacuated both the sensorial and affective aspects of remembering and the articulated network for their conceptual generalization and transmission. This tension between the conceptual and the sensorial is of great importance for mnemotechniques, which activate the reservoirs of memory differentially according to their material potentials. The implications of this distinction in kinds of memory have been addressed most forcefully by the French historian Pierre Nora in discussing what he calls the "*lieux de mémoire*" (1984) the sites or places of memory. Such "realms of memory" hold the past at a distance by externalizing what has taken place. They mark a discontinuity between an event and its recall rather than a lived memory where there is a direct continuity, often through oral transmission, but also through ongoing rituals or practices sustained over time and linked closely to place. There are *"lieux de mémoire,"* he contends, because there are no longer *"milieux de mémoire,"* quickened by the bonds of affect and custom in thick social relations.

Consequently, a major problem in memorialization is how to make memory vital, alive. The question of "living" memory comes up repeatedly, for instance, in specifications for the creation of memorials. A commonly stated objective is that of creating a "living memorial," something with the power to touch the intended audience, draw them under the spell of affect, so that the memory will be revivified and its temporal span extended. Such a stirring memory will replace what has become, as Nora says, a *"mémoire devoir,"* an empty memorial obligation or abstract debt to the past that is perceived only as an official duty to a collectivity rather than an act that carries immediate and intimate meaning. The sensory appeal of a mnemonic is important for forging a link between individual and collective memory by increasing the immediacy of involvement in memorialization, which heightens its affective force by intensifying personal engagement. Paradoxically, links with the past must be broken so that through acts of memory the past may be made more alive and its significance be projected into the future. The forcefulness of these traces is what is at stake in any memorializing practice as groups take up their positions and counter-positions in a contested field. Nonetheless, the fault line, which separates present from past into a before and after, gives the past to us as radically different, a world from which we are removed. Acknowledging the rupture, working with the gap, makes possible a new critical history that no longer participates in creating compensatory rituals or monuments but that studies these activities as mediations constructing the past. Such a critical project informs the fiction, visual art, and theatrical performances I consider here. How we choose to remember is as significant as what we recall.

Whose memory? This is an important related question, since memory is fragmented and reordered from the diverse perspectives of the different participants in any event. There have been close links between feminist activism and women's cultural production in Canada since the founding of the Toronto Women's Literary Association in the 1870s, which soon after morphed into the Toronto Women's Suffrage Association. While the performances of first wave feminism and the utopias of second wave feminism envisioned a brighter future for women with expanded rights as citizens, feminist culture at the end of the twentieth century became memory-obsessed. The backward glance was not just a function of the prominence of historians in the production of feminist knowledge. Major changes in government policy in the early 1990s, with cuts in funding to women's organizations that had worked toward women's greater financial and social autonomy, made the 1980s, with hindsight, seem a brighter period for women's aspirations in view of the significant gains in legal recognition of equality rights in the Charter (1982) and access to abortion (1988) won during that decade. But it was a major event in the history of women in Canada at the end of the decade that made memory and memorialization a major focus of feminism in Canada since the 1990s. On December 6, 1989, fourteen women engineering students at the Université de Montréal were killed precisely because their ambition to become engineers was perceived as feminist and a limitation on the prospects of young men. Through my research into the kinds of practices of memorialization that developed in the feminist community at that time and have subsequently oriented feminist action around issues of overcoming trauma, I have become interested in the issues of public memory more broadly. "*Se souvenir pour agir*," the mandate of the Montreal community and the slogan for the commemorations for the 10th anniversary of the "Montreal Massacre," emphasizes the paradox of memory work and its pedagogical function, instructing people to remember so as to act in the future. "Looking forward, reaching back"— the slogan of the Canadian Women's Movement Archives located at the Université d'Ottawa—underlines this constitutive work of memory in creating a history for women by making the past usable to write women into the historical trajectory of humanity. Such an elastic present constitutes the grounds for a future perfect through the repetition of an annual commemoration, the National Day of Remembrance and Action on Violence Against Women, December 6.

Marking Time: The Archive

Founded in the 1970s in the holdings of a feminist editorial collective in Toronto at the time, the Canadian Women's Movement Archives was one of the earliest efforts to gather the traces of feminist activism and cultural production and so spare future generations the dilemma of Virginia Woolf, who, in *A Room of One's Own* (1929), lamented her inability to find any documents in the archives on the history of women in Renaissance England nor any texts in the library by women writing in that period that would give her "mothers to think back through." Luce Irigaray has reiterated the necessity for such a genealogy in the feminine to enable women to relate to each other as social subjects through an alternate symbology not only through the Oedipal contract as objects of men's desire, which denies them subjectivity and excludes them from the production of knowledge. The archive, which has such an important role in the gathering and preservation of the traces of the past, is thus the first of the mnemotechniques to command attention in the production of new knowledges and new knowing subjects both in the history of feminism and in the activities of Canadian feminists. Indeed, the innovative aspect of the Canadian Women's Movement Archives is revealed in any Internet search for women archives, which shows it to have been a pioneer in collecting records of a social movement of its own time. Even as the writing of the history of women in Canada and the creation of an archive of second wave feminism were taking place, the archive became of considerable interest to Canadian women writers as well. Dwelling in the beyond of another moment is to inhabit a different space that functions as a space of critical intervention in the here and now, enabling a re-description of our cultural contemporaneity, the shared space of the body politic, in a project of constituting new forms of sociality. In the last twenty years, women writers have been engaged in such critiques of received knowledge as they seek to establish women as knowing subjects, not just objects of inquiry. Among the frequent protagonists in their fictions has been the archivist or archival researcher, mediating the temporal gap, keeping a record of past violence timely by "bearing witness." Beyond a concern with the gaps in the public record, which such novels interrogate and bring to light, there has been a more general concern with epistemology, about how we make history and to what ends. Introducing a reflexive analysis of archiving processes into the long-standing evidentiary function of the archive in the historical study of empirical reality, these novelists shift the emphasis from metaphysics and identity to questions of politics or ethics, refusing a logic of sacrifice or victimization for one of critique of the operations of violence in the everyday.

The archive itself is undergoing radical changes at present that have made it a widely used figure for thinking through debates over the transformations in contemporary society with the apparent dematerialization and infinite reach of a virtual "reality." The advent of digital technologies, with their shift in the techniques of conservation and classification and a consequent rhetoric of instantaneity and simultaneity, has provoked a sense of imminent breakdown in the protocols of transmission of the traces of the past, even as digitization renews the utopian impulse of the archive in its embodiment of desire for the mastery of a quasi-infinity of cultural materials. This dialectic of totality and partiality, of accumulation and dissemination, of hierarchy and destabilization, is one of the many paradoxes of the archive. As *arkhe*, housed by the *Arkhon* or chief magistrate, the archive both commences and commands, creating and enforcing power. A physical site, the archive is not only an institutional space enclosing the material traces of the past, but also an imaginative site and a conceptual space of changing limits. As both noun and verb, both what is preserved and gathered and the simultaneous action of its gathering, the archive amplifies the dialectic of the operations in this space that confers order in creating a system of classification. Although the material traces are structured as the archive comes into existence and in its relationship to the future, the signs of this sifting and interpretation are often invisible. Nonetheless there are inevitably omissions, restrictions, repressions, and exclusions. They incite recall in an attempt to uncover the accidents or intentions in structuring even as the gaps thwart such totalizing aims by exposing the ever-present relations of power inherent in processes of selection and assemblage. The work of memory is predicated thus on a necessary forgetting, the condition of possibility of remembrance.

As the novelists take up the dialectic of the archive as the problematic of temporality in any act of narrativizing, they have focused on the epistemology of selecting, ordering, and exhibiting material traces. What is at stake is not just the repetition of the past with its many secrets and gaps within a reflection on the problematic of representation's truth claims, but rather what such recall and repetition portend for the future, with their potential for reconfiguring the knowable through their powers of inclusion/exclusion. In narrativizing the practices of archivization, the novelists attempt to fill a gap they have observed between history and memory, between fact and fiction, and between the individual document and the discursive formation whose connections the narrative forges. The novel's power of generating hypotheses to test and expand the limits of the real has much in common with the destabilizing effects of the virtual archive, albeit to a lesser degree of simultaneity.

Among the several novels in question here, the earliest of these fictions, Marian Engel's *Bear* (1976), highlights some of the specific issues in knowledge production, especially those between the encyclopedia and the fragment, as well as between culture and nature. The novel is an account of the adventures of an archivist who leaves the dusty stacks of an urban archive to catalogue a collection located in a house on an island in northern Ontario. In some respects a typical Canadian "cabin gothic" or pastoral retreat into an idyllic green world from which the protagonist emerges transformed, *Bear* is also a novel about the history of settlement along the northern shore of the Great Lakes, drawing as it does on archival documents pertaining to the pioneer family of William Kingdom Rains, whose strange story of life on St. Joseph's Island near Sault Ste. Marie involved a possible case of bigamy. Transgressing boundaries also occurs in the fictions of the archive as contradictions are confounded. What is missing in the traditional archive is the body and the senses that make memory vital, living. In her northern retreat, Lou, the woman archivist, literally gets under the skin and into the flesh of the records she is sifting and documenting and her life is changed in the process. What she finds in the books on the library shelves is a series of documents about bears that is virtually encyclopedic: drawn as it is from many different cultures across time and space, this information holds out a dream of totality, if only she can find all the parts. However, the information is fragmentary, written as brief notes on scraps of paper, which are stuffed inside the books. Ever iterable, reproduceable, this is the promise of the archive: meaning that is never closed and open to the future, but which consequently undermines every form of order as it is contingently assembled from shards of the past.

As Lou describes her activities, she frames another dialectic that structures the novel, reason/passion, which in the context of the narrative translates into masculine/feminine, city/country. "Methodically because passion is not the medium of bibliography, she finished cataloguing the book she was working on, made a small mark in its card to indicate a bear clipping had been found in it, started a new card and marked on it what page and what book she had found this slip of paper and curiously the time and date" (77). Is she making a kind of "*I-Ching*" for herself, she muses, dismissing such a "non-rational" process so opposed to the bibliographer's concern for accuracy. She wonders then if there will be a moment in the future when she will look back on this experience and make a "mystical acrostic" out of the titles and dates of these books, believing that she had found the "elixir of life" (55). In such reflections on their interestedness, the hermeneutics of archival practices—selection, preservation, and classification—along with the implicit ideological valuation are exposed to critical scrutiny. A dialectic of life and its absence, of the presence or absence of the body, is a key structuring element of all these fictions of the archive. In *Bear*, it additionally involves an opposition between Amerindian and Eurocanadian cultures. On her arrival on the island, Lou is introduced to the resident bear by an old Anishinabe woman, Mrs. Leroy, who advises her to get to know the bear in its animality. Over the summer, Lou swims and walks with the bear outside and inside reads through the archive of bear-lore while the bear lies beside her. She slowly slips into the skin of a bear, approaching the ambiguously gendered bear sexually. This encounter transforms Lou so that she renounces the mechanical sex with the director of the archive of her previous life, to reclaim her body and independence, the embodied knowledge of bear-life inducing change by making her more attentive to what she experiences through her senses.

Daphne Marlatt's *Ana Historic* also dramatizes a sexual transformation accompanied by a new authority as writer as her protagonist steps into the shoes of the pioneer woman she is researching in the archive and invents new possible scenarios for both lives. Like Lou, Annie moves beyond the pages of the book, writing "into the page ahead" (153), the unknown that becomes possible when one is no longer repeating the same old script but stands critically in its silences confronting its mediations. Annie, who does the archival research for her husband, Richard, a historian, looks in vain in the archive for the history of pioneer women of Vancouver. All she finds is a brief entry saying that Mrs. Richards had come to Vancouver in 1873 as school teacher and then had become Mrs. Springer (39). However, her first name is never mentioned and nothing is known about her life after this marriage. As is frequently the case in archives, the only trace of women's lives is in the documents pertaining to their fathers or husbands, silent testimony to the patriarchal power operative in the processes of selection or appraisal of documents to be preserved. The archive holds records of a sailboat race in the harbour on Dominion Day, but none recalling the birth of the first white child in the colony, an important event in the story of settlement. Annie gets frustrated with the absence of women in the history of the city's origins and eventually starts to write a fiction of her own about such alternate women-centred beginnings, giving the name of Ana to Mrs. Richards and imagining what her life might have been like. The gap in the archival record exposes its lacunae and opens it up to speculation, to the "as if" of hypothesis and fiction. This is the "gap [Annie] keep[s] coming to" (49), the place where the questions arise about what is "wanting in [her]," what "wantonness" does she display when she claims not to "want history's voice" (48), the voice of the marriage plot, "Mrs. Richards marries Ben Springer" (48). Through Annie's punning and questions, the novel explores the dialectic of lack/excess, of fact/fiction in the production of knowledge. The facts of the historical record are only partial, both fragmentary and interested, giving substance to the lives of only a section of the population according to their "want," leaving the other half "wanting" historical status. Since the archive has not preserved what she wants to know, the only way for Annie to connect with the past is through the empathic power of the esemplastic imagination. However, this is a challenge given the force of what Marlatt calls "the f stop of act." As she writes: "but once history's on stage, histrionic as usual (all those wars, all those historic judgements), the a-historic hasn't a speaking part. What's imagination next to the weight of the (f) actual?" (139)

Trying to wedge into this gap between fact and fiction to make visible the operation of desire determining which fictions are taken for real is Marlatt's principal concern in the novel. The marriage plot regulating the valuation of archival documents and the norms of the novel is not the only possible script for women's lives, which remain the invisible within the fold of the visible. Desire may shape other endings for women as it does when Annie writes that Ana Richards becomes the lover of Birdie Stewart, the saloon keeper, even as Annie leaves Richard for Zoe, changing her own name to Torrent as she follows the new plot of the fiction she is imagining, stepping into the shoes and immersing herself in the life of her "character," reading "into the page ahead" (153).

Marlatt also becomes aware that there are women of whom there is no trace in the archive at all. Amerindian women in particular who are the oldest inhabitants of the place have been rendered completely invisible. Yet the gaze may be returned, as Annie's fiction shows, so that the dominant Eurocentric take on the world is not the only one possible. In one scene, she imagines Mrs. Richards encountering along the path on her way into the settlement an old Amerindian woman whom the white men call the Virgin Mary. This woman does not meet her gaze, indeed does not notice her, but looks through her as though she were transparent. The old woman sees not a white woman on the path, but only the trees, the sky, the mountains around her.

> [S]he had given her a singularly flat look, a look not at her but through as if she were a bush or fern. At first she had thought the old woman was blind, but no one blind could find the path like that. There had been a large amount of sky in those eyes…. She would like to know what those eyes saw. (96)

As Marlatt observes in this passage, there are many people left out of the archive because they are not perceived as fully human but, as with the "Virgin Mary," are thought to be closer to nature, immanent in the landscape.

What this nameless woman's life is like can only be reconstructed through this kind of imaginary empathic attempt to get into the body of an other and see the world through her eyes. The gaps and silences exposing the limits of the archive to the critical researcher nonetheless reveal none of the oppositional stories which would contest the "facts" of colonization. Space is contested at a later period, as we shall see, when there are so many white women occupying it that it is no longer possible for the Amerindian women to look through them.

Other groups excluded from the archive as repository of the collective memory have read its silences not as the indifference of sexual difference ordering the selection of "facts" and documents, but as the operations of systemic racism, which has excluded certain kinds of bodies and knowledges. In *Looking for Livingstone* (1991), NourbeSe Philip's traveller learns to inhabit her silence, which proves a richer repository of embodied traces of the past than the word in the journals of the white explorer into Africa, David Livingstone. Joy Kogawa's Naomi in *Obasan* (1981) turns to the letters and documents of her Aunt Emily, which make use of material in the fond of Muriel Kitagawa in the Public Archives of Canada, to study the record of the duplicities of language through which officials "whitewashed" their exclusion of the Japanese Canadians and expropriation of their property during World War II, leaving silence as the legacy of the slipperiness and distortions in their double talk. Kogawa's novel ends with an archival document, providing a lesson in exotopic reading across the boundaries of fact and fiction, document and novel. However, Marlatt's reflexive examination of the critical work of fiction in probing the limitations of public memory most fully develops the metatheoretical issues of the epistemic violence in the operations of desire constructing "(f)acts" out of fictions.

Making Space: The Monument

Monuments are not just markers contending for mastery over time, but in their concrete materiality they instantiate social relations by appropriating space and so function as sign of collective temporality and/or as marker of social violence. Placed outdoors in widely accessible sites, monuments fulfill one aspect of public art as a landmark enacting relations of power. However, the public domain is complex and fractured, not utopianly inclusive. Artworks acquire their public dimension not from an artist's claim to reflect society but from the acknowledgement of their audiences. An artwork takes on the function of monument when within public space it creates meaning and shared values and so becomes a device by which communities make their place in history. Indeed, the public itself becomes a sculpture: spatial experience is made the very subject of the art by bringing the audience into it as a participant—a "living" work of art.

Historically public art has served to monumentalize violence in the form of war or conquest, presenting the triumphant hero on arches and columns. In addition to representing the trace of past violence, public artwork may itself be a weapon of violence and a device for forcibly or subtly dislocating or fracturing public space. Indeed, inviting dialogue, public artists implicitly, if not explicitly, engage in confrontation with or challenge their surroundings. The artwork may be an intrusion into a community that does not sympathize with the activity that is being memorialized in the particular monument. It may also serve as an object of violence or vandalism: the materials of granite and steel from which monuments are traditionally made presume that, when erected in a particular place, a monument may provoke retaliatory violence, even inciting people to respond by destroying the monument. An example of such a commemoration of triumph (*denkmal*)—and a highly masculinist victory too—is the National War Memorial on Parliament Hill in Ottawa. Positioned in the capital, close to the seat of government, the monument stakes out claims to symbolic centrality to the nation and its imaginary. Relationships of gender are elaborated in this high stone tower through whose archway bronze soldiers pull a gun carriage. Vying with the transcendent thrust of the tower, the forward orientation of the soldiers along a horizontal axis traces the movement of history. Bringing up the rear, next to the gun, is a nurse, a solitary woman, indeed one of the rare women in Canadian public art. Walking alongside the large gun, the woman is linked to violence and death, the chthonic realm, where the feminine mediates the forces of life and death and makes reparation for sacrifice.

Against that kind of public monument are the counter-monuments (*mahnmal*) commemorating the victims of the violence of December 6, at least twenty-six permanent monuments across the country from Charlottetown on Prince Edward Island to Nanaimo on Vancouver Island. Among the last to be built, *Nef pour quatorze reines* by Rose-Marie Goulet sits at the foot of the mountain close to the Université de Montréal site of the massacre of 1989. Well integrated into a neighbouring park with its pathway cutting across from Côte des Neiges, a major city thoroughfare, and linking it to the gates of the university, the minimalist monument acts as a reminder in their everyday lives to the students as they come down from the campus heading out into the city, just as the news travelled down and out to the city in shock waves on the fateful day. But additionally the site acts as a ritual place of mourning where people from the city and students going to class mount the slight incline heading up to the university on the mountain between the individual steel and arcing granite ribs, bearing the inscription of the fourteen women's names. Bending to read them, the witnesses' bodies adopt the posture of mourning. The arcs rise from the grass tumulus like archaic burial mounds or the hull of ancient Viking grave ships (*nef*). They evoke thus an important Montreal feminist collective performance, *La nef des sorcières* (1975), even as they mark the advancing waves of news of the violence. The rhythmical movement connects the site of knowledge production to the body politic conjoining them in the violence and its reparation. The construction of this monument after a public silence of a decade during which questions of institutional responses to the violence had been repeatedly repressed created the space for what has subsequently become also a site for commemorative events that now involve the city and entire university, no longer just the students of l'École Polytechnique, in the annual memorial ceremonies.

Such public recognition and reparation have not been as fully achieved in Vancouver, site of another contested monument to December 6 and the victims of patriarchal violence throughout the world. *Marker of Change* by Beth Alber, the National Women's Monument, as it was first called, was one of the first monuments to be commissioned following a national competition. Alber responded to the specific invitation of the organizers to create a "living monument." Among the design features soliciting a sensory response to intimately engage the viewer are fourteen sarcophagi-like stone elements crafted the length of a woman's body out of pink granite, which looks like flesh with a scar cut into its polished surface. What the women commissioning this monument became aware of very late in the project, which took over seven years to complete, was that there were many First Nations women living in the Downtown Eastside, where this monument was to be installed in Thornton Park, a place of transit near train and Skytrain stations and close to the troubled intersection of Hastings and Main. In their attempt to create a universal monument that would address violence to women throughout the world (it was dedicated, controversially, "for all women who were murdered by men"), they chose to make Chinook one of the seven world languages to inscribe on the standing stones in recognition of the First Nations' women's prior occupancy of this space. As a vehicular trade language used by many coastal groups, this language indexed the many First Nations communities who had lived in the place, linking monument to site. The organizing committee also placed a tile of commemorization to acknowledge the difficult lives of the neighbourhood women—dwellers in the most impoverished area in Canada—in the protective circle of donors names surrounding the standing stones, encircling what was intended as sacred space with its visual parallels to the ancient feminine sites of Stonehenge and Avebury. As the title reads, "In loving memory of the women killed on Vancouver's Downtown Eastside. So many women lost to us. We dream a different world when the war on women is over." Belatedly, the organizers had become aware that a great number of women had disappeared mysteriously from these streets. Subsequently, it has become known that many had been murdered. A man who is charged with killing twenty-six of them is on trial at the time of this writing. However, many of the women have never been found. Indeed, they are among the more than 500 missing First Nations Women across the country who have been at the centre of the campaign of Sisters in Spirit, organized by the Native Women's Association of Canada in 2004–5 to draw public attention to the official silence that for years has rendered this racist and misogynist violence invisible. Their project of naming all these sisters to bring them to life through language as individuals has been accompanied by demands for the state and its institutions to take action, to make the connections between all these deaths and to bring the killers to justice.

The attempt to link this particular site to the community living there under conditions of violence and to provide a ritual space for mourning its traumas has not been effective. *Marker of Change* remains confrontational, persisting as a flashpoint, a sign of contested space, rather than as a gathering point for the reconciling of differences. Official feminist events, such as International Women's Day, still take place at the Vancouver City Hall, symbol of state power to which feminists address their demands for inclusion. Moreover, even before *Marker of Change* was dedicated in the summer of 1997, in February of that year, the First Nations women from the Downtown Eastside erected another monument, *The Heart Has Its Own Memory*, four blocks north on Main Street on a site overlooking Burrard Inlet. Its dedication emphasizes the racialized aspects of violence over the gendered ones: "In honour of the spirit of the people murdered in the Downtown Eastside. Many were women and many were Native Aboriginal women. Many of these cases remain unsolved. All my relations." Each year on Valentine's Day, the 14th of February, they hold a memorial march for the missing women, with a parade of colourful quilted banners for each woman, attended by increasingly large numbers of Vancouverites who are acknowledging their relations with these women and complicity in the violence. Within the space of a few blocks in Vancouver are played out the contested social relations dividing First Nations and Euro-Canadian women in their memorializing practices. The profound misogyny of the community, which both of these monuments attempt to recall and to renegotiate, is nonetheless lived very differently in the daily lives of the women according to their differential position on the racialized hierarchy with its sanctioned violence structuring the Canadian public sphere.

The proliferation of monuments to the women of Montreal's École Polytechnique highlights a paradox, the fact that so much women's artmaking in this last decade has focused on these acts of violence. The monuments could be read as evidence of successful feminist organizing to negotiate for public space and for funding or within a triumphal narrative of women's emergence in the field of public art. Yet the subject of their artmaking is the feminine mutilated body, the founding exclusion or sacrificial logic of our culture. What these monuments make visible is women's troubling position in the symbolic economy, where they are legitimated by the state, accorded a place in the public sphere in their dismemberment, rather than in their affirmation as citizens in emancipatory projects. For the monuments are all situated on government land, whether civic or provincial, and a "National Day of Remembrance and Action on Violence Against Women" was declared by the federal government in 1991. The same Conservative government had the previous year, just after the massacre in Montreal, slashed funding for the Women's Bureau of the Secretary of State, which supported many women's centres and shelters across the country that, among other things, helped women escape situations of domestic violence. In creating such monuments, feminist organizations and women artists are trying to model an ethos by which to imagine differently the structural and relational possibilities of social exchange and sacred ritual on grounds that would make possible the emergence of women as subjects.

Performing Subjects: Redressing the Balance

"Redressing the balance" is the project of First Nations' performance, in this particular case to redress what Paula Gunn Allen (1986) considers the fatal unbalancing in the culture when the female principle has been lost. Individually and collectively these performances establish an articulated network for conceptualizing an alternate line of transmission troubling the national imaginary. Performance, it has been suggested by Diana Taylor (2003), works in a way against the archive precisely because what it does is to enact memory through the senses as embodied memory with greater power than the recall of the word or the image on its own despite attempts to link the conceptual and the sensory in the novels and monuments, as we have seen. Through the addition of gestures, performance brings the body back onto the stage and into the public space. In the process of performance itself, identity is fashioned and negotiated as energy is gathered, bound, and then dispersed. In a ritual, participants in the performance are mutually energized, formed as subjects through their action of repeating sacred rites, which transport them into a liminal space from which they emerge transformed. In a theatrical performance, it is the audience relating in the play of desire to the actors on the stage as transitional objects who are made into subjects through the dynamics of subject-object interaction. Performance is itself a repetition, "twice told behaviour," as Richard Schechner (1985) has suggested, a stylized re-accentuation of the relations of address. As such, it is particularly appropriate within a psychoanalytic framework for dealing with the *nächtraglichkeit* or afterwardness of trauma by "working through" the horror of the past in a kind of guided repetition in order to effect transformation by means of a reworking and redirecting of energy/desire. This form of staged repetition avoids the uncontrollable repetition of melancholy with its attendant nostalgia by effecting transference of the unbounded affects through recognition of the profound loss of the other, of the object of desire, which reorients the energies of the drives into accommodation with the reality-principle to accept the distance of the past.

The work of Rebecca Belmore, an Anishinaabekwe installation and performance artist, which was exhibited in the Canadian Pavilion at the Venice Biennale in 2005, belongs to three fields: visual art, monument, and performance. An image called "Blood on the Snow," from her installation exhibition *The Named and the Unnamed* at Vancouver and the Art Gallery of Ontario (2002–3), engages with a long history of violence against Amerindian women in stylized reworkings of significant events. A red stain on an expanse of white cloth represents the blood on the blanket of snow covering all the women and children at Wounded Knee, South Dakota, who were slaughtered in December 1890 by the United States cavalry while they were dancing the Ghost Dance. Their bodies lay for four days under the snow before being thrown into a mass grave, an end from which they thought they had been protected by the ritual. A syncretic religion produced under colonized oppression, the Ghost Dance was believed to protect them from the white invaders of their land. If they put on white shirts to participate in the dance, they would not be touched by any bullets that might be shot at them. This history of the events at Wounded Knee is significant in the theatrical performances of First Nations women playwrights who, like Belmore, link this traumatized pain of the past to the violence still suffered by many Amerindian people today, especially to the many women who have disappeared violently in the Downtown Eastside of Vancouver.

Vigil, a video of a performance by Belmore on June 23, 2002, National Aboriginal Day, and projected during the exhibition, addresses the unspeakable nature of violence, the silence of its physicality and the subsequent silence of the conspiracy that conceals its occurrence from public knowledge. Belmore has created a number of such performances in which she offers herself and her body as a surrogate sacrifice for different violent acts that have been carried out against First Nations peoples. Most recently, for an installation at Toronto's *Nuit Blanche* in September 2006, she carved the letters forming "Stonechild" into blocks of ice in commemoration of Neil Stonechild, a Saskatchewan Cree youth, who was picked up by police and abandoned outside the city to freeze to death in the bitter winter of Saskatoon. In *Vigil*, she performs a ritual for the women of the Downtown Eastside whose names she has marked on her body. The performance took place at a street corner in the district where they lived. Belmore first carefully swept and scrubbed the site to purify it for the ritualized performance. Then she placed candles around it in order to control the energy of the violence by marking this off as a sacred place. Reciting the names of some of Vancouver's missing women, which she had marked on her arms, she drew a rose with its thorns through her lips as she sounded each name. Subsequently, she nailed her bright red dress to a post in the adjacent laneway and ripped it off a piece at a time, repeating the gestures of nailing and tearing in an evocation of the kinds of rituals of the Sundance of Prairie First Nations in which their flesh is torn. What she exposes here in a kind of repetition of these propitiatory acts, as well as of an initial violation, is the work of defacement and desecration necessary in order that the "public" secret may be made visible, tangible, and apparent to those who would deny it. Repetition is key to the process of stylizing and ritualizing the violence, as well as to "working it through" toward the public acknowledgement of the pervasiveness of violence and the culture's complicity in its continuation. The performance ends with Belmore back in her own clothes, out on the sidewalk leaning against a truck from which blares the music of "It's a Man's World." Out on the street, she presents herself as yet another potential victim for the serial killer, just another Aboriginal woman with a body for the taking. Leaning against the truck, however, she has entered the "man's world" differently by taking back the streets. The applause of the circle of witnesses who have gathered around to watch her, stopping as they pass by on the street, holds out the promise that this time the ending may be different, that the cycle of violence will not be repeated.

The plays by First Nations' women that have been performed on stage in recent years also make use of repetition to expose the desecration and to redress the imbalance with the loss of so many women's lives. A key figure behind the three plays that are my concern here is Yvette Nolan, currently the artistic director of Native Earth Performing Arts and a past president of the Playwrights Union of Canada, who is the author of *Annie Mae's Movement* (1999). Nolan's first play, *Blade* (1990), which shows how a young university student murdered by a serial killer is reconfigured as a prostitute by the media, relates explicitly to the Montreal Massacre of the preceding year in its focus on a student, but links more to the plays about such violence involving Aboriginal women in its attention to the subsequent defilement by the media. Not only has Nolan's own most performed play, *Annie Mae's Movement*, extended her work to attract public attention to the long history of systemic racist and misogynist violence, but she has also been involved in the production of several other related plays by First Nations women playwrights, which she has strategically programmed on the Toronto stage in the weeks leading up to and overlapping December 6, the National Day of Remembrance and Action on Violence Against Women. As such, these performances contest the prominence of Eurocentric women in the dominant memory of the nation proposing an alternate line of historical transmission that critiques its racialized imaginary.

Memory is important as history in *Annie Mae's Movement*, not only the history of Amerindian struggles against imperialism but also the technics of history making in the dialectics of oral/written traces of the past. Annie Mae Aquash, a Mi'kmaq woman from Nova Scotia, was the only woman among the leadership of the American Indian Movement. Her important contribution to its work of resistance to Euro-American society was to establish survival schools to educate First Nations peoples about their history and rights. The authority of the written word and the related devaluation of Amerindian traditional oral cultural transmission is key to several scenes in this play, which dramatizes Annie Mae's activities in AIM and probes the mystery of her death at Wounded Knee in 1976, site of the ancient slaughter and of a confrontation between AIM and the U.S. government in 1973.

Although someone was arrested in 2006, it remains unclear whether it was the FBI or members of AIM who killed her. Both groups had motives for doing so, the U.S. authorities because of her influence in AIM and possible knowledge about the killing of some FBI agents, while AIM suspected her of being a traitor or double agent because of her interrogations by the FBI. The play maintains, indeed highlights, the ambiguity by having a single actor play all the male roles, those of the FBI, a double agent, and various men in AIM. The scene at the end of the play where Annie Mae is murdered on stage deliberately blurs the boundary between characters, leaving it unclear who killed her. There is even a lingering suspicion that it might have been the Rugaru or spirit being who appears as a dark omen at critical times, his enormous image barely visible in a shadow play behind scrims—a vestigial trace of the magic thinking of the Ghost Dance, the kind of belief system against which Annie Mae has been fighting with her struggle for historical and cultural literacy. This ambiguity generalizes responsibility for her death: everybody, including the audience, may possibly have collaborated in it.

Collective involvement is also established through the question of history, of whose version of history has the greatest claim on truth. In the opening scene of the play, Annie Mae, in a classroom, is trying to convince Laurence that studying Amerindian history and learning about his rights is more important than going off to participate in the AIM-led resistance at Wounded Knee. As she argues, because the Amerindians have relied on oral transmission of their culture, their word has little authority and their rights to their land and resources have been constantly violated. A scene later in the play confirms her understanding of the power of the imperial archive with its written documents when, as she is being interrogated by the FBI, an avalanche of paper falls from the ceiling. A vast amount of knowledge about Amerindian peoples is held in the archives of the repressive state apparatuses. Whoever holds the written records has evidence to support their claims and establish their version of the story as fact, so demonizing in this instance rather than heroizing First Nations peoples for upholding their rights. The problem of the archive is restaged here as performance, drawing paradoxically on the power of the sensorial—the performer's body as supplement—to argue for the greater conviction of the conceptual reach of memory. Significantly, as the play ends with her rape and murder, Annie Mae sums up the importance of the survival schools she started to help "rebuild" an autonomous "Indian Nation" and recites her genealogy, beginning with her mother and then her daughters, father, and brother. "You cannot kill us all," she declaims: "My sisters live." Prominent among the many sisters she names are First Nations women writers. Living sisters in spirit, their texts honour Annie Mae's legacy by giving Amerindians, through their words, "a sense of pride in who they were, where they come from" (41).

The form Nolan has chosen is a repetition of the violence on stage, but in a way that generalizes it by making the audience participants. However, the other plays I am concerned with have opted instead for a First Nations tradition of avoiding tragedy. According to Delaware playwright Daniel David Moses (2001), tragedy is conservative because it helps people adapt to the situation as it is. Instead, what he advocates, and Marie Clements and the Turtle Gals have adopted, is trickster logic, the trickster holotrope, which plays on inversions and duplicity, treating horror in a slapstick manner, as the Turtle Gals have done, or in a surreal manner, as Marie Clements has, to create distance—a kind of "safe space"—through laughter or defamiliarization. This aesthetic poses a challenge to the dominant English Canadian "realism" in the theatre, drawing on ritual to effect a temporary triumph over death and destiny as the action on stage alternates between spirit world and earth plane.

In 2004, Marie Clements's play *Burning Vision* won the Japan–Canada Award, building on the success of her earlier Jessie Richardson/New Play Centre Award (1999) for *The Unnatural and Accidental Women*. Adapted by Clements for the screen in a version released in the first week of December 2006, this play is about another serial murderer who killed First Nations women from the Downtown Eastside over twenty years between 1965 and 1987. "Unnatural and accidental" was what the coroner wrote on the death certificates of his victims after recording an excessively high rate of alcohol in their blood, but "no evidence of violence, or suspicion of foul play." When his own daughter, a white woman, was killed in this way, the murderer's family put pressure on the police, who finally apprehended him. Convicted of the murders, the Vancouver barber spent only four years in prison out of a six-year term. When he died in the summer of 2006, there was a long obituary about him in the *Globe and Mail*, but his many victims remained nameless, as is so frequently the case with First Nations women who are first violated and then defiled again by the media.

The women are not nameless in Clements's play, however, nor in the *Scrubbing Project*, both of which seek to write the dead women into history by naming them. Indeed, *The Unnatural and Accidental Women* goes beyond the habitual litany of names in the monuments to the Montreal students and in the project of Sisters in Spirit to create complex individualized narratives about the lives of the dozen or so murdered women. Their names, ages, and blood alcohol levels at the time of their death, as well as its "accidental" cause as determined by the coroner, are projected onto the theatre walls during the performance. The audience is invited to make the connections between the individual cases and to see a systemic pattern of racism, which the police have failed to do. In a trenchant critique of the state's negligence and its tacit approval of gendered and raced violence, these performances help to make both crimes visible and so to compel the government to take responsibility for enforcing the law and bringing the perpetrators of violence to justice. Commemorization as such is a political project of "redressing the balance."

Among Clements's principal strategies is that of humanizing the First Nations women, which she does through her portrayal of them not as victims but as vibrant, sensual, and funny individuals whose dreams have been thwarted by complex circumstances. Framing the central action of the women's deaths is the story of Rebecca, an aspiring writer, who is searching for her mother, who disappeared suddenly one day, leaving the young girl with her father, a white logger. In her quest for her mother, the Aunt Shadie of the play, portrayed as a strong and loving woman, Rebecca learns from people on the streets and in the bars of the Downtown Eastside about the various women's disappearances, which are dramatized surrealistically throughout the first act during which Rebecca sits writing at a café table on a platform overlooking the main arena of action. Soft-hearted but sharp Rose, one of the victims, an English woman who worked in a seedy hotel in the neighbourhood, acts as a spectral telephone operator performing at her switchboard the central action of the play—establishing connections. As she says: "I am between people."

Between voices and between worlds, Rose connects the earthbound with its limited vision to the expansive spirit world where, even after death, these women are vital, life-affirming beings, freed from the constraints of time and space. Aunt Shadie's account of the racist exclusion she was subjected to as a First Nations woman living with a white man, which drove her to leave home, is symptomatic of the stories of many of these women who became separated from the children they loved and the better lives they dreamed. Their monologues and the circumstances of their encounters with the barber vary as these are presented through word, gesture, dance, and fantastic stage furniture with such devices of the unreal as drawers that open and close on their own. The means of their deaths are all the same, however.

Repeatedly on stage, the barber pours alcohol down their throats while they are in his chair, then slashes them with his razor as he cuts off their long hair and conceals it in a light fixture. In the second act, Rebecca comes down from the platform into the dream world where she meets up with the barber in a bar and is almost caught in his lure when she goes to retrieve her wallet from his shop. However, Rebecca turns the tables and repeats while inverting the actions of the first act. She ties the barber into his chair as she wields his razor to shave him, then plunges it into his throat. Within the historical temporality of the action, *The Unnatural and Accidental Women* is a revenge tragedy. In the spirit world, the performance enacts a ritual for the dead. Following the death of the barber, the action shifts to another level. Dressed in white parkas with hoods, recalling the shirts worn in the Ghost Dance, the barber's victims move in a stately manner across the stage and up onto the platform at the rear, where Rebecca eventually finds her mother again. The women form a circle for a picnic in what becomes a ritual feast for the dead. As "sisters in spirit," they form a community that recognizes and honours each woman in her vitality, not her victimhood. Through their costumes, which forge the links, the performance mourns not only the women from Vancouver but also those killed a century earlier at Wounded Knee.

It is to such a feast of the dead that the Turtle Gals in the *Scrubbing Project* have been called by Lydia, the tattooed lady, a kind of divinity who takes them from the "star world" down onto the "earth plane," in a playful reworking of creation stories about the descent of Sky Woman to the Earth World, for their vaudevillian representation of the violence experienced by First Nations women. Like Clements's play, the *Scrubbing Project* works the space between aesthetic performance and ritual: it both renders visible as spectacle the long history of violence in a stylized manner, inciting the audience to see a pattern in the repetitions and to demand justice so as to bring the cycle to an end, and it enables the First Nations women acting the roles to perform the rituals of their cultural traditions, especially the Haudenosaunee and Anishinabe with their feasts for the dead, their most solemn and important ceremonial.

The relation between performance and ritual has been a central concern for the Turtle Gals in their collective creations. Indeed, it was an interest in finding new theatrical ways for responding to the violence of racism and its impact on First Nations women that first brought them together as a collective. Monique Mojica, Jani Lauzon, and Michelle St. John (who played the role of Annie Mae in the 2006 production of the play at NEPA) created the collective after a devastating experience they had when performing in the CBC television film, *Conspiracy of Silence* (1990), about the gang rape and murder of Betty Osborne, a young Manitoba First Nations woman. The title of the film highlights the conspiratorial silence about the events, especially about the names of the guilty men kept secret by the white community for many years, which further desecrated the memory of the dead woman. Michelle St. John was especially troubled by the representation of these events. Playing the part of Betty Osborne, she was distressed at the detachment she felt on seeing her body on the snow, that is, on viewing the plastic mannequin made to look like her, which was lying bloodied on the snow, apparently dead. The split between subject and object experienced by St. John as she watched the enactment of "her" murder was also felt by the other two women. In the dressing rooms, they spoke together about the difficulty they were having in acting their parts because of the objectification and dehumanization entailed. It was good for an Amerindian actor to have work playing culturally relevant roles, but to be obliged to relive the violations of generations of First Nations women was to be excluded and victimized all over again. To counteract this defacement, they needed to create positive energy for themselves out of the horror. In the play, the juxtaposition of grief with hilarity is one creative response to this dilemma. The trickster laughter produced by such radical incongruity effects a kind of Brechtian distancing as they represent the violence for a Euro-Canadian audience in order for the secret to be made public. Within the clowning, however, they perform rituals of mourning through which they give a face to the violated and affirm their own subjectivity. Moreover, both in their sessions of improvisation to generate the material for the play and in rehearsals and performances, they carry out rituals such as smudging and praying before and after acting out the scenarios in order to contain the violence and to protect themselves from its destructive force.

A tension between ritual and performance structures *The Scrubbing Project*, which takes its name from one of the sketches in which the three mixed-race actors relate stories about ways Amerindian women literally attempt to scrub their skins to make them white. In this way, the performance focuses as much on the internalized racism of Amerindian women, which they seek to overcome through an assertion of their creative authority as on its many externalized forms that structure social relations hierarchically by means of sanctioned violence. Ritual provides the frame for *The Scrubbing Project* as the three women follow the instructions of Lydia, the tattooed lady, to gather up their bundles. Composed of their own pain and trauma and of those who have suffered before them, represented in each scene, the bundles are direct prayer offerings evocative of ritual traditions of self-inflicted torture as well as of the bundles of bones brought for reburial in the feast of the dead. Carried to the front of the stage at the end of each scene, the pile of bundles gradually forms a monument. As the play comes to an end, the women gather around what has been transformed into an altar to trauma, and begin to prepare food for a ritual feast of the dead. The entire performance, then, is translated into a ceremony in which, echoing tradition, the dead of a previous decade (or century in this case) are remembered, honoured in story and song, reburied, and so released into the spirit world. In the crossing between worlds, which is at the heart of the ceremony, the spirits of the upper world enlighten the earth world so that participants in the ritual acquire power to enable them eventually to rise to the highest plane, the Land of Souls.

Such a double movement ensuring that spirit co-exists simultaneously on multiple planes propels the action in each scene to reoccupy the site of trauma and transform its negatives into signs of survival. As the play opens, three warrior women, from different cultural traditions, winged Niki, Valkyrie, and a siren named Dove, are sent flying through the air on swings to the tune of "Swinging on a Star." They land in an abandoned vaudeville theatre on Earthplane to embody a different kind of star, Esperanza Rosenberg, Branda X, and Ophelia Squannakonk Dove. Subsequently, they engage aspects of the performance styles of other well-known trios; the three Stooges with their slapstick, Charlie's Angels and their valour, and the vaudevillian style of the Marx Brothers. In the "In Between" world of performance, the incongruities between subject and treatment are heightened as, for example, in one scene, performed to the music of the pop song "High Hopes," a prisoner desperately pleads with her guards to let her go to the bathroom, or in another lists of the locations of strategically placed tattoos of bureaucratically sanctioned violations of human rights from Rwanda to Ipperwash are sung to the tune of "Lydia the Tattooed Lady." In later scenes, the laughter struggles in vain to drown out the horrors of the Holocaust or the annihilation of the North American Indian enacted to the ironically titled "Genocide Waltz." A rare moment of pathos marks the end of the play with the women gathering around the memorial they have built as they voice their dream of a better future to the tune of "Somewhere Over the Rainbow" chanted to a Native beat. With the allusion to the rainbow, a powerful symbol in both First Nations and Eurocentric traditions, the irony is minimal, all the more so in that the song gives way to the recitation of a litany of women's names, which are simultaneously scrolled down a blackboard, in one staging of the play, or are inscribed on streamers thrown out into the audience in another staging. The dead and the living come together here as the long list of names includes both women who have been murdered and women writers who have survived: resistance to oppression and violence lives on powerfully in the actors' gestures and writers' words, which, in their combination of anger and memory, embody the living spirit of generations of sisters.

In their current project, "The Only Good Indian," the Turtle Gals are exploring the implications of the tension between theatrical performance and traditional ritual as it has developed historically. In doing so, they turn to the archive of the state and its holdings of the recorded history of "deviant" Amerindians. The "good Indian" in question is not the clichéd "dead Indian" of North American policies of genocide, but rather the "Hollywood Indian." Extensive archival research in the holdings of the U.S. Library of Congress has helped them unearth the little known history of many Canadian and American indigenous actors whose stories they are developing for performance. A possible motivation for Amerindians' participation in performances on stage and screen, so the Turtle Gals posit, is that one way to avoid death of body and soul was to become a Hollywood Indian. Surviving well financially, the Amerindian on screen could also covertly perform ritual practices, which had been banned by the state.

There is a risk, nonetheless, in turning traditional rituals into a spectacle for white audiences, the risk of internalizing the split for the actor engendered by such a double action that positions her between object and subject, as experienced by Michelle St. John. The performer may not be able to sustain the traditional ethos of ritual and undergo an inner spiritual transformation in actions lacking resonance or "manitou" when her words and gestures are received by the audience as spectacle. The balance between spectacle and ritual is uneasy in these twice-told tales, which are further reworked so that they mark a break with the past, acknowledge a history of violence, while transforming relations to it by re-scripting the modes of performance and their attendant affects. In this dialectic of memorializing, the Turtle Gals stage a history of Amerindian performance from the masks, songs, and dances of tradition, through the Wild West shows, medicine shows, and vaudeville, which they propose as a genealogy of contemporary First Nations theatre. Syncretic rituals responding creatively to imperialist oppression, these duplicitous performance modes embodying trickster logic promise a more positive outcome for the future than the Ghost Dance.

So these are some of the traces of Canada's haunted present in and out of the archive. If women are left out of the archive, their absence from public history is lived as trauma by subsequent generations. If women are kept in the archive, however, and not brought up from the dead, out into the public space as living memory through the mnemonotechniques of narrative, monument, or performance, the trauma is projected through the future. At present, these sisters in the spirit are dancing in downtown Toronto, continuing traditions of both ritual and performance and so making public their subjectivity in the act of assuming it. Redressing the balance in the public memory, they write the history of First Nations women into the story of the body politic.

Note

This chapter first appeared in *The Annual Review of Canadian Studies* 27 (2007): 59–88, published by the Japanese Association of Canadian Studies, with whose kind permission it is reprinted here. Barbara Godard presented versions of the essay as keynote lectures at the German Association of Canadian Studies, February 26, 2005; the Spanish Association of English Professors ADEAN, December 17, 2005; and the meeting of the Japanese Association of Canadian Studies, September 9, 2006.

Works Cited

Alber, Beth. *Marker of Change.* Vancouver. 1997. Print.
Allen, Paula Gunn. *The Sacred Hoop: Recovering the Feminine in American Indian Traditions.* Boston: Beacon, 1986. Print.
Anderson, Benedict. *Imagined Communities: Reflections on the Origin and Spread of Nationalism.* London: Verso, 1983. Print.
Belmore, Rebecca. 2002. *The Named and the Unnamed: Vigil.* Vancouver and Toronto.
Benjamin, Walter. "Theses on the Philosophy of History." 1955. *Illuminations: Essays and Reflections.* Ed. Hannah Arendt, trans. Harry Zohn. New York: Schocken, 1969. 253–64. Print.
Birney, Earle. *Collected Poems.* Vol. 1. Toronto: McClelland and Stewart, 1975. Print.
Blais, Marie-Claire, et al. *La nef des sorcières.* Montreal: Editions Quinze. First performed March 5, 1976, Théâtre du Nouveau Monde, Montreal, 1976. Print.
Clements, Marie. *The Unnatural and Accidental Women.* Vancouver: Talonbooks, 2005. Print.
———. *Unnatural and Accidental.* Dir. Carl Bessai. Laguna Films. 2006. Film.
Engel, Marian. *Bear.* Toronto: McClelland and Stewart, 1976. Print.

Freud, Sigmund. "The Psychical Mechanisms of Forgetfulness." *The Standard Edition of the Complete Psychological Works of Sigmund Freud*. Vol. 3. Trans. James Strachey. London: Hogarth, 1953. 287–98. Print.
Goulet, Rose-Marie. *Nef pour quatorze reines*. Montreal, 1999. Sculpture.
Granatstein, Jack. *Who Killed Canadian History?* Toronto: HarperCollins, 1998. Print.
Halbswach, Maurice. *La mémoire collective*. 1920. Paris: PUF. 1968. Print.
Hobsbawm, Eric. *The Invention of Tradition*. Cambridge: Cambridge UP, 1983. Print.
Huyssen, Andreas. *Twilight Memory: Marking Time in an Age of Amnesia*. London: Routledge, 1995. Print.
Kogawa, Joy. *Obasan*. Toronto: Lester and Orpen Dennys, 1981. Print.
Marlatt, Daphne. *Ana Historic*. Toronto: Coach House, 1988. Print.
Moses, Daniel David. "A Syphilitic Western: Making ... 'The Medicine Shows.'" In *(Ad)dressing Our Words: Aboriginal Perspectives on Aboriginal Literatures*. Ed. Armand Garnet Ruffo. Penticton: Theytus Books, 2001. 153–56. Print.
Nolan, Yvette. *Annie Mae's Movement*. Toronto: PUC's Play Service, 1999. Print.
———. *Blade, Job's Wife, and Video*. 1990. Toronto: ArtBiz Communications 1995. Print.
Nora, Pierre. *Les lieux de mémoire*. Paris: Gallimard, 1984. Print.
Philip, M. NourbeSe. *Looking for Livingstone: An Odyssey of Silence*. Toronto: Mercury, 1991. Print.
Renan, Ernst. "Qu' est ce qu'une nation?" 1882. *Nation and Narration*. Ed. Homi Bhabha. Trans. Martin Thom. London: Routledge, 1990. 8–22. Print.
Schechner, Richard. *Between Theatre and Anthropology*. Philadelphia: U of Pennsylvania P, 1985. Print.
Taylor, Diana. *The Archive and the Repertoire: Performing Cultural Memory in the Americas*. New York: Routledge, 2003. Print.
Turtle Gals. *The Scrubbing Project*. 2002, 2005.
Woolf, Virginia. 1929. *A Room of One's Own*. London: Penguin, 2004. Print.

Coda

In the Stacks of Barbara Godard, or Do Not Confuse the Complexity of This Moment with Chaos

LISA SLONIOWSKI

> How we choose to remember is as significant as what we recall.
> (Godard, "Contested Memories" 7)

Barbara Godard first appeared in my library office doorway a year and a few months before her death in May 2010. She was in remission from cancer but had retired from York University and was trying to sort out her home before her son Alexis moved in with her. She needed to make space because, as I was soon to discover, every available piece of wall, closet, and storage in her narrow Victorian home in Toronto's Annex neighbourhood had been completely overrun by her books and attendant papers: newspaper clippings, exhibition catalogues, programs, correspondence, student papers, meeting minutes, and working drafts of her own work.

She had ostensibly come to talk to me about digitizing *Tessera*, a project our Digital Initiatives unit would complete six months later, but at the end of our conversation, she offered to donate a few books she was carrying in her bag to York Libraries. She mentioned her home library and the difficulties she thought she might have in paring it down to a more manageable size, and I offhandedly offered to lend a hand sometime, wondering what sort of treasures and oddities might be found in the library of one of Canada's foremost feminist literary scholars.

Over the next few months, every time I saw Barbara she would hand me a book or two from her personal library, again to donate to York Libraries. It was only after a few months of these gifts that I realized she intended to

Figure 1: From the library of Barbara Godard (Kate Eichhorn photo)

donate a large part of her collection to us, seemingly one item at a time. I hastily suggested the benefits (for both of us) of donating everything at once, and she invited me down to Major Street to take a look at the collection. What followed was a transformative, fascinating, sometimes sad, and sometimes frustrating experience for me as the librarian fortunate enough to find herself in the thick of Barbara's personal and idiosyncratic library.

Barbara's collection was large, loosely organized, and interspersed throughout her house. Although she had been working closely with our archivists in the Clara Thomas Archives and Special Collections in collating her personal fonds and the *Tessera* fonds for over a decade,[1] in her personal library she had not yet been asked to collude with institutional practices and, as such, her books were jammed full of notes and photocopies, and the papers of colleagues and students were tucked in-between them, connected in ways perhaps clear only to Barbara herself.

We tend to distinguish between books and papers in libraries and archives. We house them separately and have significantly different processes for arrangement and description. Barbara maintained no such institutional illusions, and in one glance her collection made visible and material the intertextual and the dialogic, as well as the historical palimpsest of her own thinking.

Upon further examination, the collection revealed a vision of community as well. Her library/archive embodies a material web of connections

Figure 2: From the library of Barbara Godard (Kate Eichhorn photo)

between writers, artists, filmmakers, editors, translators, and academics engaged in various forms of feminist cultural production and activism. And thus began a process that would rapidly turn into a project that raised larger intellectual questions about feminist history, feminist archives, and archival theory. The acquisition of her collection allows us, as do other feminist archives and collections, to confront the reality of libraries and archives as sites of a hegemonic rationalization that excludes certain forms of lived experience and fixes others into place. "There is no political power without control of the archive, if not of memory," as Derrida says in *Archive Fever* (4). At the same time, libraries and archives may also be approached as places integral to the destabilization of subjects. As Barbara herself said in "Contested Memories: Canadian Women Writers in and out of the Archive,"

> A physical site, the archive is not only an institutional space enclosing the material traces of the past, but also an imaginative site and a conceptual space of changing limits. As both noun and verb, both what is preserved and gathered and the simultaneous action of its gathering, the archive amplifies the dialectic of the operations in this space that confers order in creating a system of classification. (10)

Barbara's collection demands that we interrogate the particular archival challenges posed by it and ask ourselves whether these seemingly logistical

Figure 3: From the library of Barbara Godard (Kate Eichhorn photo)

issues cast a unique light upon the hegemonic nature of our technologies of organization, access, and preservation. As a feminist I wonder how the archivization of this collection might also destabilize the subject in as much as it fixes the collector into place and assures her legacy? As a practitioner, I hope to make institutional or professional change as a result of such reflection. I don't know that Barbara intended for me to ask these questions or not, but I like to think she would be pleased to know that her collection made such interrogation possible.

More specifically, in her library we see a resistance to the ways in which our ordering schemas work to disrupt the intertextual relationships carefully uncovered and preserved by the collector. Also, as we struggle to absorb and manage her eight thousand volumes and many metres of paper records, I see a particular problem with the ways in which the archival tradition of emphasizing the provenance of the material buries the connections not only between a whole constellation of texts but also among the web of relationships in feminist communities. In fixing one context for her books and papers, all the other possible contexts are broken. In attempting to process her sprawling, delightfully textually promiscuous collection—and in so doing also document the network of Canadian feminist cultural production of which she was an integral node—the ways in which our technologies of archivization form an oddly rigid disciplinary system become clear. Archival systems actively collude in making statements inert, and as Foucault reminds us in the *Archaeology of Knowledge*, the archive may govern enunciability itself (129). My postscript to this Festschrift in honour of Barbara Godard will therefore attempt to resuscitate this collection by describing both our acquisition of it and our struggles to absorb it into the larger Library. Finally, I will attempt to elaborate upon some of the issues for feminist archivization raised by the Godard library. It is my hope that my story will inspire scholars to visit and engage with Barbara's mysterious, bursting texts full of cryptic notes and various academic and cultural ephemera and, in so doing, formulate new enunciations.

The House

> She talks and cities move behind her as on a screen with words and a lot of women walking at a good pace so that they can reach a life of their own in this world. (Brossard)

When I visited Barbara's home in the Annex, I was delighted to receive a personally guided tour through her space. We began on the second floor, where she had a large room devoted to reading, lined with her theory books, art books, and her Québécois collection. Next we visited the attic, where she kept her desk and computer, and there I found two rooms lined with Canadiana. The basement was half-lined with books on translation and post-colonial and race theory, various fiction and poetry. This description sounds very tidy, however, and doesn't do justice to the visceral impact of her space, which was utterly overwhelming. There were piles of books and papers on the floor, and photocopied journal articles, news clippings, and student papers jammed between and inside the books on the shelves like feathers about to lift the whole collection to some alternate space. Being there felt like being inside a conversation with Barbara, never sure what was related to what, trying to find patterns and connections in a seemingly endless barrage of information organized around a central core of feminist cultural activism and production, but sometimes only in the most esoteric of ways. A mind and a collection always in a process of becoming, never finding an end point. Resisting end points. One might open a closet door and find the closet lined with books. One might take a book off the shelf, only to find a row of books lined behind the first row. One might worry that there was another row behind the second. One might have walked into Borges's Library of Babel. One might wonder what kind of karmic punishment it was to be the librarian whose job it was to sort all this out.

Adding to the confusion, Barbara talked throughout the tour, alternating between descriptions of her struggles to keep trees from being cut down in the Annex, her plans for where her son's belongings might go, and explanations of why she had particular items in the collection. I was struck, as I moved through the space with her at my side, at the sheer volume of people she knew, seemingly every editor at every feminist press, every feminist journal, dealers/owners at various specialized bookstores, librarians, archivists, and library staff, literary scholars, feminist scholars, poets, filmmakers, writers, artists. The tour and the contents of the collection itself, as I will describe shortly, made manifest for me the Canadian feminist cultural and political community of which we were both a part, and the ways in which Barbara had collected the production of this community through the assemblage and curation of her personal library and archive.

Once I left her house that day, and after I had had a rather stiff drink, I began planning to go back into the house with a camera and/or a filmmaker, and perhaps some other academics who might ask different questions of her than I had—but Barbara died unexpectedly a month later, before I could make the arrangements.

The Acquisition Process

It was clear when I first revisited the house after her death that we would not be able to absorb Barbara's complete collection. Aside from the fact that many of her books were duplicated within our own collection, we struggle with limiting space constraints. However, Barbara's son Alexis very generously agreed to fund Jay MillAr (noted Toronto-based experimental poet, book publisher, antiquarian dealer, York alumni, and librarian) to complete an inventory of the collection, while simultaneously looking for items that could be placed in the Clara Thomas Archives and Special Collections and, of course, boxing up the books as he got through them. This project took a long time and eventually, at Alexis's request, we boxed up the rest of the still un-inventoried collection and papers and brought them up to York, where MillAr continued his work and then several student assistants after him. Our criteria for keeping books were developed by archivist Anna St. Onge, in conjunction with myself, and were as follows:

Books that are:

- rare (first editions, signed, and/or including ephemera)
- heavily annotated by Barbara

- formative to her thinking (i.e., her collection of fine editions of works by Cixous)
- representative of her scholarly and/or political "reach" (i.e., internationally published journals or anthologies with articles by Barbara included)
- not duplicated in our circulating collection, or additional copy needed

In all cases materials from the Godard collection are catalogued with a special note attached to the bibliographic record indicating provenance of the item.[2] MillAr also attempted in his inventory to keep track of the original spatial order of her collection: Where were items kept in the house? Which room? Or, in some cases, as part of what subject area? He also indicated if any associated ephemera were tucked inside particular books. The purpose of this unusually detailed inventory is to help future researchers get a sense of the web of connections that Barbara herself may have been trying to make in organizing her books this way and, of course, to keep some sort of record of how she organized and spatialized her own collection. In this case we attempt to align at some level with the archival principle of original order defined as "the organization and sequence of records established by the creator of the records" whose goal lies in "preserving relationships among the records and to respect the context in which the records came to be" (Millar 100). So where we cannot keep the whole library and all of its records, we have attempted to keep at least a partial record of what was there.

Why a Godard Collection? What's in There?

> For 30 years, Barbara Godard has been a turning platform in the academic life, the literary and the activist life of Toronto. (Brossard)

Barbara's importance as a scholar and author is easy to uncover. One can point to her critical accomplishments in translation studies, for instance, or her many journal articles, her important translations, or even the way she effortlessly bridged various scholarly and poetic traditions, languages, and communities. However, what became increasingly clear after my visit with Barbara and subsequent sorting of the books and papers left behind was less the archive as a document of Barbara's legacy as a scholar—in some ways she seemed to resist organizing this particular set of material around herself as a central figure—but more like what Marlene Kadar calls an "epistolary constellation," which documents and draws a skein of connective tissue between particular kinds of feminist and literary cultural activism/production across a wide-ranging set of borders, materialities, and geographies ("An Epistolary" 103–13). Indeed many of Barbara's notes are, unfortunately, written on bits of tissue, tucked between pages of books, word traces resting on top of the print, fragile, perishable, ephemeral, but nonetheless stubbornly there, superimposing something new not over the text so much as beside it. In her collection we see papers or books from (now defunct) feminist or Canadian literary publishing houses, feminist journals, women's bookstores, photocopies and books by obscure women writers found at Library and Archives Canada (and from libraries across North America). We also have discovered theses, student papers, and published articles from present and former graduate students.

Our preliminary skim of Barbara's collection also reveals correspondence with writers and artists, signed first editions of novels and books of poetry by many contemporary experimental Canadian writers, exhibit catalogues and posters for avant-garde art shows, as well as ticket stubs and programs for showings of the works of feminist avant-garde filmmakers such as Barbara Sternberg and Cheryl Sourkes.

Of course one also finds in the book collection the range of interests and influences one might expect—a large collection of material by Deleuze and Guattari, for instance, and a collection of fine French editions of works by Hélène Cixous. We've also found tattered, underlined, and torn teaching copies of books by important feminist thinkers like Judith Butler and Julia Kristeva, full of sticky notes, photocopied journal articles, news clippings, and tissue fragments with little notes scribbled upon them; these books are often bound together by elastic bands, clearly after intense engagement with the texts therein. Each of these books full of papers operates like a miniature archive in and of itself, an almost incomprehensible "inter-text," making material the ways in which the meaning of a text is constructed within different discursive formations.

And then there are the many waterlogged books—damaged, according to her son Alexis, from being placed behind the sink to read while washing dishes, or while falling asleep in the bathtub reading. One has the sense that Barbara, when alone, continued talking to her books, scribbling notes everywhere, continually and actively engaging with texts at even the most quotidian of moments. These moments themselves are documented as we also find notes in the books from her son's school or his soccer coach intermingled with meeting agendas and postcards from friends far and wide. In this collection we see the life of a working single academic mother unfolding before our eyes and wonder at how she juggled so much labour—dashing from classroom to committee meeting to parent-teacher interview to conferences, maintaining relationships all over the world—all the while stealing time for the focused reading and writing necessary to prepare her classes and write her many articles and presentations.

Other fragments noticed in the collection so far are the set of international anthologies with chapters by Barbara in many languages, evidence of her reach beyond Canadian borders. Interestingly, we also find scholarly works sent to Barbara from academics working abroad with notes from the authors pleading with her to review the book for a Canadian journal, evidence of her role as an international feminist literary hub. We also find small collections of materials documenting feminist academic/cultural production in other countries, such as a radical feminist journal from Delhi, either gathered while she was there or sent to her in hopes that she could disseminate the word from her turning platform in Canada.

Feminist Archivization

Aside from the academic, cultural, and historical significance of the feminist constellation documented in Barbara's collection, attempting to grapple with Barbara's unique, stubborn approach to her own archivization needs to be considered through a feminist theoretical lens. In the later stages of her career, Barbara began teaching a graduate course called "Theorizing the Archive" at York University, while at the same time actively beginning to archive her own papers with the Clara Thomas Archives and Special Collections. In the introduction to the course syllabus she speaks to the archival turn in critical theory, our current societal obsession with memory, and how archival processes transform documents into monuments with symbolic function for the nation. She is interested in how digitization has renewed the utopian hope that all information can be captured and represented in some way, and suggests that therefore display has or will become the central preoccupation of the contemporary archive rather than accumulation and classification. Barbara notes that this shift leads to the processes of archivization going on display themselves. In adding films and novels with archivist characters to the course, she argues that archivists and archival processes are now as much the subject of cultural production as they are a part of the process of cultural production. For Barbara, this shift makes increasingly visible the epistemological and ideological bases of selecting, ordering, and exhibiting material traces.[3]

Unsurprisingly then, given her intellectual engagement with theories of the archive, Barbara's own papers and library challenge our institutional practices in various ways and resist some of the ideologies underlying traditional practices. For instance, archivists struggle with the "flatness" of her papers—the way everything relates to everything—a flatness that reveals, perhaps, her refusal to organize her materials within any hierarchical epistemological schema that might fix subjectivity and relationships in rigid, finite ways. She resisted end points. The flatness of the records also challenges the archival principle of maintaining original order—archivists are forced to order the material themselves so as to store it and make it accessible somehow—which, of course, underscores their role as order-makers. As Derrida indicates in *Archive Fever*, the technologies of archivization produce the historical event as much as they store it (17). Barbara's archive renders that production more visible.

Her book collection vexes us in other ways. It was interesting, as the librarian working from within her collection, to discover that for Barbara, reading was an act of self-inscription ("Becoming My Hero" 142). Such self-inscription was a necessary feminist project if one was to escape one's father's library and become autonomous. And because archives organize books held in Special Collections by provenance as well as through standardized Library of Congress headings, Barbara has now written herself into the institutional library catalogue as well—she has invaded "the library fortress" ("Women of Letters" 258). Every bibliographic record for every item we kept from her collection, regardless of location in our library, has a note indicating the book came from Barbara's collection. The special items with notes and ephemera will be kept and collocated all together in our Special Collections vault. And while a collection of damaged books full of uncatalogued papers is slightly unorthodox in institutional archives, it is certainly not unheard of, and our archivists wisely suggested, wherever possible, in keeping notes, clippings, and papers inside books as we found them, in accordance with both principles of original order and provenance. Provenance matters because

> the archivist does not reorganize groups of archives by subject, chronology, geographic division or other criteria, [as] to do so would be to destroy the context in which the archival record came to be, diminishing the role of the creator and the relationships that person had with other people or agencies. (Millar 98–99)

These traditional principles allow us to keep the books full of notes and clippings intact so that future researchers can examine them—each one an open-ended archive in miniature, a set of corresponding inter-texts, each one also documenting how a reader wrote herself into the library.

However, this notion of a stable, centred subjectivity, emphasized by the principle of provenance, seems at war with feminist postmodern understandings of subjectivity as multiple and discursively produced. It does not capture that which constitutes the subject and assumes a certain unity. It ignores the collectivity of labour and the ways in which feminist collectivity empowers women to speak, to articulate one's own voice as Barbara herself described of the *Tessera* editorial collective (Cotnoir 12). The provocation posed by feminist understandings of subjectivity also challenges the archival belief that provenance does not affix meaning to materials. In her death should Barbara's library fix her identity forever into place? Is this collection only about Barbara? Who and what is lost if we consider this collection of materials solely as the record of one woman and her thinking? In privileging the individual record creator over other kinds of content and context in our ordering schemas, how do we provide access to the relationships or proximities that are produced through the collection? This emphasis on the individual is particularly problematic when dealing with a collector who is understood to be a cultural and political turning platform, a dissemination mechanism in a larger feminist community. As Hope Olson indicates in her article examining the logic behind Library of Congress subject headings, all classification schemas are themselves socially embedded, gendered, and actively construct subjects ("How We Construct Subjects" 509). How does the archive collude in erasing communities and collectivity while rationalizing the subject?

Barbara herself once defined archives as "the words of others" (Letter to Kate Eichhorn). She studied with Barthes, who is known to have killed the Author. I feel haunted by these awarenesses now in my work. She also said of Marian Engel's representation of the archive in her novel, *Bear*:

> The information is fragmentary, written as brief notes on scraps of paper which are stuffed inside the books. Ever iterable, reproduceable, this is the promise of the archive, meaning which is never closed and open to the future, but which consequently undermines every form of order as it is contingently assembled from shards of the past. ("Contested Memories" 12)

Here she recognizes and celebrates the archival resistance to subject cataloging and the resulting open-endedness of meaning that this allows. It seems possible to extend this open-endedness to a reconsideration of provenance as constitutive of subjectivity in the archive and to begin to think how we might undermine or decentre these stable subjects gathered in our facilities. Typically, feminist archival research methodologies have been about locating the female subject, examining the subject position of the researcher, and interrogating and reclaiming authority for those voices excluded from the canon (Kadar, "Afterward" 116). There is room yet for work thinking through how we might rethink the subject in a feminist archival theory, which might insist upon both locating the female subject and destabilizing her at the same time. Certainly the emergence of the digital archive shows great promise for opening up the closed stacks of the archive and making the texts that lie within fonds more accessible, visible, and infinitely reorderable. It also heartens me to know that Barbara's collection will live in our archive alongside the fonds of Deborah Britzman, Kate Eichhorn, Didi Khayatt, Barbara Sternberg, Clara Thomas (to name just a few feminist thinkers in our collection), and to imagine the bridges that could be built across these collections and the epistemological ruptures that might ensue.

All told, I suspect that this collection, if explored, used, and reconnected to the wider community, will tell us as much or more about a certain kind of feminist activism and cultural production over the last thirty years than it does about Barbara herself. In reading Barbara's essay "Becoming My Hero, Becoming Myself," however, I was struck by the strangeness of my own positionality as a librarian, feminist, reader, and writer in this process. She talks in that paper about the ways in which women are able to speak to one another in and across texts. One might say that she writes about how she assembles her own library—and there I stood, day after day, in the middle of skimming her textual notes and, with my many colleagues, largely dismantling her library, so carefully and intimately gathered, attempting to translate its provocations and possibilities between archivists, librarians, staff, and scholars. I was distraught at times, to be a part of this process, while honoured and challenged by it at others. On the whole I feel quite fortunate to have had this expansive conversation with Barbara from inside her library, mostly posthumous though it has been. Despite my growing conviction that I need to decentre the creator from her collection, it is still useful to remember Walter Benjamin, who insists that only in extinction is the collector fully comprehended ("Unpacking my Library" 67). I feel certain somehow that many of us will benefit from continuing to try to comprehend Barbara, her work, and her collection/collective. As Brossard said, "she talks, and cities move behind her." It is an intimate and haunting experience, not only to use an archive but to be a part of its absorption into a public institution and in so doing make public what was once private.

Despite her extinction, or perhaps strangely because of it, I can't help but feel touched by the collector.

Notes

1   For an inventory of the Godard fonds, see the finding aid at: <http://archivesfa.library.yorku.ca/fonds/ON00370-f0000236.htm>.
2   Acquiring, organizing, and preserving Barbara's collection was possible only because of the collective labour of many people across many of the York University Libraries' departments and beyond. Particular thanks need to be given to all of the archivists in the Clara Thomas Archives, and especially Anna St. Onge, whose assistance and guidance was crucial at the outset of the project and throughout. Karen Cassel, manager of Monograph Acquisitions, went through every one of eight thousand titles brought from the house on Major Street. Paul Harrison and his staff in Shipping carried dozens of boxes up and down stairs in Barbara's house to bring them to us. Jay MillAr's work in a hot attic for many weeks established best practice for our student workers to follow later in the project. Bobby Noble, Kate Eichhorn, Philip Kiff, and Jackie Buxton were invaluable external collaborators throughout. Catherine Davidson, associate university librarian (Research and Collections) and Michael Moir, university archivist, funded the student staff who worked on the project. And lastly, none of this work would have been possible without the generosity and patience of Alexis Godard and his partner Melissa Dagleish.
3   Archivists themselves have debated these issues at length. As Terry Cook reminds us, archives have their historical origin as record-keepers for the state "as part of the state's hierarchical structure and organizational culture. Archival science not surprisingly found its early legitimization in statist theories and models, and from the study of the character and properties of older state records" ("Archival Science" 18). Summarizing Ketelaar, he suggests that the twenty-first-century archive must transform itself into archives for the people, of the people, perhaps even *by* the people, and notes as well the tension between postmodernist thinkers and their questioning of meta-narratives and archival theory's positivism, which embraces concepts such as "universality, logical autonomy, interiorization, and anti-historicity" ("Archival Science" 18). Cook would like us to work harder to make transparent the ways in which archival appraisal, arrangement, and description is an act of historically and socially situated interpretation and narration ("Fashionable Nonsense" 28). Other archivists disagree with a postmodern approach to archives and continue to insist on the evidentiary role of the archive for many reasons, including the contradictory possibility of both the establishment and destabilization of subjectivity and identity made possible by the preservation of records that contradict dominant meta-narratives (Hardiman 36).

Works Cited

Benjamin, Walter. "Unpacking My Library." *Illuminations*. Trans. H. Zohn. New York: Schocken, 1969. Print.

Brossard, Nicole. "La Petite Musique de Barbara." Inspiring Collaborations, The Barbara Godard Symposium, Toronto. December 2008. Keynote address.

Cook, Terry. "Archival Science and Postmodernism: New Formulations for Old Concepts." *Archival Science* 1.1 (2001): 3–24. Web. February 11, 2011.

———. "Fashionable Nonsense or Professional Rebirth: Postmodernism and the Practice of Archives." *Archivaria* 51 (2001): 14–35. Web. February 11, 2011.

Cotnoir, Louise, Barbara Godard, Susan Knuton, Daphne Marlatt, Kathy Mezei, and Gail Scott. "Introduction: Women of Letters." *Collaboration in the Feminine: Writing on Women and Culture from Tessera*. Ed. Barbara Godard. Toronto: Second Story, 1994. 9–19. Print.

Derrida, Jacques. *Archive Fever: A Freudian Impression*. Trans. Eric Prenowitz. Chicago: U of Chicago P, 1998. Print.

Foucault, M. *The Archaeology of Knowledge*. New York: Pantheon, 1972. Print.

Godard, Barbara. "Becoming My Hero, Becoming Myself." *Tessera* 3 (1986): 142–49.

———. "Contested Memories: Canadian Women Writers in and out of the Archive." *Annual Review of Canadian Studies* 27 (2007): 59–88. Print.

———. Letter to Kate Eichhorn. November 26, 2009.

———. "Theorizing the Archive in the Canadian Context: Course Syllabus." English 6997/03 Social and Political Thought 6672/03. Winter 2006.

———. "Women of Letters (Reprise)." *Collaboration in the Feminine: Writing on Women and Culture from Tessera*. Ed. Barbara Godard. Toronto: Second Story, 1994. 258–306. Print.

Hardiman, Rachel. "En mal d'archive: Postmodernist Theory and Recordkeeping." *Journal of the Society of Archivists* 30:1 (2009): 27–44. Web. February 11, 2011.

Kadar, Marlene. "Afterword." *Working in Women's Archives: Researching Women's Private Literature and Archival Documents*. Ed. Helen M. Buss and Marlene Kadar. Waterloo: Wilfrid Laurier UP, 2001. 115–18. Print.

———. "An Epistolary Constellation: Trotsky, Kahlo, Birney." *Working in Women's Archives: Researching Women's Private Literature and Archival Documents*. Ed. Helen M. Buss and Marlene Kadar. Waterloo: Wilfrid Laurier UP, 2001. 103–14. Print.

Millar, Laura A. *Archives: Principles and Practices*. New York: Neal-Schuman, 2010. Print.

Olson, Hope A. "How We Construct Subjects: A Feminist Analysis." *Library Trends* 56.2 (2007): 509–41. Web. February 11, 2011.

Contributors

PHANUEL ANTWI teaches and carries out research in the literatures and cultures of the black Atlantic (with a focus on the North American quadrant of the Americas and, in particular, on Canada) in the English Department at Saint Mary's University. He is co-editor with Sarah Brophy, Helene Strauss, and Y-Dang Troeung of a special issue of *Interventions: International Journal of Postcolonial Studies* titled *Postcolonial Intimacies* (forthcoming). He has published work in *Studies in Canadian Literature, Affinities: A Journal of Radical Theory, Culture, and Action*, and *PRECIPICe: A Literary Journal*.

ALESSANDRA CAPPERDONI teaches modern and contemporary literature in the Department of English at Simon Fraser University. She specializes in Canadian and anglophone literature, feminist poetics and translation, avant-garde studies, postcolonialism and diaspora, modernism and psychoanalysis, and critical theory. She is currently working on a book manuscript, "Shifting Geographies: Poetics of Citizenship in the Age of Global Modernity." Articles have appeared in *Translation Effects: The Making of Modern Canadian Culture* (forthcoming 2013), *Cultural Grammars of Nation, Diaspora, and Indigeneity in Canada, Translating from the Margins/Traduire des marges, Convergence and Divergence in North America: Canada and the United States*, and the journals *Canadian Literature, Open Letter, TTR: Traduction, traductologie, rédaction*, and *West Coast Line*.

JASON DEMERS is currently a visiting research fellow in the Humanities Research Institute at the University of Regina. He completed his Ph.D. at York University in 2010 under the supervision of Barbara Godard. He has taught in both English and Criminology departments. His writing appears in *Angelaki, Theory & Event*, and *The Semiotic Review of Books*.

MICHAEL DORLAND is professor of communication in the School of Journalism and Communication at Carleton University. He is the author, most recently, of *Cadaverland: Inventing a Pathology of Catastrophe for Holocaust Survival: The Limits of Medical Knowledge and Memory in France* (University Press of New England, 2009) on sixty years of (failed) attempts by psychologists to come to terms with Holocaust survival. Previous publications include *Law, Rhetoric, and Irony in the Formation of Canadian Civic Culture* (University of Toronto Press, 2002), and *So Close to the State/s: The Emergence of Canadian Feature Film Policy* (University of Toronto Press, 1998). He is the editor of *The Cultural Industries in Canada* and the co-editor of *Dialogue, cinéma canadien et québécois*. Before returning to graduate school in the late 1980s, he was associate editor of *Cinema Canada* magazine from 1980 to 1985.

RAY ELLENWOOD is a retired professor of English at York University and the author of ten books of translation, French-to-English, mostly of Québec literature, including the manifesto *Refus global*, by the Montreal Automatist Movement. In addition to a number of articles on the Automatists, he has published *Egregore: A History of the Automatist Movement of Montreal* (Exile Editions, 1992) and expects to see an augmented French version published in 2013. Meanwhile, he amuses himself by writing catalogue essays on the Automatists in general, on visual artists such as Pierre Gauvreau, Rita Letendre, Ludwig Zeller, and Peter Por, as well as texts for the Toronto archive, Dance Collection Danse, on choreographers Jeanne Renaud and Françoise Riopelle.

LEN M. FINDLAY is president of Academy One (Arts and Humanities) of the Royal Society of Canada and chair of the Academic Freedom and Tenure Committee of the Canadian Association of University Teachers. He is a founding member of the Indigenous Humanities Group at the University of Saskatchewan and co-investigator on a SSHRC-sponsored research project entitled "Animating the Mi'kmaw Humanities," led by Marie Battiste. He has published extensively on nineteenth-century literature, the theory and practice of decolonization, and the responsibilities and vulnerabilities of universities. His revised translation and edition of *The Communist Manifesto* was published by Broadview in 2004. Recent essays include "Academic and Artistic Freedom and the Israel-Palestine Conflict: Towards a Canadian Pedagogy of the Suppressed" (*Cultural and Pedagogical Inquiry* 2.2 (2010): 5–18) and "What Is to Be Drummed? Dialectic, Ceremony, and the Grounds of Commonality in Canada" (*Journal of Canadian Studies*, Fall 2012).

Contributors 341

LOUISE H. FORSYTH is professor emerita and adjunct professor in the departments of French and Women's and Gender Studies at the University of Saskatchewan, where from 1991 to 2003 she was dean of the College of Graduate Studies and Research. Until 1991 she was a tenured professor at the University of Western Ontario, serving as chair of the Department of French for five years. She was president of the Humanities and Social Sciences Federation of Canada (1998–2000) and has received several awards, including YWCA Woman of Distinction, Teaching Excellence Award, Alumni Achievement Award (U of S), and Canadian Association for Theatre Research Lifetime Achievement Award. She has been a committed feminist scholar throughout her career. Her areas of academic specialization have been Québec women playwrights and poets (with particular interest in the work of Nicole Brossard), translation, semiotics, and cultural studies. Her professional friendship with Barbara Godard has been a source of sustained inspiration throughout her career.

DANIELLE FULLER is senior lecturer in Canadian Studies in the Department of American and Canadian Studies and director, Regional Centre for Canadian Studies, at the University of Birmingham (UK). Her chief research areas are contemporary Canadian writing, particularly Atlantic Canadian literary culture; the politics of cultural production in Canada; and reading communities in present-day North America and the UK. Her many publications include *Writing the Everyday: Women's Textual Communities in Atlantic Canada* (McGill-Queen's UP, 2004), winner of the Gabrielle Roy Award for Criticism. She has also co-authored a monograph with her Canadian-based research collaborator DeNel Rehberg Sedo entitled *Reading Beyond the Book: The Social Practices of Contemporary Literary Culture* (Routledge, 2013). The book draws upon extensive research into large-scale reading events and contemporary cultures of reading in the US, Canada, and the UK conducted as part of the Beyond the Book project (www.beyondthebookproject.org).

BARBARA GODARD, until her death in 2010, was the Historica chair of Canadian literature and professor emerita of English, French, social and political thought, and women's studies at York University in Toronto. She published widely on Canadian and Québec literature and culture, on feminist and literary theory, and translation studies. She edited and co-edited many books, including *Gynocritics/Gynocritiques: Feminist Approaches to Writing by Canadian and Québécoise Women* (ECW, 1987), *Collaboration in the Feminine: Writings on Women and Culture* (Second Story Press, 1994),

Intersexions: Issues of Race and Gender in Canadian Women's Writing (Creative Books, 1995), and *Wider Boundaries of Daring: The Modernist Impulse in Canadian Women's Poetry* (Wilfrid Laurier University Press, 2009). Her collection of essays, *Canadian Literature at the Crossroads of Language and Culture*, was published in 2008 by NeWest Press. She was the recipient of many awards, including the Gabrielle Roy Prize (twice) and the Northeastern Association of Graduate Schools Award. As translator, she introduced experimental works by Québec women writers to an English readership. She was inducted posthumously in the Royal Society of Canada.

JENNIFER HENDERSON is associate professor in the Department of English Language and Literature at Carleton University, with cross-appointments to the School of Canadian Studies and the Department of Sociology and Anthropology. From 1993 to 2001, she was a co-editor of the journal *Tessera*. Her work in Canadian cultural studies uses tools of feminist and genealogical critique, usually to address questions at the intersection of liberal government and settler colonialism. She is the author of *Settler Feminism and Race Making in Canada* (University of Toronto Press, 2003) and the co-editor of *Reconciling Canada: Critical Perspectives on the Culture of Redress* (University of Toronto Press, 2013). Recent essays appear in *Canadian Literature*, *Atlantis*, and *English Studies in Canada*, as well as in the collection *Unsettled Remains: Canadian Literature and the Postcolonial Gothic* (Wilfrid Laurier University Press, 2009).

KARL E. JIRGENS is associate professor in the Department of English Language, Literature, and Creative Writing at the University of Windsor. He is the author of *Strappado* (Coach House), *A Measure of Time* (Mercury), *Bill Bissett and His Works*, and *Christopher Dewdney and His Works* (ECW). He has edited books on the Canadian painter Jack Bush (Coach House) and the poetry of Christopher Dewdney (*Children of the Outer Dark*, Wilfrid Laurier UP). With Beatriz Hausner he guest-edited an issue of *Open Letter* magazine on artistic collaboration. His articles appear in journals such as *World Literature Today* (US), *La Revista Canaria de Etudio Ingleses* (Spain), *Q/W/E/R/T/Y* (France), *Canadian Literature*, and *Open Letter* (Canada), as well as the *Dictionary of Literary Biography* (entry on Jacques Lacan). His fiction and poetry are published in Australia, Europe, and North America, and his inter-media performance pieces have been presented internationally, including at the prestigious INTER Fest (Quebec City). He has edited *Rampike*, an international journal of art and writing, since 1979.

EVA C. KARPINSKI teaches in the School of Gender, Sexuality, and Women's Studies at York University in Toronto. Her research interests include postmodern fiction, autobiography and life writing, translation studies, and feminist theory and methodology. She has published articles in edited collections and journals, including *Literature Compass, Review of International American Studies, Men and Masculinities, Studies in Canadian Literature, Canadian Woman Studies, Atlantis, Canadian Ethnic Studies,* and *Resources for Feminist Research,* and co-edited, with Jennifer Henderson, Ian Sowton, and Ray Ellenwood, a special issue of *Open Letter,* "Remembering Barbara Godard." Her book *"Borrowed Tongues": Life Writing, Migration, and Translation* was published by Wilfrid Laurier University Press in 2012.

GILLIAN LANE-MERCIER is associate professor of French literature at McGill University and associate dean (academic) of the Faculty of Arts. Her research and teaching interests include literary theory, translation studies, twentieth-century French literature, contemporary Anglo-Québec literature, Canadian writer-translators (other articles on Gail Scott have appeared in *Voix et images, Québec Studies, Studies in Canadian Literature,* as well as in several volumes of collected essays), and the history of literary translation in Canada. Author of *La parole romanesque* and co-author of *Faulkner: Une expérience de retraduction,* she has published numerous articles in European and North American journals and has co-edited special issues for *Québec Studies* and *TTR.* She is currently completing a book-length study of the issues raised by the translation into English of *joual,* a non-standard register of French spoken in Québec, and is embarking on a large-scale project on the emergence of traditions of literary translation in Canada since 1980.

CATHERINE LECLERC is associate professor in the Department of French Language and Literature at McGill University, where she teaches Canadian and Québec literatures and translation. Her research focuses on literary multilingualism and its translation, particularly in Anglo-Québec, Franco-Ontarian, and Acadian writing. She has published articles on France Daigle in the journals *Voix et images* (2004) and *TTR* (2005), as well as in the book *Traduire depuis les marges/Translating from the Margins* (Merkle et al., Éditions Nota Bene, 2008). She won the Gabrielle Roy Prize 2010 (in French) and was shortlisted for the Governor General's Literary Awards in 2011 for her book *Des langues en partage? Cohabitation du français et de l'anglais en littérature contemporaine* (XYZ, 2010).

SUE LLOYD is a visual artist and educator. Her visual practice is photo-based, a hybrid form open to the influence of other media, characterized by plurality rather than purity. She has constructed her images digitally, using original and found imagery. Her areas of interest are subjectivity, perception, and language. Currently, her work explores ways of knowing that are considered intuitive, non-verbal, and beyond the bounds of the rational. Her visual work has been exhibited locally and nationally: solo shows include Gallery TPW in Toronto, 2001; Hartnett Gallery in Rochester, 2002; Platform Gallery in Winnipeg, 2003; and Kamloops Art Gallery and Presentation House in Vancouver, 2004. Her work has been published in *Brick* and *Public*. Lloyd has been affiliated with the Red Head Gallery, numerous artist collective projects, and SPIN Gallery in Toronto. Her work is in private and public collections, and since 1997 she has received Arts Council grants. She received her Master of Fine Arts from York University in 1997. She is an associate professor in the Visual Studies Program in the Department of Art at University of Toronto.

SOPHIE MCCALL is associate professor in the English Department at Simon Fraser University. Her research interests include contemporary Canadian and Indigenous literatures, post-colonial studies, and textualized oral narrative. Her book, *First Person Plural: Aboriginal Storytelling and the Ethics of Collaborative Authorship* (University of British Columbia Press, 2011), was a finalist for the Gabrielle Roy Prize and the Canada Prize. She is co-editor, with Christine Kim and Melina Baum Singer, of a collection of essays entitled *Cultural Grammars of Nation, Diaspora, and Indigeneity in Canada* (Wilfrid Laurier UP, 2012). She has published other articles in *Essays on Canadian Writing, Canadian Review of American Studies, Resources for Feminist Research, Canadian Literature, West Coast Line*, and *C.L.R. James Journal*.

PAMELA MCCALLUM is professor in the Department of English, University of Calgary. She is interested in problems of representation, particularly around history and globalization. Recently, she has published articles on Zadie Smith, Raymond Williams, and Jacques Derrida, and a book, *Cultural Memories and Imagined Futures: The Art of Jane Ash Poitras* (University of Calgary Press, 2011). She was editor of *ARIEL: A Journal of International Literature* from 2001 to 2011.

LIANNE MOYES is professor and chair in Études anglaises at the Université de Montréal. She specializes in Canadian and Québec literatures with a focus on women's writing. She is editor of *Gail Scott: Essays on Her Works* (Guernica, 2002) and of a special issue of *Open Letter* devoted to Scott's writing (2012); and co-editor of *Adjacencies: Minority Writing in Canada* (Guernica, 2004), as well as of two special dossiers on Anglo-Québec literature in *Québec Studies* (1998/1999; 2008). From 1993 to 2003 she was a co-editor of the bilingual feminist journal *Tessera*. Her research has appeared in *Voix et images*, *Études canadiennes*, and *Canadian Literature* (2007), as well as in the collections *Language Acts* (Véhicule, 2007), *Trans.Can.Lit* (WLUP, 2007), *Wider Boundaries of Daring* (WLUP, 2009), *Contemporanéités de Gertrude Stein* (Éditions des archives contemporaines, 2011), *Failure's Opposite: Listening to A.M. Klein* (McGill-Queens's UP, 2011), and *Transmission et héritages de la littérature québécoise* (Presses de l'Université de Montréal, 2012).

CLAUDINE POTVIN is Professor Emerita at the University of Alberta, where she taught Québec and Latin American literatures, gender theory and women's writing, visual arts and literature. She was Chair of the Women's Studies Program between 1995 and 1998. She has published a book on medieval Castilian poetry and an edition of *Rédempteurs* by Hubert Aquin, various anthologies of critical essays, among them a book on *Literary Institutions and Women's Writing*, and a collection on *Angéline de Montbrun*. She is also the author of three collections of short stories, *Détails*, *Pornographies* (*L'instant même*), and *Tatouages* (to be published in 2013). She is a member of the Royal Society of Canada.

TRISH SALAH lectures at the Ontario Institute for Studies in Education at the University of Toronto. Her current research addresses the emergence of transsexual and transgender minor literatures and relationships between transnational feminist organizing and internationalized sexual governance. Her writing appears in the journals *Aufgabe*, *Descant*, *Drunken Boat*, *Eoagh*, *Feminist Studies*, *Fireweed*, *The Journal of Medical Humanities*, *No More Potlucks*, *Open Letter*, *Queen Street Quarterly*, *Tessera*, *Torquere*, *West Coast Line*, and in the recent collections *Contested Imaginaries: Reading Muslim Women and Muslim Women Reading Back* (Palgrave Macmillan, 2013), *Féminismes électriques* (2012), *Selling Sex: Canadian Academics, Advocates, and Sex Workers in Dialogue* (UBC Press), and *The Anthology of Trans and Genderqueer Poetry* (2013). Her first book of poetry, *Wanting in Arabic*, was published in 2002 by TSAR, and her second, *Lyric Sexology*, is forthcoming.

LISA SLONIOWSKI is the English literature librarian at York University Libraries and the chair of York University Libraries' Special Collections Working Group. She was instrumental in the acquisition of the Barbara Godard library. Her research interests surround feminist archives and special collections, information literacy for civic engagement, and advocacy for librarians. She is co-investigator on the SSHRC-funded Feminist Porn Archive and Research Project. She is also interested in the role of libraries in the public sphere and in the formation of counter-publics. She holds a master of arts in English (York) and a master of information studies (University of Toronto). Recent articles have appeared in *Access: The Magazine of the Ontario Library Association* and in the forthcoming Library Juice Press book entitled *Information Literacy and Social Justice: Radical Professional Practice*.

IAN SOWTON is professor of English emeritus and senior scholar at York University, and a long-time friend and colleague of Barbara Godard in the graduate programs of English and social and political thought there. He taught in the Department of English at the University of Alberta from 1956 to 1968, and in the Department of English at Atkinson College, York University, from 1968 to 1994. His major academic interests are early modern literature, with special emphasis on Spenser, Donne, Elizabethan and early Jacobean drama, and writing by women; literary theory, especially feminist literary theory; and modern and contemporary Canadian literature, with a gender-inclusive emphasis on poetry.

Index

Aarseth, Esapen, xiii; *Cybertext: Perspectives on Ergodic Literature*, 62
Aboriginal/Indigenous/Native/First Nations/Amerindian peoples, viii, xvii, xxii–xxxiii, 16, 152–54, 158–64, 165n3, 179, 230–31, 238, 245–59, 259n1, 260nn2–3, 261n8, 10, 262nn11–13, 297, 305, 307–8, 310–23; Indian Residential Schools Settlement Agreement, 247; indigenous humanities, 149; Inuit, 163, 263n16, 297; A. languages, 151, 153, 158–59, 236–38, 257, 310; A. literature, x, 16–17, 151, 153–54, 261n6, 314–19; Métis, 162–64, 245, 248, 250, 252, 259, 297; reconciliation, xxiii, 246–47, 254, 258–59, 260n3, 263n15–16; Truth and Reconciliation Commission, 255; violence against A. women, xxv, 90n10, 161, 310–22. *See also* colonialism; culture
Abraham, Nicolas, 231
Acadian literature, x, xv, 28, 96–99, 101–10, 11n6, 112n10, 196–99
Adenauer, Konrad, 48
Adorno, Theodor, 53–54
affect, xii, xvi, 12, 41, 44–45, 47, 120–22, 128–29, 131, 134, 137, 141–42, 169, 171–72, 174–75, 177, 179, 183n2, 194, 268–69, 278, 300–301, 313

Ahmed, Sarah, 122, 125
Ahokas, Pirjo, 283n3
Akenson, Donald Harman, 130
Alber, Beth: *Marker of Change* (National Women's Monument), 310–11
Alfred, Taiaiake, 159
Algerian war, xii, 41–42, 45, 52, 54, 268, 277; Front de la libération nationale (FLN), 56n5
Allen, Paula Gunn, 312
Alloucherie, Jocelyne, 89n3
Alonzo, Anne-Marie, 84
Amagoalik, John, 263n16
American Association of Canadian Studies, 201
American Indian Movement (AIM), 315–16
American Sign Language, 63–64
Amiskouevan, Marie, 153
Anderson, Benedict, 298
Anderson, Lori, 62
Annual Review of Canadian Studies, xxv, 323n
Antwi, Phanuel, xvi
Aquash, Annie Mae, 315
Aquin, Hubert, 99, 111n8
Arbour, Magdeleine, 60
Arbour, Rose-Marie, 90n13
archive, xv–vi, xxii, xxv, 119–22, 126, 141, 179, 267–68, 273–74, 277,

279–80, 293–94, 296–97, 299, 302–8, 313, 316, 322–23, 326–36, 337n3; feminist archival theory, 327, 329, 333–36
Arendt, Hannah, 278
Aristotle, 73
Armstrong, Jeannette: *Slash*, 17
Art Gallery of Ontario, 313
arts, vii, xvi, xviii, 14, 27, 79–80, 83, 103, 178, 295, 300, 309; Canadian art, 16, 59; feminist a.,185n12; a. installations, xiii, xxiv, 64, 80, 313–14; inter-media a., vii, xiii, 59–62, 67; public a., xxv, 295, 308–9, 312; transsexual a., 172–74, 176–80, 185n11; visual a., xiv, 7, 77–79, 81, 84–89, 90n8, 11, 134, 287, 291–92, 296n3, 301, 313
Association des professeurs de français des universités at collèges canadiens, 36, 201
Association for Canadian and Québécois Literatures, 5, 32
Association for Canadian Studies, 2
Association of Canadian University Teachers of English, 32
Atelier d'études feminists, 36
Atwood, Margaret, ix
Austin, Al, 172
Automatistes, 59–60; *Refus global* (*Total Refusal*), 59

Backhouse, Constance, 129
Bakhtin, Mikhail, x, 29, 197, 261n6
Barbusse, Henri: *Le Feu*, 282
Barnes, Djuna: *Nightwood*, 203
Barthes, Roland, 9, 219, 276, 283n13, 335; *Mythologies*, 276
Bartley, Alan, 125–30, 139–40, 143n3
Barzman, Paolo: *Emotional Arithmetic* (film), 283n14
Basile, Elena, 180, 186n15

Baton, John, 252
Baton, Shirley, 252
Baudrillard, Jean, 61
Beaulieu, Gérard, 113n24
Beaulieu, Victor-Lévy: *Jack Kerouac: essai-poulet*, 28
Beaumier, Jacques, 113n24
Beausoleil, Claude, 113n24
Beck, Julian, 221
Beckett, Samuel: *Krapp's Last Tape*, 61
Bell, Shannon, 178; *Reading, Writing, and Rewriting*, 183n2
Bellamy, Elizabeth, 268
Bellefleur, Léon, 89n3
Belmore, Rebecca, viii, xxv, 313–15; *The Named and the Unnamed* (installation), 313; *Vigil*, 314–15
Benjamin, Walter, 298, 336
Bergson, Henri, 61
Berkeley Free Speech Movement, 220
Berlant, Lauren, 122
Berlioz, Hector: *Damnation of Faust*, 62
Berman, Antoine, xxi, 150, 164n2, 225, 228
Bernini, Gianlorenzo, 61
Bersianik, Louky, 206n12
Bertrand, Monique, 89
Bhaggiyadatta, Krisantha Sri. *See* Brand, Dionne
Bibliotheca Alexandrina, 185
Binhammer, Katherine, xxii
Birnbaum, Pierre, 276
Birney, Earle, 297
Biron, Michel, 105, 110, 114n34
Bishop, Ted, 119
Bizot, Jean-François, 220
black history, xvi, 125–26
Blais, Marie-Claire, xxviin8, 12, 95
Blanchot, Maurice, xiii, 61; *The Gaze of Orpheus*, 68
Blondin, Ethel, 263n17

Blondin, George, 246–47, 249–50, 252, 254, 257, 261n9–10, 262n12; *Trail of the Spirit*, 247; *When the World Was New*, 247, 250, 260n9; *Yamoria the Lawmaker*, 247, 261n10
Blow, Peter: *A Village of Widows* (film), 247, 252, 258, 262n11–12
Boehringer, Monika, 112n17
Bond, David, 56n4
Border/lines (journal), xvii
Boréal (press), 105, 108, 112n16, 113n19
Borges, Jorge Luis, 329
Bornstein, Kate, 169, 176, 184n8
Boudreau, Raoul, 96, 107, 112n11,15,17, 113n24, 114n34
Bouillon de culture, 107–8, 110
Boundas, Constantin, 213–14
Bourdieu, Pierre, xvi, 11, 15–16, 131, 174; *Distinction: A Social Critique of the Judgement of Taste*, 168, 174–75, 177
bpNichol, 196
Braidotti, Rosi, 85
Branach-Kallas, Anna, 55n1
Branchard, Claudette, 207n18
Brand, Dionne, and Krisantha Sri Bhaggiyadatta: *Rivers Have Sources*, 138, 140
Brandt, Di, 3
Brault, Jacques, 37n4, 205n6
Brecht, Bertolt, 44, 174, 320
Brisset, Annie, 164n2
British Association for Canadian Studies, 11
British Empire, 125, 130–31
Britzman, Deborah, 336
Brossard, Nicole, viii, x–xi, xiii, xix–xx, 2, 5, 11, 23–24, 26, 28–30, 32–35, 37n5, 59, 62, 67–68, 71, 84, 89n4, 150, 193–94, 200–205, 205n1, 206n11, 212–14, 217, 329, 331, 336; *Amantes (Lovhers)*, xii, xx, 36, 201–3, 206n13; *Baroque at Dawn*, 66–67; *French Kiss: Étreinte-exploration (French Kiss. Or: A Pang's Progress)* xi, 29, 32–33; *Journal Intime (Intimate Journal)*, xii, xx, 36, 201–4, 206n15; *L'Amer ou le chapitre effrité (These Our Mothers)*, xi–xii, xx, 5, 10, 34–35, 196, 199–202, 206n14, 213–14, 217–18, 221; *Un Livre (A Book)*, xi, 30–31, 33; *Mauve Desert*, 67, 193; *Mécanique jongleuse/ Daydream Mechanics*, 29, 32–32; *Picture Theory*, xii–xiii, xx, 36, 59, 62, 66–74, 202–3; *Sold-Out. Étreinte/illustration (Turn of a Pang)*, xi, 28, 31; *Les Stratégies du réel. The Story So Far 6*, 35. *See also* language
Browning, Christopher, 280
Bryson, Norman, 88
Buddies in Bad Times Theatre, 176
Burroughs, William, 219–22
Butler, Judith, 332
Buxton, Jackie, 337n2

Cage, John, 220
Canada Council, xiv, 10, 12, 14, 28, 96, 101–3, 106, 110, 112n13–14, 150
Canadian Association of American Studies, 201
Canadian Association of Translation Studies, 151
Canadian Charter of Rights and Freedoms, 158, 230, 237, 239n5, 302
Canadian Comparative Literature Association, 32
Canadian Fiction Magazine, 37n5, 205n4
Canadian literature, vii, ix, xiv, 2–3, 5, 8, 10, 14, 23–24, 34, 95–100, 103, 111n1, 155, 297; African Canadian

writing, x, 16; Canadian literary criticism, ix, xi, 2, 8, 24–25, 123, 248, 260n5; canon, x, xi, 23; Franco-Ontarian literature, 97, 99–100, 105, 111n7; literary theory, ix, 5, 34; relations between francophone and anglophone literatures, ix, xi, xv, xx, 9, 11–12, 25, 28, 34–35, 95–100, 150. *See also* Aboriginal literature; Acadian literature; Québec literature; women's writing
Canadian Literature (journal), 17
Canadian Women's Movement Archives, 293–94, 302–3
Capperdoni, Alessandra, xix–xx
Carani, Marie, 90n8
Carbon 14 (theatre), 60
Cardiff, Janet, and George Büres Miller, viii, xiii, 59, 62; *Paradise Institute*, 64; *Forty*, 65
Carrera, Carlos: *Backyard* (*El traspatio*) (film), 90n10
Carson, K.B., 135
Caruso, Barbara, 196
Cassel, Karen, 337n2
CBC (Canadian Broadcasting Corporation), 256–57, 320
Central Commission of Jewish History, 279
Centre de recherche interuniversitaire sur la litérature et la culture québécoises (CRILCQ), 101–6, 108–10
Chamberland, Paul, 37n4, 205n6
Chard-Hutchinson, martine, 283n1
Cheshire, Neil M., 165n3
Chiasson, Herménégilde, 102, 112n11
Chirac, Jacques, 269, 277
Chou En-lai, 268
Chrétien, Jean, 13
citizenship, xvii–xviii, 6, 149, 155–56, 159–60, 162, 226, 228, 235, 238, 245, 249, 260n2, 297, 301, 212

Citron, Suzanne, 283n7
Cixous, Hélène, xxviin8, 9, 126, 129, 143n3; *La venue à l'écriture*, 205n3; *Vivre l'orange*, 214, 216
Clara Thomas Archives and Special Collections, 326, 330, 333, 337n2
Clements, Marie, viii, xxv, 245–46, 248–53, 255, 258–59, 260n2–3, 261n7,9, 262n10–11, 263n16; *Burning Vision*, xxiii, 245–54, 260nn2–3, 5, 317; *The Unnatural and Accidental Women*, 317–19
Cloutier, Cécile, 207n18
Cohen, Matt, 283n14
Cohn-Bendit, Daniel: *Obsolete Communism*, 220
Cold War, 43
Coleman, Daniel, 142n
colonialism, viii, 16, 25, 51–53, 73, 113n20, 152–54, 156, 159, 163, 165n6, 179, 235, 246, 248–51, 254, 260n4, 261n8, 268, 297, 300, 306, 308, 313; anti-colonial struggle, xiv, 52; decolonization, 6, 17, 154; neo-colonial relations, xviii, 163; settler-colonial state, xviii, xxiii, xxv, 248, 260n2, 263n16
commemoration, xxiv, 269–70, 273–77, 282, 295–97, 302, 209–11, 318
Conference of Inter-American Women Writers, 205nn1–2
Conference on Literary Translation, 201
Conservative Party, 126, 163
Conspiracy of Silence (film), 320
Cook, Terry, 337n3
Cormier, Pénélope, 113n18
Corso, Gregory, 221
Cossey, Caroline (Tula), 169
Cotnoir, Louise, xx, 97, 195, 202, 335
Counting Past 2 Performance-Film-

Video-Spoken Word with Transsexual Nerve, xvi, 172–81, 185n10, 186n14, 16
Coutivron, Isabelle, 206n7
Crawford, Isabella Valency, ix
CRIAW (Canadian Research Institute for the Advancement of Women), x
Cronin, Michael, xxi, 225–31, 234–35, 238–39, 240n9; *Translation and Identity*, 225. *See also* microcosmopolitanism
Crowley, Blair, 142
Cubism, xiii, 70–71, 74
culture, xiv, 7, 13–16, 124, 134, 137, 149, 156, 160, 162, 168, 178, 195, 228, 231, 238, 249, 251, 271, 273, 275, 288–89, 292, 295, 300, 303–5, 312, 314, 319; Aboriginal c., 154, 159, 236; black c., 134, 136; cultural memory, xii, xxi, 8, 228; cultural production, xiv, xv, xviii, xxii, 4, 15–16, 95, 98, 123, 175–77, 183n3, 296, 301–2, 327–28, 332–33, 336; cultural studies, viii, 2, 4, 248; Quebec c., 102; trans c., xvi–xvii, 167, 173, 177, 184n4, 9, 185n12. *See also* feminist culture
Cummings, Ron, 142n
Curran, Beverley, 261n8
Curry, Bill, 163
Cusset, François: *French Theory*, 220
Cuthand, Doug, 163
Cvetkovich, Ann, 122

Dagleish, Melissa, 337n2
Daigle, France, viii, xv, 89n4, 95–99, 101–10, 111n4, 112nn14–18, 113n19, 114nn25–29; *Un fin passage*, 108, 112n16, 113n19; *La Vrai vie*, 105; *Pas pire (Just Fine)*, 107–8, 110, 113n19, 114nn25–29; *Petites difficultés d'éxistence (Life's Little Difficulties)*, 108–9, 113n19, 114n30, 32, 33; *Pur sûr*, 113n19
Dallimore, Maegan, 250, 261n7
Davey, Frank, xi, 10, 25, 28–30, 111n1, 196
Davidson, Catherine, 337n2
da Vinci, Leonardo, 61
Davis, Rae, xiii
Dean, Amber, 142n
de Beauvoir, Simone, 41–42, 54, 56n6, 278; *Mémoires d'une jeune fille rangée* and *Le deuxième sexe*, 18
Debord, Guy, 221
de Gaulle, Charles, 41, 276–77
De Gagné, Mike, 247
Delacourt, Susan, 163
Delanty, Gerard, 228
Deleuze, Gilles, x, xiii, xviii–xxi, 9, 61–62, 66, 199, 211–22, 231, 332; *Différance et repetition*, 218; *The Fold*, 61; *Logique du sens*, 218; *Negotiations*, 211; and Claire Parnet: *Dialogues*, 213; *Pourparler*, 220; and Félix Guattari: *Anti-Oedipus: Capitalism and Schizophrenia*, 213, 222; *Mille Plateaux (A Thousand Plateaus)*, 213, 220–22; *What Is Philosophy?* 215, 217
De l'Incarnation, Marie, xxii, 151–55, 158
Demers, Jason, xx–xxi
Denault, Anne-Andrée, and Linda Cardinal, 114n24
Den Toonder, Janet, 112n17
Derrida, Jacques, 9, 73, 151, 199, 205, 219; *Archive Fear*, 327, 334; *The Ear of the Other*, 73; *La vérité en peinture*, 86
Desautels, Denise, viii, xiii–xv, 77–84, 88–89, 89n3, 4, 5, 8; *Leçons de Venise*, xiii, 78, 80–83, 88, 89n5; *Ce fauve, le Bonheur*, 81

Desh Pardesh (festival), 180
de Sousa, Mike, 162
Dewar, Jonathan, 247
Dialogue Conference, xxvin3, 36, 37n6, 202, 206n9
Dickson, Robert, 111n7
Dictionary of Canadian Biography, 295
Didi-Huberman, Georges, 278–79, 281, 284n17; *Images malgré tout*, 278
di Felice, Attanasio, 61
di Michele, Mary, 97–98
Dorland, Michael, xxiii–xxvi
Dornier, Carole, 282, 284n25
Douzou, Laurent, 283n12
Downes, Gwladys, 207n18
Doyon-Gosselin, Benoît, 96, 110, 113n18, 114n31–35
Dubnov, Simon, 279
Duchamp, Marcel, 221
Ducharme, Réjean, 99, 111n8
Duguay, Raoul, 37n4
Dulong, Renaud, 281–82, 284n25; *Le témoin oculaire*, 281–82
Dumont, François, 105, 110, 114n34
Duncan, Dwight, 163
Dupré, Louise, xx, 80–81, 89nn5–6, 195
Duras, Marguerite, 112n15
Dylan, Bob, 220–21

Écrits des Forges (press), 114n24
Éditions les Etincelles (press), 284n26
Éditions Perce-Neige (press), 114n24
Egginton, William, 61
Eichhorn, Kate, xxv, 3, 233, 238, 335–36, 337n2
Eichmann, Adolf, 280, 284n23
Einstein, Albert, xiii, 61, 69
Eisenhower, Dwight, 43
Elder, Jo-Anne, 112n12
Ellenwood, Ray, 59–60; *Egregore: A History of the Montréal Automatist Movement*, 59
Elliot, Beth, 169
Ellipse (journal), 25, 201, 206n9
Engel, Marian, 304; *Bear*, 304–6, 335
Enlightenment, 43, 45, 53–54, 272, 277
Ertel, Rachel: *Dans la langue de personne*, 284n22
Escarpit, Robert, 9
Éthier-Blais, Jean, 97
Evans-Pritchard, Edward Evan, 141

Fanon, Frantz, 56n5; *The Wretched of the Earth*, 52
Farnand, Debbie, 161
Fehr, Michael, 87
Feinberg, Leslie, 176, 182n
Felman, Shoshana, 284n19
Felski, Rita: *Doing Time: Feminist Theory and Postmodern Culture*, 185n12
feminism, viii, x, xiii, xvii, 5, 9, 15, 24, 26–27, 32, 34, 74, 167, 234, 294, 299, 301–3, 311; feminist culture, xi, 7, 10, 27, 181, 186n15, 195–96, 202, 301, 327–28, 332–33; f. epistemology, xiv, 77, 303–4, 333, 336; f. literary criticism, ix–x, 3, 325 (*see also* Godard, Barbara); f. and memory, xxv, xxviin9; f. periodicals, 2, 15, 96, 180, 183n3, 330, 332–33 (*see also Tessera* and other titles); f. politics, 2; f. theory, xi, xix–xx, xxvi, 4, 11, 24, 33, 78, 95, 167, 175, 183n3, 201–2, 214, 216, 287–88, 333, 335; f. writing in Québec, 33–34, 223; post-feminism, 167, 181, 183–84n3
Ferlighetti, Lawrence, 220
Findlay, Len, xvii–xviii, 162, 165n4
Finkelkraut, Alain, 269
Finkiel, Emmanuel, 284n25; *Voyages* (film), 282

Fireweed (journal), 2, 6, 32
FitzGerald, James, 132
Fitzhugh, William, 261n8
Flaherty, Jim, 156
Flaubert, Gustave: *Madame Bovary*, 45
Foreman, Richard, 219
Forsyth, Louise, xi, 11
Foucault, Michel, 9, 138, 171, 177, 219, 275, 328; *Archeology of Knowledge*, 329
Francis, Cécilia W., 114n34
Freedgood, Elaine, 125
French Revolution, 44, 268, 276, 283n14
Frenkel, Vera, viii, xiii, 59, 62, 64; *Messiah with the Right Credentials*, 63; *This Is Your Messiah Speaking*, 62
Freud, Sigmund, 214, 267, 275, 299
Friedman, Philip, 279
Frost, Corey, 235
Frye, Northrop, 9
Fugitive Slave Act, 136
Fuse Magazine, xvii, 14

Gagnon, Madeleine, xx, 84, 89n4, 195; *New French Feminisms*, 197, 205n3
Galerie Barbara Weiss, 65, 66
Gauvin, Lise, 112n17, 114n34
Gavreau, Claude: *Bien-être (The Good Life)*, 59–60
Gavreau, Pierre, 60
gay and lesbian community, 167–68, 172, 174–75, 180, 184n8, 9; Gay and Lesbian Archives, 294. *See also* lesbians; LGBTQ
gender, xvi–xvii, xix–xx, xxiv, 5, 7, 11, 15, 32, 74, 88, 96, 98, 127, 160–61, 167–70, 172–73, 175, 177, 182, 182n, 182n1, 184n4, 185n12, 194–96, 201–2, 206n10, 216, 287–93, 296n4, 297, 306, 309, 311, 318, 335

Gender Troublemakers: Transsexuals in the Gay Community (McKay and Ross) (video), 168–73; 184n4, 5, 8
Genette, Gerard, 9
genre, ix, xi, xix, 4, 14, 17, 24, 27, 106, 154
German Association of Canadian Studies, 323n
Giacometti, Alberto: *Femmes de Venise*, 82
Gill, Gillian, 214
Gilroy, Paul, 127
Ginsberg, Allen, 219–20
Giroux, François, 112n17, 114n34
Glissant, Edouard, 230, 239n4
globalization, xxi, 12, 225–28, 239
Globe and Mail, 163, 175, 317
Godard, Alexis, 325, 330, 332, 337n2
Godard, Barbara, vii–xxix, 1–20, 23–40, 54, 55n, 66–67, 69–70, 72–73, 77, 95–100, 111n2, 4, 8, 123–24, 126, 129, 143n2, 149–55, 157–60, 163–64, 164nn2–3, 167–68, 175, 177, 180, 182n, 183n3, 185n12, 193–205, 206nn9–10, 206nn12–13, 206n16, 207n18–19, 211–18, 222–23, 225–26, 229–34, 237–39, 239n2, 240n9, 248, 253, 260–61n6, 262n14, 267–68, 287, 293, 296n1, 323n, 325–36, 337nn1–2; *Canadian Literature at the Crossroads of Language and Culture*, vii, ix, 1, 3, 8–12, 16–19, 29, 32, 34, 77, 95–98, 100, 111n2, 150; *Collaboration in the Feminine*, x, 2, 29, 36, 37n5, 230, 239n2; and comparative literature, xiv, 2, 4, 6, 9, 26, 28, 123; and cultural criticism, xvii, 7; and Deleuze, xx, 211–18; as editor, 2–3, 10; and feminist criticism, x–xi, xix, 3, 15, 18, 98, 194–95; *Gynocritics/La gynocritique*, x, xiii, 3, 37n6, 202;

and institutional analysis, xiv–xv, 9, 11, 97–99; and mnemotechniques, xiii, 267, 297–98, 300, 313, 323; as public intellectual, vii, xi, 8, 34; *Re: Generations: Canadian Women Poets in Conversation*, 3; and relational logic, ix, xvi, 8, 16, 73, 123–24, 129, 131, 262n14; G.'s scholarship, vii, ix, 2, 24; and semiotics, vii, xvii, 2, 2, 9, 24, 26, 155, 194; and student activism, xv, 6–7; and translation studies, xi, xvii–xix, xxi–xxii, 11, 28–29, 149–55 ("Writing Between Cultures"), 193–96, 200–205, 223, 225–26, 331; as translator, xi–xii, xix, 2, 6, 10, 24, 28, 35, 73–74, 194–205, 213–14, 218, 240n9
Goelnicht, Don, 142n
Gould, Deborah, 45
Goulet, Michel, xiv, 80–83, 88, 89n3, 7
Goulet, Rose-Marie: *Nef pour quatorze reines* (monument), 309
government, of Canada, xvii, 13, 27–28, 107, 149, 155–56, 158–64, 230, 246, 257, 260n3, 309, 312; federal funding, 12–13, 101–3, 106–7, 161, 183n3, 303; *Gathering Strength—Canada's Aboriginal Action Plan*, 260n3; g. or state policy, viii, xiv, xvii–xviii, xxii, 12–15, 261n8, 302; *Study-Guide: Discover Canada/ Guide d'étude: Decouvrir le Canada*, xvii–xviii, 149, 155–63, 165nn4–5. *See also* Harper, Stephen
Grace, Sherill, 259
Gramsci, Antonio, 8, 126
Granatstein, Jack, 162; *Who Killed Canadian History?* 299
Grant, Cat, 178, 180
Grant, Joanne: *Confrontation on Campus*, 219
Group of Seven, 60

Guattari, Félix, x, xxi, 212–13, 215–16, 219–22, 231, 332. *See also* Deleuze, Gilles
Guilbaut, Muriel, 60
Guy, Chantal, 112n17
Gysin, Brion, 221
Gyurcsik, Margareta, 112n17

Hakluyt, Richard, 152, 164n3
Halberstam, Judith, 176
Halbwachs, Maurice, 267, 270–72, 274, 298; *Les cadres sociaux de la mémoire*, 270; *Mémoire collective*, 270
Halley, Janet: *Split Decisions*, 183n3
Hallows, Joanne, 184n3
Hamilton Public Library, 119–20, 142n
Hardiman, Rachel, 337n2
Harding, Jim, 251
Harmon, Hérve, 56n5
Haroun, Ali, 56n5
Harper, Stephen, xvii, 156, 160, 162–63, 164n1, 260n4
Harrison, Paul, 337n2
Haussman, Baron, 42
Havercroft, Barbara, 81
Heart Has Its Own Memory (monument), 311
Hébert, Anne, ix, xxviin8, 12, 95
Heidegger, Martin, 164n2
Heller, Monica, 113n21
Henderson, Jennifer, 142n, 260n4
Henderson, Sakej, 159, 162
Herman, Judith Lewis: *Trauma and Recovery*, 46–47
Herndon, April, 182n
Hilberg, Raul, 278–80; *Sources of Holocaust Research*, 280
Histoire de la littérature québécoise (Biron, Dumont, and Nardout-Lafarge), 104, 112n17, 110, 115n36

Hobsbawn, Eric, 282, 298; *The Age of Extremes*, 282
Holbrook, Susan, 73
Hölderlin, Fiedrich, 164n2
Hollier, Denis, 219
Holocaust, xxii–xxiv, 267–70, 275, 277–83, 284n22–23, 321
Houghton, Margaret, 142n
Houston, Cecil, 130
Huffer, Lynne, 68
Hungarian revolution, xii, 45
Hunt, Lynn, 274, 283n10–11
Hunter, Lynette, 5
Hurwitz, Elise, 179
Huston, Nancy, viii, xii, 41, 55; *Losing North*, 56n4; *The Mark of the Angel*, xii, 42, 45–55, 56n3; *Tale-Tellers*, 56n7
Hutcheon, Linda: *Narcissistic Narrative: The Metafictional Paradox*, 68
Huyssen, Andreas, 300

Inside/Out Lesbian and Gay Film Festival, 180, 184n4
interdisciplinarity, xii, 7, 59
International Association of Comparative Literature, 9
International Conference on Research and Teaching Related to Women, 36
International Transgender Film and Video Festival, 172, 181, 185n10
In the Feminine: Women and Words/ Les femmes et les mots, 202
Irigaray, Luce, xx, xxvn8, 178, 212, 214–17, 221, 303; *Speculum de l'autre femme*, xx, 214–16; *This Sex Which Is Not One*, 214
Isacson, Magnus: *Uranium* (film), 261n9, 262n13
Iser, Wolfgang, 61

Jack the Ripper, 66
Jakobson, Roman, 193
Japanese Association of Canadian Studies, 323n
Jenkins, William, 130
Jim Crow laws, 139
Jirgens, Karl, xii–xiii
Johnson, Stephen, 133
Jones, Ernest, 170, 184n6
Jospin, Lionel, 277
Joyce, James: *Ulysses*, 70

Kadar, Marlene, 331, 336
Kamboureli, Smaro, vii, xxvn6, 8, 18–19, 32, 37n2, 97–98, 149–50
Kant, Immanuel, 53
Karbusicky, Mark, 180
Karpinski, Eva C., 142n
Kaufmann, Eric, 131
Keeshig-Tobias, Leonore, 17
Kellett-Betsos, Kathleen, 112n17
Kelly, Fred, 263n15
Kenney, Jason, 162–63, 164n1
Ketelaar, Eric, 337n3
Khayatt, Didi, 336
Kiff, Philip, 337n2
Kitagawa, Muriel, 308
KKK (Ku Klux Klan), xvi, 119–21, 124–31, 133, 137–41, 142n1
Kloran: Knights of the Ku Klux Klan, 129–30, 144n6
Kluger, Ruth: *Refus de témoigner*, 284n21
Kodak, Boyd, 178, 180
Kogawa, Joy: *Obasan*, 308
Kristeva, Julia, xiii, 61, 74, 332
Kroker, Arthur, 59
Kui, Kam Wai, 181, 186n16

La Barre du jour (journal), 25–26, 32–35, 201–2, 206n11, 207n20; *NBJ: Nouvelle Barre du jour*, 205n4, 5, 206n9, 11, 14

La Bine, Gilbert and Charlie, 253
Lacan, Jacques, 66, 70, 197, 214, 219
L'Actualité, 108, 112n16
La Duke, Winona, 262n13; *All Our Relations*, 259n1
Laframboise, Alain, 89n3
La Grace Volcano, Del, 176
Lalonde, Michèle, 37n4, 205n6
Lamb, Laura, 142n
Lambert, Gregg: *The Return of the Baroque in Modern Culture*, 62
Lamy, Suzanne, x, xx, 36, 201, 205n1
Lanctôt, Mireille, 206n12
La nef des sorcières (performance), 207n20, 310
Lane-Mercier, Gillian, xxi, 239n6–7
language, 77, 79, 87, 96, 99, 104, 136, 193–94, 197–99, 203–5, 232, 234, 238, 260n6, 284n22, 298, 311; code-switching, xxiii, 248; French- and English-speaking Canada, viii, xv, 2, 6, 26–27, 113n22, 100, 107, 149, 156–61, 203, 232, 249, 297; l.-based art, xiii, 28, 59, 64; in Brossard, 68–69, 72–73; l. of lack, 125–26, 140; as proposition in Wittgenstein, 71–72; l. rights, xxi, 6; Official Languages Act, 28, 150; poststructuralist view of, 73; and power, xvii, 5, 27, 29, 98, 151, 153, 155, 158, 195, 204; and translation, xix–xxi, 29, 194, 196–97, 199–200; and women, 32–34, 195–97, 199. *See also* Aboriginal languages
Languages of Criticism and the Science of Man Conference, 218
Lanzmann, Claude, 278–79; *Shoah*, 278, 284n19
Laplanche, Jean, and J.B. Pontalis: *The Language of Psychoanalysis*, 184n6
La Presse, 112n16

La Révolution tranquille, 26
Latour, Bruno: *Reassembling the Social*, 222
Laub, Lori, 50, 280–81
Lauzon, Jani, 319
Laytner, Anson: *Arguing with God: A Jewish Tradition*, 281
Leavis, F.R., 9
Lebel, Jean-Jacques, 221–22
Leblanc, Gérald: *Moncton Mantra*, 102, 112n12, 114n24, 27
Le Blond, Josée, 201
Lecaine, Hugh, 59
Leclerc, Annie: *La venue à l'écriture*, 205n3. *See also* Cixous, Hélène
Leclerc, Catherine, xv, 112n10, 12, 14, 114n34
Le Debat (journal), 276
Lee, Christopher, 172, 176, 180, 186n16; *Alley of the Tranny Boys* (video), 179; (and Elise Hurwitz) *Trappings of Transhood* (video), 179
Lee, SKY: *Disappearing Moon Café*, 260n5
Leibniz, Gottfried Wilhelm, 61, 273
Lepage, Robert, viii, 59, 62; *Far Side of the Moon*, 62; *Geometry of Miracles*, 62; *Ka*, 62; *Polygraph*, 62; *Tectonic Plates*, 62; *Zulu Time*, 62
Lequin, Lucie, 90n12
lesbians, xii, x, 35, 73, 169, 171–80, 184n8, 185n11, 288–89. *See also* gay and lesbian community; LGBTQ; queer theory: queer community
Les Éditions d'Acadie, 105
Les Herbes rouges (press), 35
Les Têtes de pioches (journal), 206n11
Levasseur, Jean, 96, 112n16
Léveillé, J. R., 113n18
Levi, Primo: *If This Is a Man* (*Si questo un uomo*) a.k.a. *Survival in Auschwitz*, 283n9

Lévi-Strauss, Claude, 219
Leys, Ruth, 269
LGBTQ, 167–68, 171, 177. *See also* gay and lesbian community; lesbians; queer community
Liberal Party, 164n1
Library and Archives of Canada, 332
Library of Congress, 334, 335
Lie, John, 261n8
Likert, Derek, 262n11
Lispector, Clarice, 215
Livingstone, David, 308
Lloyd, Sue, xxiv; *Arms (Monumental) for Montreal* (installation) xxiv, 289–92, 294–96
Lotringer, Sylvère 218–20
Lott, Eric, 133
Love, Heather, 122
Luhring Augustine Gallery, 65–66
Lyotard, Jean-François, 73

Mackay, Eva, 127
MacKay, Xantra, 168–72
MacKenzie, Gordene Olga, 182n
MacMillan, Margaret, 162
Madahbee, Patrick, 163
Maheu, Gilles: *Hamlet machine*, 60; *Le Dortoir*, 60
Maillet, Antonine, xix, 2, 28, 32, 150, 194, 206n10; *Don l'original*, 28, 150, 196–99, 206n8
Majzels, Robert, 113n19, 114n25
Malina, Judith, 221
Manzo, Shadmith: *Shadmith Manzo Performance*, 178–79
Mao Zedong, 43
Maracle, Aiyyana, 176, 179; *Chronicle of a Transformed Woman*, 179
Maracle, Lee, 11, 260n5; *I Am Woman*, 17
Marlatt, Daphne, xx, 195–96, 202; *Ana Historic*, 5, 306–8; *Readings from the Labyrinth*, 206n9

Martí, José, 143n2
Martinez, Mauricio, 142n
Marxism, xii, 42, 44
Massey Commission, 16
Matisse, Henri, 87
McCaffery, Steve, 196
McCall, Sophie, xxiii
McCallum, Pamela, xii
McLaren, Norman, 59
McLuhan 100 Festival, 63
memorializing, viii, xxii, xxiv–xxv, 141, 268, 274, 287, 289–91, 293–94, 300–302, 309, 312, 322. *See also* commemoration
memory, xxii, xxiv–xxv, 47–48, 71–72, 79, 86–87, 104, 121, 131–32, 137–38, 141, 157, 195, 203, 258, 267–78, 280–82, 283n3–4, 291, 293, 297–302, 304–5, 313, 315–16, 323, 333; collective m., xiv, 270–27, 293, 289–99, 301, 308; cultural m., xii, 41–42, 298; public m., xvi, xxii, xxiv, 119–21, 140–41, 267, 269, 287, 289, 292–94, 297–98, 302, 308, 323; m. work, xxii–xxiii, 293, 298
Meschonnic, Henry, 150, 164n2
Mezei, Kathy, xix–xx, 24, 28, 35, 37n2, 196, 202, 206n18
micro-cosmopolitanism, xxi, 225–31, 234–35, 238
MillAr, Jay, 330–31, 337n2
Millar, Laura, 331, 334
Miller, George Büres. *See* Cardiff, Janet
Miller, Jim, 162
minor literatures, x, xvi
Mitchell, W. J. T. , 88
Mitterand, François, 277
modernism, x, 90n8, 195; modernity, 104, 106, 163, 203, 249
Moir, Michael, 337n2
Mojica, Monique, 319

Monette, Madeleine, 89n4
Monture, Patricia, 159
Morris-Suzuki, Tessa, 261n8
Moseley, Rachel, 184n3
Moyn, Samuel, 278
multiculturalism, 138, 155–56, 230, 237, 239
Montreal Massacre, viii, xxii, xxiv–xxv, 82, 90n10, 287, 290–91, 303, 309–11, 315, 318
Morancy, Jean, 112n18, 114n31
Morante, Elsa: *History: A Novel*, 55n1
Moses, Daniel David, 151–55, 159, 317; *Almighty Voice and His Wife*, xxii, 153
Moyes, Lianne, xv, 11n9, 115n36, 233
Muñoz, José Esteban, 122
Munro, Alice, ix

Namaste, Viviane, 175–76, 182–83n1; *Invisible Lives*, 182n, 184n7; *Sex Change*, 183n2, 184n4, 9; *Social Change*, 186n14
Nangeroni, Nancy, 185n10
Nataf, Zachary, 172, 181, 185n10, 186n16
Nardout-Lafarge, Élizabeth, 104–5, 110, 112n17, 114n34, 115n36
nation, 96, 127, 137, 141, 149, 152, 154–56, 165n4, 195–96, 226, 253, 157–58, 271, 274–77, 296–300, 309, 315, 333; n.-building, 127; n.-state, 6, 17, 138, 155–56, 175, 183n3, 231, 246, 267, 297, 311, 316, 318 (*see also* colonialism; government, of Canada); national literature, 106–7
nationalism, xxiii, 12, 24, 102, 104, 138, 140, 235, 257, 300; Acadian, 114n27; cultural, 13, 17
National Gallery of Canada, 65
National War Memorial, 309
Native Earth Performing Arts, 315, 319

Native Women's Association of Canada, 311
Nazism, xii, 43, 46, 48–53, 268, 277–78, 284n15, 22
Neo-baroque, xii–xiii, 61–62, 64, 66, 68–69, 74
neoliberalism, xiv, xviii, 14–16, 181, 183n3
Netherlands Transgender Film Festival, 181
Newton, Isaac, 225
New Woman Conference, 184n8
New World Coming: The Sixties and the Shaping of Global Consciousness Conference, xxvin6
Ngai, Sianne, 125
Nietzsche, Friedrich, 272
Nikiforuk, Andrew, 252
Noble, Bobby, 337n2
Nolan, Yvette, vii; *Annie Mae's Movement*, 315–17; *Blade*, 315
Nora, Pierre, 273–76; 283nn10–11, 300–1; *Les Lieux de mémoire*, 237, 276
Norman, Jessye, 276
North American Free Trade Agreement (NAFTA), 123
Norton Cru, Jean: *Witness: An Essay of Analysis and Critique of the Memoirs of Combatants Published in French, 1915–1926*, 282
Nova Scotia Arts Council, 14
Novick, Peter, 283n8

October Crisis, 30
Olson, Hope, 335
O'Neill, Patrick, 133
Ontario Arts Council, xiv, 12, 14
Open Letter (journal), 2–3, 10, 25, 28, 37n4, 196, 201
Orange Order (The Loyal Orange Lodge), xvi, 121–22, 124–32, 133–40

Osborne, Betty, 320
Oulette, Pierre, 80
Out on Screen Film Festival, 184n5
Owens, Louis, 261n6

Pagès, Irène, 36
Papon, Maurice, 277, 284n16
Paquin, Nycole, 78
Paré, François, 82, 11n4, 6, 9, 112n17, 113n21; *La Distance habitée*, 100, 104
Paris Is Burning (film), 172
Parizeau, Jacques, 162
Parmenius, Stephen, 152, 164n3
Parnet, Claire, 212–13, 215, 217, 220–21. *See also* Deleuze, Gilles
Parti Québécois, 27
Paz, Octavio, 197
performance, viii, xiii, xvii, xxv, 5, 14, 16, 59–62, 64–67, 72, 74, 78–79, 89, 127, 131, 154, 174, 179–80, 185n11, 235, 267, 295, 297, 302–10, 312–16, 318–23
Perloff, Marjorie, 67
Perron, Maurice, 60
Philip, NourbeSe, 17; *Looking for Livingstone*, 308
Picasso, Pablo, xiii, 70
Pivot, Bernard, 107
Plato, 61
Playwrights Union of Canada, 315
PMLA (journal), 61–62
Pontalis, J.B. *See* Laplanche, Jean
postcolonial theories, xix, 156, 186n3, 329
postmodernism, xiv, 61, 77, 80, 85, 184n3, 335, 337n3
post-structuralism, xi, xxiv, 4, 9, 19, 24, 164n2, 183n3, 194, 217–19
Potvin, Claudine, xiii–xiv
Povinelli, Elizabeth, 122
Prise de parole (press), 11n7

Prism International (journal), 201, 206n13
Probyn, Elspeth, 97
Proseer, Jay, 183n1
Proulx, Monique, 84
Proulx, Patrice J., 56n4
Proust, Marcel, 299
Public Archives of Canada, 308. *See* Library and Archives of Canada

Québec, ix–xi, xiii, xv, 3, 6, 11, 25–27, 30–31, 96–110, 11n3, 5–6, 8, 112nn13–14, 16–18, 113n19–20, 22–24, 114n27, 115n36–37, 151, 161, 195, 230, 234, 291; Québec Act, 158
Québec literature, viii, xv, 1, 10–11, 95–110, 11n1, 113n23, 196. *See also individual writers*
Queer Sites Conference, 168, 172
queer theory, 169–71, 173, 175–78, 181, 182n1, 183–84n3; queer community, 172–73, 176. *See also* LGBTQ
Quinn, David B., 165n3

Rabelais, François, 177
race: and racialization, viii, 133–34, 138, 143n3, 144n9, 161, 259, 260n5, 311–12, 329; blackface minstrelsy, xvi, 121–22, 124–27, 132–37, 139, 142n1, 144n8; institutionalized racism, 17; race politics, 123, 126, 136; racial imaginary, xvi; racial or anti-black feeling, xvi, 120, 122, 124–33, 137, 141; racism, 52, 113n20, 122, 126–27, 136, 138–39, 143n3, 246, 260n2, 261n6, 283, 308, 311, 315, 318–20; racist stereotypes, 16, 133–34. *See also* KKK; Orange Order; whiteness

Rains, William Kingdom, 305
Rajchman, John, 219
Rampike (journal), 64
Raphael, 53
RAT Subterranean News, 220–22
Raymond, Janice: *The Transsexual Empire*, 182n1
Reaney, James, 59, 60; *Colours in the Dark*, 60
Reinders, Robert C., 137
Reinhart, Anthony, 142n1
Renaissance, 53, 61, 302
Renan, Ernest, 298–99
Resnais, Alain: *Hiroshima mon amour* (film), 282
Resnick, Marjorie, 206n7
Response, Responsibility, and Renewal, 247
Revel, Jacques, 274, 283n11
Rich, Adrienne, 201
Richard, Chantal G., 112n17
Ricoeur, Paul: *La Mémoire, l'histoire, l'oubli*, 270–74
Riel, Louis, 162
Rights on Reel: The Toronto Human Rights Film Festival, 180
Robin, Martin, 125, 128–29
Robinson, Sir John Beverley, 136
Room of One's Own (journal), 201, 205n2, 4
Rosenblum, Robert: *Cubism and Twentieth-Century Art*, 70
Ross, Malcolm, 8
Ross, Mirha-Soleil (Jeanne B.), 168–77, 179–80, 186n16
Rotman, Patrick, 56n5
Roudebush Marc, 273, 283n10–11
Rousseau, Frédéric, 282
Rousseau, Henry: *Le Syndrome de Vichy*, 275
Rousseau, Jean-Jacques, 55n3
Roy, Gabrielle, 12, 95, 97

Rubin, Henry: *Self-Made Men: Identity and Embodiment among Transsexual Men*, 171, 181–82n1
Rudd, Mark, 219
Rudy, Susan, 11

Sadowski-Smith, Claudia: *Globalization on the Line*, 143n2
Saint-Hilaire, Mélanie, 108, 112n16
Salah, Trish, xvi–xvii, 170, 183n1
Sartre, Jean-Paul, 41, 278
Saul, John Ralston, 158, 165n5
Scarry, Elaine: *The Body in Pain*, 46
Schechner, Richard, 313
Scheemann, Carolee, 221
Schiller, Friedrich, 53
Schizo-Culture Conference, 218, 220
Schladow, Sarah, 283n15, 284n24
Scott, Gail, viii, xx, 11n5, 196–96, 202, 225–26, 229–39, 239nn1–3, 6, 240nn8–9; *Biting the Error*, 239n1; *Heroine*, 234, 239n1, 240n9; *La théorie, un dimanche*, 239n1; *Main Brides*, 226, 229, 231–34, 239n1, 7; *My Paris*, 239n1, 240n9; *The Obituary*, xxi, 226, 229–30, 235–38, 239n1, 3; 240n9; *Spaces Like Stairs*, 239n1; *Spare Parts*, 233, 239n1
Seaborn, Tad, 142n1
Semiotext(e), 219–20
Semprun, Jorge: *Le mort qu'il faut*, 270
Sheard, Charles and Joseph, 137
Sher, Julian, 125, 129
Shinjuku Boys (film), 172
Shouldice, Larry, 201
Simon, Roger, 119
Simon, Sherry, 201, 239n6
Simonin, Francine, 89n3
Singer, Sandra, 55n
Sloniowski, Lisa, xxv–xxvi
Smith, Patti, 220

Smith, William J., 130
Snyder, Timothy, 268, 283n2
Sophocles, 164n2
Sourkes, Cheryl, 332
Soviet Revolution, 44
Spanish Association of English Professors (ADEAN), 323n
Spillers, Hortense: *Comparative American Identities*, 143n2
Spivak, Gayatri Chakravorty, 151, 184n3; *The Postcolonial Critic*, 73
Stalin, Joseph, 44
St. Andrews College, 132, 135–36
Stapells, Cathy, 143n5
State Museum of Auschwitz-Birkenau, 284n18
Stein, Gertrude, xiii, 67, 70, 74
Steiner, George, 278; *The Death of Tragedy*, 43
Steiner, Jean-François: *Treblinka: The Revolt of an Extermination Camp*, 278
Stendhal: *Le Rouge et le noir*, 45
Stern, Anne-Lise, 279, 284n21
Sternberg, Barbara, xiii, 98–99, 111n4, 332, 336
Stiles, Kristine, 221
St. John, Michelle, 319–20, 322
Stone, Sandy, 176, 182–83n1, 184n7
Stonechild, Neil, 314
St. Onge, Anna, 330, 337n2
Structuralist Controversy, 219
Stryker, Susan, 170; *(De)Subjugated Knowledges*, 1777
Sullivan, Shannon: *Race and Epistemology of Ignorance*, 144n9
Taylor, Diana, 313
Tessera (journal), x, xiii, xxiii, 2, 5, 36, 37n5, 96–98, 11n4, 151, 195–96, 202, 205n2, 4, 206n11, 239n2, 325–26, 335
testimony, xxiii–xxiv, 246, 279–80, 282, 284n19, 23, 306

Thaler, Danielle, 207n18
Théoret, France, x, xix, 32, 36, 84, 194, 204–5, 206n11; *Bloody Mary*, 203; *Of Necessity a Whore*, 203; *The Tangible World*, xx, 203; *A Voice for Odile*, 203
Theweleit, Klaus, 49
Thézé, Ariane, 89n3
Thomas, Audrey, ix, 206n10
Thomas, Clara, 336
Todorov, Tzvetan, 9
Topia (journal), 2
Torok, Maria, 231
Toronto Area Women's Research Colloqium, 32
Toronto Scream Festival, xiii
Toronto Women's Literary Association, 301
Toronto Women's Suffrage Association, 301
Tostevin, Lola Lemire, 3, 97–100, 111nn8–9, 112n10; *Frog Moon (Kaki)*, 111n7
Townsend, Martha, 89n3
Tranny Fest, 172–73, 180–81, 184n5
TransCanada Conferences, 111n6
transgender, viii, xvii, 167–70, 172–74, 176–78, 180–82, 182n, 182n1
translation, viii, xix, xvii–xviii, xxiii, 5, 77, 79, 88, 90n13, 95–96, 111n2, 149, 164nn2–3, 267; and Deleuze, xx–xxi, 211–17; feminist t. theory, ix, xviii–xx, 2, 11, 24, 32, 149–63, 193–96, 200–205, 212–18, 223, 225–31, 234–35, 238–39 (*see also* Godard, Barbara); gender in t., xi, xix, 194–96, 201–2; indigenous, xxii, 153–55
transphobia, 171, 178, 182n1, 183n2, 184n8
transsexuality, viii, xvii, 167–82, 182n, 182n1, 183n2

trauma, viii, xii, xxiv, 46–51, 245–46, 253, 269, 275, 280, 282, 299, 302, 311, 313–14, 320–21, 323
Trudeau, Pierre, 113n6
Tsilitsky, Boris, 270, 283n6
Tuana, Nancy: *Race and Epistemology of Ignorance*, 144n9
Tuff, Martha, 142n
Turtle Gals, xxv, 322; *Scrubbing Project* (performance), 317, 319, 320

Uncle Tom's Cabin, 133
Underground Railway, 127, 131, 143n3, 5
University of Toronto Quarterly, 150
Upper Canada College, xvi, 132–37, 142n

Valerio, Max Wolfe, 176; *The Testosterone Files*, 179, 185n11
Van Gogh, Vincent: *La chambre à Arles*, 81
Van Herk, Aritha, 55n
Van Pelt, 284n24
Venice Biennale, 64–65, 80, 83, 90n7, 313
Venuti, Lawrence, xxi, 150, 225, 228
Verthuy, Maïr, 36
Villemaire, Yolande, 206n12
Voaden, Herman, 59–60; *Ascend the Sun*, 60; *Hill-Land*, 60; *Murder Pattern*, 60; *Rocks and Earth Song*, 60
Voix et images (journal), 80, 89n6, 112n18
Wakeham, Pauline, 260n4
Walcott, Rinaldo, 140
Walden, Riisa, 142n
Walker, James W., 129
Warland, Betsy, xx, 201–2
War Measures Act, 31, 157
Warren, Louise, viii, xiii, 77–79, 84–89, 90nn11–12; *Bleu de Delft*, 90n11; *Interroger l'intensité*, 85–86; *La Forme et le deuil*, 90n11; *La poésie mémoire de l'art*, 88; *Objects do monde*, 90n11; *Tableaux d'Aurelie*, xiii–xiv, 78, 84–87, 89n5, 11
Watson, Sheila, ix, 206n10
Weber, Max, 132
Wheeler, Ann-Marie, 11
whiteness, 132–34, 136–37, 248, 260n2, 5, 307–8, 314, 317–20; white supremacy, viii, 128–29, 131, 140
Wiedmer, Caroline, 277, 283n3
Wiesel, Elie, 278, 281
Wieviorka, Annette: *L'Ere du témoin*, 279
Wilchins, Riki Ann, 184n8
Williams, Raymond, xii, 42, 49, 52, 54–55; *Marxism and Literature*, 122; *Modern Tragedy*, 43–44, 55n2; *The Long Revolution*, 45
Wilson, David, 131
Wilson Robert, 62
Wiseman, Adele, 206n15
Wittgenstein, Ludwig, xiii, 67, 69–70, 74; *Tractatus*, 70–72
Womak, Craig, 261n6
Women and Words Conference, 5, 36, 202
women's writing (in Canada), ix, xi, xiii, xv, xviii, xxvin7, 2, 4, 12, 32, 77, 84, 89n5, 96–97, 194–95, 202, 297, 302–3; *écriture au féminin*, 193, 200, 202–3, 205, 205n1; fiction-theory, xx, 2, 35, 37n5
Wong, Rita, 259, 260n5
Woolf, Virginia, xvii, 7; *Mrs. Dalloway*, 46; *A Room of One's Own*, 294, 302
World Trade Organization, 12
World War I, 46, 70, 136, 282, 300

World War II, 31, 55, 245, 256, 268, 308
Writers in Dialogue Conference, 201

Yerushalmi, Yosef Hayim: *Zakhor: Jewish History and Jewish Memory*, 271–73
Yiddish Scientific Institute (YIVO), 279

York University, xxii, xxiv–xxv, xxvin1; 2, 5, 10, 28, 32, 287, 293, 295, 325, 330, 333, 337n2
You Don't Know Dick (film), 172
Young, James E., 283n3
Younging, Gregory, 247, 260n3

Zumthor, Paul, 77

Books in the TransCanada Series
Published by Wilfrid Laurier University Press

Smaro Kamboureli and Roy Miki, editors
Trans.Can.Lit: Resituating the Study of Canadian Literature / 2007 / xviii + 234 pp. / ISBN 978-0-88920-513-0

Smaro Kamboureli
Scandalous Bodies: Diasporic Literature in English Canada / 2009 / xviii + 270 pp. / ISBN 978-1-55458-064-4

Kit Dobson
Transnational Canadas: Anglo-Canadian Literature and Globalization / 2009 / xviii + 240 pp. / ISBN 978-1-55458-063-7

Christine Kim, Sophie McCall, and Melina Baum Singer, editors
Cultural Grammars of Nation, Diaspora, and Indigeneity in Canada / 2012 / viii + 276 pp. / ISBN 978-1-55458-336-2

Smaro Kamboureli and Robert Zacharias, editors
Shifting the Ground of Canadian Literary Studies / 2012 / xviii + 350 pp. / ISBN 978-1-55458-365-2

Kit Dobson and Smaro Kamboureli
Producing Canadian Literature: Authors Speak on the Literary Marketplace / 2013 / xii + 208 pp. / ISBN 978-1-55458-355-3

Eva C. Karpinski, Jennifer Henderson, Ian Sowton, and Ray Ellenwood, editors
Trans/acting Culture, Writing, and Memory: Essays in Honour of Barbara Godard / 2013 / xxx + 364 pp. / ISBN 978-1-55458-839-8

www.ingramcontent.com/pod-product-compliance
Lightning Source LLC
Chambersburg PA
CBHW020349080526
44584CB00014B/956